People and piety

SEVENTEENTH- AND EIGHTEENTH-CENTURY STUDIES

General editors

Ladan Niayesh and Marie-Jeanne Rossignol

Founding editor

Anne Dunan-Page

Seventeenth- and Eighteenth-Century Studies promotes interdisciplinary work on the period c.1603–1815, covering all aspects of the literature, culture and history of the British Isles, colonial and post-colonial America and other British colonies. The series welcomes academic monographs, as well as collective volumes of essays, that combine theoretical and methodological approaches from more than one discipline to further our understanding of the period and geographical areas. It is supported by the Société d'Études Anglo-Américaines des XVIIe et XVIIIe siècles.

Previously published

Bellies, bowels and entrails in the eighteenth century
Edited by Rebecca Anne Barr, Sylvie Kleiman-Lafon and Sophie Vasset

Writing and constructing the self in Great Britain in the long eighteenth century
Edited by John Baker, Marion Leclair and Allan Ingram

Radical voices, radical ways: Articulating and disseminating radicalism in seventeenth- and eighteenth-century Britain
Edited by Laurent Curelly and Nigel Smith

Frontiers of servitude: Slavery in narratives of the early French Atlantic
Michael Harrigan

The challenge of the sublime: From Burke's Philosophical Enquiry to British Romantic art
Hélène Ibata

English Benedictine nuns in exile in the seventeenth century: Living spirituality
Laurence Lux-Sterritt

People and piety

Protestant devotional identities in early modern England

Edited by
Elizabeth Clarke and Robert W. Daniel

Manchester University Press

Copyright © Manchester University Press 2020

While copyright in the volume as a whole is vested in Manchester University Press, copyright in individual chapters belongs to their respective authors, and no chapter may be reproduced wholly or in part without the express permission in writing of both author and publisher.

Published by Manchester University Press
Oxford Road, Manchester M13 9PL
www.manchesteruniversitypress.co.uk

British Library Cataloguing-in-Publication Data
A catalogue record for this book is available from the British Library

ISBN 978 1 5261 5012 7 hardback
ISBN 978 1 5261 8260 9 paperback

First published 2020
Paperback published 2025

The publisher has no responsibility for the persistence or accuracy of URLs for any external or third-party internet websites referred to in this book, and does not guarantee that any content on such websites is, or will remain, accurate or appropriate.

Typeset
by New Best-set Typesetters Ltd

Contents

List of figures and tables	page viii
List of contributors	x
Foreword – John Coffey	xv
Acknowledgements	xxiii
List of abbreviations	xxiv
Introduction – Elizabeth Clarke and Robert W. Daniel	1

SECTION I: SITES

Part I: Devotional identities in religious communities

1	What was devotional writing? Revisiting the community at Little Gidding, 1626–33 – David Manning	25
2	'HERSCHEPT HET HERT': Katherine Sutton's *Experiences* (1663), the printer's device and the making of devotion – Michael Durrant	43

Part II: Devotional identities in the household

3	'A soul preaching to itself': sermon note-taking and family piety – Ann Hughes	63
4	The Act of Toleration, household worship and voicing dissent: Oliver Heywood's *A Family Altar* (1693) – William J. Sheils	79

CONTENTS

Part III: Devotional identities in the theatre

5 Devotional identity and the mother's legacy in
  A Warning for Fair Women (1599) – *Iman Sheeha*   97
6 Devotion, marriage and mirth in *The Puritan
  Widow* (1607) – *Robert O. Yates*   114

Part IV: Devotional identities in the prison

7 'O this dark dungeon!': murderers, martyrs and
  the 'sacred space' of the early modern prison –
  Lynn Robson   135
8 Editing devotional identity: the compilation and
  reception of the prison prose of George Fox's
  Journal (1694) – *Catie Gill*   151

SECTION II: TYPES

Part V: Devotional identities in spiritual autobiographies

9 Fathers and sons, conscience, and duty in early
  modern England – *Bernard Capp*   169
10 Dissenting devotion and identity in *The Experience
   of Mary Franklin* (*d.* 1711) – *Vera J. Camden*   185

Part VI: Devotional identities in religious poetry

11 Loyalist and dissenting responses to George Herbert's
   The Temple (1633) in the devotional writing of the
   1640s–50s – *Jenna Townend*   205
12 'Whom I never knew to Poetrize but now': grief and
   passion in the devotional poetry of Richard Baxter –
   Sylvia Brown   222

Part VII: Devotional identities in the *ars moriendi*

13 'My sick-bed covenants': scriptural patterns and
   model piety in the early modern sickchamber –
   Robert W. Daniel   241

14 'Now the Lord hath made me a spectacle': deathbed
   narratives and devotional identities in the early
   seventeenth century – *Charles Green*   259

Afterword – *N. H. Keeble*   275

Select bibliography   285
Index   289

Figures and tables

Figures

1.1 Page from the 'story books' of Little Gidding, held at the Archives of Clare College, University of Cambridge (CCPP/FER). Reproduced by kind permission of Clare College, Cambridge. *page* 32

2.1 Title page to Katherine Sutton's *A Christian Woman's Experiences* (Rotterdam, 1663), held at the Cambridge University Library (R.11.89). Reproduced by kind permission of the Syndics of Cambridge University Library. 46

8.1 Page from the Spence Manuscript, Library of the Society of Friends, London, MS, fol. 87^r. © 2019 Religious Society of Friends (Quakers) in Britain. 158

10.1 Page showing the handwritten title Franklin's granddaughter gave to her writings as well as the stamp of the Congregational Library that later received it. Held at the Congregational Library (at the DWL), London (CL MS 33 I. h. fol. 3^r). Reproduced by kind permission of the Trustees of the Congregational Memorial Hall. 186

10.2 Page from Mary Franklin's papers illustrating her use of the letter 'X', held at the Congregational Library (at the DWL), London (CL MS 33 I. h. fol. 17^v). Reproduced by kind

	permission of the Trustees of the Congregational Memorial Hall.	193
13.1	Woodcut scene of a man in his sickbed from the ballad *An hundred godly lessons* (1684–95?). Held at the British Library (C.20.f.7.144–145). Reproduced by kind permission of The British Library Board.	252
13.2	Woodcut scene of a woman in her sickbed from the ballad *An hundred godly lessons* (1674–79). Held at the University of Glasgow Library (Euing Ballads 143). Reproduced by kind permission of the University of Glasgow Library, Archives and Special Collections.	252

Tables

4.1	Sermons preached by Oliver Heywood in addition to his normal Sunday preaching, 1665–1701.	81–82

Contributors

Sylvia Brown is Professor of English at the University of Alberta. Her publications include *Women's Writing in Stuart England: The Mothers' Legacies* (ed.) (Sutton, 2000), and the edited volume *Women, Gender, and Radical Religion in Early Modern Europe* (Brill, 2007). She has published on a number of other topics involving seventeenth- and eighteenth-century annotated books, Bunyan and Milton. She is also editing 'The Life of Christopher Love by Mary Love' and is part of the editorial team tackling Richard Baxter's correspondences.

Vera J. Camden is Professor of English at Kent State University, Training and Supervising Analyst at the Cleveland Psychoanalytic Center and Clinical Assistant Professor of Psychiatry at Case Western Reserve University. Her publications include *Trauma and Transformation: The Political Progress of John Bunyan* (ed.) (Stanford University Press, 2008); 'Carnality into Creativity: Sublimation in John Bunyan's "Apology" to *The Pilgrim's Progress*', in *Immortality and the Body in the Age of Milton* (Cambridge University Press, 2017); and *She Being Dead Yet Speaketh: The Franklin Family Papers*, for The Other Voice Series (University of Toronto Press, 2020).

Bernard Capp is a Fellow of the British Academy and Emeritus Professor in History at the University of Warwick. His research focuses on early modern English history, especially in the period 1560–1700. His publications include *The Fifth Monarchy Men* (Oxford University Press, 1972), *Astrology and the Popular Press*

(Faber, 1979), *Cromwell's Navy: The Fleet and the English Revolution, 1648–1660* (Oxford University Press, 1992), *The World of John Taylor the Water-Poet, 1578–1653* (Oxford University Press, 1994), *When Gossips Meet* (Oxford University Press, 2004), and *England's Culture Wars: Puritan Reformation and its Enemies in the Interregnum, 1649–1660* (Oxford University Press, 2012). His latest book is *The Ties that Bind: Siblings, Family and Society in Early Modern England* (Oxford University Press, 2018).

Elizabeth Clarke is Professor Emeritus in English and Comparative Literary Studies at the University of Warwick. She specialises in seventeenth-century religious poetry, spirituality and religious writing, particularly by nonconformists and women. She led the Perdita Project for early modern women's manuscript compilations as well as the John Nichols Project at Warwick University, resulting in the five-volume *Progresses of Queen Elizabeth I* (Oxford University Press, 2014). Her publications include *Politics, Religion and the Song of Songs in Seventeenth-Century England* (Palgrave Macmillan, 2011) and, with Danielle Clarke, *The Double Voice: Gendered Writing in Early Modern England* (Palgrave Macmillan, 2000). Her most recent work includes *The Complete Works of Lucy Hutchinson: Vol. 2* (Oxford University Press, 2018).

John Coffey is Professor of Early Modern History at the University of Leicester. He is the author of monographs on the Scottish Covenanter Samuel Rutherford and English Independent John Goodwin, as well as *Persecution and Toleration in Protestant England, 1558–1689* (Longman, 2000), and *Exodus and Liberation: Deliverance Politics from John Calvin to Martin Luther King Jr.* (Oxford University Press, 2014). He edited *The Cambridge Companion to Puritanism* (Cambridge University Press, 2008), and *Heart Religion: Evangelical Piety in England and Ireland, 1690–1850* (Oxford University Press, 2016). With N. H. Keeble, Tom Charlton and Tim Cooper he is a co-editor of Richard Baxter's *Reliquiae Baxterianae*, 5 vols (Oxford University Press, 2020).

Robert W. Daniel is Associate Tutor in English Literature at the University of Warwick, where he holds the Vice Chancellor's Award for Teaching Excellence. His publications examine the religious and literary culture of post-Reformation Britain, with an emphasis on cross-confessional practices. As well as Associate Editor of *Bunyan Studies*, he is a co-editor of 'Liminality and Domestic Spaces in Early Modern England' (*Special Issue: Early Modern Literary Studies*, 29, 2020). His recent book project is entitled *Popular Piety and Religious Writing in Early Modern Britain, 1558–1720*. He is currently co-editing the Stockton diaries held at the Dr Williams's Library.

Michael Durrant is Lecturer in Early Modern Literature at Bangor University. He researches and writes on print and printers, materiality, and the book, as well as seventeenth-century religion and dissent. His publications include 'Henry Hills and the Tailor's Wife: Adultery, Hypocrisy, and the Archive', in Lucia Nigri and Naya Tsentourou (eds), *Forms of Hypocrisy in Early Modern England* (Routledge, 2018), and his monograph *The Dreaded Name of Henry Hills, Printer (c.1625–1688/9)* (Manchester University Press, forthcoming 2021).

Catie Gill is Lecturer in Early Modern Writing at Loughborough University. Her research has appeared in a number of books and collections, including *Women in the Seventeenth-Century Quaker Community* (Ashgate, 2005), *Theatre and Culture* (Ashgate, 2010), *Expanding the Canon of Early Modern Women's Writing* (Cambridge Scholars, 2010), *Radical Voices* (Manchester University Press, 2016), *The Oxford Handbook of Literature and Religion* (Oxford University Press, 2017), and, with Michele Lise Tarter, *New Critical Studies on Early Quaker Women, 1650–1800* (Oxford University Press, 2018).

Charles Green gained his PhD at the University of Birmingham in 2020. His research focuses on early modern commemorative writing (particularly by and about John Donne), literary afterlives and *ars moriendi* texts. In early 2019 he published an award-winning paper on early print and manuscript elegies for Donne in the *John Donne Journal* (volume 35), and undertook a three-month fellowship at the Huntington Library in California. He has also undertaken spells working at the National Archives, the Arden Shakespeare, and the *Guardian*.

Ann Hughes is Emeritus Professor of Early Modern History at Keele University. Her research interests include the culture, religion and politics of the English Civil War. She is the author of many books and articles, including *Gangraena and the Struggle for the English*

Revolution (Oxford University Press, 2004) and, co-edited with Tom Corns and David Loewenstein, *The Complete Works of Gerrard Winstanley* (Oxford University Press, 2009), and most recently *Gender and the English Revolution* (Routledge, 2012). She is now principally working on preaching during the English Revolution.

N. H. Keeble is Emeritus Professor of English Studies at the University of Stirling, Scotland. His publications include studies of *Richard Baxter: Puritan Man of Letters* (Oxford University Press, 1982), *The Literary Culture of Nonconformity in Later Seventeenth-Century England* (Leicester University Press, 1987), *The Restoration: England in the 1660s* (Blackwell, 2002) and, with Geoffrey F. Nuttall, a two-volume *Calendar of the Correspondence of Richard Baxter* (Oxford University Press, 1991). He has edited five collections of original essays; texts by John Bunyan, Daniel Defoe, Lucy Hutchinson, Andrew Marvell and John Milton; and is co-editor of Richard Baxter's *Reliquiae Baxterianae* (Oxford University Press, 2020).

David Manning is Lecturer of History at the University of Leicester. His research interests include the history of Christian thought and culture in Britain and British Colonial America, *c*.1500–*c*.1800. His recent publications include 'Reformation and the Wickedness of Port Royal, Jamaica, 1655–*c*.1692', in Crawford Gribben and Scott Spurlock (eds), *Puritans and Catholics in the Trans-Atlantic World, 1600–1800* (Palgrave Macmillan, 2015), and 'Anglican Religious Societies, Organisations, and Missions', in Jeremy Gregory (ed.), *The Oxford History of Anglicanism, Volume II: Establishment and Empire: The Development of Anglicanism 1662–1829* (Oxford University Press, 2017).

Lynn Robson is Fellow and Tutor in English Literature at Regent's Park College at the University of Oxford. Her current research focuses on the stereotype of the penitent murderer in early modern cheap print. Her publications include '"Now farewell to the Lawe, too long have I been in thy subjection": Early Modern Murder, Calvinism and Spiritual Authority' (*Literature and Theology*, 2008), and '"We'll build in sonnets pretty rooms": Early Modern Literature, the "Spatial Turn" and Ecocriticism' (*Literature Compass*, 2010). She co-edited 'Still Kissing the Rod?', a special edition of *Women's Writing* (2007). She collaborated in developing a liturgy based on

A Midsummer Night's Dream, which was published in *New Places: Shakespeare and Civic Creativity* (2018).

Iman Sheeha is Lecturer in Shakespeare and Early Modern Literature at Brunel University London. She has published articles in *Early Theatre*, *Early Modern Literary Studies*, *The Apollonian: Journal of Interdisciplinary Studies*, and *American Notes and Queries*. Her first monograph is entitled *Household Servants in Early Modern Domestic Tragedy* (Routledge, 2020).

William J. Sheils is Emeritus Professor in History and was Leverhulme Fellow 2014–16 at the University of York. His publications include *The Puritans in the Diocese of Peterborough 1558–1610* (Northampton Record Society, 1979), *Restoration Exhibit Books and the Northern Clergy 1662–1664* (Borthwick Institute of Historical Research, 1987) and *The English Reformation 1530–1570* (Routledge, 1989). He has co-edited several volumes and authored several articles. The most recent was entitled 'From Reformation to Restoration, 1539–1660', in David Brown (ed.), *Durham Cathedral: History, Fabric and Culture* (Yale University Press, 2015). He is also the recipient of a festschrift volume entitled *Getting Along? Religious Identities and Confessional Relations in Early Modern England* (Ashgate, 2012).

Jenna Townend completed her doctorate in the Department of English and Drama at Loughborough University in 2018. Her research examined the admirers of the seventeenth-century devotional poet George Herbert in light of their textual borrowings from *The Temple* (1633). Her publications include '"[S]weet singer of our Israel": George Herbert, Music, and the Formation of Dissenting Communities', *Bunyan Studies* (2018), and 'Quantitative and Qualitative Approaches to Early-Modern Networks: The Case of George Herbert (1593–1633) and his imitators', *Literature Compass* (2016). She is preparing her first monograph for publication, entitled *George Herbert and Seventeenth Century Reading Culture*.

Robert O. Yates is a Mellon Humanities Public Fellow and doctoral student in the Department of English at the Graduate Center, City University of New York. His research focuses on early modern literature and culture, with particular interests in drama, embodiment and popular festivities.

Foreword

John Coffey

The devotional turn

In recent years, literary scholars have spoken of a 'religious turn' in their discipline, just as historians have commented on 'the return of religion' in theirs.[1] Less often noted is what one might call 'the devotional turn'. Yet scholars in different fields have been showing a renewed interest in devotional texts.[2] As the essays in this volume testify, the study of piety is no longer the preserve of church historians.

Various factors have contributed to this upsurge. Scholars study early modern piety for the same reason that George Mallory set out to climb Everest: 'Because it's there', looming large. If we follow the sources, we find an abundance of neglected devotional writings that call for serious scrutiny. One can study seventeenth-century devotional literature because 'the past is a foreign country, they do things differently there'.[3] However, there is also a 'post-secular' recognition that religion is not 'a thing of the past', that it demands renewed attention. Hard secularisation theory has fallen on hard times as social theorists reckon with 'multiple modernities' and the religious genealogy of the secular. And scholarly interest in past religion has arguably grown with the new salience of religion in the present; we are more alert to its presence and importance in past societies, including ones that we think of as early modern.[4]

Other trends are at work too, including a fresh preoccupation with the self and personal identity. Spiritual diaries, testimonies and autobiographies are valuable sources in the study of interiority. And scholars who write of the emergence of the modern self are often (though not always) alert to its religious sources.⁵ A related development is the rise of 'emotions' scholarship in various fields. Here again, one of the unintended by-products has been a re-engagement with personal piety, ranging from case studies (such as Thomas Dixon's analysis of the weeping evangelist George Whitefield) to an Oxford Handbook.⁶ Alongside this, there has been the rediscovery of 'lived religion'. Turning away from elite statements about how religion ought to be practised, historians have trained their sights on how it was actually practised on the ground, in the popular religion of hymn-singing, prayer, devotional reading, burial customs, festivals and processions.⁷ In scholarship on early modern England, this has involved a new awareness of the spatial dimension, with work on the worship and the 'soundscape' of parish churches and dissenting chapels, as well as domestic settings and household religion.⁸ The latter development has been assisted by the recovery of women's history and women's writing and reading. This has led to an encounter with religious texts, which constitute such a large proportion of early modern women's literary output.⁹ During the English Revolution, for example, prophecy was the single largest genre in the 1640s, and together with Quaker works in the 1650s comprised more than half of the printed writings of women between 1640 and 1660.¹⁰ Finally, there has been the fashion for reception history, especially reception history of the Bible; while this has often focused on 'the political Bible', it has also led to a rediscovery of the devotional Bible.¹¹

Of course, the suddenness and extent of the 'devotional turn' can be exaggerated. Devotional texts have always formed part of the canon of English literature, above all for the age of Herbert, Donne and Milton. Indeed, today's students may be less likely to grapple with piety than a previous generation. John Bunyan's place in the English literary canon, and especially in the classroom, is now much less secure than it once was. In the latest 'Major Authors' edition of the *Norton Anthology of English Literature*, Bunyan is still entirely absent.¹² His displacement by Pepys, Rochester and Aphra Behn reflects the fact that those latter authors are more accessible and appealing to a post-Christian readership. Moreover, the exponential growth of scholarly publication in all directions can lead us to overplay the market share of religious studies. Nevertheless, as this volume indicates, both historians and literary scholars are now dedicating serious attention to devotional writing, and the devotional identities such works espoused, across different genres, spaces and contexts.

Piety and polemic

The 'devotional turn' is not without its controversies. One area of debate is the relationship between piety and polemic. Over the past generation, historians have made major advances in understanding 'the politics of religion' in early modern England. The emphasis has been on religious conflict and factionalism. By contrast, the study of piety can look like the past in soft focus, with the edges blurred. That is certainly how Peter Lake and Isaac Stephens have seen Alec Ryrie's *Being Protestant in Reformation Britain* (Oxford University Press, 2013). In Lake's view, historians like Ryrie and Ian Green present post-Reformation Protestantism as far too consensual and pietistic. Lake detects a tendency to downplay divisions between puritan and conformist Protestants, in favour of a religious tradition that is constructed to appear 'inherently moderate and timeless'. Piety is divorced from polemic, so that spirituality becomes a matter of 'ineffability' rather than being subject to rigorous historical analysis.[13] Ryrie denies the charges, and suggests that he and Lake are often arguing at cross purposes, but he does assert that his critics have 'a tin ear for spirituality in their sources, and a frustratingly reductive insistence on reading all of those sources exclusively through the lens of confessional conflict'. In his view, post-Reformation Protestants did not regard such divisions as 'their religion's beating heart'.[14] Protestants, as he has written in his major history of that tradition, should be understood as both 'fighters and lovers'.[15]

Ryrie and Lake represent different tendencies in contemporary scholarship, though given the subtlety of their scholarship, it would be unfair to suggest that they represent different extremes. The tendencies, however, are worth holding in check and in tension. Piety should not be reduced to polemic, nor divorced from it. In the context of intellectual history, Quentin Skinner claims that 'no one is above the battle, because the battle is all there is'. As a maxim, this may work for the history of political thought, but it is problematic when applied to the full range of religious texts and practices. There is reason to question Skinner's statement that 'The only histories of ideas to be written, are histories of their uses in argument.'[16] As David Bebbington has noted, this can lead to 'a concentration on the polemical' at the expense of 'other styles of exposition'. In the field of religion, in particular, it can lead us to overlook the various uses to which texts are put: for contemplation, prayer and consolation, as well as refutation. Thus 'the contemplative works of Teresa of Avila ... call for appreciation in a different mode from that brought to the study of argumentation'.[17]

The other extreme is to see religious devotion as something that rises above the murky world of doctrinal and ecclesiastical controversy, and exists on a mystical plane of spirituality, like an ethereal spirit escaping the confines of a body. 'Anglicanism' has often been praised (mainly by Anglicans) for escaping the unpleasant dogmatism of other traditions, achieving a serene 'moderation, balance, equipoise, and order'.[18] Recent trends in religious history (such as the emphasis on lived religion or the history of emotions) can also serve to marginalise the shaping influence on piety of confessions, catechisms and institutions. The concept of 'devotional identities' might help us here, because it recognises that piety and polemic are distinct but interrelated. Devotion never existed in abstraction, but was always practised in particular communities using specific texts, concepts and practices with their own contested history.

Description and explanation

Of course, the language of 'identities' is our language, not the language of our subjects, and it reflects our preoccupations, not least with the politics of identity. This raises a further problem: do modern interpretations of the religious past explain it or misrepresent it? The classics of spirituality have often been subjected to social scientific readings, and women's devotional writings are frequently read through feminist eyes, being set within emancipation narratives or narratives of agency. What is gained and what is lost by such interpretive approaches?

In the field of religious studies, it is not uncommon to distinguish between description (an account of how one's subjects understand themselves), and explanation (a social scientific account of religious experience). Conceptually, this can be helpful, for we need to be clear as to the task we are engaged in, and distinguish sharply between our categories and those of our subjects. Of course, the line between description and explanation can blur as readily as the one that divides 'fact' from 'interpretation', or 'news' from 'opinion'.

Yet the worry persists that modern explanatory frameworks can facilitate misrepresentation and misappropriation. As the historian Amy Hollywood has observed, social scientific accounts 'are often subtly at odds with the experiences they purport to describe'. Thus a feminist construal of medieval female mystics (or Quaker women prophets) may not chime with how the women themselves understood their experience. 'How seriously do we take the agency of the other', Hollywood asks, 'when the other seems intent on ascribing her agency to God?' 'If part of the project of women's history is to hear the other – in all her alterity – we cannot unquestionably presume that our own explanatory and descriptive categories are valid and those of our subject are invalid.'[19]

Anthropologists refer to the problem as the difference between the 'emic' (seeing things from the point of view of the subject) and the 'etic' (seeing them from the point of view of the observer). It might also be seen as mapping on to the 'insider/outsider' distinction, with insiders to a religious tradition taking the 'emic' view of their ancestors, and outsiders taking the 'etic' perspective. In reality, however, insiders can be strongly inclined to project their own contemporary religious outlook on to their subjects, especially if those subjects are prestigious enough to validate a contemporary cause. And outsiders are capable of taking an 'emic' view of their subjects, devoting themselves to 'seeing things their way', and in their terms.[20] In practice, it is difficult to be so chaste that we deploy no modern categories in our description of early modern piety, but we should distinguish clearly between our terms and those available to our subjects.[21] And a major part of our task, whether we are historians or literary scholars, is to respect the otherness of our subjects by attending very closely to their own accounts of their experience and practice (and the accounts of their contemporaries). This involves immersion in their worlds (including their mental worlds), and learning their language; though it also requires some translation, with its attendant challenges and risks. The essays in this volume are exercises in immersion and translation, and they reflect the current vitality of this field.

Notes

1 Ken Jackson and Arthur Marotti, 'The Turn to Religion in Early Modern English Studies', *Criticism* 46 (2004), 167–90; Alister Chapman, John

Coffey and Brad Gregory (eds), *Seeing Things Their Way: Intellectual History and the Return of Religion* (Notre Dame, IN: University of Notre Dame Press, 2009); Mark Knight (ed.), *The Routledge Companion to Religion and Literature* (Abingdon: Routledge, 2016); Julia Reinhard Lupton, 'Religion and the Religious Turn', in John Lee (ed.), *A Handbook of English Renaissance Literary Studies* (Oxford: Wiley-Blackwell, 2017), pp. 70–85.

2 See for example two recent collections on early modern Britain and Ireland: Jessica Martin and Alec Ryrie (eds), *Private and Domestic Devotion in Early Modern Britain* (Abingdon: Routledge, 2012); John Coffey (ed.), *Heart Religion: Evangelical Piety in England and Ireland, 1690–1850* (Oxford: Oxford University Press, 2016).

3 The novelist L. P. Hartley as cited in David Lowenthal, *The Past is a Foreign Country* (Cambridge: Cambridge University Press, 1985), p. xvi.

4 See Devorah Baum, 'The Return of Religion: Secularization and its Discontents', and Lori Branch, 'The Post-Secular', in Knight (ed.), *The Routledge Companion to Religion and Literature*, pp. 80–8, 91–101.

5 See the classic study of Charles Taylor, *Sources of the Self: The Making of Modern Identity* (Cambridge: Cambridge University Press, 1989). Other studies tell what Taylor would call a 'subtraction story', in which the modern self is created following 'the retreat of God and the decline in the immediacy of the divine order of things'. Dror Wahrman, *The Making of the Modern Self: Identity and Culture in Eighteenth-Century England* (New Haven, CT: Yale University Press, 2004), p. 202.

6 Thomas Dixon, *Weeping Britannia: Portrait of a Nation in Tears* (Oxford: Oxford University Press, 2015), pp. 69–81; John Corrigan (ed.), *The Oxford Handbook of Religion and Emotion* (Oxford: Oxford University Press, 2008); Alec Ryrie and Tom Schwanda (eds), *Puritanism and Emotion in the Early Modern World* (Basingstoke: Palgrave Macmillan, 2016).

7 See David D. Hall (ed.), *Lived Religion: Towards a History of Practice* (Princeton, NJ: Princeton University Press, 2007). See also the classic study of Robert Orsi, *The Madonna of 115th Street: Faith and Community in Italian Harlem, 1880–1950* (New Haven, CT: Yale University Press, 3rd edn, 2010).

8 John Craig, 'Psalms, Groans and Dogwhippers: The Soundscape of Worship in the English Parish Church, 1547–1642', in Will Coster and Andrew Spicer (eds), *Sacred Space in Early Modern Europe* (Cambridge: Cambridge University Press, 2005), pp. 104–23; Jonathan Willis, *Church Music and Protestantism in Early Modern England: Discourses, Sites and Identities* (Farnham: Ashgate, 2010); Isabel Rivers and David L. Wykes (eds), *Dissenting Praise: Religious Dissent and the Hymn in*

England and Wales (Oxford: Oxford University Press, 2011); Andrew Cambers, *Godly Reading: Print, Manuscript and Puritanism in England, 1580–1720* (Cambridge: Cambridge University Press, 2011).

9 A striking example is 'My Booke of Rememberance' by Elizabeth Isham, a 60,000-word spiritual autobiography analysed most fully in Isaac Stephens, *The Gentlewoman's Remembrance: Patriarchy, Piety and Singlehood in Early Stuart England* (Manchester: Manchester University Press, 2016). See also the works of two influential historians: Caroline Walker Bynum, *Holy Feast and Holy Fast: The Religious Significance of Food to Medieval Women* (Berkeley: University of California Press, 1987); Phyllis Mack, *Visionary Women: Ecstatic Prophecy in Seventeenth-Century England* (Berkeley: University of California Press, 1992); Phyllis Mack, *Heart Religion in the British Enlightenment: Gender and Emotion in Early Methodism* (Cambridge: Cambridge University Press, 2008).

10 Richard Bell and Patricia Crawford, 'Statistical Analysis of Women's Printed Writings, 1600–1700', in Mary Prior (ed.), *Women in English Society, 1500–1800* (London: Routledge, 1991), pp. 265–82 (268–9).

11 See especially Elizabeth Clarke, *Politics, Religion and the Song of Songs in the Seventeenth Century* (Basingstoke: Palgrave Macmillan, 2011); Kevin Killeen, Helen Smith and Rachel Willie (eds), *The Oxford Handbook of the Bible in Early Modern England, c.1530–1700* (Oxford: Oxford University Press, 2015); Victoria Brownlee, *Biblical Readings and Literary Writings in Early Modern England, 1558–1625* (Oxford: Oxford University Press, 2018).

12 Stephen Greenblatt (gen. ed.), *The Norton Anthology of English Literature: The Major Authors*, 2 vols (New York: W.W. Norton, 10th edn, 2018). I am indebted to Robert W. Daniel for bringing this to my attention.

13 Peter Lake and Isaac Stephens, *Scandal and Religious Identity in Early Stuart England: A Northamptonshire Maid's Tragedy* (Woodbridge: Boydell & Brewer, 2017), pp. 174, 295. For a similar critique of a church historian by a political historian see Mark Goldie's review of Gordon Rupp, *Religion in England, 1688–1789* (Oxford: Oxford University Press, 1986): 'too often pious, even sentimental, where a greater historical astringency was required. It is a book of worthies … There is no grasp of the manifold ramifications of politics upon religion … Rupp shows too little stomach for theological and ecclesiological controversy.' *Journal of Ecclesiastical History* 39 (1988), 151–2.

14 Alec Ryrie, 'On Lake and Stephens' "Scandal and Religious Identity"', Alec Ryrie's blog, 26 August 2016. http://alecryrie.blogspot.com/2016/08/on-lake-and-stephens-scandal-and.html. Accessed 11 March 2018.

15 Alec Ryrie, *Protestants: The Radicals Who Made the Modern World* (London: Harper Collins, 2017).

16 Quentin Skinner, *Visions of Politics, Volume 1: Regarding Method*, 3 vols (Cambridge: Cambridge University Press, 2002), I:7.
17 David Bebbington, 'Response', in Chapman *et al.* (eds), *Seeing Things Their Way*, pp. 240–57 (252).
18 See the critique of Anthony Milton, 'Introduction: Reformation, Identity, and "Anglicanism"', *c.*1520–1662', in Anthony Milton (ed.), *The Oxford History of Anglicanism, Volume I: Reformation and Identity, c. 1520–1662*, 5 vols (Oxford: Oxford University Press, 2017), I:1–27 (1). See also Ethan H. Shagan, *The Rule of Moderation: Violence, Religion and the Politics of Restraint in Early Modern England* (Cambridge: Cambridge University Press, 2011).
19 Amy Hollywood, 'Gender, Agency, and the Divine in Religious Historiography', *Journal of Religion* 84 (2004), 514–28 (524).
20 See Russell T. McCutcheon (ed.), *The Insider-Outsider Problem in the Study of Religion* (London: Continuum, 1999); George Chrysiddes and Stephen E. Gregg (eds), *The Insider/Outsider Debate: New Perspectives in the Study of Religion* (Sheffield: Equinox, 2019).
21 For reflections on this see Skinner, *Visions of Politics*, I:27–56.

Acknowledgements

We are extremely grateful for the aid, support and encouragement offered by our colleagues at the University of Warwick. We also express our gratitude to the University of Warwick's Centre for the Study of the Renaissance and the Humanities Research Centre for their generous financial assistance during this endeavour, and the continued support of the Société d'Études Anglo-Américaines des XVIIe et XVIIIe siècles. We are extremely thankful to Birmingham University Library, the British Library, Cambridge University Library, Clare College Library, Dr Williams's Library, Derbyshire Record Office, University of Glasgow Library and the Religious Society of Friends (Quakers) in Britain, whose archivists and librarians were a tremendous source of help in acquiring permissions and answering various queries. We would like to thank the contributors for their outstanding scholarship, enthusiasm and commitment to this project, many of whom we count not just as colleagues but as dear friends. Finally, our gratitude to our families for patiently allowing this work to steal us away for these past three years – without you this would not be possible.

Abbreviations

BCP   *The Book of Common Prayer: The Texts of 1549, 1559, and 1662*, ed. Brian Cummings (Oxford: Oxford University Press, 2009)
BL   British Library
CJ   *The Journal of George Fox*, ed. Norman Penney, 2 vols (Cambridge: Cambridge University Press, 1911) (referred to as the *Cambridge Journal*)
DRO   Derbyshire Record Office
DWL   Dr Williams's Library
EJ   *A Journal or Historical Account of the Life, Travels, Sufferings, Christian Experiences and Labour ... of ... George Fox* (London, 1694) (referred to as the *Ellwood Journal*)
ODNB   Oxford Dictionary of National Biography
OED   *Oxford English Dictionary Online*
SJ   *The Short Journal and Itinerary Journals of George Fox*, ed. Norman Penney (Cambridge: Cambridge University Press, 1925) (referred to as the *Short Journal*)

Introduction

Elizabeth Clarke and Robert W. Daniel

In a dedicatory epistle to *The Mystery of Self-Deceiving* (1615), Jeremiah Dyke, the Church of England clergyman of Epping, Essex, remarked on the benefit and impact devotional writing possessed. Endorsing this treatise, penned by his elder brother and fellow clergyman Daniel Dyke, who had died the year previously, and having read Daniel's diary, 'a catalogue ... of his sinnes against God', Jeremiah hailed such literary endeavours as necessary spiritual acts because 'surely wee never beginne to know Divinitie or Religion, till wee come to know our selves'.[1] Jeremiah's message – that in order to understand 'Religion' people had to write about their own experience of it – clearly resonated with many Protestants, as by 1642 *The Mystery of Selfe-Deceiving* had reached eleven editions. Increased access to this kind of literature ensured, and not just amongst the literate class, that a large number of spiritual guides and religious books were read (or heard read aloud) during the Tudor and Stuart reigns. This was part of a pan-European appreciation for and consumption of printed devotional works following the printing boom of the Reformation.[2] In England, and to English Protestants like Jeremiah, devotional reading was a means and not an end; it helped shape devotional writing, which cultivated an individual or shared sense of devotional identity.[3]

The devotional exercises of England's lay and clerical Protestants have always fascinated scholars. As Roger Pooley has observed, it is the 'mixture of fury and faith' exhibited in early modern religious writings that makes 'many ... Christians so magnetic' as figures for historical study.[4] This notion is not a modern symptom of nostalgia for the past. As the contemporary poet and pamphleteer John Milton put it, 'For Books are not absolutely dead things, but doe contain a potencie of life in them to be as active as that soule was whose progeny they are; nay they do preserve as in a violl the purest efficacie and extraction of that living intellect that bred them.'[5] Milton's notion could be extended to the 'living intellect' exhibited in manuscript writings such as diaries, sermon notes, commonplace books, wills and poetic miscellanies.[6] One may question whether printed and scribal works, which in Milton's age so often defined themselves by their shared *sententiae* and religious verbiage, provided the 'purest' portraits of those who wrote them.[7] To seventeenth-century English men and women, however, devotional writing was a vital tool by which they could know their 'Religion' by better knowing '[them]selves'.

People and Piety is a collection of essays that examines the complexities and contingencies of Protestant devotional identity in religious writings during post-Reformation England. It brings together fresh investigations from established scholars and early-career researchers from sixteen institutions on either side of the Atlantic. Interdisciplinary in approach, their research shows how devotional acts and attitudes manifested themselves in a variety of spaces, literary styles and material forms.

Definitions and parameters

What are Protestant 'devotional identities'? Such a broad term requires categorisation. On the one hand, it serves as a useful distinction from Protestant 'denominational identities'. While the former demarcates religious rituals, texts, songs, gestures and gnomic phrases shared by a variety of writers, the latter marks out the rigid and often uncompromising practices of religious groups. In this way, 'devotional identities' accommodates scholarship that has shown how putatively Roman Catholic prayers and precepts were incorporated within Protestant devotional regimens in intriguing ways.[8] The term also allows for studies that nuance our understanding of the wide assimilation of certain kinds of religious reading, writing and acting that occurred within the 'broad church' of Protestantism during early modern England. In short, it enables researchers to better elucidate what Debora Shuger called 'the sociocultural imbrications of religion'.[9]

On the other hand, Protestant devotional identities could be tied to, and be a symptom of, denominational ones. The heat of Church- and State-sponsored persecution in England, particularly after the Restoration in 1660, which saw the triumphant return of monarchic rule under Charles II, stiffened rather than eroded the pietistic practices of several religious groups, especially those who came to be known as 'dissenters'.[10] These groups rejected the rituals and liturgy of the Established Church and sought to maintain their own spiritual codes of conduct. A rooted sense of devotional exceptionalism took hold as Presbyterians, Independents, Quakers, Baptists and other religious movements each independently saw themselves as a select band of saints. Their congregational and domestic devotional performances crystallised their sense of religious identity and sharpened their resolve. Each saw their own pious beliefs and practices as above reproach and disputed those of others. This ensured that their religious communities narrowed, even if their social circles did not.[11] Though recent studies have shown how the boundary between the Established Church and moderate dissent was 'highly porous', it must be remembered that a great many dissenters were still willing to suffer fines, imprisonment, transportation or even death rather than recant their religious beliefs and cease their devotional activities.[12]

The tensions within Protestant devotional identities can be demonstrated in two examples from pre- and post-Restoration England. The first is the inclusion of the biblical passage in Exodus 18 – where Jethro, Moses' father-in-law, celebrates the Israelites' crossing of the Red Sea – in the parliamentarian victory hymns of the 1640s–50s. Here early hymn writers such as George Wither, John Goodwin, William Barton, Thomas St Nicholas and a balladeer by the name of 'R. P.' all paraphrased Exodus 18:11 ('Now I know that the LORD is greater than all gods: for in the thing wherein they dealt proudly he was above them')[13] in their songs to celebrate Parliament's various victories over the Royalists, the Scots and the Dutch during the English Civil Wars and Interregnum.[14] Though these authors all subscribed to the parliamentarian cause – some, like Wither and St Nicholas, even served as officers in it – they came from different religious groupings and traditions. Goodwin, although later shunned by Parliament as an 'Arminian puritan', was a dependable supporter of the Commonwealth and his Coleman Street congregation were influential in the City of London.[15] Wither was a fiery religious 'radical' and a friend to Levellers.[16] By comparison, Barton was part of a godly, popular and 'experienced parish clergy' who later conformed to the Church of England.[17] St Nicholas was an ardent Independent, part of the landed gentry, who fell out of favour with the Protector Oliver Cromwell.[18] 'R. P.' was a London minister, likely of the Congregational persuasion.[19]

This demonstrates how devotional, and to some extent political, identities could be shared by any number of people who did not share the same religious identities. These writers may very well have ignored, or been ignorant of, the earlier and alternative uses of Exodus 18, but regardless it was these antecedent echoes that gave their use power and recognition, a profound sense that they conveyed a tangible truth as old as time itself. In doing so, English Protestants made religion their own by practising their own spiritual devotions, in spite of (or perhaps because of) the apparent historic continuity of those devotions with other strands of Protestantism.

Another example of the fluidity of Protestant devotional identities is the occasional and partial Prayer Book worship practised by some Presbyterians. This is evidenced in the life of the dissenting minister and diarist Philip Henry. When his son printed Philip's autobiography in 1698, he remarked on his father's fondness for the phrase 'In the midst of Life we are in Death' in his preaching and writing, openly acknowledging that it was an 'expression of our English Liturgy in the Office of Burial' that appeared in the revised 1662 version of the *Book of Common Prayer*.[20] The phrase formed part of an anthem said or sung at the graveside as the body was lowered into the ground. It was one of the few survivals of the medieval Catholic Prayer Book for the offices of the dead.[21] Philip Henry's use of the Prayer Book's phraseology may have given his High Church opponents ammunition enough. Its repeated use, however, did not indicate that he, a dissenting clergyman, was an avid supporter of the Prayer Book or its burial service. He attended church funerals only to hear the sermon and left before the rubric could be read out over the coffin.[22] His use of the Prayer Book's quasi-scriptural *dictum* for his own pastoral and personal purposes did not make him less Presbyterian – or more Anglican. It did not indicate that he was more amenable to the possible comprehension of Presbyterians in the Church of England. Instead, the partial use of the Prayer Book cemented rather than discounted Henry's

INTRODUCTION

credentials as a thoroughgoing Presbyterian, for this practice was not uncommon amongst his brethren after 1662.[23] The above cases provide a useful spotlight on the shared and piecemeal ways English Protestants lived out their faith in early modern England, revealing how religious heterodoxy did not preclude occasional spiritual accommodation.[24]

As our definition of Protestant devotional identities suggests, this volume encompasses the whole range of religious traditions, evolving denominations and competing faith systems in Reformation England. Contributors discuss puritanism (chapters 3, 6) Catholicism (chapters 6, 7, 13, 14), Anglicanism (chapters 11, 13) and a hybrid post-Calvinism (chapter 1), with a view to exploring the formation of Protestant devotional identities as either trans-confessional or distinct denominational exercises.

As Alec Ryrie has posited, 'Christians are more than credal statements on legs,' and this volume of essays both complements and challenges that claim.[25] This collection's title – *People and Piety* – reflects the 'lived religion', or rather the 'lived devotion', as men and women of the period described it. Though their world was factious and refractory, their words describe a struggle of a different kind – to defend their own beliefs (to kin, kirk, God and themselves) rather than attack those of others. Denominational communities were important. They served as surrogate families, when blood relations were of a contrary faith. However, religious allegiances, just like political ones, were susceptible to change and contingent upon circumstance. In a similar way, devotional identities were not static. They were often a messy bricolage of experimental, folkloric and doctrinal concepts. In this way piety did not define people, it was people who defined their piety. This volume shows how Protestant authors worked out their faith in deeply personal, painstaking and sometimes painful ways. This approach allows scholars, as John Coffey has noted, to understand 'early modern religion in its own terms' and by its own devotional writings.[26] In doing so one discovers that English Protestantism was at once segregational and social, fixed in principle yet fluid in practice.

Sources

The volume's sources include a rich array of manuscript and printed devotional works including hymns and poems, prayers and covenants, sermons and sermon notes, journals and diaries, martyrologies, and ballads and plays, as well as spiritual guides. This balance reflects the now voluble scholarship on how scribal culture could exist side by side with print.[27] Manuscript texts were just as devotionally potent and important as printed ones. Contributions to this volume (especially chapters 1, 3, 8, 10) reinforce Andrew Cambers' assertion that there existed a significant paradigm within religious manuscript writing which consisted of 'sociability and the self'.[28] William Sherman's research on the 'dynamic ecology of use and reuse' of printed books equally applies to manuscript life-writing, a major theme in this volume, whereby the use of devotional texts leads to their frequent 'transformation' and 'preservation'.[29] A wealth of recent research, outlined by Zeynep Tenger and Paul Trolande, shows how manuscript authors were not 'dead set against print' but 'made strategic choices' and 'deployed texts tactically'.[30] Through a study of various religious authors and their texts, *People and Piety* shows how this was just as true for manuscript writers when writing about their devotions.

Although this volume does not address the devotional practices of the illiterate, the subjects of it reflect a variety of social backgrounds, which include landed gentlemen and gentlewomen, clergymen and their wives, physicians, lawyers, apprentices, and printers. Thus, readers are presented with an eclectic gamut of English authors playing a variety of gendered roles (father, son, mother, daughter, husband, wife) who sought to express their faith in surprising, and sometimes surprisingly similar, ways. In this way, readers are introduced to the lives of rarely discussed male religious figures, such as the Cambridgeshire clergyman Isaac Archer (1641–1700) (chapter 9) and the Kent-born lawyer and religious poet Thomas St Nicholas (*bap.* 1602, *d.* 1668) (chapter 13). Its various case studies also reveal the intellectual culture and writings of under-investigated early modern women.[31] These include the printing strategies, formats and designs employed in the work of the Baptist prophetess Katherine Sutton (*fl.* 1630–63) (chapter 2), the voluminous sermon notes and correspondences of the puritan patron Katherine Gell (*bap.* 1624, *d.* 1671) (chapter 3), and the recently discovered life in manuscript of the London dissenter Mary Franklin (*d.* 1711) (chapter 10). The literary output of these individuals furthers our understanding of how Protestant devotional identity was shaped through familial, domestic and congregational settings. Such biographical portraits are glimpsed here on a small but important canvas. These figures sit alongside more familiar devotional authors of the period such as Oliver Heywood (chapter 4), George Fox (chapter 8), George Herbert (chapter 11) and Richard Baxter (chapter 12). Together these studies nuance our thinking about the role prosopography, poetry, letters and pamphlets played in encapsulating and shaping Protestantism and devotional identity in Reformation England.

Scope and structure

This collection brings new examinations into the field of devotional writing, which, as Susan M. Felch has argued, is sorely 'underrepresented'.[32] This area is vital to our understanding of how individual and corporate selfhood was expressed and incorporated into the socio-religious landscape of early modern England. Miri Rubin has argued, in her study of Medieval England, that 'identity is as elusive as it is central to individual lives and collective experience', and this includes identities forged through 'devotional traditions'.[33] As Linda Tredennick has averred for the seventeenth century, there is 'still no single issue more central' to the study of that period today than the 'definition and history of identity' exemplified in religious writings.[34] The 'devotional turn' in recent scholarship is further evidence of the growing importance of studying the formation of Protestant identities and the literary styles that expressed them.[35]

Previous studies have mined many fragmentary and variegated aspects of devotional identity in early modern England. This volume engages with this work in several ways. Where scholars such as Andrew Cambers have explored the 'godly reading' of this period, the essays in this volume investigate a corresponding 'godly writing'.[36] Where John Doran, Charlotte Methuen and Alexandra Walsham's edited volume examines *Religion and the Household*, this work broadens its scope by looking at religious practices within and beyond the home.[37] The studies in this collection build on Jessica Martin and Alec Ryrie's edited volume *Private and Domestic Devotion* by examining performances of piety that were not confined to the domestic realm or defined by a narrow regimen of psalm-singing, prayers or Bible reading.[38] The scholarship in this volume also complements the work of Kate Narveson by revealing the creativity and ingenuity of lay devotional readers and writers.[39]

The time period covered by this volume (roughly 1517–1700) is of notable import. Suzanne Trill has been right to argue that while a lot of work has recently been done on the 'intersection between public and private devotions', with a special focus 'on lay practice', for the most part 'general studies make 1640 their endpoint'.[40] While there are good reasons for this, the essays collected here, by contrast, represent a longer view of religious history by examining the devotional writings during sixteenth- and seventeenth-century England. The investigations here also both confront and complement historiographical work since the 2000s that has stressed cross-confessional modes of religious expression.[41]

People and Piety is divided into two central sections: 'Sites' and 'Types'. The 'Sites' section broadens our understanding of the places in which religious devotions and writings were performed. From the 2010s onwards, scholars have paid renewed attention to the home as the centre of religious life. In particular, as 'new historicism' gave way to 'new materialism', researchers have illustrated the physical objects, decorative styles and functional roles specific rooms within the home played in facilitating Protestant devotional activities.[42] Chapters in this section provide an additional and alternative treatment whereby domestic religious activities were fostered by material texts such as storybooks, letters and sermon notes.

Whilst scholarship has elucidated the Protestant domestic sphere as a mediatory space that could serve both secular and sacred functions, not enough attention has been paid to the devotions performed outside the home – with perhaps the exception of the parish church.[43] For this reason, the 'Sites' section also examines other, often under-investigated, devotional spaces. The academy (chapter 1), the printing house (chapter 2), the theatre (chapters 5 and 6) and the prison (chapters 7 and 8) were all important zones in which devotional identities were forged, rehearsed, read and performed. The findings presented in this section open up these spaces as being equally crucial to the devotional lives, identities and writings of men and women of faith.

The 'Types' section explores some of the genres in which devotional identities were couched. These offer new ways of thinking about the various receptacles of religious expression: spiritual autobiographies (chapters 9 and 10), religious poetry (chapters 11 and 12), and accounts tied to the *ars moriendi* (chapters 13 and 14).[44] Chapters in this section reveal the persistent use of and reliance of authors on devotional writing during moments of personal loss or public persecution. They add to an emerging scholarship that is revealing the heterogeneity of texts, writings styles and mediums in which people chose to defend or better comprehend their devotional acts.[45] Ultimately, the division of the 'Sites' and 'Types' sections is not intended to provide exhaustive coverage of these areas, nor are they mutually exclusive, rather they serve as springboards for further research.

Overview of chapters

Devotional identities through religious writing could be communal in character. Recent work has sought to re-evaluate the perceived insularity and introspective writing practices of some strands of English Protestantism.[46] It is in this vein that David Manning's essay in chapter 1 examines the understudied writings of the little academy at Little Gidding (*c.*1631–33). He reveals how the Ferrar family's use of oral, handwritten and printed forms of devotional expressions constituted a hybrid blend of Humanist, post-Calvinist and Arminian influences. Their cerebral musings foraged the past to feed their present, as part of a cycle of social and textual re-appropriation. Here Manning's work provides a unique insight into the trajectory of devotional endeavours from minority to mainstream, and how these were dissected and assimilated by the industrious learners at Little Gidding.

Michael Durrant's essay in chapter 2 continues this theme by demonstrating the social and material production (rather than just the literary or spiritual exercise) of devotional identities. By showcasing Katherine Sutton's Particular Baptist conversion account *A Christian Woman's Experiences* (1663) as a highly crafted and visually sophisticated product, Durrant adduces a lively interaction between what might be described as the 'physicality' of the text and the model of godly selfhood that it advanced. Manning and Durrant reveal how materially and socially imbricated devotional polemics were, pointing to the religious communities that forged them.

The Protestant household, itself a micro-community and 'little church', was a site where devotional selfhood was frequently practised, regulated and monitored in Reformation England.[47] Ann Hughes in chapter 3 examines how lay scribal practices of sermon note-taking linked individual spiritual crises to collective experience and became a family project. Through examining the sermon notes kept by the Gell household from the 1640s to the 1710s, Hughes reveals them as devotional prompts that sustained the family's Presbyterianism across two generations. In evaluating the figure of Katherine Gell, Hughes demonstrates the crucial role played by women within the home in sustaining a nonconformist devotional culture both before and after the Restoration. Similarly, William J. Sheils in chapter 4 examines the domestic worship of Presbyterians both before and after the Act of Toleration (1689). By investigating the dissenting clergyman Oliver Heywood's diary and his printed treatise *A Family Altar* (1693), Sheils provides a case study on how centralising prayer became within the godly home. In particular, Sheils reveals how, through his writing on prayer, Heywood configured household worship as a substitute for chapel worship in dissenting circles, blurring the lines between corporate and domestic devotion. Hughes and Sheils demonstrate how the performance of household piety could be a unifying force that helped galvanise the faith of families during trying periods and periods of great change.

Unlike the home, the early modern theatre might seem a strange place to encounter devotional identities. Post-Reformation plays were often seen as inciting sin with their performance of lewd acts, adulteries and bedevilments.[48] Yet the English stage, like the English household, could be a site where the rituals of piety were re-enacted. Iman Sheeha in chapter 5 examines the modelling out of mothers' legacies, a genre of conduct books penned and left by mothers for their children, in the anonymous domestic tragedy *A Warning for Fair Women* (1599). Sheeha reveals how the play frames the 'gallows speech' of a convicted murderess – Mistress Saunders – as exemplifying this genre, and culminates in Saunders leaving a copy of John Bradford's *Meditations* (1560) to her children. This act, coupled with her dying words, completes Saunders' journey of rehabilitation from adulterous and murderous wife to redeemed and devoted mother. Sheeha emphasises the play's function as a proselytising tool that sought to reinforce the importance of godly motherhood by depicting those who had transgressed it.

Thomas Middleton's city comedy *The Puritan Widow* (1607) attacked puritan devotional practices and derided Catholic ones. This did not go unnoticed. William Cranshaw denounced the play in his Paul's Cross sermon, later printed, for irreligiously bringing 'religion and holy things vpon the stage'.[49] In chapter 6 Robert O.

Yates takes a different view. He reveals how Middleton attempted to reconcile the conflicting religious roles of the play's protagonist – Lady Plus – as chaste widow to her sexualised potential as a remarried wife. The play wryly subsumes what Yates terms 'devotion to mirth' with devotion to God, whereby the dramatisation of communal feasting, festive combat and the wearing of livery leads to the marriage altar, the re-establishment of Protestant religious values and the play's denouement. In this way, audiences could be taught to adopt religious conformity through dramatic and festive re-enactment – satire could (and often did) point to the sacred. In doing so, English playwrights could mock devotions and model them too. Yates's and Sheeha's findings suggest that the sermonising of plays was arguably as important in inculcating Protestant devotional practices as the preachments of the pulpiteers who detested them.

Those who did not heed these minatory messages, and refused to conform to the Church of England, were frequently imprisoned. For, in an age of religious persecution, English prisons were not just for traditional criminals.[50] As one Quaker pamphleteer observed, 'Prisons turned into Churches' as the Word was regularly preached by inmates within (to their fellow cellmates) or without (to the wider public).[51] As a result, several inmates became fervent devotional writers and readers. Lynn Robson in chapter 7 examines how early modern prisons in the sixteenth and seventeenth centuries could sometimes serve as sacred spaces. Through her engagement with elite and popular texts, Robson draws the frequent connection between profane incarceration and the consecration of space achieved by an individual's pious actions: self-examination, religious conversation, praying, reading and writing. Robson further posits that the prison texts themselves that recorded these devotions might have been read more than other traditional Protestant works, thus propelling godliness across thresholds: from the prison into the booksellers, and finally into the home. Catie Gill in chapter 8 explores the autobiographical writings of the Quaker leader George Fox during his series of imprisonments in the 1650s. Through a detailed analysis of the textual variants in three editions of his prison accounts – found in the *Short Journal*, the *Cambridge Journal* and the *Ellwood Journal* – Gill adduces the role that Thomas Ellwood (as editor) played in shaping, and not just ventriloquising, the devotional identity of this dogmatic religious leader. In doing so, Gill reveals to what extent

Fox's representation of imprisonment – and his own devotional character – had been censored, and the effects these changes had on the reception of him and his journal. Robson and Gill reveal how religious prison writing created a recognisable form of carceral piety that connected English prisoners textually, spatially and historically too.

Devotional identities were defined not just by where they were recorded and performed, but by the literary forms they came in. Arguably the most prolific of these during the period was autobiographical writing and its corollary, spiritual autobiographies.[52] Bernard Capp in chapter 9 examines how internal disputes within families over devotional practices, particularly between fathers and sons, were played out in the confessional spaces of their diaries. Financial and filial concerns, rather than soteriological and casuistical ones, might emerge as the deciding factors in one's choice of faith. Capp shows that behind closed doors many agonised, deliberated and fought over the kinds of piety they were expected to perform, revealing how domestic piety could be coerced as well as co-opted. Vera J. Camden in chapter 10 shows how Mary Franklin, a newly discovered female voice, used her private manuscript devotions to create an identity that could defy and defend against State persecution. As a Presbyterian mother and wife, living in a Restoration London notoriously dangerous to dissenters, Franklin chronicles the trials her family endured for their religious beliefs in a manuscript account, later titled by Franklin's granddaughter 'The Experience of my dear grandmother, Mrs Mary Franklin'. A recourse to scripture proofs, coupled with her own dramatic experiences, allowed Franklin to write a spiritual autobiography that situated her belief in a distinct Protestant past as well as in the present tumultuous times she was living in. Franklin's writing provided an enduring material record that sustained not only her own faith, but that of successive generations of her family. Camden, through meticulous research, brings the hitherto unknown devotional life of Mary Franklin to bear with vivid detail and sensitivity. Capp and Camden reveal how religious autobiographical writing served as a pivotal spiritual exercise to defend one's own devotional identity, and contend with the devotional identities of others.

Like autobiography, poetry served as an appropriate form of both devotional expression and religious exercise.[53] Jenna Townend's essay in chapter 11 examines the political and religious fluidity of George Herbert's *The Temple* (1633) to link the devotional expressions of Royalists and Roundheads during the Civil Wars and Interregnum. Readers integrated Herbert's verse into their own piety, as they responded to unprecedented religious and political upheavals. Ironically, as Townend reveals, this meant that there was often more that united Herbert's admirers than divided them. This causes us to re-evaluate how religious verse was adaptable to, as it was contiguous with, the devotional needs of those on either side of England's truculent political aisle. Sylvia Brown in chapter 12 investigates the role 'passions' played in the life of the eminent dissenter Richard Baxter and his devotional works: *Poetical Fragments* (1681) and his *Additions* (1683). Like Herbert's, Baxter's poetry was defined by passions inspired by the Holy Spirit, but was also grounded in more earthly emotions. Baxter used the occasion of the devastating personal loss of his wife Margaret to present his readers with a new kind of practical divinity: consolation – of self as much as others – through a poetics of the passions. Brown shows how Margaret was intricately bound up with Baxter's sense of his own devotional identity, and how her figure loomed large over the hymns and poems he wrote, thus drawing important attention to the intimate role their connubial relationship played in inspiring his sacred poetry for a public audience. Townend and Brown remind us that the potency of religious verse was situational, linked to either the biographies of its authors or those of its readers.

The *ars moriendi*, or 'the art of dying well', was arguably the figurative end and literal pinnacle of religious writing in early modern England.[54] The Ludlow clergyman Robert Horne summed up the sentiment of the age well when he preached: 'I know not when I shall die, and therefore every day shall be as my dying day.'[55] A life of piety was thus the best preparation for a good death, and one never knew whether an illness would prove fleeting or fatal. Robert W. Daniel in chapter 13 examines the devotional identities exhibited through the acts and attitudes performed in the early modern sickchamber. Through exploring the manuscript accounts of various valetudinarians, he reveals a shared biblicism employing the same scriptures as sacred acts that mirrored or contested those outlined in printed devotional works which governed the correct behaviours during illness. He finds that one did not have to be a co-religionist to appreciate or practise the same kind of sickbed devotions. By recording their similar reading habits, covenants, prayers, gestures, speeches and praises, the laity more than the clergy made their piety recognisable and thus repeatable. While Daniel examines the sickbed, Charles Green in chapter 14 examines the deathbed. Green explores the generic fluidity of Protestant deathbed narratives, and the devotions they described, in late Elizabethan and early Jacobean England. He sees such texts as deriving rhetorical power from the persuasive and cultural capital of the sermonic, liturgical and biographical genres in which they were enshrined in print. He argues that these accounts were polemically charged, describing not just how their subjects died, but how readers might also die a holy death. Empowered lay authors, and omnivorous readers, could see themselves as exemplifying the archetypal pious death in recorded dying speeches. Daniel and Green reveal the denominational parity in the Protestant piety performed within the early modern sick- and death-chamber. Though the ill might be treated and ministered to differently, if they were to perish they wanted to be seen to die in similar ways.

By elucidating the various 'sites' of devotional identities, and the various 'types' of religious writings that espoused them, *People and Piety* demonstrates the complexities and continuities of faith in early modern England: that individual or corporate devotion was not always driven by competition or distinction, but by a genuine and deep desire, in Jeremiah Dyke's words, 'to know our selves'.

Notes

1. Daniel Dyke, *The Mystery of Self-Deceiving* (London, 1615), A3^r, B1^r. He is not to be confused with Daniel Dyke (1614–88), General Baptist minister, who was Jeremiah Dyke's (*bap.* 1584, *d.* 1639) son.
2. As Matthew P. Brown avers, 'devotional steady sellers must be reckoned a, perhaps the, canon of popular reading in the early modern West'. Matthew P. Brown, 'The Thick Style: Steady Sellers, Textual Aesthetics, and Early Modern Devotional Reading', *Publications of the Modern Language Association* 121.1 (2006), 67–86 (69).
3. Jeremiah Dyke was not alone in this thinking. The Presbyterian minister Isaac Ambrose insisted that 'If we were read in the Story of our own lives, we might have a Divinity of our own, drawn out of the observation of God's particular dealings towards us.' Isaac Ambrose, *Media, or the Middle Things* (London, 1649), p. 93 (mispaginated as 98).
4. Roger Pooley, *English Prose of the Seventeenth Century 1590–1700* (London: Longman, 1992), p. 4.

INTRODUCTION

5 John Milton, *Areopagitica* (1644), in Don M. Wolfe et al. (eds), *Complete Prose Works of John Milton*, 8 vols (New Haven, CT: Yale University Press, 1953–82), II:492. Milton was defending the liberty to publish and the tyranny of censorship. His argument, however, had an obvious devotional dimension. Nearly half of all books published during this period were about religious subjects. See Debora K. Shuger, *The Renaissance Bible: Scholarship, Sacrifice, and Subjectivity* (Berkeley: University of California Press, 1994), p. 1.

6 Margaret Ezell compares the survival of scribal documents to 'flies in amber'. Such glimpses, Ezell asserts, of a 'long since deceased literary landscape', ensure a 'continuation of that presence which survives destruction, that matter which the living are permitted still to embrace'. Margaret J. M. Ezell, 'The Posthumous Publication of Women's Manuscripts and the History of Authorship', in George Justice and Nathan Tinker (eds), *Women's Writing and the Circulation of Ideas: Manuscript Publication in England, 1550–1800* (Cambridge: Cambridge University Press, 2002), pp. 121–36 (128).

7 Such questions were posed by Stephen Greenblatt, who argued that Renaissance texts demonstrated 'an increased self-consciousness about the fashioning of human identity' as a 'manipulable, artful process'. Stephen Greenblatt, *Renaissance Self-Fashioning: From More to Shakespeare* (Chicago: University of Chicago Press, 1980), p. 2.

8 See Elisabeth Slater, 'What Kind of Horse Is It? Popular Devotional Reading during the Sixteenth Century', in Matthew Dimmock and Andrew Hadfield (eds), *Literature and Popular Culture in Early Modern England* (London: Routledge, 2009), pp. 105–20; Janel Mueller, 'Prospecting for Common Ground in Devotion: Queen Katherine Parr's Personal Prayer Book', in Micheline White (ed.), *English Women, Religion, and Textual Production, 1500–1625* (Burlington, VT: Ashgate, 2011), pp. 127–46; Micheline White, 'Dismantling Catholic Primers and Reforming Private Prayer: Anne Lock, Hezekiah's Song and Psalm 50/51', in Jessica Martin and Alec Ryrie (eds), *Private and Domestic Devotion in Early Modern Britain* (Abingdon: Routledge, 2012), pp. 93–113. Also see chapters 7 and 13.

9 Shuger, *The Renaissance Bible*, p. 2.

10 For comprehensive histories of this movement and its literary by-products see N. H. Keeble, *The Literary Culture of Nonconformity in Later Seventeenth-Century England* (Leicester: Leicester University Press, 2nd edn, 1991); Margaret J. M. Ezell, *The Oxford English Literary History, Volume V: 1645–1714, The Later Seventeenth Century* (Oxford: Oxford University Press, 2017), pp. 54–70; Michael Davies, Anne Dunan-Page, and Joel Halcomb (eds), *Church Life: Pastors, Congregations, and the Experience of Dissent in Seventeenth-Century England* (Oxford: Oxford

University Press, 2019); John Coffey (ed.), *The Oxford History of Protestant Dissenting Traditions, Volume I: The Post-Reformation Era, c.1559–c.1689* (Oxford: Oxford University Press, 2020).

11 See Alexandra Walsham, 'Supping with Satan's Disciples: Spiritual and Secular Sociability in Post-Reformation England', in Nadine Lewycky and Adam Morton (eds), *Getting Along? Religious Identities and Confessional Relations in Early Modern England* (Farnham: Ashgate, 2012), pp. 29–56. For the interlinking social circles of radical religious groups see William E. Smith III, 'Henry Hills Goes Ranter', *Seventeenth Century* 32.3 (2017), 257–68. Also see chapter 2. There also existed, however, friction between competing religious groups at the local level. See William Sheils, 'Religious Divisions in the Localities: Catholics, Puritans and the Established Church before the Civil Wars', in Trevor Dean, Glyn Parry and Edward Vallance (eds), *Faith, Place and People in Early Modern England* (London: Boydell and Brewer, 2018), pp. 29–42.

12 Roger Morrice, *The Entring Book of Roger Morrice (1677–1691)*, ed. Mark Goldie et al., 7 vols (Woodbridge: Boydell & Brewer in association with the Parliamentary History Yearbook Trust, 2007), I:229–30.

13 King James Bible.

14 See Robert W. Daniel, 'The Manuscript Poetry of Thomas St Nicholas and the Writing of "Scripturalism" in Seventeenth-Century England' (unpublished PhD thesis, University of Warwick, 2018), pp. 182–232. This furthers Nigel Smith's hypothesis about 'battle hymns' as a popular religious genre composed during Cromwellian England. Nigel Smith, *Literature and Revolution in England, 1640–1660* (London: Yale University Press, 1994), pp. 260–76. It also supports John Coffey's assertion about the persistence of the Exodus story as an expression of political liberation during the 1640s and beyond. John Coffey, *Exodus and Liberation: Deliverance Politics from John Calvin to Martin Luther King Jr* (Oxford: Oxford University Press, 2014), esp. pp. 25–55.

15 John Coffey, *John Goodwin and the Puritan Revolution* (Suffolk: Boydell and Brewer, 2006), pp. 4, 168–98.

16 David Norbrook, *Writing the English Republic: Poetry, Rhetoric and Politics, 1627–1660* (Cambridge: Cambridge University Press, 1999), pp. 384–6.

17 A. B. Grosart, revised by D. K. Money, 'Barton, William (1597/8–1678)', *Oxford Dictionary of National Biography* (hereafter *ODNB*). https://doi.org/10.1093/ref:odnb/1606. Accessed 12 March 2019.

18 H. Neville Davies, 'St Nicholas, Thomas (*bap.* 1602, *d.*1668)', *ODNB*. https://doi.org/10.1093/ref:odnb/66680. Accessed 12 March 2019.

19 Biographical details can be gleaned from R. P., *Berachah, or Englands memento to thankefulnesse being a hymne* (London, 1646), broadside.

20 Matthew Henry, *An account of the life and death of Mr. Philip Henry* (London, 1698), pp. 194–5.
21 Church of England, 'The Book of Common Prayer, 1662', in *The Book of Common Prayer: The Texts of 1549, 1559, and 1662*, ed. Brian Cummings (Oxford: Oxford University Press, 2009), pp. 183–666 (455). For an earlier version of this prayer in the 1559 Prayer Book see p. 171.
22 See Richard L. Greaves, 'Henry, Philip (1631–1696)', *ODNB*. https://doi.org/10.1093/ref:odnb/12976. Accessed 12 March 2019.
23 Philip Henry records attending Presbyterian meetings where parts of the Prayer Book were read and states they were only occasionally omitted through 'hast[e] and careles[s]nes[s]'. Philip Henry, *Diaries and Letters of Philip Henry, M.A. of Broad Oak, Flintshire, A.D. 1631–1696*, ed. Matthew Henry Lee (London, 1882), pp. 135, 156. Also see Keeble, *The Literary Culture of Nonconformity*, p. 36; Robert W. Daniel, 'Prayer "Bills" in Seventeenth-Century Britain', *Notes & Queries* 66.4 (2019), 554–8.
24 Other examples can be found in devotional reading habits of the period. Printed devotional texts written by High and Low Church authors were read and recommended in the same breath by such contrasting figures as Anne Halkett, Lucy Hutchinson and Richard Baxter. See respectively, Suzanne Trill, *Lady Anne Halkett: Selected Self-Writings* (Aldershot: Ashgate, 2007), p. xxvii; Robert Wilcher, 'Lucy Hutchinson', in Andrew Hiscock and Helen Wilcox (eds), *The Oxford Handbook of Early Modern English Literature and Religion* (Oxford: Oxford University Press, 2017), pp. 360–73 (361); John Coffey, 'Between Puritanism and Evangelicalism: Heart-Work in Dissenting Communion Hymns, 1693–1709', in John Coffey (ed.), *Heart Religion: Evangelical Piety in England and Ireland, 1690–1850* (Oxford: Oxford University Press, 2016), pp. 29–49 (note 22, p. 33). Readers also crossed the confessional divide in selecting texts that provided them with spiritual comfort. This was the case with the Whig Member of Parliament for Chester (1689–97) and ex-Royalist army officer Roger Whitley. Whitley records in his diary owning both the Protestant devotional bestseller *The Whole Duty of Man* (1658) alongside the Catholic hagiography *The Life of the Blessed Virgin, Saint Catharine of Siena* (1609). Bodleian Library, Ms Eng Hist C 711, fols 42^v, 51^v.
25 Alec Ryrie, *Being Protestant in Reformation Britain* (Oxford: Oxford University Press, 2013), p. 3. For a contrasting view see Peter Lake, 'Anti-Puritanism: The Structure of a Prejudice', in Kenneth Fincham and Peter Lake (eds), *Religious Politics in Post-Reformation England* (Suffolk: Boydell and Brewer, 2006), pp. 80–97. For the ongoing debate surrounding the nature of religious identity during this period see the foreword.

26 John Coffey, *Persecution and Toleration in Protestant England, 1558–1689* (London: Longman, 2000), p. 10. This point is developed more fully in John Coffey's 'Quentin Skinner and the Religious Dimension of Early Modern Political Thought', in Alister Chapman, John Coffey and Brad Gregory (eds), *Seeing Things Their Way: Intellectual History and the Return of Religion* (Notre Dame, IN: University of Notre Dame Press, 2009), pp. 46–74.

27 For the overlapping and competing mediums of print and manuscript during this period see Arthur F. Marotti and Michael D. Bristol (eds), *Print, Manuscript, Performance: The Changing Relations of the Media in Early Modern England* (Columbus: Ohio State University Press, 2000); Zeynep Tenger and Paul Trolande, 'From Print versus Manuscript to Sociable Authorship and Mixed Media: A Review of Trends in the Scholarship of Early Modern Publication', *Literature Compass* 7.11 (2010), 1035–48 (1040); Margaret J. M. Ezell, *Social Authorship and the Advent of Print* (Baltimore: Johns Hopkins University Press, 2nd edn, 2011).

28 Andrew Cambers, 'Reading, the Godly, and Self-Writing in England, circa 1580–1720', *Journal of British Studies* 46.4 (2007), 796–825 (802).

29 William H. Sherman, *Used Books: Marking Readers in Renaissance England* (Philadelphia: University of Pennsylvania Press, 2009), p. 6.

30 Tenger and Trolande, 'Print versus Manuscript', p. 1038.

31 For the growing scholarship on female interpretative and literary agency during this period see Erica Longfellow, *Women and Religious Writing in Early Modern England* (Cambridge: Cambridge University Press, 2004); Johanna Harris and Elizabeth Scott-Baumann (eds), *The Intellectual Culture of Puritan Women, 1558–1680* (Basingstoke: Palgrave Macmillan, 2011); Sarah C. E. Ross, *Women, Poetry, and Politics in Seventeenth-Century Britain* (Oxford: Oxford University Press, 2015).

32 Susan M. Felch, 'English Women's Devotional Writing: Surveying the Scene', *ANQ: A Quarterly Journal of Short Articles, Notes, and Reviews* 24.1–2 (2011), 118–30 (122).

33 Miri Rubin, 'Identities', in Rosemary Horrox and W. Mark Ormrod (eds), *A Social History of England, 1200–1500* (Cambridge: Cambridge University Press, 2012), pp. 383–412 (383, 386). For devotional identities within the Henrician context see Peter Marshall, *Religious Identities in Henry VIII's England* (London: Routledge, 2006), pp. 1–18.

34 Linda Tredennick, 'Exteriority in Milton and Puritan Life Writing', *SEL* 51.1 (2011), 159–79 (159). Tredennick is primarily concerned with the development of the spiritual autobiography as a manifestation of the birth of modern subjectivity.

35 For a fuller discussion of the 'devotional turn' see the foreword.

36 Andrew Cambers, *Godly Reading: Print, Manuscript and Puritanism in England, 1580–1720* (Cambridge: Cambridge University Press, 2011). For Cambers' exploration of religious writing as a product of devotional reading see 'Reading, the Godly, and Self-Writing in England', pp. 796–825. For similar investigations see Kathleen Lynch, *Protestant Autobiography in the Seventeenth-Century Anglophone World* (Oxford: Oxford University Press, 2012), pp. 179–232; Femke Molekamp, *Women and the Bible in Early Modern England: Religious Reading and Writing* (Oxford: Oxford University Press, 2013), pp. 119–50.

37 John Doran, Charlotte Methuen and Alexandra Walsham (eds), *Religion and the Household* (Woodbridge: Boydell (for the Ecclesiastical History Society), 2014).

38 Martin and Ryrie, *Private and Domestic Devotion*.

39 See Kate Narveson, *Bible Readers and Lay Writers in Early Modern England: Gender and Self-Definition in an Emergent Writing Culture* (Farnham: Ashgate, 2012), pp. 199–215.

40 Suzanne Trill, 'Lay Households', in Hiscock and Wilcox, *Oxford Handbook of Early Modern English Literature and Religion*, pp. 397–413 (398).

41 See C. Scott Dixon, Dagmar Freist and Mark Greengrass (eds), *Living with Religious Diversity in Early Modern Europe* (Farnham: Ashgate, 2009); Thomas Max Safley (ed.), *A Companion to Multiconfessionalism in the Early Modern World* (Leiden, Netherlands: Brill, 2011); Randall J. Pederson, *Unity in Diversity: English Puritans and the Puritan Reformation, 1603–1689* (Leiden, Netherlands: Brill, 2014).

42 The pioneering work of Tara Hamling exemplifies this shift. See Tara Hamling, *Decorating the 'Godly' Household: Religious Art in Post-Reformation Britain* (London: Yale University Press, 2010); Tara Hamling, 'Seeing Salvation in the Domestic Hearth in Post-Reformation England', in Jonathan Willis (ed.), *Sin and Salvation in Reformation England* (London: Taylor and Francis, 2016), pp. 223–44; Tara Hamling and Catherine Richardson, *A Day at Home in Early Modern England: Material Culture and Domestic Life, 1500–1700* (New Haven, CT: Yale University Press, 2017).

43 See John Craig, 'Psalms, Groans and Dogwhippers: The Soundscape of Worship in the English Parish Church, 1547–1642', in Will Coster and Andrew Spicer (eds), *Sacred Space in Early Modern Europe* (Cambridge: Cambridge University Press, 2005), pp. 104–23; Amanda Flather, *Gender and Space in Early Modern England* (Woodbridge: Boydell, 2nd edn, 2011), pp. 135–60; Natalie Mears and Alec Ryrie (eds), *Worship and the Parish Church in Early Modern Britain* (Farnham: Ashgate, 2013), *passim*. A notable exception is Alexandra Walsham's *The Reformation of the Landscape: Religion, Identity, and Memory in Early Modern*

INTRODUCTION

Britain and Ireland (Oxford: Oxford University Press, 2nd edn, 2012), esp. pp. 236–40, 431–54.

44 One could include in this list devotional genres explored in section I: sermon notes (chapter 3), printed prayer manuals (chapter 4), salvific plays (chapter 5), murder pamphlets (chapter 7) and spiritual journals (chapter 8).

45 There has been much recent work, for example, on the devotional mediums, genres and writing styles of lay religious women. See Narveson, *Bible Readers and Lay Writers*, pp. 101–30; Susan M. Felch, '"Halff a Scrypture Woman": Heteroglossia and Female Authorial Agency in Prayers by Lady Elizabeth Tyrwhit, Anne Lock, and Anne Wheathill', in White, *English Women, Religion, and Textual Production*, pp. 147–66; Victoria Brownlee, *Biblical Readings and Literary Writings in Early Modern England, 1558–1625* (Oxford: Oxford University Press, 2018), pp. 143–68.

46 See Cambers, *Godly Reading*, pp. 1–7; Narveson, *Bible Readers and Lay Writers*, pp. 11–13; Robert W. Daniel, '"Have a little book in thy Conscience, and write therein": Writing the Puritan Conscience, 1600–1650', in Willis, *Sin and Salvation*, pp. 245–58.

47 For variations on this theme see Christopher Hill, *Society and Puritanism in Pre-Revolutionary England* (Harmondsworth: Penguin, 1986), pp. 443–81, Cambers, *Godly Reading*, pp. 84–6; Bernard Capp, 'Republican Reformation: Family: Community and the State in Interregnum Middlesex, 1649–60', in Helen Berry and Elizabeth Foyster (eds), *The Family in Early Modern England* (Cambridge: Cambridge University Press, 2007), pp. 40–66.

48 For contemporary anti-theatrical polemics see Stephen Gosson, *The School of Abuse* (London, 1579); William Prynne, *Histriomastix* (London, 1632). For a comprehensive survey of this topic see Peter Lake and Michael Questier, *The Antichrist's Lewd Hat: Protestants, Papists and Players in Post-Reformation England* (London: Yale University Press, 2002), esp. pp. 425–82.

49 William Cranshaw, *The sermon preached at the Crosse* (London, 1608), p. 171.

50 See Lake and Questier, *The Antichrist's Lewd Hat*, pp. 187–228; Peter Lake and Michael Questier, 'Prisons, Priests, and People', in Nicholas Tyacke (ed.), *England's Long Reformation, 1500–1800* (London: University College London University Press, 1998), pp. 195–234.

51 *A narrative of the cruelties & abuses acted by Isaac Dennis, keeper, his wife and servants, in the prison of Newgate* (London, 1683), p. 28. A century earlier the martyrologist John Foxe made the same observation that 'all the prisons in England were become right Christian schools & Churches'. John Foxe, *Acts and Monuments of the English Martyrs*

(London, 1583), p. 1521. For preaching by and to prisoners see: Samuel Clarke, *A Generall Martyrologie* (London, 1651), pp. 400–1; Sharon Achinstein, *Literature and Dissent in Milton's England* (Cambridge: Cambridge University Press, 2003), p. 61; Nigel Smith, 'Introduction', in *A Collection of Ranter Writings of the 17th Century*, ed. Nigel Smith (London: Pluto, 2014), pp. 1–31 (15).

52 For autobiographical religious writing during this period see John Stachniewski, 'Introduction', in *Grace Abounding with Other Spiritual Autobiographies*, ed. John Stachniewski with Anita Pacheco (Oxford: Oxford University Press, 1998), pp. ix–xliii; Lynch, *Protestant Autobiography*, pp. 1–30; Abigail Shinn, *Conversion Narratives in Early Modern England: Tales of Turning* (London: Palgrave, 2018), pp. 1–28.

53 For religious verse during this period see Barbara Kiefer Lewalski, *Protestant Poetics and the Seventeenth-Century Religious Lyric* (Princeton, NJ: Princeton University Press, 1979); Elizabeth Clarke, *Theory and Theology in George Herbert's Poetry: 'Divinitie, and Poesie, Met'* (Oxford: Clarendon, 1997); R. V. Young, *Doctrine and Devotion in Seventeenth-Century Poetry* (Rochester, NY: D. S. Brewer, 2000); Sarah C. E. Ross, 'Epic, Meditation, or Sacred History? Women and Biblical Verse Paraphrase in Seventeenth-Century England', in Kevin Killeen, Helen Smith and Rachel Willie (eds), *The Oxford Handbook of the Bible in Early Modern England, c.1530–1700* (Oxford: Oxford University Press, 2015), pp. 483–97.

54 For the religious tradition of, and literary works associated with, the *ars moriendi* see chapters 13 and 14.

55 Robert Horne, *Life and Death, Foure Sermons* (London, 1613), p. 116.

SECTION I
Sites

Part I: Devotional identities in religious communities

1

What was devotional writing?
Revisiting the community at Little Gidding, 1626–33*

David Manning

> And what the dead had no speech for, when living,
> They can tell you, being dead: the communication
> Of the dead is tongued with fire beyond the language of the living.
> Here, the intersection of the timeless moment[1]

T. S. Eliot's *Four Quartets* turned ontological angst into a poetic meditation that begot prophetic historiographical insight in *Little Gidding*. This response to the modernist malaise resonated with George Herbert's sense of eschatological crisis that had been articulated over three hundred years before: 'The second Temple could not reach the first: / And the late reformation never durst / Compare with ancient times and purer yeares; / But in the Jews and us deserveth tears.'[2] Such a synergy was no coincidence. During the early 1930s Eliot had been deeply affected by his reading of *The Temple* (1633), the original publication of which had been arranged by Herbert's close friend, Nicholas Ferrar (1593–1637), who had founded the

---

*This essay has been developed through papers delivered at Magdalene College, Cambridge; the Institute of Historical Research, London; and the University of Warwick: many thanks to all those who supported me in these endeavours and provided feedback on my work. I am also very grateful to Joyce Ransome, Tom Webster and Robert W. Daniel for commenting upon a draft typescript: I take full responsibility for the final text. The work of Elizabeth Clarke, Isabel Rivers and N. H. Keeble continues to be a source of great inspiration. Much love and thanks to my parents.

community at Little Gidding, Huntingdonshire (act. 1626–57).[3] Whilst this historical enterprise in collective piety has been the subject of romanticised Anglican apologia since the nineteenth century, any historians who seek to study the devotional culture of the Ferrar family would do well to take Eliot as their Clio.

Eliot understood all too well what academic research into early modern religion often struggles to appreciate: that the devotional culture at issue here was suffused with divinity.[4] In this case, the ache of Saint Augustine's restless soul throbbed in the hearts and minds of Christians in a way that passed through, between and beyond both the confessional dogmatics of Catholicism, Calvinism and Arminianism and the religio-political structures of conformity and nonconformity, puritanism and anti-puritanism. The Neoplatonic metaphysics of God in Trinity transcended the power of scholastic theology, liturgical authority and biblical hermeneutic to give expression to mystical traditions in divine participation. Notwithstanding the anti-papist mantra of *sola fide*, the legacy of Augustine's anti-Pelagianism could be complicated by the pragmatics of activities such as communal religious learning in a way that tacitly supported the kind of synergism advocated by conformist post-Calvinist thought. Personal and cosmological experience could be conflated so that the theologico-cultural forces of thoughts, words and deeds bled into each other as they became manifest in both corporal and spiritual dimensions to highlight an intersect between past memory, present insight and future expectation in a prophetic, or timeless, moment. Considering these impulses has the potential to complicate some contemporary academic thinking on the historical progression from Catholicism to Protestantism in England;[5] for the devotional identities that arose from them complemented modes of appropriating and adapting sixteenth-century Catholic piety to engender a new sense of Christianity as English Protestantism. Moreover, at the close of the second decade of the twenty-first century, Eliot's intervention now dares historians to re-engage with those past spiritualities of devotional culture that are all but denied by the evaluative paradigm of 'new materialism' that has come to dominate much of the research agenda in both literary and historical approaches to early modern religion.

In taking inspiration from the Eliot–Herbert–Ferrar nexus, this essay will draw attention to a world beyond the materialistic mediation of stimulus and response that typically shapes working assumptions about early modern religion as 'lived experience'. What follows is not concerned with how religious writing informed devotional identity, or how religious identity informed devotional writing. Instead, its focus will be the supposed conflation of worldly endeavour and spiritual action that gave meaning to the way in which self-selecting agents came together through discourse as they dwelt in the presence of God.[6] Given both the inevitable brevity of this essay and the complexity of its subject matter, the objective here is not to offer a fully explicated discussion with a neat conclusion, but rather to constitute a new experiment in interdisciplinary historiography (not literary studies) that will craft three interrelated provocations about how lives and writings came together at Little Gidding to engender themselves with a devotional quality.[7]

To make good with this focus, a basic appreciation of how the community at Little Gidding came into being is required. The precocious Nicholas Ferrar served as the deputy of the Virginia Company from 1622 until its demise in 1624. He subsequently found his family's capacity to save his brother from bankruptcy as something of a providential sign. Ferrar turned anew to God. In 1626 he was ordained deacon by William Laud at Westminster Abbey and then set about creating a pious community at Little Gidding with his widowed mother, Mary Ferrar (1553/54–1634), and much of his extended family, including his brother, John Ferrar (c.1588–1657), and his married sister and brother-in-law, Susanna and John Collett (d. 1657 and d. 1650, respectively), as well as their daughters, including Mary (c.1600–80) and Anna (c.1602–38/39), and their younger sons. In the same year, George Herbert (1593–1633) had been made non-resident canon of Lincoln Cathedral and prebendary of Leighton Bromswold, Huntingdonshire. The latter office served as something of a pretext for George Herbert and Nicholas Ferrar to befriend one another before embarking upon a mutually formative exploration of faith which was to last the rest of their lives. At Little Gidding a post-Calvinist spiritual aesthetic combined with the legacy of a Jacobean sensibility for pastoral care in the midst of other more idiosyncratic impulses in charity, edification and asceticism to forge an implicit rejection of the kind of supercilious religiosity advocated by the Caroline court. Crucially, it is within this setting that the Ferrars found a sense of devotion.

What was devotional writing?

As part of the multifaceted process to found the community at Little Gidding, the newly ordained Nicholas Ferrar delivered a 'solemn vow' to God that was 'written and signed with his own hand' and then 'read' aloud to his mother, who in reply, and in the presence of other friends, 'devoutly blessed him' and prayed 'most heartily', that 'he might be filled with God's Holy Spirit daily more and more, to his greater glory and good of her and his Family'.[8] This vignette subtly complicates the established view that the devotional experience of the Ferrars was governed by the way in which they took the prescriptions of the *Book of Common Prayer* and brought them to life through a series of daily exercises. For, here, a design to triangulate the Church, the State and the community was augmented by a phenomenon where embodied words, writing and action not only flowed through each other but found meaning in and through God at a site where worldly and spiritual place-time met.[9]

Devotional discourse – whether oral, handwritten or printed – was, then, invariably not just about God, or directed at God, but something which gained meaning through the grace of God and in the presence of God. In this context, devotional writing was, *pace* Alec Ryrie and Ian Green, much more than a category of literature that governed the practice of devotion in relatively uncontroversial ways.[10] Indeed, whilst devotional writing may be understood through its capacity to act as a driving force of that practical divinity which supported both practical predestinarianism and experimental synergism, historians remain basically silent when it comes to thinking about the transformation of a piece of writing into a devotional text.[11] By contrast, in the wake of Kate Narveson's reframing of biblically inflected reading and writing, it has become almost de rigueur for literary scholars to utilise the innovations of 'new materialism' to advance insightful, albeit still awkwardly present-centred, investigations into the lives and texts of Little Gidding.[12] Suzanne Trill has re-envisaged the community as a site where household management was mediated through devotional writing.[13] Adam Smyth has focused on the Ferrars' cut-and-paste production of biblical harmonies to probe the materiality of rhetoric where the supposed destructive act of cutting became the premise for new forms of *inventio* and text production.[14] Furthermore, Michael Gaudio has lavished attention on the visual culture of the Ferrars' biblical concordances in a way that dwells upon the rend between pictures and words, matter and meaning.[15] As fascinating as all this may be, twenty-first-century theories about how material interactions harboured deeper epistemological and ontological forces should not be conflated with or used as a substitute for historical insights into Reformation theology. Indeed, by appreciating how the adjective 'devotional' emerged through seventeenth-century debates about the dialectic between theological principles and sincerity of belief, what may be referred to as devotional writing should, first and foremost, be viewed as a function of spiritual discernment.[16]

Such a reorientation of thinking has at least two implications for the study of those devotional lives and writings which will be advanced here through a meditation on the community at Little Gidding. One, that which scholars have come to see as devotional writing in contrast to polemical writing needs to be reassessed, for any manifestation of spiritual discernment in the world was surely subject to the contingencies of religio-political controversy.[17] Two, that which scholars have come to view as secular writing in contrast to religious writing also needs to be reassessed, for there has yet to be much consideration of what it meant to write by means of the grace of God and in the presence of God.[18] Whilst Joyce Ransome's depiction of the community at Little Gidding as a voluntary religious association of family and friends 'united not only in cohabitation but in hearts' is a better description than the old caricature of a quasi-monastic Arminian outfit, there is still much to be said about the Ferrars' communal divinity.[19] The ebb and flow of the Ferrars' religiosity was surely a complex business and yet the wellspring of that divinity flowed as much from their enduring fellowship in Christ than any performative inter-action or inter-subjective experience, including those grounded in the bonds of family and friendship.

Words beyond authorship

In 1626 Nicholas Ferrar composed a handwritten prayer to commemorate the start of a new life at Little Gidding. In being read at home on the first Sunday of every month, this prayer constituted a spiritual speech act with a commemorative subtext; yet the prayer's substantive content also reflected and gave further expression to an extra-liturgical piety that established a formative contrast with the Ferrars' public worship. Following thanksgiving for God's grace, the prayer made a subtle petition for enhanced learning through divine participation: 'The Knowledge of thee [oh God] & of thy son Jesus Christ is everlasting Life, & how surpassing then is the Riches of thy mercy that compel us to the study of this Knowledge? ... how unspeakably gracious is Thy love that dost Invite us daily & hourly the participation thereof'.[20] Here, the temporality of the discourse was twisted into a spiritual dimension to offer a vision of eternity, whilst setting the processes of petitioning and learning into a context where Christian love became a condition of divine participation, or that 'mutual inward hold which Christ hath of us and we of him'.[21] Whilst Laudianism envisaged the sacrament of the Lord's Supper as the ultimate expression of this experience, Richard Hooker had also stressed 'how we are made partakers of Christ both otherwise and in the sacraments them selves'.[22] Set against this backdrop, the Ferrars' more secular discourses pertaining to education and edification may still be understood within the context of an extra-liturgical 'communion of spirits' which aimed at 'the perfection of the minds'.[23]

A heightened sensitivity to the theology of communal learning at Little Gidding provides an opportunity to reconsider why the Ferrars began heading manuscript letters and documents with the IHS Christogram. It is plausible that this move was either a relatively benign quirk in the evolution of dating correspondence Anno Domini, or a more provocative attempt to appropriate a symbol that had become most readily associated with the Jesuits.[24] However, in paying attention to works such as Thomas Bentley's *Monument of Matrones* (1582), Richard Vennar's *Right way to Heaven* (1601) and John Cosin's *Collection of Private Devotions* (1627), it was also the case that the print culture of English Protestantism had given rise to a trend in book decoration whereby title pages and border edges could be adorned with the Christogram.[25] To render IHS incarnate in the blood of ink and the body of paper was surely something of an anti-puritan intervention in the theology of Reformation semiotics; that said, when crafted in manuscript within the domestic realm of Christian fellowship, the letters arguably revealed not merely a symbolic yearning to have Christ close at hand, but an active example of divine participation where human words were transfigured in the presence of IHS as *Logos*. In such a Johannine light, the Humanist performance of rhetoric and virtue was shot through with the edifying love of Christ. Hence, the hierarchical relationships between priest and parishioner, tutor and pupil, man and woman, adult and child, speaker and listener, writer and reader, would have been complicated by and mediated through an active affirmation of fellowship in Christ. Such dynamics would have resonated with not just the heterodox sodality of Juan de Valdés (*d.* 1541), who was so admired for his practical divinity by Nicholas Ferrar and George Herbert, but the diffuse heritage of the *devotio moderna*.[26] Here, words could emanate from mouths, pens and printing presses without much thought given to what was perceived to be the impious audacity of human authorship. Processes of writing, copying, collating and editing, as well as tasks such as active reading, note-taking, and cutting and pasting, were supposedly all inflected by a spiritual endeavour that invariably confounds the labels that contemporary scholars might wish to impose upon them based solely on their material function.[27] With this in mind, it may be posited that those patterns of Neoplatonic synergy between human and divine activity that had once been displaced by predestinarian theology found fresh meaning in the post-Calvinist expression of extra-liturgical life at Little Gidding. Indeed, the Ferrars' sense of communion with Christ serves as a potent theological rationale for the way IHS appeared not only at the head of the Ferrars' private correspondence but also at the top of every page of the written accounts, or 'story books', of the apparently secular discourses of their 'little academy' (*c.*1631–33) (see figure 1.1).

The little academy was ostensibly a domestic enterprise in civil learning, in both form and content, eliciting readings, monologues and dialogues of 'some part of history, such as was appointed, either some chronicles of nations, journeys by land, sea voyages, and the like' and then 'for the better retaining in memory or what which shall be read ... a summary collection shall be kept in writing'.[28] This endeavour was borne of 'collaborative authorship' with the defining impetus coming from female minds, voices and hands.[29] Debora Shuger has ingeniously drawn the little academy out from the shadows of the Great Tew circle to show how its 'spirit of heroic Christian feminism' engaged with 'republican political thought' to foster a practical conviction that 'intellectual labour could become integral to the devout life'.[30] However, this avant-garde principle was not solely the product of the kind of forces that Shuger identifies. Group discussions, which appear to have gained their critical momentum from mealtime readings, followed in the wake of saying

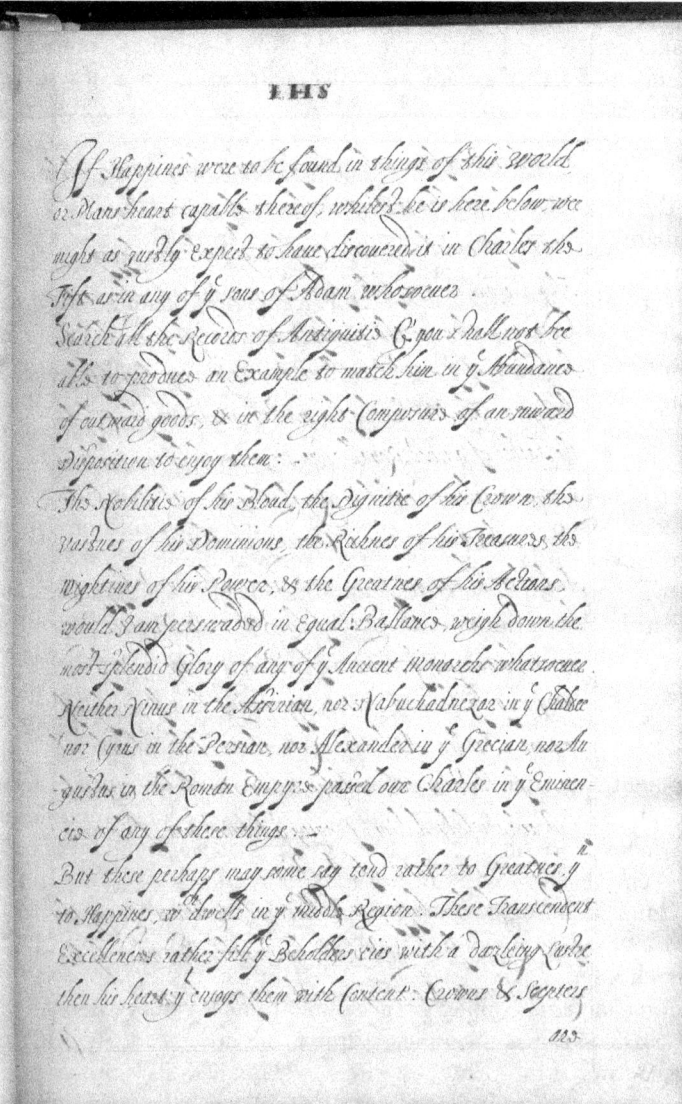

Figure 1.1 Page from the 'story books' of Little Gidding.

grace. The method of learning was in keeping with post-Calvinist, post-scholastic theological epistemology, which shunned 'speculation' in favour of acquiring knowledge that moved beyond the mind to 'stir up the affections to the embracement of virtue'.[31] IHS, then, was no simple embellishment to the written record of the little academy but an actualisation and affirmation of devotional discourse in the presence of Jesus Christ (gendered male). In sum, there is value in complementing Shuger's intervention with a vision of how the Humanist form and rationalist content of the 'intellectual labour' of the Ferrars could have been transfigured through the presence of the divine to become devotional discourse. Within this frame of reference, issues of gendered agency, secular politics, and both individual and collective authorship arguably give way to an appreciation of the worldly and spiritual place-time that the Ferrars inhabited to participate in that 'mutual inward hold which Christ hath of us and we of him'.[32]

In acknowledging that 'the greatest bar of Perfection was Ignorance of truth', members of the little academy entered into a 'joint Covenant between themselves and some others of nearest Blood' to 'confer together of some such subject as should tend either to the information of the understanding or to the exciting of the Affections, to the more ready and fervent prosecution of virtues and better performance of all … duties'.[33] As much as there were valuable lessons to be learned from the subject matter of those discussions, which laid bare the foibles and veracity of human agents set against the measure of God's providence, there was much about the process of learning in and of itself. Discipline and eloquence entreated disputants to exemplify the pious qualities that they discussed; a point underscored by the way in which contributions were advanced not under the actual names of individuals but ventriloquised through allegorical characters such as 'chief', 'patient', and 'cheerful'.[34] Allusions to the classical virtues were imbued with and elevated by their theological counterparts to ensure that understanding could be an affective and practical endeavour that was piously aspirational and suffused with divine love. In all, the Ferrars' escapades may have helped to stave off becoming one of those forsaken 'imperseverant and relapsing righteous persons'.[35] Indeed, the prominent female members of the group were certainly keen to discover 'those false Opinions wherewith the world misleads all Mankind, especially our weaker sex'; and, here, there is a certain implication that the principle of spiritual discernment ultimately governed the processes and benefits of worldly learning.[36] In turning edifying discussion into devotional writing, Mary and Anna Collett addressed Mary Ferrar as founder of the study group 'to accept now in writing that which you were so favourably pleased to approve in the rehearsing ... [for] you have taught us often that which we hope shall ever remain as firm[ly] written in our minds as in this Book, That there is nothing but the Practices of Virtue and Religion that can in the end yield comfort'.[37] Nicholas Ferrar later praised the chastity and learning of his pious nieces, 'with perfect Love and Unity of Mind to go on cheerfully in these good paths' such that their 'Labour is not in Vain in the Lord[,] But through Patient Continuance in well-doing we shall obtain Glory and Honour and Immortality'; adding that he hoped 'by God's grace to be to you wards in the search and study of true wisdom and perfection in Christ Jesus – Not as a Master but as a Partner and fellow student with you'.[38] With echoes to Saint Clement of Alexandria's seminal approach to pedagogy, the Ferrars and Colletts found a collaborative spirit of learning in Christ that was a defining feature of their devotional community.[39]

Words beyond stories

The little academy bequeathed to posterity a series of conversations on historical subjects that were written up as didactic stories. The distinction between 'dialogue', 'story' and 'history', here, was as fluid as it is open to interpretation and debate.

For a start, there are weighty and unexplored questions about how a traditional fourfold model of biblical hermeneutic – literal, moral, allegorical and spiritual – shaped the meaning of the discourses. Set against the work undertaken to produce the biblical concordances, the story books produced by the discussion group certainly aimed to 'judge worldly activities purely by scriptural standards'; and, although this ambition was considerably diluted by a formative non-scriptural inter-textuality, Joyce Ransome has rightly emphasised how the little academy was often preoccupied with exemplifying the 'value of temperance'.[40] But such a virtuous undertaking was also readily transfigured through scriptural decree: 'vanity of vanities; all is vanity' (Ecclesiastes 1:2)[41]. By this measure the little academy was singularly attentive on those 'illustrious examples' from times past 'which God hath continually set forth before our eyes for the full reformation of our understanding touching the Vanity of all earthly things, still making this application to our own hearts'.[42]

In contrasting fashion, Reid Barbour has persuasively shown that not only were the Ferrar–Collett symposia part and parcel of a distinctly 'Caroline search for the elusive marks of the genuine church heroic', but that they were 'deeply influenced' by John Foxe's *Acts and Monuments* (1563–83) to the extent that they crafted a novel appreciation of 'heroic sufferings' so as to bear witness to 'memorable examples of constancy in the name of faith and in opposition to the world'.[43] Yet, here too, there are further dimensions of intrigue to consider. As early Stuart England found novel ways to critique the political machinations of current affairs through reading histories of ancient Rome, a Platonic intellectual tradition in storying (i.e. a curious and protean synthesis of *mythos* and *logos*) threatened to unsettle authoritative Humanist discourses in poetry and history, whilst also finding itself destabilised by Reformation strains of prophetic historiography. As the members of the little academy found themselves at the intersect of these forces, so they would have deployed all the parts of rhetoric to splice together multiple textual sources for edifying ends. However, such activities were also elevated through the group's participation in Christian fellowship in a way that made their words transcend the worldly boundaries of 'history' and 'story' to dwell in a moment where mortification turned to near-prophetic insight. For, on one noteworthy occasion, Mary Ferrar had cause to interject:

> What the Authority of this History is I will not contend. Let every man believe as he please, so he deny me not that for which this History, if it be made History, seems chiefly intended: That it becomes them to whom much is forgiven to love much – that is CHRIST his own Law; and that for great sins the repentance ought to be long continued – that was David's practise, who every night washed his bed and watered his couch with tears and professed to have his heavens ever in his sight [Psalm 6:6].[44]

Here, a loving embrace of the supposed divine messages of the past transcended temporal historiography to serve as a testament to that divinity engendered by dwelling in the presence of Christ, which in turn advanced a convergence of the holy virtues of historical and eternal truth.

With this in mind, it is worth evaluating the longest and most prominent of the 'stories' crafted by the little academy: the one that focused on the 'retirement' of Charles V, who famously abdicated from his position as Holy Roman Emperor two years before his death in 1558. The rationale for such a selection by the group was surely multifaceted, even if it remains a matter of speculation amongst contemporary scholars. Having spent time travelling on mainland Europe in the years leading up to the outbreak of the Thirty Years War, Nicholas Ferrar may have had a personal interest in the fate of the Holy Roman Empire. More significantly, William Camden's *History of Elizabeth* (1625) had already begun the process of recasting the reputation of Charles V in a favourable light by drawing attention to the piety of his final years without reference to the divisive features of confessional politics. For, as Camden put it, the 'honours' of Charles V were 'rare example of all Caesars, and more glorious than all his victories', viz. 'conquering himself' to renounce his empire, thus 'withdrawing himself from this mortal life, to live for ever wholly with God'.[45] Whilst historians are now well aware that 'Protestantism was much better equipped than Catholicism to be devotionally omnivorous, and that Catholic Materials were better suited to cross-confessional adaption than Protestant ones', the phenomena at work here have yet to receive due attention by contemporary scholars.[46]

The little academy was fascinated by the story of a layman whose seemingly unprecedented wealth and status did not prelude eventually finding a measure of that temperance that allowed him to negotiate the corrupting vanity of worldly things. For it was written, 'search all the records of Antiquity and you shall not be able to produce an Example to match him in the Abundance of outward goods, and in the right Composition of an Inward Disposition to enjoy them' (see figure 1.1).[47] The presentation of this moral exemplar of history was, therefore, transformed into a devotional discourse that held this interest in tension with the enaction of that spiritual discernment which adjudged the sincere commensurability of inward and outward virtues. The leading narrator of the 'story' then spoke for the whole group: 'I perceive (said she) by the Affectionateness of your Countenances, that there is a Fire of Love kindled in your hearts towards the memory of this Heroical Prince.'[48] Set against Augustine's theology of memory, the Spirit of truth took the present of past things in memory and elevated it through the store of affection to connect it with the present of present things, all to excite the present of future things. Before too long, the character of Charles V was being lauded as an ectype of King Solomon and a sort of spiritual foil for the members of the little academy: for 'would the better sort of men (those I mean of pure souls and Elevated understandings) esteem themselves in any mean Conformity to his Excellent Virtues and in any weak Participation of those Certain Pledges, which he had of being partaker of that better life above'.[49] Here, the beginnings of a self-reverential quality to the discussion would have been as much about the providential workings of grace as the rhetorical machinations of self-interest. Indeed, this dialectic was further enmeshed in the spiritual practice of the little academy as it was implicitly refracted through the Ferrars' own retrospective perception of the failed Virginia Company, and built up into a searing critique of the propensity of colonial projects to be poisoned by the evils of mammon. For as 'Divine Providence contrived in the Admirable Resignation on Charles [V] ... thus he become like Solomon a Royal and Everlasting Preacher to these younger Sons of Nature. Vanity of Vanities all is Vanity, shall for ever be as often proclaimed as the Name of Charles [V] repeated in the Newfound World.' And, in damning the 'Gallant Tobacconist' just as those other symbolic material substances and experiences of colonial wealth which were deemed to be 'vain pleasure, not of real worth', so the symposia focused on the 'Remembrance of Eden ... being propagated not only by sacred History, but by continued Tradition hath in all Ages brought forth a strong and ravishing conceit; that there was yet remaining in the world a place of Perfect Happiness'.[50] Thus, the little academy worked in the presence of God to turn the storying of a history of Charles V's 'retirement' into a pattern of devotional discourse and identity that helped to engender and affirm Little Gidding as a place of righteousness.

Afterword

The provocations set forth in this essay challenge historians and literary scholars alike to reconsider the relationship between lives and writing in the context of past spiritualities. The discussion above seems to have opened up a curious conversation with Tom Webster's 'Writing to Redundancy' article of 1996.[51] Then the bogeyman of those trying to historicise spiritual writing was 'new historicism';

now it is 'new materialism'. There the focus was on the narratives of conversion borne of experimental Calvinism; here the preoccupation has been with a spiritually inflected practice of historiographical storying that advanced strands of post-Calvinist conformist culture. That article destabilised scholarly principles about how to critique a historical relationship between writer and text in the crafting of anglophone puritan diaries; this essay has questioned assumptions about the classification of literature to explore how some of the transnational and meta-confessional forces of Reformation allowed devotional text to find its meaning in a spiritual context. Set against these contrasts, the two endeavours share a common commitment to deep and reflexive thinking about how to expand the limited capacity of contemporary historiography and literary studies to craft historically sensitive insights into a supposed spiritual reality imbued with the Christian metaphysics of presence such that the Word gave meaning to words. All this shows that Eliot's poetical maxim about the transfigured power of 'the communication of the dead' extending beyond the insights of 'the living' is not necessarily true for academic scholarship, but therein lies the point.[52] To historicise devotional lives and devotional writing is a complex business which arguably requires a creative and critical appreciation of Christian meta-history.[53]

Notes

1 T. S. Eliot, *Little Gidding* (London: Faber & Faber, 1942), pp. 8–9. *Little Gidding* was later incorporated into T. S. Eliot's *Four Quartets* (New York: Harcourt, 1943), pp. 31–9 (32), i.e. *Little Gidding*.
2 George Herbert, *The Temple: Sacred Poems and Private Ejaculations*, ed. Nicholas Ferrar (Cambridge, 1633), pp. 184–91 (190), i.e. 'The Church Militant' (drafted *c.*1623–24).
3 For details see Ronald Schuchard, '"If I think again, of this place": Eliot, Herbert and the Way to "Little Gidding"', in Edward Lobb (ed.), *Words in Time: New Essays on Eliot's Four Quartets* (London: Athlone, 1993), pp. 52–83; Joyce Ransome, *The Web of Friendship: Nicholas Ferrar and Little Gidding* (Cambridge: James Clarke, 2011).
4 For complementary supporting discussions see Tom Webster, 'Writing to Redundancy: Approaches to Spiritual Journals and Early Modern Spirituality', *Historical Journal* 39.1 (1996), 33–56; Elizabeth Clarke, *Theory and Theology in George Herbert's Poetry: 'Divinitie, and Poesie, Met'* (Oxford: Clarendon, 1997), pp. 224–67; Torrance Kirby,

Richard Hooker, Reformer and Platonist (Aldershot: Ashgate, 2005), pp. 29–44; Katrin Ettenhuber, *Donne's Augustine: Renaissance Cultures of Interpretation* (Oxford: Oxford University Press, 2011), pp. 105–36; John Coffey, 'Introduction: Sources and Trajectories of Evangelical Piety', in John Coffey (ed.), *Heart Religion: Evangelical Piety in England & Ireland, 1690–1850* (Oxford: Oxford University Press, 2016), pp. 1–28.

5   For details see Jessica Martin and Alec Ryrie (eds), *Private and Domestic Devotion in Early Modern Britain* (Abingdon: Routledge, 2012), *passim*; Elisabeth Salter and Robert Lutton (eds), *Pieties in Transition: Religious Practices and Experiences, c.1400–1640* (Abingdon: Routledge, 2016), *passim*.

6   See Clarke, *Herbert's Poetry*, p. 267.

7   N.B. Reformation discourse was not beholden to the kind of scepticism about the relationship between life and text which permeates through contemporary academic thinking: see Clarke, *Herbert's Poetry*, p. 264.

8   [John Ferrar (*c*.1588–1657)], 'Life of Nicholas Ferrar', in *The Materials for the Life of Nicholas Ferrar: A Reconstruction of John Ferrar's Account of his Brother's Life Based on all the Surviving Copies*, ed. and intro. Lynette Muir and John White (*Proceedings of the Leeds Philosophical and Literary Society* 24.4) (Leeds: Leeds Philosophical and Literary Society, 1996), pp. 41–118 (67).

9   See Matthew 18:20; Revelations 1:19; 2 Peter 3:18.

10 Ian Green, *Print and Protestantism in Early Modern England* (Oxford: Oxford University Press, 2000), pp. vii, 223, *passim*; Alec Ryrie, *Being Protestant in Reformation Britain* (Oxford: Oxford University Press, 2013), p. 8, *passim*.

11 N. H. Keeble, *Richard Baxter: Puritan Man of Letters* (Oxford: Clarendon, 1982), pp. 37–8, 73–6, 132–48; Leif Dixon, *Practical Predestinarians in England, c.1590–1640* (Farnham: Ashgate, 2014); Isabel Rivers, *Vanity Fair and the Celestial City: Dissenting, Methodist, and Evangelical Literary Culture in England 1720–1800* (Oxford: Oxford University Press, 2018), pp. 248–74.

12 See Kate Narveson, *Bible Readers and Lay Writers in Early Modern England: Gender and Self-Definition in an Emergent Writing Culture* (Farnham: Ashgate, 2012), pp. 151–76, *passim*.

13 See Suzanne Trill, 'Lay Households', in Andrew Hiscock and Helen Wilcox (eds), *The Oxford Handbook of Early Modern English Literature and Religion* (Oxford: Oxford University Press, 2017), pp. 397–413 (399–404).

14 See Adam Smyth, '"Shreds of Holinesse". George Herbert, Little Gidding, and Cutting Up Texts in Early Modern England', *English Literary Renaissance* 42.3 (2012), 452–81.

15 See Michael Gaudio, *The Bible and the Printed Image in Early Modern England: Little Gidding and the Pursuit of Scriptural Harmony* (Abingdon: Routledge, 2017), p. 5, *passim*.
16 See 1 Corinthians 14:1–4 and 1 John 4:1.
17 For example, see *The Arminian Nunnery* ... (London, 1641).
18 See Peter Lake, 'Religion and Cheap Print', in Joad Raymond (ed.), *The Oxford History of Popular Print Culture, Volume 1: Cheap Print in Britain and Ireland to 1660*, 9 vols (Oxford: Oxford University Press, 2011), I:217–41.
19 *The Virginia Company Archives Online*, 'The Ferrar Papers' (hereafter 'Ferrar Papers'), 665: John Ferrar to Mary Ferrar, 26 February 1628/29. www.virginiacompanyarchives.amdigital.co.uk. Accessed 12 March 2018. Also see Ransome, *Web of Friendship*, pp. 50–79; David Manning, 'Anglican Religious Societies, Organisations, and Missions', in Jeremy Gregory (ed.), *The Oxford History of Anglicanism, Volume II: Establishment and Empire, 1662–1829*, 5 vols (Oxford: Oxford University Press, 2017), II:429–51.
20 Cambridge University Library, Add. MS 4484, fols 62–67.
21 Richard Hooker, *Richard Hooker: Of the Laws of Ecclesiastical Polity: A Critical Edition with Modern Spelling*, ed. Arthur Stephen McGrade, 3 vols (Oxford: Oxford University Press, 2013), II:158 (i.e. *Laws*: V.56.1). Also see 2 Corinthians 13:14.
22 Hooker, *Laws*, II:152 (i.e. *Laws*: V.55.1).
23 Ferrar Papers, 676: Nicholas Ferrar to Anna Collett, 18 June 1629.
24 On the former point see James Daybell, *Manuscript Letters and the Culture and Practices of Letter-Writing, 1512–1635* (Basingstoke: Palgrave Macmillan, 2012), pp. 104–5.
25 Margaret Aston, *Broken Idols of the English Reformation* (Cambridge: Cambridge University Press, 2016), pp. 582–92.
26 See Juan de Valdés, *The Hundred and Ten Considerations*, trans. Nicholas Ferrar with notes by George Herbert (Oxford, 1638).
27 Maximilian von Habsburg, *Catholic and Protestant Translations of the Imitatio Christi, 1425–1650: From Late Medieval Classic to Early Modern Bestseller* (Farnham: Ashgate, 2011), pp. 31–3, 127–78.
28 *Materials for the Life of Nicholas Ferrar*, pp. 83–4. Also see Isaac Archer, 'The Diary of Isaac Archer, 1641–1700', in Matthew Storey (ed.), *Two East Anglian Diaries 1641–1729* (Woodbridge: Boydell, 1994), pp. 41–200 (91). Thanks to Robert W. Daniel for this reference.
29 Debora Shuger, *Religion in Early Stuart England, 1603–1638: An Anthology of Primary Sources* (Waco, TX: Baylor University Press, 2012), pp. 590–5.

30 Debora Shuger, 'Laudian Feminism and the Household Republic of Little Gidding', *Journal of Medieval and Early Modern Studies* 44.1 (2014), 69–94 (89, 80, 90).
31 *Materials for the Life of Nicholas Ferrar*, pp. 83–4.
32 Hooker, *Laws*, II:158 (i.e. *Laws*: V.56.1).
33 'Feast of the Purification 1630/1', in *The Story Books of Little Gidding, being the Religious Dialogues Recited in the Great Room, 1631-2. From the Original Manuscripts of Nicholas Ferrar*, ed. and intro. E. Cruwys Sharland (New York, 1899), pp. 1–2.
34 'Christmastide 1631', in *Story Books*, pp. 103–4.
35 Lancelot Andrewes, 'A Sermon Preached before Queen Elizabeth, at Hampton Court, on Wednesday, being the VI of March AD MDXCIIII [*Memores estote Uxoris Lot*, Luke 17:32]', in *Lancelot Andrewes: Selected Sermons and Lectures*, ed. and intro. Peter McCullough (Oxford: Oxford University Press, 2005), pp. 108–21 (109).
36 'Prefatory Epistle' to the Story Books, Mary and Anna Collett to Mary Ferrar, 2 February 1630/31, in Story Books, p. li.
37 *Ibid.*, pp. li–liii.
38 Ferrar Papers 788: Nicholas Ferrar to Anna Collett, 1 June 1631.
39 Clement of Alexandria, *Christ the Educator*, trans. and intro. Simon Wood (The Fathers of the Church, vol. 23; Washington, DC, 1953), p. 4.
40 Ransome, *Web of Friendship*, p. 132; also see pp. 134–58.
41 King James Bible.
42 'Conversations on the Retirement of Charles V', conducted between Ash Wednesday and St Stephen's Day 1631, in *Conversations at Little Gidding*, ed. and intro. A. M. Williams (Cambridge: Cambridge University Press, 1970), p. 17.
43 Reid Barbour, 'The Caroline Church Heroic: The Reconstruction of Epic Religion in Three Seventeenth-Century Communities', *Renaissance Quarterly* 50.3 (1997), 771–818 (772, 778, 787, 787).
44 'St Andrew's Day 1632', in *Story Books*, p. 212. Psalm 6:6 reads: 'I am weary with my groaning; all the night make I my bed to swim; I water my couch with my tears' (King James Bible).
45 William Camden, *Annales the True and Royal History of the famous Empress Elizabeth Queen of England France and Ireland &c ...* (London, 1625), sig. C2^r. For invaluable context see C. Scott Dixon, 'Ideas of Empire: Charles V and His Reign in British Historical Thought', in C. Scott Dixon and Martin Fuchs (eds), *The Histories of Emperor Charles V: Nationale Perspektiven von Persönlichkeit und Herrschaft* (Münster, Germany: Aschendorff, 2005), pp. 159–90 (159–69).
46 Ryrie, *Being Protestant*, p. 287.
47 'Conversations on the Retirement of Charles V', p. 29.

48 *Ibid.*, p. 33. Cf., *Augustine: Confessions, Books 9–13*, ed. and trans. Carolyn J. B. Hammond (Cambridge, MA: Harvard University Press, 2016), p. 231 (*Conf.* XI.20.26).
49 'Conversations on the Retirement of Charles V', p. 49. Cf., Proverbs 1–9.
50 'Conversations on the Retirement of Charles V', pp. 69–72.
51 Webster, 'Writing to Redundancy', pp. 33–56.
52 Eliot, *Four Quartets*, p. 32.
53 See David Manning, '"That Is Best, Which Was First": Christian Primitivism and the Reformation Church of England', *Reformation & Renaissance Review* 13.2 (2011), 153–93.

2

'HERSCHEPT HET HERT': Katherine Sutton's *Experiences* (1663), the printer's device and the making of devotion

Michael Durrant

Katherine Sutton (*fl.* 1630–63), an English governess, is best known for her Particular Baptist conversion account, *A Christian Woman's Experiences* (1663), which was printed in Rotterdam in the year of Sutton's death.[1] We know nothing about Sutton's parentage or her socio-economic origins; what we do know about Sutton's life comes from her *Experiences*. In this text, we learn that Sutton was married (although her husband remains unnamed); she had children, but lost at least two of them to unknown causes. Evidence from this text suggests that Sutton rejected Laudian reforms at a very early age, and that this prompted years of agonising heart searching and autobiographical cataloguing, as well as geographical roaming, first around England and then later to the Dutch Republic. A key aspect of the *Experiences* is its account of Sutton's providential 'gift' for 'spiritual singing', which she first experienced 'in the year 1655 in the Moneth of February', possibly while serving as a governess in Lancashire.[2] Ten spiritual songs pepper the central section of Sutton's text, which runs to thirty-nine pages, and a further seven songs are reserved for a Sutton-authored five-page coda, in which she updates the reader on her spiritual condition, and, through her songs, warns of a calamitous future under a Restoration regime. Another notable feature is the text's three-page introductory address to the 'COURTEOUS READER', written by the London-based Baptist pastor Hanserd Knollys (1599–1691), who, following the Restoration, was in self-imposed exile in the Dutch Republic alongside Sutton. Sutton may have been a member of Knollys' congregation, based in Bishopsgate, but this is not affirmed in the *Experiences* itself. What is clear is that Knollys' presence within the text is designed to buttress Sutton's central narrative, shepherding the *Experiences* into the public domain and codifying it as a devotional product of her devotional identity, one that – despite, or perhaps because of, the doctrinally stark subject of predestination – was preserved and disseminated on behalf of self-identified Protestant saints 'watchful' over their own spiritual security.[3]

The vehicle of Sutton's life was pitched towards English dissenting groups recently disenfranchised by the collapse of the godly Commonwealth. This aspect of the text's political dimensions has already served as a point of interest in early modern criticism, and the power dynamics between Sutton and her pastor-editor, and the interrelated issues of voice, meaning, and collaborative authorship, have also been scrutinised.[4] Considerably less attention has been paid to this text's visual layout and design. Indeed, what I have found noteworthy is that Sutton's *Experiences*, which appeared in just one edition in the seventeenth century and survives today in only three exemplars, is a highly crafted, visually sophisticated product, and careful thought and consideration went into its aesthetic and functional dimensions. There is a lively interaction between what might be described as the 'physicality' of the text and the model of godly selfhood advanced by Sutton in her central narrative.[5] I argue that this is particularly evident in the *Experiences*' title page and its five-page coda, which, like Knollys' introduction, would have been printed separately from the main body and added towards the end of the printing process. By shifting focus towards exchanges between the material and the literary, my chapter highlights instances where we might see the bibliographical coordinates of the printing house and the devotional coordinates of the convert coming into expressive alignment. There is – to quote a phrase that I will return to below – an 'Ebbing & flowing' between the book's physical qualities and linguistic content, between its beginnings and endings, as well as its inner and outer dimensions.[6] It is in this 'back-and-forth flow of influence' that we might spot the contours of cooperative making between Sutton and her Dutch printer flickering into view.[7]

'HERSCHEPT HET HERT'

In early modern literary criticism, title pages have often been treated as the most 'disposable bits' of a printed text, conceptually 'separated' out from the text proper.[8] The design of early modern title pages has been considered to have been the responsibility of printers, and so the title page has been relegated to the realms of artisanal self-promotion, advertisement and marketing.[9] We are beginning to think more creatively, however, about the printed title page not only as a vehicle for commercial content but also as an essential meaning-making zone, designed to appeal to readers' minds as well as their purses.[10]

The title page to Sutton's *Experiences* is orderly and neat (see figure 2.1). The font appears to remain consistent, varying from upper-case lettering ('WOMAN') to lower-case ('Gods free grace') in order to distinguish main title from subtitle, subject and object. The author's name and the name of the printer are both capitalised, and details about space and place of production are clearly presented: the text was '*Published*' by 'SUTTON' and 'Printed by HENRY [or Henricus] GODDÆUS [or Goddaeus]' (*d.* 1682), a 'ROTTERDAM'-based printer-bookseller operating 'in the Newstreet' (or de Nieu-westraat). Perhaps the most visually strikingly aspect of this title page is Goddæus' highly detailed printer's device (or mark, or emblem). It takes up much of the title-page space, sitting above the imprint and just beneath a biblical excerpt from the post-resurrection narrative about female witnessing: '*And they found it even so, as the VVomen had said*' (Luke 24:24).[11]

Goddæus' device features three interlocking layers, which can be read from outside in, or inside out:

1. At its centre is a standing man, who is dressed like a gardener or pilgrim, holding a shepherd's shovel over his left shoulder, and he has his right hand placed on a kneeling woman's head. The kneeling woman's face is in profile, and we can make out the faint glimmer of a smile. The two figures are pictured in a garden, featuring potted plants, a palm tree and birds. Echoing the biblical quote from Luke 24:24, the image clearly offers a visual counterpart to the encounter, recorded in John 20:15, between Mary Magdalene and the resurrected Christ, and her misrecognition of Christ as a gardener.[12] Goddæus' device appears to have been

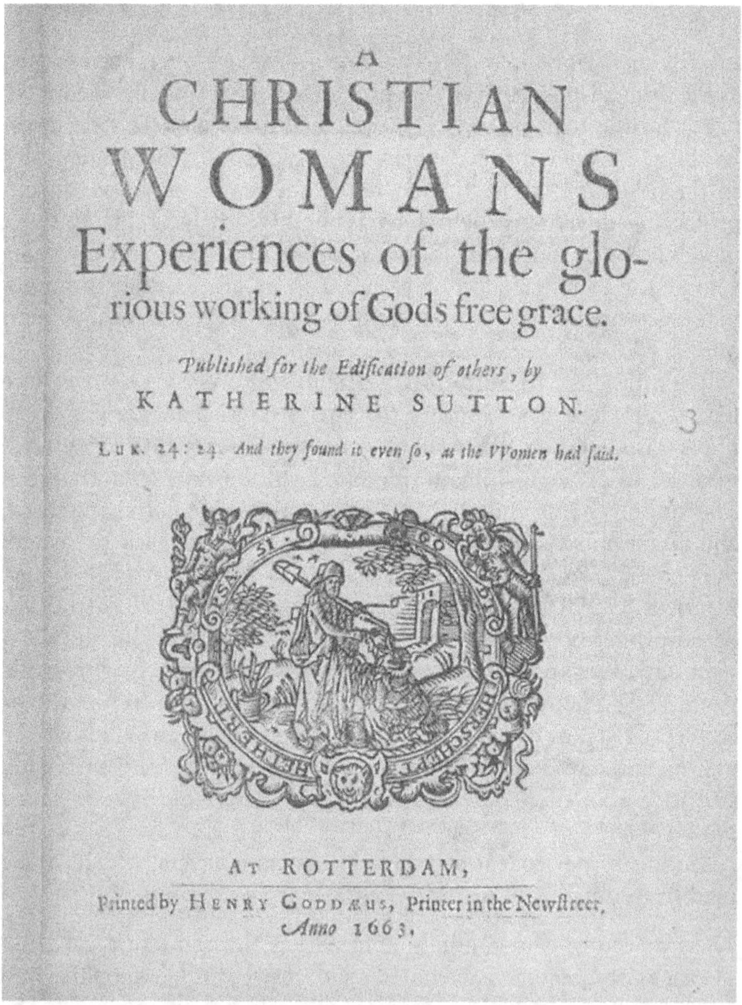
A
CHRISTIAN
WOMANS
Experiences of the glo-
rious working of Gods free grace.

Published for the Edification of others, by
KATHERINE SUTTON.

LUK. 24: 24. *And they found it even so, as the VVomen had said.*

AT ROTTERDAM,
Printed by HENRY GODDÆUS, Printer in the Newstreet,
Anno 1663.

Figure 2.1 Title page to Katherine Sutton's *A Christian Woman's Experiences* (1663).

directly influenced by Albrect Dürer's woodcut, 'Christ Appears to Mary Magdalene [or "*Noli me tangere*"]' (*c.*1509–11), although it is part of a broader visual engagement with John 20:15 in medieval and early modern visual cultures.[13]

2. Bordering and enclosing the edges of the central scene is a strip of text, printed not in English but in Dutch, which redirects us to another biblical referent. What first appears, running clockwise around the image's edge, and possibly punning on Goddæus' name, is the word 'GODT'. Following on from this and printed beneath the central image is the motto 'HERSCHEPT HET HERT', which roughly translates as 'God remakes [or rebuilds/recreates] the heart.' Finally, as the border completes its circumference of the garden, we encounter the psalm to which this motto alludes: 'PSA[LM]:51', or the *'Miserere mei Deus'*, in which King David is forced to confront his sin of adultery with Bathsheba before the Prophet Nathan.[14]
3. On the outermost edge, two classical figures look on, figures who were both frequently associated with the spirit of European printing, and frequently deployed in early modern printer's devices.[15] On the left, we find Mercury, the god of financial gain, communication, travellers and boundaries; on the right, we find Minerva, the goddess of wisdom, poetry, commerce and crafts. At the bottom of the device, sitting centrally, is a lion's head.

Printer's devices had at the time broadly practical purposes, deployed as a means by which printers could authenticate a text's provenance, offering visual assurances of quality;[16] but they could also be used to strategically 'train' readers 'to follow a path' through the book, visually evoking thematic concerns found in the text that readers are about to enter.[17] The device on the title page to Sutton's *Experiences* does not reappear on the title pages to any of Goddæus' print products from the same period, or, indeed, from any other point in his career. Goddæus usually deployed a device featuring an image of a squirrel in profile, which is surrounded by a heart-shaped border of flowers and branches. This leaves open the possibility that the device on the title page to Sutton's *Experiences* was specifically selected for Sutton as an individual client, and used not only because it is visually appealing, but because it interacts with her devotional self-fashioning.

Such a reading is, of course, not without its complications. The presence of a pagan god, Mercury, and a goddess, Minerva, whose twofold gaze activate generic associations between crafting and financial productivity, might suggest concerns quite apart from those emphasised as important by Sutton, who casts aside 'the vain profits of the world'.[18] Her burden of emphasis falls on the personally felt and the emotionally lived as useful barometers of authentic faith. She repeatedly juxtaposes outer and inner, and like many other devotional writers of the century, she warns about the dangers of spiritual pride, drawing on well-worn sartorial metaphors to link the 'outward performance' of insincere piety to 'monstruous cloathes, and filthy raggs'.[19] Early on in the narrative, Sutton casts aside the prescriptive straightjacket of her 'prayer-book', signalling her broader 'resistance' to outward conformity, embodied in particular by the reintroduced *Book of Common Prayer*.[20] Books and reading remain absolutely central to Sutton's faith, but only in terms that continue to resonate with her broader promotion of the interior. Like Saint Augustine, Sutton hears God's disembodied voice telling her to 'go in and read', a phrase that neatly encapsulates a sense of pious (scripture) reading as a movement through 'outside' surfaces towards inner wisdoms and meaning.[21] Within this context, my current emphasis on the *Experiences*' title page, and in particular its printer's device, could be read as a counter-intuitive move. However, we know that 'the task of spiritual autobiography is to demonstrate the eventual coherence of inner and outer'.[22] Lest a convert be faced with the label of '*Hypocrite*', as Sutton fears, true faith must be premised on the certainty of an achieved correlation between surfaces and depths.[23]

In the *Experiences*, these doubts over inner and outer are narratively positioned as having been defeated, both in Sutton's coda, in which she makes a claim to completeness – '*I am what I am*', she says – and in Knollys' introduction, where he justifies Sutton's status as a regenerate 'godly Woman'.[24] Knollys posits that Sutton's inner experience finds outward expression in her narrative style: 'In the Reading of her Book,' he warns, 'thou wilt meet with some suddain and unexspected Transition from one thing to another (and thou mayest think it to be some what abruptly).'[25] Like Sutton's body, which manifests signs of her inner degenerate state through physically debilitating illnesses, the body of Sutton's 'little Book' becomes itself a source and sign of the shifting 'course of ... Heavenly communications', which for Sutton did not run smooth, but rather took on the figurative qualities of the sea, 'Ebbing & flowing' like the tide.[26] The difficulty of Sutton's 'suddain and unexspected' style is, in Knollys' paratextual framing, designed to lend authenticity through an impression of unmediated speech, an issue echoed in Sutton's own concluding assertion that her spiritual songs were 'not stud[i]ed things' but came to her 'immediately'.[27] These corroborating statements bookend the central narrative but are deeply implicated in qualifying the truth claims made within, suggesting, in turn, that anxieties about inside/outside could find linguistic outlet in the text's 'paratextual architecture'.[28]

We can move this idea forward by acknowledging that in the material properties of the printed codex, we might see the concepts of inner and outer falling not into a neat binary but instead into a kind of kinetic negotiation. To 'go in' to a book involves the physical process of turning over each new leaf, a repetitive interaction that relies on the stability of load-bearing structures 'physically outside the printed text proper'; the paper on which Sutton's own words were printed owes its existence to those abject 'raggs' of the outside world, as paper at the time was made using the recycled 'residue' of old 'sheets and clothes'.[29] As Juliet Fleming has lucidly argued, by reflecting on the absorbability of paper – that is to say, Sutton's inky words do not sit on, but sink into, the rag-based paper that makes up her 'little Book' – we can challenge the notion of paper as 'surface', which, in turn, helps us to think of text as 'being-within, rather than being-on'.[30] If we think of the *Experiences*' title page as similarly 'being-within, rather than being-on', we can read it as less a passive surface than an integrated element of the book's meaning, one that begins by reflecting the text's inner workings.

This is possible because Sutton specifically references the repentant sinner, Mary Magdalene, who served as an 'exemplar of perfect penance' in English Protestantism, and whose encounter with the resurrected Christ is visually evoked at the centre of Goddæus' device.[31] In her coda, Sutton asserts her spiritual authority, proclaiming that '*I own a Prophetical voice of Christ*,' and she reinforces the point by conjuring Magdalene as a useful model of feminine duty and responsibility: Magdalene '*followed Christ to the last*', and '*Christ put this honour upon her, that she must bring the first glad tidings of the Gospel of the resurrection unto the Disciples*'; his '*appearance to her ... shewed* [Christ's] *great Love to sinners*', '*she being a poor ignorant woman, though full of affection*'.[32] Rachel Adcock notes that since Magdalene's report of her encounter with Christ was initially 'dismissed' by the disciples, Sutton's reference to her, situated right at the end of her text, serves as a useful scriptural corrective to congregational scepticism over Baptist women's claims to discipleship.³³ Pre-empting the text's movement into a community of (potentially censorious) readers, Sutton's *Experiences* closes by asserting biblical precedent for female witnessing and reliable reporting. Clearly, though, that work has already begun on the text's title page, which, in the form of a printer's device, offers the consumer a navigational tool, one that anticipates (or prophesies) the book's closing movements, right at the point of initial paratextual encounter.

Sutton also models her own sinful yet penitent self on the biblical King '*David*', whose confession of guilt served as a key penitential model in early modern Protestant cultures of devotion, capturing complex confrontations between individual Christians and their inner spirituality.³⁴ Psalm 51's focus on 'personal sinfulness', and on 'inner penitence over outward, physical sacrifices', helped to structure an experiential language of interiority in Protestant cultures of devotion, one that privileged the 'introspective' over the worldly.³⁵ Sutton picks up on these meanings, representing her David-like suffering – including her troubled marriage to an ill-matched, 'practical' husband – as a key aspect of her devotion and as a necessary corollary of authentic faith, claiming to have 'found in times of greatest outward trouble and affliction … the onely times of greatest inward and spiritual joy'.³⁶ Echoing David's mental anguish, Sutton repeatedly refers to her heart's 'brokenness', and indeed the word 'heart' is used at least 103 times throughout main body of the text.³⁷ Or perhaps that should be 104 times? That is, if we take into account the Dutch word 'HERT' circling the garden in Goddæus' device, which offers a paratextual context and a gloss for Sutton's biblical coordinates even before the reader has reached them. Understood in these terms, Goddæus' device might be seen to unfold the stakes of Sutton's inner transformation, a transformation that must be experienced in the 'HERT' but also acknowledged externally. One way in which this might be achieved is for a printer to relocate that inner 'HERT' to the text's title-page surface.

'END'/'FIN'

Sutton's narrative proper 'conclude[s]' on the thirty-ninth page with 'So shal I leave this to the blessing of the Lord, and the consideration of the vvise.'³⁸ The text, however, does not end there. As suggested, the *Experiences* ends with a short narrative coda, in which Sutton updates the reader about her spiritual condition. This is then followed by three pages of additional songs, which have been subdivided using horizontal and vertical rules as well as pithy headings, like 'As I was waiting on the Lord … this following short Hymne was immediately given,' and 'This was November the 20. in the Year 1656.'[39] This section of the coda then concludes with a typographically amplified 'END' on page forty-three, although Sutton's songs actually spill over onto a forty-fourth page, where two further songs, this time lacking headings, have been documented. This additional page ends with another sign that we have reached the end of the text: a capitalised 'FIN'.[40]

What happened here? Some answers may lie in the *Experiences*' collation statement ([4], 44 p.; 4°), which remains the same across all three surviving exemplars. This statement tells us that the text contains four unnumbered leaves, which include the title page and Knollys' introduction. These are followed by forty-four numbered pages, thirty-nine of which are devoted to Sutton's *Experiences*. A further five pages make up the text's conclusion, split between Sutton's coda and a short register of her additional songs, which is itself interrupted by that 'END' on page forty-three. We know that the text was published in quarto format (4°); as such, if we were to think of Sutton's text in terms of the number of sheets required to produce it, we can deduce that, with each sheet containing eight pages of text, four on each side, and with the sheet folded twice to produce four leaves or eight book pages, a total of six sheets were required. Had Sutton's *Experiences* ended at the 'END' – that is, the text's forty-third page – there would have been a final blank page. The absence of a catchword in the lower right-hand corner of the text's penultimate page suggests that at some point during production the forty-third page may have marked the text's terminating boundary. However, there appears to have been a recognition that an extra blank page offered additional space in which Sutton could continue to testify to her providential gift of singing without interfering with the central narrative or incurring extra paper costs.

To think of Sutton's *Experiences* in these terms is to (re)position it as, to quote Stephen Orgle, 'less a product than a process'.[41] This 'process' begins at the end of writing; or, with that 'END'/'FIN' standing as a case in point, perhaps this process is always trying to catch up with the scene of writing, to offer an end, or sometimes two. One can at least say that, as is characteristic of the early modern printing process, there is evidence of 'improvisation' here, at least in the sense that the 'END'/'FIN' opens up the possibility of a late-stage renegotiation of the text's spatial dimensions in response to evolving circumstances.[42]

What those circumstances were, it is difficult to say. It has been suggested that Sutton's *Experiences* was 'published posthumously', and so, depending on how we interpret 'posthumous' here, it is possible that the text's makers were confronted, at some point during the production process, with the author's death.[43] We know, perhaps with greater certainty, that Psalm 51's particular emphasis upon repentance and redemptive grace made it 'highly popular as a preparation for death', and it should not go unnoticed that Sutton's text is deeply concerned with what she describes as life's 'latter end'.[44] Death circles, like the birds in Goddæus' device, throughout her main narrative, and so we might want to reread the text's doubly reiterative 'END'/'FIN' as a sign that we have reached the terminal boundary not only of the printed book, but also of the life that the book comes to represent, a life that has been brought to conclusion by divine grace, and an identity that has now been fixed in print as a monument. Sutton's death might actually help to explain why her text did not go through any subsequent reprints after its first and only edition in 1663: there was simply no more life to attest to, an issue that was perhaps an ideal publication scenario in terms of this text's proselytising potential as a stable model of inner transformation.

Equally, however, the text's narrative ending is less a fixed, terminating boundary, and more like a 'dilatory and deferred' point of departure.[45] I would suggest that another meaningful feature of Goddæus' title-page device is that it directly appeals to, and helps to produce, a looping teleology. For instance, Sutton signs off her narrative coda by calling on readers to 'seek [Christ's] face', which implies a 'desirably direct, intimate encounter' that, as we come to end of the text, must be sought after through self-examination, as readers are deposited back out into 'the World'.[46] Sutton proposes that we must 'look up' to meet His revelatory gaze; this 'looking' enables an introspective turn towards 'what is in [the] heart'.[47] We have, though, already encountered a face at the centre of Goddæus' device. Gracing the book's title page is a head-on image of the resurrected Christ, who shares a face-to-face encounter with the penitent woman genuflected before him. The text ends by pointing towards new beginnings embodied in the promise of seeing Christ's face, but that face has been there all along, right from the very start. This is revealed by physically turning back to the book's title page, and to the image placed near its centre, which visually cues associations between endings and/as beginnings, implying, too, a model of 'reading ... from beginning to end, and then starting again', which is a crucial feature of Protestant devotional writings.[48]

This arrangement suggests that a printer's device may have been selected to endorse Sutton's discursive approach. This evidence, in turn, suggests a printerly response to the experiential, which sees the role and function of, say, ornament and decoration as of crucial importance to the authority of Sutton's inner life. Particularly when it comes to women's self-writings from this period, such modes of authorisation have been associated with the kinds of paratextual defences offered by co-authorial figures like Knollys, who, as pastor-editor, serves as witness and gatekeeper in Sutton's movement into the public realm of print. However, the implication of looking at, rather than through, the *Experiences*' title-page surface, and focusing in particular on its printer's device, is that it offers a more complex picture of the way in which Sutton's writing self has been manufactured and (re)produced. Invocating, and giving outward shape to, the broken but ultimately contrite heart found within, collapsing distinctions between outside and inside, beginnings and endings, this outwardly facing commercial sign related to the printer's identity has been used to elevate Sutton as an object of spiritual emulation.

'GODDÆUS'

As Elizabeth Skerpan-Wheeler points out, while early modern religious self-narratives were made 'cheaply', there appears to have been an almost unusual degree of care put into the making of Sutton's *Experiences*, which was, she says, 'beautifully produced'.[49] Highly legible printing, ornamental headpieces, running headers and subheadings together imply an alertness amongst the text's makers to the lucidity of its *mise-en-page* arrangement, and suggest that the compellingness of the text's autobiographical data extends into the realm of the material, established, here, at the level of visual layout and design. These material features combine with scriptural references, specific dates and place names to make Sutton's account authoritative and legible evidence of inner transformation. The broader implication is that, to return to Skerpan-Wheeler's thinking, the 'acknowledgement and recognition Sutton received from others' is not only 'evident' in Knollys' three-page introduction, where he positions himself as a key witness, but also in the physical properties of 'the book itself'.[50]

This is a striking argument, since early modern printers are often reduced to serving a purely mechanical function. Peter Blayney, for example, assigns little more agency to the figure of the printer than he does to the machine at his or her disposal: as a hired hand, employed by a text's publisher, 'the printer bore no more responsibility', he argues, 'than does a photocopier'. Blayney suggests that the printing house should be conceptualised as 'a copying machine: a text, a heap of clear paper, and the required payment were inserted at one end, and the paper emerged from the other end with the text on it'.[51] In this context, the title-page designation of Goddæus as printer would imply that he was appointed to manufacture Sutton's *Experiences* for a one-off payment, and that his agency extended to print-house management, but that he would not have been invested, ideologically, emotionally or financially, in the text's promotion or its future in the marketplace. However, as Skerpan-Wheeler's point astutely suggests, it is possible that this distinction might belie or negate more integrated forms of collaboration.

Goddæus is an intriguing figure. He made himself available as manufacturer for local and international print markets and reading communities, making Dutch books and pamphlets on mathematics and astrology, puritan piety and Reformation history, works in French by Huguenot exiles, and Dutch-language editions of English-language texts. With Sutton's *Experiences* standing as a case in point, Goddæus' business model also included manufacturing English-language texts, which were produced for the English community settled in the Dutch Republic, but could just as easily have been smuggled into England for binding and distribution.[52] These practices do not make Goddæus an outlier in the seventeenth-century Dutch publishing trade, and nor should we be surprised that Sutton was drawn to the Dutch Republic in an effort to publicise her form of dissent. By the mid-1600s, Dutch commercial centres like Amsterdam and Rotterdam were 'at the epicentre of separatist life', home to 'thriving expatriate churches', and a 'well developed' network of local printing establishments, which sprung up to support the dispersal of radical propaganda during periods of exile.[53] What is interesting, however, is that Goddæus' printing house – Blayney's 'copying machine' – sometimes served as a place where his expatriate clients could lodge.

Having escaped a violent marriage with the London lawyer Robert Hampson (1627–88), Mary Wingfield (1639–98) took up lodgings with Goddæus above his 'Newstreet' printing house in 1681. In 1682, Goddæus (identified by Wingfield as 'Mr. Godens' in one of her letters home) printed the first English-language edition of Wingfield's extraordinary account of domestic abuse at Hampson's hands.[54] The fate of that first edition, which was entirely self-funded by Wingfield, suggests something about official perceptions of Goddæus' printing house as a location for the making of texts but also as a bolthole for sedition. In 1682, the turncoat informer and former Popish Plot conspirator Edmund Everard (fl. 1673–1711), who had close connections with Wingfield's abusive husband, Hampson, lodged with Goddæus as part of a mission to monitor activities amongst the English dissenting community in Rotterdam.[55] It was a sting operation, and one that had consequences for Goddæus, who was compelled by Everard to burn products likely considered dangerous in English readers' hands. This included copies of the first edition of Wingfield's self-narrative.[56]

After 1660, Sutton's affiliations placed her on the wrong side of Charles II's restored regime, and her *Experiences* is, like the second edition of Wingfield's self-narrative, deeply informed by a sense of discrimination. She protests against the post-1660 legislative clampdown on dissenting 'Teachers', who, Sutton laments, were being 'persecuted' and 'thrown into prisons'.[57] That Sutton's *Experiences* is, at least in part, a justificatory response to the scrutiny of authoritative men – men who, we are told, repeatedly stymied her attempts to aurally 'declare' the works of God before her own 'Church' – attests to a sense of deep frustration with the systems of witnessing practised by her English co-religionists.[58] These discriminatory forces brought Sutton, like Wingfield after her, to Goddæus' 'Newstreet' printing house, perhaps on the basis of shared perception of that house as a safe space in which foreign clients could lodge. The burning of Goddæus' books in 1682 highlights, however, that such perceptions could come at the printer's own detriment, and that a safe space could easily become quite the opposite. There could be consequences for printers like Goddæus when he agreed to serve as 'a photocopier' for a foreign client/lodger, and we might also glean from the fate of the first edition of Wingfield's text a sense of drama and risk and, perhaps, a perception of shared responsibility between author and printer, which Blayney's earlier analogy might not totally accommodate.

These reflections also underline an often-overlooked aspect of early modern printing houses: they were 'busy' and 'noisy' spaces of mechanical making, but they were also domestic places, housing printers, their wider families, employees and, on occasion, authors.[59] Mixing domestic and occupational quarters, the printing house sat on an intersection between privacy and publicity, a coincidence of spheres that is materially reproduced as a text like Sutton's passed from the delimited sphere of manuscript circulation and into the more public realm of print.[60] While we do not know if Sutton lodged with Goddæus, the possibility of their domestic propinquity remains active, and potentially suggestive. The rhetoric of personal witnessing – 'I my self have some experience of this,' writes Knollys – is, in women's self-writings of the period, generally associated with the narrative interventions of established ecclesiastical authorities, husbands or other male relatives who claim to have known those writer(s) personally.[61] But did printers like Goddæus, who opened up their houses to exiled lodger-authors, have their own bibliographical codes to express acknowledgement and recognition? I have already proposed that Goddæus' device imagistically enacts some of Sutton's devotional themes, animating parallels between textual appearance and substance. We might add to this that the promotion of the printer as a skilful artisan and the promotion of the convert as a reliable exponent of experience are not altogether separate issues, but are instead implicated in each other. Sutton's *Experiences* encapsulates how the identities and affiliations of an author and printer could converge in devotional works, and how this confluence perhaps added to the promotional and spiritual appeal of such texts.

Notes

1 Katherine Sutton, *A Christian Woman's Experiences of the Glorious Working of God's Free Grace* (Rotterdam, 1663). My base copy is held at Cambridge University Library (R.11.89).
2 Sutton, *Experiences*, p. 13, sig. B3^r.
3 *Ibid.*, p. 17, sig. C1^r.

4   See Helen Ostovich and Elizabeth Sauer (eds), *Reading Early Modern Women: An Anthology of Texts in Manuscript and Print, 1550–1700* (London: Routledge, 2004), pp. 170–2; Rachel Adcock, '"Gathering up the Fragments, that nothing be lost": "Memorable" Women's Conversion Narratives', *Early Modern Women: An Interdisciplinary Journal* 6 (2011), 209–15; Rachel Adcock, Sara Read and Anna Ziomek (eds), *Flesh and Spirit: An Anthology of Seventeenth-Century Women's Writing* (Manchester: Manchester University Press, 2014), pp. 218–35; Rachel Adcock, *Baptist Women's Writings in Revolutionary Culture, 1640–1680* (London: Routledge, 2015), pp. 69–116; Elizabeth Bouldin, *Women Prophets and Radical Protestantism in the British Atlantic World, 1640–1730* (Cambridge: Cambridge University Press, 2015), pp. 33–9.
5   G. Thomas Tanselle, *Bibliographical Analysis: A Historical Introduction* (Cambridge: Cambridge University Press, 2009), p. 2.
6   Sutton, *Experiences*, sig. *1^v.
7   Adam Smyth, *Material Texts in Early Modern England* (Cambridge: Cambridge University Press, 2018), p. 12.
8   Tiffany Stern, *Documents of Performance in Early Modern England* (Cambridge: Cambridge University Press, 2009), p. 62.
9   See Gérard Genette, *Paratexts: Thresholds of Interpretation*, trans. Jane E. Lewin (Cambridge: Cambridge University Press, 1997), p. 16; Margaret Smith, *The Title-Page: Its Early Development, 1460–1510* (London: British Library, 2000), p. 11.
10 See Helen Smith, '"Imprinted by Simeon such a signe": Reading Early Modern Imprints', in Helen Smith and Louise Wilson (eds), *Renaissance Paratexts* (Cambridge: Cambridge University Press, 2011), pp. 17–33; Lucy Razzall, '"Like to a title leafe": Surface, Face, and Material Text in Early Modern England', *Journal of the Northern Renaissance* 8 (2017). www.northernrenaissance.org/like-to-a-title-leafe-surface-face-and-material-text-in-early-modern-england/. Accessed 18 February 2019.
11 Exact wording appears in both the Geneva and King James Bibles.
12 For Luke 24:24, see below. John 20:15 reads: 'Jesus saith unto her, Woman, why weepest thou? whom seekest thou? She, supposing him to be the gardener, saith unto him, Sir, if thou have borne him hence, tell me where thou hast laid him, and I will take him away' (King James Bible).
13 A similar image found its way into one of Little Gidding's Gospel Harmonies. See Nicholas Johnson, '*Anima*-tion at Little Gidding: Thoughtful Inconsistency as Ecological Ethos in an Early Modern Bible', in Thomas Hallock, Ivo Kamps and Karen L. Raber (eds), *Early Modern Ecostudies: From the Florentine Codex to Shakespeare* (London: Routledge, 2008), pp. 145–66 (150). For the devotional writings of the academy at Little Gidding see chapter 1.

14 This is not a direct quotation but rather a reworking of the twelfth line of Psalm 51 as it appears in the 1637 Dutch Bible – the official *Statenvertaling*, or *States Translation* – which reads: 'Schep mij een rein hart, oh God!' ['Create in me a clean heart, oh Lord!'] (Psalmen 51:12). Goddæus' motto plays with the meanings of the word 'schep', which as a noun can mean shovel or spade, and as a verb, 'scheppen', means to dig up; to lay open; to make, construct or manufacture; or to give material shape and form.
15 See the frontispiece of Prosper Marchard, *Histoire de l'origine et des premiers progrès de l'imprimerie* (The Hague: Pierre Paupie, 1750), in which the technology of printing is shown to have been delivered to earth under the influence of Minerva and Mercury. Elizabeth Eisenstein's *The Printing Revolution in Early Modern Europe* (Cambridge: Cambridge University Press, 1983) deploys this image on its own frontispiece. See also Paul Hoftijzer, '*Pallas Nostra Salus*: Early Modern Printer's Marks in Leiden', in Anja Wolkenhauer and Bernhard F. Scholz (eds), *Typographorum Emblemata: The Printer's Mark in the Context of Early Modern Culture* (Berlin: De Gruyter Saur, 2018), pp. 169–96 (186–8).
16 M. Smith, *The Title-Page*, pp. 93–4; Sarah Werner, *Studying Early Printed Books, 1450–1800: A Practical Guide* (Chichester: Wiley Blackwell, 2019), p. 95.
17 Lee Palmer Wandel, 'John Calvin and Michel de Montaigne on the Eye', in W. S. Melion and Lee Palmer Wandel (eds), *Early Modern Eyes* (Boston: Brill, 2010), pp. 135–56 (141).
18 Sutton, *Experiences*, p. 15, sig. B4^v.
19 Ibid., p. 33, sig. E1^v.
20 Ibid., p. 1, sig. A1^r; Adcock, *Baptist*, p. 95.
21 Sutton, *Experiences*, p. 29, sig. D3^r; p. 7, sig. A4^r.
22 Katherine Hodgkin, 'Abject Hypocrisy: Gender, Religion, and the Self', in Lucia Nigri and Naya Tsentourou (eds), *Forms of Hypocrisy in Early Modern England* (London: Routledge, 2018), pp. 119–37 (131).
23 Sutton, *Experiences*, p. 3, sig. A2^r.
24 Ibid., p. 41, sig. F1^r; sig. *1^v.
25 Ibid., p. 33, sig. E1^r; sig. *2^r.
26 Ibid., sig. *1^r; sig. *2^r.
27 Ibid., p. 44, sig. F2^r.
28 Helen Smith and Louise Wilson, 'Introduction', in Smith and Wilson, *Renaissance Paratexts*, pp. 1–14 (7).
29 Razzall, '"Like to a title leafe"', paragraph 5; Margreta de Grazia and Peter Stallybrass, 'The Materiality of the Shakespearean Text', *Shakespeare Quarterly* 44.3 (1993), 255–83 (280).
30 Juliet Fleming, *Cultural Graphology: Writing after Derrida* (Chicago: University of Chicago Press, 2016), p. 140.

31 Patricia Badir, *The Maudlin Impression: English Literary Images of Mary Magdalene* (Notre Dame, IN: University of Notre Dame Press, 2009), p. 6.
32 Sutton, *Experiences*, p. 40, sig. E4^v.
33 Adcock, *Baptist*, p. 93.
34 Sutton, *Experiences*, p. 14, sig. B3^v. For an analysis of the cultural uses of Psalm 51, see Hannibal Hamlin, *Psalm Culture and Early Modern English Literature* (Cambridge: Cambridge University Press, 2004), esp. pp. 173–217.
35 Femke Molekamp, *Women and the Bible in Early Modern England: Religious Reading and Writing* (Oxford: Oxford University Press, 2013), p. 142; Hannibal Hamlin, 'Sobs of Sorrowful Souls: Versions of the Penitential Psalms for Domestic Devotion', in Jessica Martin and Alec Ryrie (eds), *Private and Domestic Devotion in Early Modern Britain* (Abingdon: Routledge, 2012), pp. 211–36 (214).
36 Sutton, *Experiences*, p. 3, sig. A2^r; p. 11, sig. B2^r.
37 *Ibid.*, p. 21, sig. C3^r.
38 *Ibid.*, p. 39, sig. E4^r.
39 *Ibid.*, pp. 40–4, sigs E4^v–F2^v.
40 *Ibid.*, p. 44, sig. F2^v.
41 Stephen Orgel, 'Textual Icons: Reading Early Modern Illustrations', in Neil Rhodes and Jonathan Sawday (eds), *The Renaissance Computer: Knowledge Technology in the First Age of Print* (London: Routledge, 2000), pp. 27–42 (63).
42 Smyth, *Material Texts*, p. 6.
43 Bouldin, *Women Prophets*, p. 34.
44 Janina Niefer, *Inspiration and Utmost Art: The Poetics of Early Modern English Psalm Translations* (Zürich: LIT Verlag, 2018), p. 280; Sutton, *Experiences*, p. 37, sig. E3^r.
45 Abigail Shinn, *Conversion Narratives in Early Modern England: Tales of Turning* (London: Palgrave, 2018), p. 10.
46 Sutton, *Experiences*, p. 42, sig. F1^v; p. 44, sig. F2^v; Razzall, '"Like to a title leafe"', paragraph 11; Sutton, *Experiences*, p. 44, sig. F2^v.
47 Sutton, *Experiences*, p. 44, sig. F2^v; p. 36, sig. E2^r.
48 Molekamp, *Women and the Bible*, p. 61.
49 Elizabeth Skerpan-Wheeler, 'Katherine Sutton', in Ostovich and Sauer (eds), *Reading Early Modern Women*, pp. 173–5 (173).
50 *Ibid.*, p. 173.
51 Peter Blayney, 'The Publication of Playbooks', in John D. Cox and David Scott Kastan (eds), *A New History of Early English Drama* (New York: Columbia University Press, 1997), pp. 383–422 (389). See also Lukas Erne, *Shakespeare and the Book Trade* (Cambridge: Cambridge University Press, 2013), esp. p. 136.

52 See Balthazar Gerbier, *A Sommary Description, Manifesting that Greater Profits are to bee done in ... America* (Rotterdam, 1660); Edward Billing, *A Faithful Testimony for God & my Country* (London?, 1665); John Brown, *Christ, the Way, and Truth, and the Life* (Rotterdam, 1677); and Francis Turner, *Sermon Preached before Their Majesties K. James II and Q. Mary at Their Coronation in Westminster-Abby* (London?, 1685).
53 David R. Como, *Radical Parliamentarians and the English Civil War* (Oxford: Oxford University Press, 2018), pp. 26–7. See also Andrew Pettegree and Arthur der Wieduwen, *The Bookshop of the World: Making and Trading Books in the Dutch Golden Age* (London: Yale University Press, 2019).
54 Jessica Malay, *The Case of Mistress Mary Hampson: Her Story of Marital Abuse and Defiance in Seventeenth-Century England* (Stanford, CA: Stanford University Press, 2014), pp. 99–100. Wingfield describes the burning of the first edition of her book in Malay's edition of her *Plain and Compendious Relation of the Case of Mrs. Mary Hampson* (1684), p. 45.
55 Alan Marshall, 'Everard, Edmund (*fl.* 1673–1711)', *ODNB*. https://doi.org/10.1093/ref:odnb/67394. Accessed 11 March 2019.
56 Malay, *Mary Hampson*, p. 99.
57 Sutton, *Experiences*, p. 30, sig. D3^v.
58 *Ibid.*, p. 20, sig. C2^v.
59 James Raven, 'Printing and Printedness', in Hamish M. Scott (ed.), *The Oxford Handbook of Early Modern European History, 1350–1750, Volume 1: Peoples and Places*, 2 vols (Oxford: Oxford University Press, 2015), 1:214–43 (226).
60 See Adrian Johns, *The Nature of the Book: Print and Knowledge in the Making* (Chicago: University of Chicago Press, 1998), esp. p. 75.
61 Sutton, *Experiences*, sig. *2^v.

Part II: Devotional identities in the household

3

'A soul preaching to itself': sermon note-taking and family piety*

Ann Hughes

In the mid-1650s the Presbyterian minister Robert Porter offered regular counselling by letter to his friend and patron Katherine Gell, who was in the throes of a prolonged spiritual crisis. Responding to Gell's complaint 'about meditation which because yu cannot doe at Mr Baxters height yu run upon a double temptation, the first is to give up your hopes of heaven, 2 is to neglect the duty of set meditation', Porter cautioned that most Christians fell short of Richard Baxter's standards, but 'yet thinke it noe ground to question their title to heaven', before advising that 'the usefullest exercise of all piety, its a soules preaching to it selfe without which the preacher from the pulpit doth little good'. In preaching to your own soul, 'to help you may use any booke or sermon notes you have upon that subject you would meditate on which will shew you the nature of [it] ... what affections to be exercised about it and what duties to be learned from it'.[1] Katherine Gell needed little prompting to keep sermon notes; from the time of her marriage in 1644 to John Gell of Hopton, Derbyshire, the son and heir of the controversial Civil War commander, if not before, she had kept full notes of sermons heard in Westminster and in Derbyshire, prompting her

---

* I am grateful to audiences at the Universities of Birmingham, Cambridge, East Anglia and Oxford, and at the Institute of Historical Research, for comments on presentations on Katherine Gell, and to Gillian Wright in particular for very helpful suggestions. In all quotations from sermon notes and correspondence I have expanded the frequent abbreviations.

husband and other members of her family to do the same. Making sermon notes across the generations shaped the Presbyterian devotional identity of the family, and sustained their commitment in difficult times after 1660.

Katherine Gell's living influence on her family was reconstructed as an exemplar after her premature death. On 16 April 1670 a private fast was held at Hopton Hall, to seek God's guidance during her serious illness. Porter, now ejected from his living, preached on 2 Peter 2:9: 'The Lord knoweth how to deliver the godly out of temptations, and to reserve the unjust unto the day of judgment to be punished,' a stern message of patience in hard times.[2] According to notes kept by Katherine's sister-in-law Eleanor Alsop, Porter noted the inevitability of suffering and persecution for the godly but reassured his hearers that God knew how to deliver his people, and delighted in the 'prosperitie of his servants'. They should 'exercise godlynes under sickness, [God] will either heale or close better, submit and resigne'; they were to 'learne by actuall distemper to make preparation for death'.[3] In July things looked brighter and a thanksgiving was held to celebrate God's mercy in Mrs Gell's recovery, but on 22 January 1671 the same note-taker, now at Alsop Hall, just over eight miles from Hopton, recorded 'the first sermon I herd after the death of my deare deare deare sister Gell which was Fridday last betwixt 8 and nine in the morning being Jan[uary] 20 1670: god tooke her to himselfe'.[4] This sermon was preached, as most weeks at Alsop, by Joseph Moore, a younger man than Porter but also ejected from a living in Derbyshire, on Psalm 48:14, a text he had expounded for some weeks, but particularly apt for the occasion: 'For this God is our God for ever and ever: he will be our guide even unto death.' A few months later, Robert Porter at Hopton was apparently still providing comfort and reflection on Katherine Gell's life and death as recorded in incoherent, broken notes by her daughter Elizabeth: 'apear as much as ever for religion, take up everything of her that is left. Let Gods calling her away. A large stock of praiers left upon the file, it is much of her left behind, there is letters, there is sermon notes, there is diaries.'[5]

Katherine Gell's devotional writings were the crucial legacy to her grieving family. She explained to Richard Baxter in November 1657 that she had for 'these 2 yeares kept a diary of spirituall matters whereby I can tell the frame of my [heart] in every duty and ordinance and what thoughts passe too and fro or stay theer'.[6]

The diary no longer survives in the unwieldy Gell archives but they do include manuscript prayers, loose correspondence and the letter book already quoted. In this last document Katherine recorded in her own hand, over 256 pages, the letters of spiritual counselling written by Robert Porter and Richard Baxter in response to her (mostly lost) requests for help.[7] Above all, however, the archives hold some sixty volumes of sermon notes, all in similar small, leather-bound notebooks opening from the top, and probably used for writing directly during the sermon.[8] The earliest sermon recorded is a parliamentary fast sermon from 27 November 1644 by Thomas Hill before the Lords in Westminster Abbey, in a notebook kept by Katherine's husband. There are three 1640s books noting sermons in both Westminster and Derbyshire, two kept by John between November 1644 and May 1645 and between June 1645 and September 1646, with one by Katherine, overlapping with John's, who 'Began this booke at Westm[inster] March 1 1645[6] and ended it at Darly in Darbyshire July 29 1646'.[9] Katherine's unmarried daughters and sister-in-law, in particular, followed her example; the latest notebook was kept by her youngest child Temperance in 1705–07, mostly recording sermons by the eminent Presbyterian Edmund Calamy III at Westminster. Temperance noted his sermon at a thanksgiving for the union with Scotland on 1 May 1707, and her book concludes with Calamy's funeral sermon for the leading Whig patron Lady Elinor Hollis, on the afternoon of 27 June 1707.[10]

This essay stresses the importance of writing, and of preserving and reflecting on writing, in shaping devotional identity using the spiritual life of Katherine Gell and her family, with a particular focus on sermon notes. Despite important scholarship on sermon note-taking, and notwithstanding the place of preaching as the 'ordinary means of salvation' for Protestants, this sort of writing features rarely in discussions of personal or 'private' devotion.[11] In his influential book on 'Being Protestant', Alec Ryrie wrote that 'the importance of sermon-noting for earnest, literate Protestants would be hard to exaggerate', but he found diaries and spiritual memoirs more illuminating for Protestants' emotional and spiritual experiences and for their personal prayer and meditation.[12] Kate Narveson has argued that 'Reading as transformation is at the heart of devotion'; lay devotional writing developed through 'reading with pen in hand'.[13] Katherine Gell's correspondence with Baxter and Porter, along with stray survivals of her books, reveals her to be a conscientious reader of puritan divinity, including many of Baxter's own works, and there is ample evidence also of her passion for writing, including verse and a recipe book written as a young woman.[14] While acknowledging the vagaries of archival survival, it does seem, however, that most of her writing as an adult developed through hearing with 'pen in hand'. Her notes do not include personal judgements, favourable or adversarial, on the sermons heard, and were rather aimed at grasping the preacher's words as effectively as she could. Note-taking aided concentration and sought to record the immediate experience of the sermon, while also offering material for enduring meditation, reflection and discussion. 'Sermon-writing' on this scale demanded a significant commitment of time, and effort, besides the cost of pens, ink and paper. Narveson has outlined a spectrum of lay writing from passive copying to more active composition, and sermon notes might seem to be at the passive end of the scale. Yet, as Narveson also stresses, the absence of creativity or originality in our terms was not the same as a lack of agency or independence. Katherine Gell's conscientious attendance at godly sermons and her choice of preachers to hear and of what elements of the sermon to record amounted to a determined personal engagement with preaching, not a passive reception of a clerical message.[15]

Katherine Gell and spiritual crisis

To understand the particular value of sermon notes to Katherine Gell, we need to explore aspects of her spiritual crisis in the 1650s. Writing to Baxter in July 1655, she explained that she was prompted to seek his help after reading his *Saints Everlasting Rest* (1650). Despite a godly upbringing she 'was as formall as any and as constant in duties tell neere 20 yeares of age that a sermon of Mr Marshalls did worke soe far as to make me seeke out for a better way then I was in'. During 'many sad troubles in my soule', 'through gods mercy many words ... supported me in my hearing the sermons', but now, and partly through reading Baxter's tract, she feared that she was neglecting other duties and could not be 'in a state of grace'. Bashfulness in admonishing her family, dullness and distraction in prayer, 'over-loving' her children, and recurring distress over the death of her infant son Thomas in 1654, all contributed to a terrifyingly persistent spiritual crisis, all the more vivid as it is revealed through a series of letters over time rather than through a retrospective spiritual memoir or godly life with its usually comforting resolution. She wrote to Baxter that at times she despaired of her life: 'my life is my burthen ... I am many times troubled to thinke what if I should live another 30 yeare how should I be able to passe in such continuall sorrow by reason of my spirituall wants.'[16]

The responses of Porter and Baxter differed to some extent, but they both combined conventional Calvinist divinity with natural or medical interpretations of her plight, and practical advice. In theological terms they both tried to convince her that her very doubts and difficulties were a good sign: only hypocrites or the reprobate felt secure or unworried by sinfulness; as Porter summed up the approach, hers were 'the infirmities of a gracious woman and not the iniquities of a graceless woman'.[17] Yet on the other hand, they stressed that excessive doubt could be an undervaluing or reproaching of God himself, and they hinted at some presumption in the high spiritual standards Katherine set for herself. Baxter was exasperated that she so soon questioned God's 'grace & acceptance of you' after a period of tranquillity, chiding 'Thats not well.'[18] Katherine Gell – like Sarah Savage, the daughter of Philip Henry – is, in Gillian Wright's words, a woman 'known to academic scholarship principally through her connection with eminent men'.[19] Although Katherine Gell had sought clerical help, she did not wholeheartedly accept their solutions. Her superior social status as well as her determined character enabled her to challenge their judgements. Gell acknowledged her 'melancholy disposition' but did not thereby discount the spiritual aspects of her troubles, and she often resisted their advice. In November 1657 she explained to Baxter 'I blesse god I am much recovered of that melancholy distemper that I used to complain of though it was by a way contrary to all advise (viz) reading I found Mr Gurnalls *Christian Armour* did soe revive me and refresh my spirits that it set me much above any such things as used to discompose me,' and in August 1658 she insisted that her current troubles did not proceed from melancholy, 'for its reall the things in it are too true and doe much perplex my spirit and discourage me else I would not thus have troubled you'. As she had previously explained, her continual sorrows came from 'spiritual wants'.[20]

The strains of this potentially unending struggle for assurance are evident. Reflection and self-examination were necessary but could become self-indulgent and self-defeating. Sermon note-taking, on the other hand, was a strenuous, intellectual activity that might put individual struggles in a broader, more manageable and externalised context. Encouraging her husband and subsequently her children and sister-in-law in the practice had specific benefits for Katherine Gell, who feared her concern for her family was one sign that she was unregenerate. At times she tried the desperate tactic of consciously neglecting them: 'the sin of inordinate affection I have long greeved under and prayed agaynst and yet cannot prevaile over it though I strive much not to let out my affection to them soe that I forbeare much ther company'.[21] Furthermore she was uncomfortable with the conventional female role of managing a household, resenting Baxter's advice to concentrate on domestic routines. When he urged her to 'Be much busye in your necessary imployments in the world, and much in cheerfull company ... be not much in secret meditation,' she retorted, 'as for my calling I find busines enough there, have a great family many children and these things must be looked after and out of pure conscience I doe very much stir about in this imployment though it would suit better with my nature, to s[i]t and read all day yet since god hath called me to such affaires ... I strive not to neglect my calling though many atime I goe about my house and amongst my servants when I had rather locke my selfe up in a roome alone amongst my bookes'.[22] Yet, as all her clerical advisers insisted, encouraging her family in godly pursuits could reconcile service to God with affection for her relatives. Porter reassured her that she had 'shamed sin out of your family' and made her house 'a receptacle for god's dispised ministers', while John Otefield, her local minister at Carsington, made the argument explicitly: 'There is a way so to impart our love to Relations as yet to reserve it intire for God, and that is when our love works this way to make them God's, such I hope yours is, at least in a prevailing degree, & thus over-love them if you can'.[23]

Porter and Baxter both worried about the effects of Gell's more introspective writing and it may be that here she did accept their advice: 'frequent recording the same infirmity over and over will make us as customary and sensles as if we recorded them not, or else will tempt us to dispaire because we live still in ye same recorded sins'.[24] She had explained to Baxter that she noted thoughts 'that stay there' in her diary. Hearing and noting sermons must have helped Gell address her personal doubts about salvation, but it was also a collective experience, a family project, and one that connected her individual crisis to the broader experiences of the community of the godly. It was a more detached written regime than keeping a diary, and a more outward-looking one, applying the minister's words to her own condition, and reflecting on the 'affections' and 'duties' implied, rather than beginning with self-examination. Taking notes at sermons was a much-valued godly practice, and for Katherine Gell, who disliked housewifery, it could combine duty and pleasure. We have seen that she loved writing, and her youthful recipe book experimented with different techniques, including shorthand. There is no systematic shorthand in her sermon notes and letters, but she often deployed drastic and idiosyncratic abbreviations. Some of these were shared with her daughters and with her sister-in-law Eleanor Alsop, while both Katherine and Eleanor occasionally used a symbol of a heart rather than writing out the word. Katherine's influence can thus be seen in the very technologies of writing as well as in her encouragement of the practice of note-taking itself.[25]

A shared endeavour

The notebooks were shared amongst family members, both immediately and in the longer term. In the 1640s Katherine and John occasionally noted the same sermons in their overlapping notebooks; their notes are clearly independent (although both grasped the same essential messages from the preacher) but they show signs of consultation and amendment. As might be expected, the university-educated John Gell kept briefer and more systematic notes, whereas Katherine's were more discursive and more personal. On the fast day of 27 May 1646, observed in Twickenham, where they frequently stayed with Katherine's parents, they both noted the sermon by Philip Nye, a leading Independent pastor. Katherine's began: 'A saint is soe intimate and god is soe intressed in his wellfare that god hath wonderfully separated him for himself. Its like an inclosed garden. That the priviledges and security of the righteous is an unknown thing to the wicked. A godly man is a person of designe for god and to god,' and she continued with some five hundred vivid words on the Saints' closeness to god: 'the Saints lay folded up in Christs bosome'. John began by writing out the text (Psalm 4.3) in full, 'but know that the lord hath set apart him that is godly for himself the lord will heare when I call unto him, obs[ervation] That the priviledges of the righteouse are unknowne to the wicked'. His notes ran to only 160 words.[26] John and Katherine were Presbyterians, but Katherine was a dedicated hearer at the morning lecture preached in Westminster Abbey by a rota that included leading Congregationalists as well as her favourite, Stephen Marshall, and other Presbyterians. Her parents lived partly in Westminster and she visited regularly until the mid-1650s. Nye's concern with the Saints' identification with Christ and God's love for them seems to have had much appeal for Katherine. She noted his sermon in the Abbey on 19 September 1650 from the text John 14:20: 'At that day ye shall know that I am in my Father, and ye in me, and I in you.' She wrote of the comfort available to those who had 'fellowship with Christ, yu come here to viset and converse with Christ in ordinances it will much raise yor heart, to come to Christ for yor ends is not soe acceptable but when you doe it only to viset and have communion ... he will then much increase your love to him and it will be noe smale advantage to you'. Attending sermons and making notes that could be pondered and remembered at home – 'a soul preaching to itself' – connected private devotion inextricably to the public ordinances of the visible church.[27]

Furthermore, this volume was shared by two more members of the Gell family. Most comprises Katherine's notes at the morning exercises in September and early October 1650, but on the family's return to Derbyshire it was taken up by John, who used it to record brief notes from John Otefield's sermons in Carsington later in October and in November. Finally it is marked with the initials of Gell's daughter Elizabeth, 'EG', within the familiar heart shape used in the writing of her mother and aunt, alongside the date '1679'. The same marks are found in all the volumes from the 1640s and 1650s; they had become precious family heirlooms to be organised and pondered by the next generation of note-takers. Katherine's younger daughters, Elizabeth and Temperance, never married, and after their father's death in 1689 they lived for most of the time with cousins in furnished rooms in Westminster. Some thirty-five years after Porter's sermon quoted at the start, Elizabeth Gell's modest property was appraised in Hopton Hall and in Westminster, where she had died in October 1704 in her fifty-seventh year. Amongst the pin cushions, the candlesticks, the damask napkins and the 'old scarlet mantle of velvet', there were – in Westminster – 'eighty books bound and some stitched books and seven small bookes'; and, in

Derbyshire, 'one little box of sermon bookes unbound' and 'five and twenty bookes bound' on a 'little hanging shelfe'.[28]

The preservation of the earliest sermon notebooks in the Gell archive is then likely due to the care that Elizabeth, 'a maid of exemplary piety', took of the notes kept by her parents, Katherine and John Gell. The most numerous later volumes are Eleanor Alsop's notes of preaching in Alsop church and hall; Eleanor did not die until 1713, and these presumably were preserved by her niece Temperance.[29] The precise function of sermon notes within family piety varied. Perhaps most common was the practice of the London artisan Nehemiah Wallington, who often took brief notes, sometimes written down from memory when he returned home, and used them immediately for 'repetition' in his household.[30] On the other hand, the Congregationalist politician Sir John Hartopp deliberately recorded the sermons of the eminent preacher John Owen, in a shorthand subsequently copied out in longhand, 'thinking them worthy of being transmitted down to posterity'.[31] The Gell notebooks are between these two extremes. The notes are often fairly full but not adequate to subsequent print or scribal publication. In the 1640s Katherine and John listened to many of the most famous preachers of the day, but they also heard local Derbyshire ministers and Katherine recorded no London sermons after 1660; there is no indication they planned to share the books beyond their intimate networks. Sermon note-taking began as a zealous individual response to a collective activity, which then prompted further reflection, sharing and discussion, further interactions of the personal and the social through hearing, writing, reading and talking within a family who preserved their sermon notebooks over the generations.

Presbyterian piety and Restoration nonconformity

Chronologically, the Gell sermon notebooks begin in years when a Presbyterian settlement for the national church was a plausible, although ultimately unfulfilled, aspiration, and broadly Presbyterian clerics retained a dominant, if contested, influence within the public ministry.[32] Notebooks also survive in large numbers for the decades between 1660 and 1689 when Presbyterianism was mostly illegal and its adherents subject to harassment and persecution, while Katherine's daughters survived to attend legal Presbyterian preaching after 1689, albeit not within a national church. In the sermons Katherine and

John Gell heard in the 1640s and 1650s, individual seeking for assurance was inextricably connected to the collective aspirations for reformation of national worship. They heard Derbyshire ministers defend a *jure divino* Presbyterian church, and they sometimes attended high-profile thanksgiving and fast-day sermons delivered to the English Parliament. This integration of personal aspiration with national reformation faltered in the 1650s and broke down with the restoration of episcopal government and the *Book of Common Prayer*. From the 1640s to the end of the seventeenth century the Gells were a prominent, 'mainstream' puritan family, broadly 'Presbyterian' in the 1640s and 1650s, and, according to recent scholarship 'Puritan Whigs' after 1660, negotiating the complex and shifting boundaries between nonconformity and adherence to the Established Church.[33] This boundary was at the time, and later, constructed as a distinction between private devotion and public conformity, a split that, as I have argued here, would have been most unwelcome to Katherine Gell. Nonconformists themselves deployed a rhetoric that distinguished between the public and the private, and then, as now, this was often seen in gendered terms as a distinction between a female-centred household religion and male public responsibilities.

We know from a long, passionate letter to Katherine from Robert Porter in January 1663 that she was extremely troubled by the prospect of attending public worship. The decision of whether to conform to the restored church after 1662 brought real anguish for moderate, church-based puritans, torn between hostility to separation and abhorrence of the Prayer Book. It was, as Porter wrote, a 'trembling subject'; his unexpected and not entirely coherent conclusion was that given the 'sad conflicts' in her spirit she should not attend public worship until her mind was more resolved.[34] Porter reinforced the importance of Gell's care for her household, given the 'many temptations to dullnesse and indevotion' in the public ordinances.[35] Sermon notes from the 1660s and 1670s reveal an enduring commitment to godly preaching in the Gells' households. The regular weekly sermons at Alsop Hall, the home of John's sister, were usually delivered by Joseph Moore, who, as Porter described: 'was forced from his publick Ministry ... by the Act of Uniformity, spent the residue of his time in divers private Families, in Praying, Preaching, Catechizing, all which he performed far beyond what might be expected from his years'. Moore was licensed as a Presbyterian at Hopton in 1672, and his family is recognised in John Gell's will of 1687, which also included bequests to Porter and to ejected ministers from further afield such as Francis Tallents of Shropshire.[36] Indeed, with very few exceptions, the Gells were noting the sermons of ministers who had not been able to conform in 1662.[37] They also recorded frequent 'private' fasts around family or personal issues, as with the illness and death of Katherine Gell, as we have seen. On 22 June 1671 Moore preached 'at a day for my father in reference to his soule and body'. This was for Katherine's aged father-in-law, Sir John Gell, one of the less godly members of the family. The value of preserving a godly household was urgently reinforced: 'keep up family duties, it makes every little house becom a bethel, where God is not called upon in a family are such as god has threatened'. There were sermons on the approaching marriage of Katherine's daughter in 1663, and a thanksgiving for the safe delivery of her ninth child in June 1680, when Joseph Moore and William Bagshaw preached.[38] A zealous regime combining puritan preaching and individual devotional writing was thus maintained in the Gell households at Hopton and Alsop after 1662, but its 'private' designation might imply a process of retreat, even a feminised retreat.

There are many reasons, however, to be cautious about this judgement, which in general rests on too simple a distinction between the private and the public, and specifically underestimates the influence of Katherine Gell. To take the specific points first, I hope I have demonstrated the crucial role Katherine Gell played in her family's scribal devotions. Sermon noting began with her marriage, and was continued by her daughters for more than thirty years after her death. As Porter reminded her: 'Religion was not in your owne memory in soe good credit at Hopton' before she came there.[39] The public activism of her husband, described by William Bagshaw when he likened Katherine and John to the biblical figures of Elizabeth and Zechariah (Luke 1:5–6), should not be overestimated.[40] He did not sit in Parliament between 1659 and a brief period in 1688 before his death in February 1689, and he was only briefly a Justice of the Peace in Derbyshire.[41] Most contemporaries agreed that he was a more restrained character than his wife. When Katherine was furious that a minister serving as chaplain and tutor at Hopton was leaving for a better position, Robert Porter urged her, without much expectation of success, to calm down and listen to her husband: 'my earnest desire to you is that as yu solicite me to write so yu would weigh what I write and consider it and that you would observe your deare husband whose holy moderation I know will appear in this as in all other his concernments and follow that wisdom and composedness which I know his good example will set before you'.[42]

Alison Searle has argued that active involvement in Restoration dissent enabled women to influence public affairs.[43] If John Gell was not a particularly active public servant, neither was the 'Bethel' at Hopton, the household in which Katherine Gell's agency was so significant, exactly private. Most obvious is the consistent support for ejected ministers, and the consequent and public estrangement from the Established Church. Alongside the fasts marking family crises, deprived ministers preached regularly on God's enduring care for his saints and his true church, explaining how individuals develop assurance of their salvation. There were sermons on avowedly public matters, as when Moore preached on 13 September 1675 at a day of 'humilitye for the Church of God in its low estate'. The note-taker, most likely Elizabeth Gell, combined concerns for her own salvation with anxieties about the overall fortunes of the church.[44]

The Gells' household religion was sustaining, private devotion that offered individual reassurance but also nurtured the strength to work for better times. It was also exemplary for the wider world of dissenting communities. Hence the praise of Katherine Gell after her death by an ejected minister for her 'near and dear relationship to the whole church of God especially poor distressed persecuted faithful ministers of Christs gospel to the whole county and neighbourhood'. Indeed, she had made Hopton one of the 'major centres of Presbyterianism in the north of England'.[45] This was no private matter.

Notes

1 Derbyshire Record Office (DRO) D3287/47/7, letter book of Katherine Gell, pp. 85, 89–90. It is clear from the survival of some of the original letters from Porter and Baxter that Gell's copies are accurate and complete versions of the words written, albeit with idiosyncratic abbreviations.
2 All biblical quotations in this chapter are taken from the King James Bible.

3 DRO D3287/24/4, no pagination. Joseph Moore (see also DRO D3287/24/5/2) also preached at the occasion on the very practical text from 1 Timothy 5:23, 'Drink no longer water, but use a little wine for thy stomach's sake and thine often infirmities.' Porter preached again on his text the following day, a Sunday. Eleanor Alsop was the sister of Katherine's husband John, who left her an annuity of £10 in his will of 1687: The National Archives, PROB 11/395/127. Katherine's children continued to support their aunt financially and were clearly very close to her: DRO D258/24/30/9–11; D258/24/50/4. There is no name in the volumes with this hand; the identification is mine on account of the declared relationship to Katherine Gell, and the reference to a sermon 'for my father' in 1671: DRO D3287/24/5/2.
4 DRO D3287/24/4, 24/5/2.
5 DRO D3287/24/5/1, 4 May 1671. The identification of Elizabeth is mine, comparing the notebook to her more polished hand in correspondence. The notes are very disorganised and the text is given incorrectly as Psalm 78 (actually Psalm 89:48: 'What man is he that liveth, and shall not see death?').
6 DWL, Richard Baxter, 'Letters', V:8. Gell often drew a heart shape instead of writing the word in her letters.
7 DRO D3287/47/7. Six letters from Gell to Baxter survive amongst the Baxter papers. See also Alison Searle, '"My Souls Anatomiste": Richard Baxter, Katherine Gell and Letters of the Heart', *Early Modern Literary Studies* 12.2 (2006), 1–26; Alison Searle, 'Writing Authority in the Interregnum: The Pastoral Letters of Richard Baxter', in Anne Dunan-Page and Clotilde Prunier (eds), *Debating the Faith: Religion and Letter Writing in Great Britain, 1550–1800*, International Archives of the History of Ideas 209 (Dordrecht: Springer, 2013), pp. 49–68.
8 The notebooks are in DRO D3287/boxes 24 and 25.
9 DRO D3287/25/19, 25/5, 24/1.
10 DRO D3287/25/14.
11 For sermon notes: Meredith Marie Neuman, *Jeremiah's Scribes: Creating Sermon Literature in Puritan New England* (Philadelphia: University of Pennsylvania Press, 2013). For England: Arnold Hunt, *The Art of Hearing: English Preachers and their Audiences, 1590–1640* (Cambridge: Cambridge University Press, 2010); John Craig, 'Sermon Reception', in Peter McCullough, Hugh Adlington and Emma Rhatigan (eds), *Oxford Handbook of the Early Modern Sermon* (Oxford: Oxford University Press, 2011), pp. 178–97; John Spurr, *The Laity and Preaching in Post-Reformation England* (London: Dr Williams's Trust, 2013).
12 Alec Ryrie, *Being Protestant in Reformation Britain* (Oxford: Oxford University Press, 2013), p. 358.

13 Kate Narveson, *Bible Readers and Lay Writers in Early Modern England: Gender and Self-Definition in an Emergent Writing Culture* (Farnham: Ashgate, 2012), pp. 82–3.
14 Gell welcomed the reading lists offered by Baxter and Porter and mentioned reading Baxter's *The Saints Everlasting Rest* (1650), *The Right Method for a Settled Peace of Conscience* (1653) and *A Call to the Unconverted* (1658), as well as works by William Gurnall and Thomas White: Baxter, 'Letters', V:5, V:8; IV:208. Her copy of Christopher Love's *Heaven's Glory, Hell's Terror* (1653) survives in the Gell archives, with an inscription by her daughter Elizabeth: 'Des livres de ma mere c'est a moy Elizabeth Gell 1679': DRO D3287/48/1. For her youthful poetry see Harvard University, Houghton Library MS Eng 107. For her recipe book, kept before her marriage and later owned by her daughter Temperance, see Folger Shakespeare Library, Ms V.a. 387.
15 Narveson, *Bible Readers and Lay Writers*, pp. 45–7, 101. Narveson discusses sermon notes on pp. 28–33.
16 Baxter, 'Letters', V:5, August 1658.
17 DRO D3287/47/7/39, February 1655.
18 Baxter, 'Letters', V:9, September 1658.
19 Gillian Wright, '"Delight in Good Books": Family, Devotional Practice and Textual Circulation in Sarah Savage's Diaries', *Book History* 18 (2015), 48–74 (50).
20 Baxter, 'Letters', V:8, V:5. William Gurnall, *The Christian in Compleat armour. Or, a Treatise of the Saints War against the Devil* (London, 1655). With many subsequent editions, this was a very popular puritan work.
21 Baxter, 'Letters', V:3.
22 *Ibid.*, IV:142; V:3.
23 DRO D3287/47/7/25; D258/38/11/2, undated and undirected letter from John Otefield but obviously connected to Katherine Gell's dilemmas in the 1650s.
24 DRO D3287/47/7/224, Baxter to Gell, 15 December 1657. For other godly women who repeatedly recorded their sins, see Raymond A. Anselment, 'Samuel Clarke's Lives and Husbands' Remembrances of Their Wives', *Seventeenth Century* (2018), 1–18. I owe this reference to Robert W. Daniel.
25 For examples see DRO D3287/24/4, 24/5/2, 25/20 (Eleanor Alsop); D3287/24/5/1 (Elizabeth Gell).
26 DRO D3287/24/1 (Katherine), fols 136^{r-v}; 25/5 (John) fols 102^{r-v}. For gender and note-taking, Narveson, *Bible Readers and Lay Writers*, pp. 28–35, 50–3.
27 DRO D3287/24/2, fols 32^{r-v}.

28 DRO D258/38/1.
29 It is not always clear whether the sermons were in the hall or the local church, a chapelry of Ashbourne, 'fit to be disused' in the 1650 church survey and controlled by the Alsop family. There are no parish registers before 1701 and it may have been, in effect, a private chapel: J. Charles Cox, *Notes on the Churches of Derbyshire*, 2 vols (London, 1877), II:368, 404–5.
30 British Library (BL), Add MS 40, 883, fol. 165^r, May 1643.
31 See the entry on MS OWE in New College Library, Edinburgh, in the *Gateway to Early Modern Manuscript Sermons* database. https://gemms.itercommunity.org/view_record.php?table=manuscript&id=893. Accessed 28 November 2018. Hartopp's granddaughter arranged for the publication of Owen sermons in the eighteenth century.
32 Ann Hughes, '"The public profession of these nations": The National Church in Interregnum England', in Christopher Durston and Judith Maltby (eds), *Religion and Society 1640–1660* (Manchester: Manchester University Press, 2006), pp. 93–114.
33 J. T. Cliffe, *The Puritan Gentry Besieged 1650–1750* (London: Routledge, 1993), pp. 56–9, 69–73, 88–9, 214. Roger Morrice, *The Entring Book of Roger Morrice (1677–1691)*, ed. Mark Goldie et al., 7 vols (Woodbridge: Boydell & Brewer in association with the Parliamentary History Yearbook Trust, 2007), I:44.
34 DRO D258/38/11/5.
35 *Ibid.*
36 Robert Porter, *The Life of Mr John Hieron ... Published by D. Burgess* (London, 1691), pp. 53–4; will of Sir John Gell: The National Archives, PROB 11/395; DRO D3287/24/5/2. For Presbyterian preaching and domestic piety after the Act of Toleration see chapter 4.
37 Exceptions are Ellis Farnworth, the master of Wirksworth Grammar School, who accepted the Act of Uniformity and preached the sermons on marriage in 1663 (see DRO D3287/25/15), and Nathaniel Boothouse, the conformist but Whig minister of Carsington whom John Gell was hearing in 1688 (see DRO D3287/24/7).
38 DRO D3287/24/5/2, 25/15. For 'Cousin Eyre's preservation of her 9th child' see DRO D3287/24/20. Katherine's eldest daughter, also Katherine, married William Eyre in 1664 (notes by Eleanor Alsop).
39 DRO D3287/47/7/26, dated 1655.
40 See William Bagshaw, *De Spiritualibus Pecci* (London, 1702), pp. 56–9.
41 See his biography from the 1660–90 volume of the History of Parliament website. www.historyofparliamentonline.org/. Accessed 12 March 2018.
42 DRO D3287/47/7/244–5, November 1657.

43 See for example, Alison Searle, 'Women, Marriage and Agency in Restoration Dissent', in Sarah Apetrei and Hannah Smith (eds), *Religion and Women in Britain c. 1660–1760* (Aldershot: Ashgate, 2014), pp. 23–40; see also Elizabeth Clarke, 'Elizabeth Jekyll's Spiritual Journal: Private Diary or Political Document?', *English Manuscript Studies* 9 (2000), 218–37; Melinda S. Zook, *Protestantism, Politics and Women in Britain, 1660–1714* (Basingstoke: Palgrave Macmillan, 2013).
44 DRO D3287/24/9.
45 DRO D258/17/31/54, James Sutton to John Gell; Cliffe, *The Puritan Gentry Besieged*, p. 69.

4

The Act of Toleration, household worship and voicing dissent: Oliver Heywood's *A Family Altar* (1693)

William J. Sheils

The ministerial career of the Presbyterian divine Oliver Heywood spanned the years from 1650, when as a young man he accepted the call of the congregation at Coley Chapel in Halifax, West Yorkshire, until his death there in 1702, a patriarchal figure respected by fellow ministers and congregations across the north of England.[1] His life has been subsequently deployed by historians as an exemplary study of the pastoral tradition within 'Old Dissent' at a time of shifting and fraught relations between that tradition, deriving as it did from puritanism, and the Established Church.[2] Heywood stood at the centre of a ministerial and spiritual cousinage extending throughout the West Riding and Lancashire for over half a century, maintaining a roving ministry throughout the area and serving his congregation at Coley and North Owram both in times of persecution and in the first decade following the Act of Toleration.

In this essay I explore Heywood's printed manual for domestic devotion *A Family Altar* (1693). Firstly, I will examine its content, revealing how Heywood envisaged the household worship of dissenters post-persecution. Secondly, I will reveal how Heywood's activities while he was writing his text in 1692 reflected his pastoral concerns and the message of this work. In doing so, I reveal the twin import printing and preaching had in propagating a devotional identity of Presbyterian domestic worship. Where Sharon Achinstein has shown how the 'domestic spaces of the family home took up the roles previously performed by the church' in periods where dissent was persecuted, this essay reveals how the home took on a new spiritual significance for family and household worship in the years following the Act of Toleration.[3]

Heywood's ministry

First it is important to situate Heywood's ministry concerning domestic devotions more broadly by examining his preaching and publications. Heywood's reputation as a powerful preacher emerged early among his followers, and his reputation was consolidated by a number of publications between 1667 and his death.[4] The earliest of these, *Heart Treasure* and the famous *Closet Prayer*, focused, as their titles imply, on the nature of prayer: how it was the foundation of Christian living generally and, more personally, how it formed the continual basis of Heywood's ministry. The first of these texts was Heywood's first venture into print and derived from a course of sermons which he preached at Coley. It was dedicated to his congregation there, his 'very loving and dearly beloved friends and neighbours the inhabitants of Coley, and the places adjacent'.[5] Clearly this was an essay designed for a specific audience, but one with general application, and Heywood gave an account of its gestation. Having heard a godly minister preach on the same text, 'A good man out of the good treasure of the heart bringeth forth good things,' Heywood addressed the text in a series of sermons 'with which some were so affected, that several of them entreated me to give them copies thereof, which I set myself to'. But the project grew in size and his supporters offered to bear the cost of publication – 'a sudden and, to me, a strange notion, for I had never yet judged any labours of mine to be of so much worth as to be expressed in the public view'. Heywood prayed and sent the text to 'some reverend Ministers' to be ruled by their judgement and advice. Support was forthcoming from 'four or five eminent men in these two counties of Yorkshire and Lancashire' and the text was published.[6] As Harold Love has shown more generally, Heywood located this text within a collective ministerial tradition, locating its origin in the sermon of a fellow minister and its ultimate textual form bearing the authority of some of his more senior colleagues. Thus the wider ministry, as validation, and the whole congregation, as supporters and encouragers, were contributors to the volume.[7] Heywood's later publications were never so directly linked to particular sermons or to his specific congregation, but were more general: thus his *Baptismal Bonds*, published in 1687, was prefaced by an epistle 'To all Christians who hope and desire to stand firm in their baptismal obligations', and *Israel's Lamentation* (1682) was dedicated to 'all the mourners in Zion that wait for the Consolation of Israel'.[8]

Heywood's published works were the result of his reputation and not the source of it. For the half-century between 1650 and 1702 he conducted an unremitting ministry of itinerant preaching and pastoral care, marked by public and family fasts and by a healing ministry among the families of his congregation at home and throughout the region, which he recorded in his autobiography, journals, common place books and day books – themselves articles of his devotional identity and writing (see table 4.1).[9] Throughout

Table 4.1 Sermons preached by Oliver Heywood in addition to his normal Sunday preaching, 1665–1701

Year	Sermons	Fasts	Thanksgivings	Miles travelled
1665	26	18	3	600
1666	60	20	3	700
1667	89	20	7	900
1668	69	18	3	900
1669	48	16	4	600
1670	53	20	8	530
1671	55	29	5	870
1672	62	28	8	728
1673	69	30	3	1070
1674	72	33	5	910
1675	48	–	–	1097
1676	67	56	12	1052
1677	60	40	8	1198
1678	64	50	4	1034
1679	77	52	7	1386
1680	91	53	8	1250
1681	105	50	9	1400
1682	100	41	12	1100
1683	109	49	7	900
1684	126	51	7	746
1685	74	8	–	70[a]
1686	132	37	15	1004
1687	124	44	15	1400

Table 4.1 Sermons preached by Oliver Heywood in addition to his normal Sunday preaching, 1665–1701 (Continued)

Year	Sermons	Fasts	Thanksgivings	Miles travelled
1688	132	42	14	1300
1689	131	34	8	1358
1690	135	40	17	1100
1691	103	37	11	853[b]
1692	97	49	14	966
1693	109	35	12	841
1694	90	38	17	735
1695	70	38	5	700
1696	85	34	15	700
1697	82	40	15	700
1698	78	34	16	410[c]
1699	67	36	9	300
1700	45	22	3	157
1701	23	14	5	no travel[d]
Total	3036	1356	317	31,465

This information is extrapolated from Oliver Heywood, *The Whole Works of the Reverend Oliver Heywood*, ed. Richard Slate, 5 vols (Idle, Yorkshire: John Vint, 1826), I:350.

[a] in York Castle, preached in prison
[b] confined to home by sickness, two months
[c] in addition, attended six meetings of ministers
[d] also attended eight conferences

his ministry, save for the last few years of his life, Heywood preached hundreds of sermons each year, and even in his seventies they numbered about one hundred a year. They were preached in chapels, houses, inns and sometimes in the open air, in both town and country, and he kept a record of them in his annual spiritual reckonings.

The varied locations in which Heywood preached demonstrate the shifting boundary between the public and the private so characteristic of dissent in the years before the Act of Toleration (1689), as it was of puritanism in the early part of the century,[10] but the Act provided a stimulus to probe that boundary more fully. It was this aspect that Heywood, by now a senior figure in the northern dissenting community, undertook in his *A Family Altar*, published in 1693,[11] with a commendatory epistle by an elder statesman of London Presbyterianism and close friend of Richard Baxter, John Howe. By this time the right to public worship nationally had been given physical manifestation in Heywood's community by the erection of a chapel for his congregation at North Owram.

A Family Altar (1693)

A Family Altar was prefaced by an epistle to the Christian reader, and especially those 'Householders Professing Religion', in which Heywood wrote, 'I know not how a minister can better employ his time, and studies, and pen better … than in pressing upon householders a care of the souls under their care. This hath a direct tendency to PUBLIC reformation: religion begins in individuals, and passeth on to relatives, and lesser spheres of relationship make up greater, churches and commonwealths consist of families … In vain do you complain of magistrates and ministers, while you that are householders are unfaithful in your trust.'[12]

The altar, of course, was not a physical object but consisted in 'all the worship of God to be performed in families', and it was to be clearly distinguished from 'public, and also secret personal altars'.[13] These distinctions were important: family worship was separate not only from the national but also the local congregational worshipping community, at which ministerial presence was required, but it was a shared worship, distinct from that personal encounter with God which Heywood had given such importance to in *Closet Prayer*, which he had written in the more fraught ecclesiastical environment of a quarter of a century earlier. Heywood addressed the term 'family', noting that sometimes the word signified a whole nation, but he chose to work with what he called a common definition 'in this house are such as are most ordinarily and familiarly conversant together, that work, eat, drink, and sleep under one roof':[14] a definition wider than a kin group, but denoting one sharing a common socio-economic and, in his words, hopefully a common religious purpose.

Heywood then embarked on a section on the justification for this family altar, which is generally uncontentious, but he did address the question of the ungodly – those prayerless and wicked household members, and their effect on the practice and how they were to be treated. The impact of such individuals on the efficacy of communal worship had long exercised the godly.[15] For Heywood, inclusion rather than exclusion was his leitmotif; drawing on an analogy from public worship to stress the efficacy for individuals of worship in wider public contexts: 'What think you of poor ministers and prayers in mixed congregations? Certainly the presence of unworthy persons prejudiceth not the reception of sincere worshippers.'[16]

Heywood then discussed the relationship to public prayer, arguing that public prayer of itself, though necessary, was not sufficient to create godliness or to overcome all those enemies of the kingdom of God in the world noted in scripture – the mockers, the hypocrites and the timid – but he made it clear that separation was not the answer, with a warning about what he called over preciseness in the attitude of the godly to the rest of society.[17] What would bridge that defect in the public ordinances was family worship and, recalling the harassment which dissenters had recently been subject to, and reflecting on his own well-recorded ministerial experience under such circumstances, Heywood concluded that 'when public persecution breaks up church assemblies, house worship will maintain religion in the world'.[18] Family worship, which he had witnessed at first hand throughout his ministry, was crucial to the maintenance of religion, but it had to be conducted alongside both more public and more personal devotional and social frameworks. This was underlined in the conditions which Heywood set out to ensure such prayer would have a fruitful outcome. First and foremost it had to be built on and attentive to powerful ministry in the public chapels, and it was to be sustained by the frequenting of the society of Christian people in the neighbourhood and congregation (a constant refrain throughout the volume); secondly, and possibly also collectively, it was dependent upon diligent study of the scripture, and especially of the Lord's Prayer; and finally, for the householders themselves, he returned to the theme of his early work on *Closet Prayer* by stressing the necessity of regular prayerful converse with God.[19] The family altar, or household worship, was therefore the arch which fortified those pillars of the godly nation: public worship and personal devotion.

Practical suggestions for ensuring the success of family worship were given both generally and specifically. In general, the usual tropes about the importance of choosing wives, servants and other household members carefully were run through.[20] This was especially important as parenthood was a responsibility with uncertain outcomes even when all care was taken, a theme that recurs in Heywood's accounts of many of the pastoral and healing visits recorded by him in his diaries and event books, in which he recounted the providential outcomes for those who accepted God's grace, as well as the fates of those who failed to do so, even when the sons of godly parents. Heywood well knew that it was the responsibility of parents to raise their children in God's ways, but also knew that, in his phrase, 'children are given' and their needs and characters were various.[21]

Having set out these general and unexceptional suggestions, Heywood then turned to what can best be described as the 'how to' part of the book, covering the conduct and form of family worship, its rules, and the best context for its practice. It was in this section that Heywood both drew on his past experiences of household worship and sought to express a distinctive form of devotional identity.

As to conduct, Heywood suggested that it should begin with a call for God's help by the master or mistress of the house or, if he or she were unable to undertake this, then a psalm might be substituted to focus the minds of the worshippers; once engaged upon, worship should be short and serious, not tedious.[22] As to the use of set forms of prayer, they were 'not absolutely unlawful', but heads of household were admonished 'not to neglect the gifts of the spirit'. These gifts, however, were the result of study and meditation, and worship was to be led in a serious, audible voice, but not in clamorous or hectoring tones. Family worship was to be a sober opportunity to reflect on God's words and the day's events, not an enthusiastic embracing of special providences. In order to ensure this, the practice of what he termed 'holy conversation' both within the family and with neighbours was to be the norm, so that worship arose naturally from that context and did not take on the character of a 'formal course' set apart from the household's usual tone.[23] As to the times for prayer, Heywood, having dismissed the formal practices of the Moslems and the Jews, recommended morning and evening prayer at set times known to all the household: 'it is a proper time for duty morning and evening, when the family come together to their stated meals'. In the evening this was best attended to before supper, 'when your spirits are more brisk and lively', for 'it will not be so seasonable to go down upon your knees, when you are fitter to lie down in your beds'.[24] It was a defining characteristic of the Christian household that it organised its daily life around family worship, and not the other way around: meeting for worship before mealtimes was advised, but the two events, prayer and dining, should be kept firmly distinct. Although God should always be invoked at meals, this was not enough in itself to fulfil the Christian's duty, and posture too marked that distinction. In common with many Anglican writers on the subject, Heywood, who usually kneeled in private prayer and while praying with his wife, enjoined kneeling at family worship: 'As for sitting in prayer, it is an unbecoming, lazy position' only allowable to the weak and sickly.[25]

The distinctiveness was also marked by location, for although the family altar was not an object, it had a preferred location in those orderly, middling-sort dissenting houses which had provided support for the ministry before the Act of Toleration. The venue varied with circumstance, and poorer families had less choice, but the ideal was that worship should take place in 'some distant place from the street, to avoid disturbance from the hurries, tumults, and confusions that may distract you'.[26] Perhaps recalling the disturbance to his prayers caused by the kitchen maids preparing the celebratory meal at the household fast marking the marriage in 1678 of James Halstead and his wife, and no doubt similar disturbances in other places and at other times, Heywood argued that household worship should always take place in a location set aside for that purpose, and that it should be known as such to all the household, whose members should treat it with respect. It was not an exclusive place, neither an oratory nor a chapel, but it was nevertheless a clearly marked space within the household with time set aside for worship and, where possible, the location was not to be that normally used for the family meal.[27]

Rules and boundaries were then set down in answer to a series of questions, two of which, about timing and posture, we have already addressed. More significant were questions of leadership, legitimacy and authority. In response to consideration about the householder's qualifications for preaching or dispensing the Lord's Supper, Heywood was, not surprisingly, unequivocal: the householder was to work alongside the minister and not usurp the latter's function, either in preaching or in administering the Lord's Supper. Accordingly, worship was to be largely catechetical in practice, and could not assume the functions of public worship, which should now take place in licensed chapels.[28] Whether the householder could delegate authority in leading worship produced an interesting response. If available and affordable, a chaplain could be appointed to lead family worship, but this was only possible in the wealthiest of households, and these were very few. More commonly leadership had to be delegated to other household members and, in an acknowledged, if qualified, departure from Calvin on this point, Heywood declared that it was also permissible to entrust the wife of the householder with that responsibility: 'I see no reason why an Abigail or a Deborah, may not at least be the mouth of a family to God. But I am not positive herein, and leave it to the consideration of others.'[29] Given the valued contribution of women, both in numbers and in support, which Heywood received during his ministry, this comes as no real surprise, and accords with the views of other dissenters of his acquaintance, such as John Angier,[30] but his antipathy to the local Quaker presence, which he feared had disrupted members of his congregation, may have influenced his hesitancy on this point, given the more public ministerial role that Quakers allowed to women.[31] To ensure the continuity of household worship on those occasions when neither the householder nor his wife was able to lead prayers, Heywood advised the employment of a suitable servant, chosen for godliness rather than by seniority, to lead worship in their absence.[32]

Heywood was also conscious that not all members of his congregation found themselves employed in godly households, and offered advice in a question-and-answer format to those placed in such unfortunate circumstances. In reply to the problem of a careless or drunken master he was unequivocal: where prayers were said then the Christian must attend despite the shortcomings of the household, but should show disapproval – though quite how this was to be done was not made clear! If reform of practice was not forthcoming, then it was the Christian's responsibility to speak directly with the head of the household and, if that failed to bring any adequate improvement, then he or she should seek the advice of the minister, who might know the household and be able to prevail upon the master to bring about the desired reform.[33] It was the minister's responsibility and his authority which came into play in such circumstances, but that authority had its limitations. Where the Christian was employed by a 'prayerless' family then the best course of action was to try to seek alternative employment within the law; in the case of the young and apprentices, not a very helpful response. Beyond that, all that Heywood offered was the suggestion that the servant should seek reform of the household through example. Clearly,

Heywood's rather unhelpful responses in these circumstances reflected the social conditions of the patriarchal household, and underlined his earlier argument about the importance to serious Christians of exercising care in their choice of household and of employer.

Heywood's advice about family prayer was unexceptional and could be found in the devotional writings of other dissenting ministers, but in the years following the Act of Toleration the opportunity to articulate the importance of the domestic devotional sphere and to distinguish it from both the public and the personal, or private, sphere was important. No longer liable to the persecution which had marked their lives for a generation and more, dissenters could build on that puritan tradition of domestic piety to establish their churches around a more secure and settled ministry. Heywood's declared intention was to provide encouragement and advice 'to those that are heads and governors of families to take up Joshua's resolution: that whatever others do, they and their houses will serve the Lord in daily, fruitful, fervent prayer', an activity which was 'both work and wages: a service that carries its reward with it (reward not of debt but of graces), it brings blessings upon a family'. This was not only upon the family, but on the wider community and the nation as a whole. Heywood's treatise was 'A word in season, for it is a common complaint and that too, by many who are not a little guilty of it themselves, that the power of godliness, the life of practical religion, is at this day under a lamentable decay: and amongst the many cases of this decay, there is scarcely any that hath been more perniciously influential thereunto, than the neglect of family worship of God'.[34] It was a theme he articulated on a number of occasions; in two sermons preached at Pontefract in February 1693 he stressed the point: 'Our holiness must appear not only in God's house, but also in our own ... Much of the power of God lies within doors, ... the noise and stir we make about religion amongst others will signify little, if those that are with us every day, and have opportunity to know us best, speak little of our holiness'.[35] The timing was perhaps significant in the context of both the sermons and the publication of *A Family Altar*.

Domestic worship post Toleration Act

The Toleration Act transformed the life of the congregation at North Owram as elsewhere: a new chapel had been opened in 1688 following

James II's Declaration of Indulgence, and a school was added in 1693. The opportunities brought about by the Act of Toleration were accompanied by concerns, however, both personal and more general. In 1691 Heywood had played a leading role in introducing into Yorkshire 'the happy union' between Presbyterians and Independents, but these optimistic beginnings were followed by Heywood's concern that the new atmosphere of toleration had permitted a falling away from that Calvinist doctrinal orthodoxy which formed the bedrock of his ministry.[36] In 1691 Heywood suffered a near fatal attack of ague, but despite being in his sixties there was little diminution of his preaching and travelling. The diaries for these years no longer survive, so we cannot reconstruct his ministry at this time in the same rich detail as we can for the years before 1685, but his annual spiritual reckonings are helpful. In these for 1692, the year in which he was writing *A Family Altar*, he recorded that he had travelled 841 miles, preached 109 weekday sermons, kept thirty-five fasts and twelve days of thanksgiving, and had baptised twenty-two children. In addition to this public ministry he also offered a rare glimpse of his domestic regime:

> I have arisen out of my bed, fallen down on my knees by my bed-side with my wife, thankt god for that nights mercys, had nothing to do but go to my chamber, read my chapter, sometimes a comment thereon, fell down on my knees, prayd, went down, made ready, had breakfast, family-prayer, went to my study (except I had some whither to goe), there I studied, read, writ till noon, dined, walkt to some neighbour an hour after dinner, came home took my pipe (in doing which I read in some book, read over many thus doing), went to my study, continued till 4, then read my scripture comment, prayd, went down, we had supper, prayer, went again to my study till 8 or 9 a clock, read some good book to my family till bed-time, then upon our knees put ourselves into the hands of god, ordinarily slept comfortably[37]

The domestic sphere had always been integral to dissenting life, and in the years before toleration, household worship was a defining and necessary characteristic, both in sustaining the tradition and supporting the ministry. Close reciprocal relationships between leading laity and their ministers were vital when public worship was prohibited, obscuring the boundary between the public and the private. Household gatherings, such as those recorded by Heywood in his journal for the years before 1688, often represented the public worship of the community, and we find Heywood preaching and praying in houses of the wealthy and the poor; in inns, market halls, and in the open air, both in town and country; as well as in licensed chapels, when permitted, and occasionally in parish churches, when invited. The fact of toleration shifted the boundary between the public and the private, and also perhaps that between minister and congregation: what might be described as a move from a community worshipping primarily in household settings to one of congregations organised around chapels. This was not confined to dissent, for John Bossy identified a similar shift occurring at about this time within the Catholic community, in which the country houses of the gentry were gradually replaced by town-based chapels served by resident priests as the location of the worshipping community, albeit in the case of Catholics without the impetus of toleration.[38]

In this new environment it was natural that ministers would seek to reconsider the boundary between public and private worship, and the purposes of each. Legalisation of public worship and the building of chapels made ministers less dependent on their congregations, in providing opportunities to preach if not for financial support, and the emergence of dissenting academies produced in time a more distinct ministerial identity, whereby ministers led their congregations from their chapel pulpits.[39] Relations between minister and congregation remained strong, but after 1689 it was the congregation which resorted to the chapel for public worship, and not the minister who travelled to the homes of his followers. The household no longer fulfilled the same public purposes that many had previously, but it remained integral to dissenting experience, albeit with a different emphasis. In this context devotional identity needed to be redefined, and especially that which took place within the household. Household worship had always involved the future of the Church through the older generations passing on their faith to the younger ones, but in the years of persecution up to 1689 it had also been essential to sustaining both the ministry and the present state of the Church. This probably explains the richness of the record about household worship in these years, or more properly of worship conducted in a household setting, and the relative decline in the recording of such activities after 1689, though there were many exhortatory writings on the subject in the generation following.[40]

This is not to say that ministers no longer engaged with household worship as before, but that the character of that worship, and its functions, had changed. Heywood devoted a long, distinguished and fruitful ministry of over half a century to preaching and voicing dissent in its public gatherings, and he continued to do so throughout the 1690s when he was in his sixties, and until the end of his life.[41] In 1700, when he was seventy, he had reduced his travelling but managed to preach forty-five weekday sermons and conduct twenty-two fasts and three days of thanksgiving, as well as attending eight conferences of ministers.[42] His commitment to the public ministry did not wane but, after the Act of Toleration, his manuscripts and his published writings reveal increasing attention to the personal and the domestic. Among the 'returns of prayer' recorded by him in 1692 two were public, nationally, for the discovery of a plot against the King in May, and, locally, for the settlement of a dispute between two members of his congregation which threatened the reputation of his church; three were personal, the settlement of a property dispute with one of his congregation, his son's recovery from illness and his own rescue after a fall from a horse; the remaining two concerned responses to his ministry.

Reflecting on the fact that he had recently been discouraged by the apparent lack of conversions attributed to his preaching, he recorded eleven such cases brought to his attention during that year, ranging across the north from Ormskirk in Cheshire and Colne in Lancashire to Halifax nearby. His final answer to prayer that year returned his attention to the young:

> I heard that god had set the faces of some young men of my hearers and neighbours heavenwards, and that they met together frequently in the night to pray, I was greatly rejoiced in that good news and sent on Lord's Day Nov 13 to speak to one of them, JW, desired him to ask his companions to come to my house on Wednesday following and spend some time in prayer with me: we began after 2, spent time till after 7 ... Oh what a presence of God there was with those hopeful youths ... such meltings of gratitude that I have seldom had with other.[43]

The experience of dissent in the years after 1662 demonstrated to Heywood that public ministry was in itself an insufficient mark of God's church, and that the household formed the essential building block if that tradition were to be sustained. Without domestic devotion the public voice of dissent would lose its force and would not be passed down to the following generations. It was this that inspired publication of *A Family Altar* in 1693. When sent to the printer publication proved problematic because of paper costs, but Heywood drew comfort from his ministry, especially among the young, and from the personal mercies shown to him, especially in his domestic life, with a convenient dwelling, 'a lovely companion, hopeful sons, faithful servant[s] ... kind friends abroad, loving neighbours at home', all sustained by household prayer in the morning and the evening and 'the reading of some good book to my family till bedtime'.[44] Though this was the bedrock of his ministry this was a rare reference to his domestic routine and, in contrast to some other ministers, Heywood's diaries are reticent about his own family worship.[45] Unsure if his books would be published, his summary of that year was nonetheless confident: 'this I can truly say, I have been industrious and spent my time for the good of the church and the glory of my good God'.[46] One of the glories of God and one of the strongest signs of the church was the domestic devotional piety which his diaries and memoranda record, and which publication of *A Family Altar* sought to strengthen.

Notes

1 Samuel S. Thomas, *Creating Communities in Restoration England: Parish Congregations in Oliver Heywood's Halifax* (Leiden, Netherlands: Brill, 2013), is the most recent study. See also William Joseph Sheils, 'Heywood, Oliver (*bap.* 1630, *d.*1702)', *ODNB*. https://doi.org/10.1093/ref:odnb/13186. Accessed 1 December 2018.

2 There are several biographies of Heywood by his fellow nonconformists, based on his own autobiographical writings. See *The Whole Works of the Reverend Oliver Heywood*, ed. Richard Slate, 5 vols (Idle, Yorkshire: John Vint, 1826), hereafter *Works*. In addition to his published works, volume I prints some of the early lives of Heywood. For a study which locates him within a broader cultural tradition see Walace Notestein, *Four Worthies* (London, 1956), pp. 211–43.

3 Sharon Achinstein, *Literature and Dissent in Milton's England* (Cambridge: Cambridge University Press, 2003), p. 223.

4 These are collected in Heywood's *Works*. The early lives are published in volume I, and volume V contains some hitherto unpublished sermons. All references to Heywood's works are made to the Slate edition cited above.

5 Oliver Heywood, *Heart Treasure, an essay comprising the substance of a course of sermons preached at Coley*, dedicatory epistle, in *Works*, II:1–282.

6 *Ibid.*, pp. xxvi–xxvii.

7 See Harold Love, 'Preacher and Publisher: Oliver Heywood and Thomas Parkhurst', *Studies in Bibliography* 31 (1978), 227–35. I am grateful to Robert W. Daniel for this reference. For a wider discussion of print and dissent see N. H. Keeble, *The Literary Culture of Nonconformity in Later Seventeenth-Century England* (Leicester: Leicester University Press, 2nd edn, 1991), esp. pp. 83–92, 143–50.
8 Heywood, *Works*, IV:1–282 and III:363–494 respectively, epistles dedicatory.
9 These are collected in *The Rev. Oliver Heywood BA, 1630–1702; His Autobiography, Diaries, Anecdote and Event Books* ..., ed. J. Horsfall Turner, 4 vols (Brighouse, 1881–85), hereafter *Diaries*.
10 Patrick Collinson, 'The English Conventicle', in William J. Sheils and Diana Wood (eds), *Voluntary Religion* (Oxford: Blackwell, 1986), pp. 223–60; John Spurr, *English Puritanism 1603–1689* (Basingstoke: Macmillan, 1998), pp. 133–43, 192–201.
11 Heywood, *Works*, IV:283–418.
12 *Ibid.*, 285.
13 *Ibid.*, 305, 307.
14 *Ibid.*, 308.
15 Alexandra Walsham, 'Supping with Satan's Disciples: Spiritual and Secular Sociability in Post-Reformation England', in Nadine Lewycky and Adam Morton (eds), *Getting Along? Religious Identities and Confessional Relations in Early Modern England* (Farnham: Ashgate, 2012), pp. 29–56.
16 Heywood, *Works*, IV:330.
17 *Ibid.*, 334.
18 *Ibid.*, 362.
19 *Ibid.*, 374–90.
20 *Ibid.*, 370–2.
21 For his record of the 'returns of prayer' for 1682 see Heywood, *Dairies*, IV:64–86. For conflict that arose over religious differences between fathers and sons see chapter 9.
22 Heywood, *Works*, IV:392, 396.
23 *Ibid.*, 396, 411.
24 *Ibid.*, 396, 407.
25 *Ibid.*, 407–9.
26 *Ibid.*, 411.
27 Heywood, *Diaries*, I:342; *Works*, IV:410.
28 Heywood, *Works*, IV:402–4. Interestingly, in his recommendatory epistle, Heywood describes the head of the household as 'a prophet, priest and ruler in the family', and describes the household as 'a little church of God', but he does not follow the logic of these descriptions at this point, adopting the more traditional distinction in the text. *Ibid.*, 289.

29 *Ibid.*, 404.
30 William. J. Sheils, 'Oliver Heywood and His Congregation', in Sheils and Wood, *Voluntary Religion*, pp. 261–78; more generally see Spurr, *English Puritanism*, pp. 195–7; Melinda S. Zook, *Protestantism, Politics and Women in Britain, 1660–1714* (Basingstoke: Palgrave Macmillan, 2013), pp. 16–58.
31 Adrian Davies, *The Quakers in English Society, 1655–1725* (Oxford: Clarendon, 2000), pp. 118–22; John Spurr, *The Post-Reformation, Religion, Politics and Society in Britain, 1603–1714* (London: Routledge, 2006), p. 321.
32 Heywood, *Works*, IV:404–6.
33 *Ibid.*, IV:411–2.
34 *Ibid.*, IV:289.
35 *Ibid.*, V:465.
36 Sheils, 'Heywood, Oliver'.
37 Heywood, *Diaries*, III:262–3.
38 John Bossy, *The English Catholic Community, 1570–1850* (London: Darton, Longman and Todd, 1975), pp. 250–77.
39 Michael R. Watts, *The Dissenters: From the Reformation to the French Revolution* (Oxford: Clarendon, 1978), pp. 366–71. For a list of those students at the academy set up by Richard Frankland at Attercliffe and from 1689 at Rathmell, and later taken on by John Chorlton at Manchester, see Heywood, *Diaries*, II:9–16. Of the 303 educated by Frankland, 110 became ministers. Watts discusses ministerial finance: in 1690 the Presbyterians and Congregationalists set up a Common Fund to establish chapels and assist poorer congregations. *Ibid.*, 342–6.
40 For a discussion of both Anglican and nonconformist texts see W. M. Jacob, *Lay People and Religion in the Early Eighteenth Century* (Cambridge: Cambridge University Press, 1996), pp. 101–6.
41 See table 4.1.
42 See table 4.1. For further details see Heywood, *Diaries*, III:254–85.
43 Heywood, *Diaries*, IV:142–6, quote at 146.
44 Heywood, *Diaries*, III:262–3.
45 See Ian Green, 'Varieties of Domestic Devotion in Early Modern England', in Jessica Martin and Alec Ryrie (eds), *Private and Domestic Devotion in Early Modern Britain* (Abingdon: Routledge, 2012), pp. 9–31, esp. p. 12.
46 Heywood, *Diaries*, III:262–3.

Part III: Devotional identities in the theatre

5

Devotional identity and the mother's legacy in *A Warning for Fair Women* (1599)[*]

Iman Sheeha

The anonymous play *A Warning for Fair Women* (1599) has attracted extensive critical attention since the middle of the twentieth century. It has been profitably examined in terms of, among other topics, its relationship to the period's didactic literature,[1] to early modern popular literature and to medieval morality plays.[2] Criticism has also considered its engagement with concerns about social mobility,[3] as well as with the position of women within domestic hierarchy.[4] Critics have also explored the play's engagement with contemporary theorisation on the domestic, arguing that the disruption of the patriarchal household in this play in particular, and more generally in domestic tragedy, the genre to which the play belongs, originates from within the house,[5] or from without, whether it is the world of business that calls household masters away from home[6] or the court whose members disrupt the orderly household.[7] Scholarly engagement with the play has so far, however, largely overlooked an aspect of it that is essential to its presentation of the disorderly woman who is, whether as a principal or accessory, involved in the murder of her husband. This aspect concerns the play's use of a devotional book in its final movement, the Protestant martyr John Bradford's *Meditations* (1560), that Mistress Saunders passes on to her children as she takes leave of them. *A Warning for Fair Women*

---

[*] I am grateful to Bernard Capp, James Carney and John T. Gilmore for their insightful comments on an earlier version of this essay.

employs this devotional book to mark Mistress Saunders' individual devotional identity, her repentance and return to godliness, visually attaching her to an object meant to be used for the godly purpose of meditation and prayer. It is also used, more importantly, to stage the transgressor's rehabilitation and reintegration into the devotional community of godly mothers from whose ranks she had withdrawn upon getting involved with her seducer, Master Browne, and giving consent to, if not explicitly being an agent of, her husband's murder.

The play, I argue, traces Mistress Saunders' degeneration from being a representation of the ideal household mistress and mother into the figure's anti-type, the murderous wife and irresponsible mother, only to ensure her repentance and return to her former role as an ideal mother conscious of her devotional duties towards her children and eager to perform them in the end. In staging this journey, the play, I show, deploys the devotional book it places on the windowsill of Mistress Saunders' prison cell, then in her hands, and finally in those of her children, as a crucial emblem of her rehabilitation and reassumption of the role of the ideal mother. Mistress Saunders' passing on of a devotional book to her children, I will show, crucially inserts the tableau comprising mother and children into the cultural and literary tradition of the mother's legacy, a genre that emerged two decades before the publication of the play and that was to continue to flourish throughout the seventeenth century. The devotional book which appears in the final scene of the play, then, ensures Mistress Saunders' recuperative insertion within the ranks of godly mothers dying a good and exemplary death and thus reversing and undoing her earlier transgression.

The execution spectacle and the 'good' death

Scenes of execution, whether staged on scaffolds erected to execute criminals, on stages surrounded by playgoers or described in early modern murder pamphlets and ballads, have received extensive critical attention from social and cultural historians. Most notable is Michel Foucault, who saw these spectacles in eighteenth-century France as a demonstration of state power.[8] Ever since, critics have either complemented or critiqued this reading.[9] As James Alsop has argued, 'the interrelatedness of stage and scaffold might be found in the very geography and architecture of early modern London'. Quoting James Shapiro, he notes how Elizabethans were acutely aware of the Roman precedent of 'using the playhouse as a site for public executions', a tradition continued in London theatres – especially when in 1588 two priests were actually executed, 'one in the theatre and the other close-by'.[10] Lynn Alison Robson, in the context of studying early modern murder pamphlets and their execution scenes, has, however, expressed a sceptical attitude towards the execution-as-demonstration-of-state-power theory, persuasively arguing that these executions 'owed more to the English Protestant "craft of dying" than to discourses of state power and theatrical performance'.[11] For Robson, if executions are to be seen as 'theatre', 'it was the theatre of dying rather than of punishment' that they embodied.[12] The power that brought condemned men and women to the scaffold, she holds, 'was not that of the law and the state but their sinful human nature and their own actions'.[13] Reading the execution scenes and the gallows speeches commonly delivered by condemned criminals in light of the discourse of the *ars moriendi*, Robson concludes that 'it is clear that most murderers were represented as having "good" deaths'.[14] The 'good' death was one where the dying man or woman was given time to prepare for that death (i.e. did not die suddenly, such as happens to Master Saunders in *A Warning for Fair Women*), displayed courage and stoic patience in the face of death, settled his or her worldly affairs, and expressed faith in salvation.[15] Building on Robson's work, I offer a new reading of *A Warning for Fair Women* that is sensitive to a particular aspect of devotional identity that situates the execution scene at its denouement within the literary and cultural context of the early modern genre of the mother's legacy.

The genre of the mother's legacy emerged in the late sixteenth century when, in 1576, Lady Frances Abergavenny, a noblewoman on her deathbed, bequeathed a set of prayers and two acrostic poems to her daughter, which then appeared in Thomas Bentley's collection of biographies of exemplary women, *The Monument of Matrons* (1582).[16] Nicholas Breton published an advice book in 1601 aimed at a young man, Thomas Rowe, naming it *The Mothers Blessing*.[17] In 1616, Dorothy Leigh, a puritan mother on her deathbed, wrote a book simply titled *The Mothers Blessing*, perhaps in a conscious effort to link it generically to Breton's book. The immediate audience for this book were her own three sons: 'My sonnes, the readers of this book', as she addresses them at the outset.[18] This proved to be a very popular book, appearing in nineteen editions in the seventeenth century.[19] It was followed by a book written by a pregnant woman, Elizabeth Jocelin, experiencing fears that she would not survive giving birth (Jocelin was twenty-eight when she wrote her *Mothers Legacie*, and did die shortly after giving birth to her daughter)[20] and worrying about the upbringing and education of the child that she would leave behind.[21] The book was *The Mothers Legacie to her Unborne Childe*, and its title came to be applied to the small group of advice books written within similar contexts and under comparable circumstances.[22] This genre proved quite popular: as late as 1670 similar works were being published.[23]

The defining elements of these texts, as Jennifer Heller notes, are that 'they feature a maternal voice, they are written to children, they are cast as deathbed advice, they provide religious counsel'.[24] '[T]hese women', as Sylvia Brown writes, 'decided to leave their advice in the form of a written "legacy" or "blessing" which would speak for them after they were gone.'[25] These mothers' legacies took the form of letters, prayers, translations, dialogues, family histories and collections of precepts.[26] Their writers seem to have drawn on such wide-ranging devotional discourses available to them as the Bible, advice books, conduct books, prayers, sermons and *ars moriendi* texts, as well as other legacies in print.[27] Perhaps the most important feature of these works, and the most relevant for my purposes, is the sense of urgency that deeply pervades them. The texts are unfailingly offered as a mother's last dying words. Whether the mother is actually on her deathbed, painfully aware of her pressing mortality, or a young pregnant mother experiencing anxieties that she will not survive the childbirth, the figure of the dying mother occupying a liminal, and thus powerful, space between life and death is crucial to the genre.[28] Importantly, the term 'legacy' that forms part of the title of Jocelin's book and which came, together with 'blessing',[29] to apply to the entire genre encompasses two important senses. 'Commonly', as Heller writes, 'the term indicated a material item bequeathed by one person to another'. A legacy could also be the 'message committed to a delegate or deputy'. 'Mothers' legacies', she elaborates, 'play upon both of these senses, becoming doubly eternal', whereby 'a legacy is an enduring, material item – a book handed down by a mother to her children – but it is also a charge to execute maternal commands'.[30]

Surviving mothers' legacies are concerned first and foremost with the religious and moral instruction of the children who are to be left behind, motherless. Leigh, for instance, states that observing 'the great care, labour, trauaile, and continuall study, which parents take to inrich their children', she has decided instead, 'being not desirous to inrich you with transitory goods[,] to exhort and desire you to follow the counsel of Christ'.[31] She defines her aim behind writing this document as that of wanting to 'make you [my children] labour for the spirituall food of the soule, which must be gathered euery day out of the Word ... By the which you may see it is a labour ... A pleasant labour, a profitable labour: a labour without the which the soule cannot liue'.[32] Similarly, Jocelin stresses the moral lesson she wishes to impart in her *Legacie*: 'I thought there was some good office I might doe for my childe more than only to bring it forth ... when I considered our frailty, our apt inclination to sin, the deuils subtility, and the worlds deceitfulnesse, against these, how much desired I to admonish it?'[33]

Nor is this concern with the religious education of children unique to Leigh's and Jocelin's documents. '[T]he prime duty of the patriarchal household' in this period, as John Morgan writes, was the 'inculcating of godliness'.[34] Contemporary moralists and writers of conduct literature frequently urged parents among their readers to give their children a godly education. Insisting that parents had a duty to provide for their children's 'spirituall good', William Gouge, writing in 1622, declares: 'Parents must traine vp their children in true pietie.'[35] He further insists that:

> The charge and office of parents bindeth them to teach their children pietie: for they are by God made watchmen ouer their children: if therefore their children liue and die in impietie through their parents negligence, their bloud shall be required at their parents hands.[36]

Failing to raise up godly children, Gouge states, is a dereliction that parents will have to answer for. It is a religious duty.[37] The genre of the mother's legacy, with its emphasis on both material devotional books and oral, religious and moral advice, is at the heart of *A Warning for Fair Women*'s representation of its rehabilitated mother, to an examination of which I now turn.

Mistress Saunders and the mother's legacy

A Warning for Fair Women traces its one and only mother's journey from familial contentment and domestic competence to her deathbed, the gallows, where the mother's legacy, both as a genre and as a devotional, physical book, features prominently. Mistress Saunders enters the play as a mother whose performance of motherhood is exemplary: in the first scene in which she substantially contributes to dialogue and action, she is cast emphatically as a mother concerned about her children's behaviour and education as well as about the proper government of her household. While Mistress Saunders is nearly mute in scene I (she has only one line to say out of the 320 that make up this scene) in the presence of her husband and the stranger (her eventual seducer), Master Browne, she is notably articulate in the dialogue she holds with her child in scene II. The theatricality of this scene aims at establishing Mistress Saunders' maternal role and stressing her domestic industry and care. Her dialogue with her child concerns his behaviour, which the mother deems it fit to check. Asked by the boy: 'when shal we goe to supper?' the mother responds firmly: 'Why, when your father comes from the Exchange'.[38] Faced by an insistent child who demands again: 'I would faine eate,' the mother reiterates her point about a household order and a domestic routine that revolves around the activities of its patriarchal head: 'Forbeare a while until your father come, / I sit here to expect his quicke returne.'[39] This glimpse into this woman's domestic devotion is, of course, emphasised later in the play when she waits for her husband's return from work again and again, experiencing different minor nuances as she waits for him, such as the meat being 'marrde' in this scene, and major ones, such as being approached by Master Browne, whose 'idle chat' with her will ultimately prove destructive to her person and marriage.[40]

As an embodiment of those good mothers that the genre of the mother's legacy features, Mistress Saunders is shown in this same scene to be a careful mother concerned with both her child's formal education and the orderly government of her household in her husband's absence at work. Seizing the opportunity of being asked by her child for some new items, a 'new bow and shafts', 'scarves' and 'rings', and 'a white feather' to go with his 'velvet cappe', the mother assents, but stipulates a condition: 'Yes, if ye learn'.[41] Mistress Saunders uses material rewards as incentives to encourage her child to do well at school. The next portion of the dialogue works to give the audience a glimpse into this mother's housekeeping and the nature of her household government: 'Goe,' she orders her son, 'go bid your sister see / My closet lockt when she takes out the fruite'.[42]

Sending this order to the sister, who is described as unlocking the closet and taking out fruit in the space imagined as the interior of the house, Mistress Saunders fulfils one of the most important duties of the household mistress in this period, as Natasha Korda's research has shown.[43] Supervising and preserving goods and items and making sure nothing perishes out of neglect or carelessness were her main duties. Mistress Saunders is depicted as a careful mistress of her household, a guardian of its domestic spaces. She exemplifies the ideal housewife praised by Samuel Rowlands's *The Bride* (1617) for 'hav[ing] domestique cares, / Of private businesse for the house within'.[44] Supervising household stuff, the government of domestic economy, was one of the mistress's most important tasks. Moralists often stressed the importance of guarding domestic spaces and considered it a marker of a careful mistress. Thomas Tusser, for example, commands mistresses to 'no doore leave unboulted'.[45]

Mistress Saunders' embodiment of the ideal of the good household mistress is further emphasised through the play's staging of her reaction to an instance of a violation of proper household hierarchy. Scene IV depicts Mistress Saunders shopping for some items together with her friend and confidant, Mistress Drury (the woman who is paid by Master Browne to aid him in his bid to seduce Mistress Saunders). The scene opens by setting in train the events that will lead to a marital row over the husband's failure to honour domestic hierarchies, a row that will eventually bring the marriage itself to a tragic end. Master Saunders cannot send his wife the money she needs to complete her purchase, he tells his unnamed servant, because he has 'to discharge the bond / Of maister Ashmores fifteene hundred pound / That must be tendered on the Exchange to night'.[46] Not only does Master Saunders decline his wife's request for money, he also chooses to send his servant to her to convey the unwelcome news. The servant anticipates trouble: 'She will not so be answered at my hand,' sensing the impropriety of the service he is being asked to perform by stressing 'at my hand' as opposed to simply stating that 'she will not so be answered'. The servant is interrupted by a master who now resorts to his superior position within the domestic hierarchy and the prerogative he has to issue orders and, it seems, to define and shape that hierarchy as he sees fit: 'Tell her I did command it should be so.'[47]

Mistress Saunders' reaction to her servant's news inserts her within the discourse of scolding and marks her as a shrew, in sharp contrast with her near mute presence in scene I and her dutiful and obedient performance of her wifely and motherly duties in scene II, as discussed above. The reaction she displays stresses her commitment to proper household government and her upholding of domestic hierarchy. Learning from the servant that 'my master gave me charge / I should deliver none [money]', Mistress Saunders retorts violently, 'Howes that sir knave?', threatening to subject him to physical violence: 'Go to, dispatch and fetch me thirtie pound, / Or I will send my fingers to your lips.'[48] Despite the efforts of Mistress Drury (the paid friend) to turn Mistress Saunders against her husband for his failure to supply the money ('I never knew, But that you had at al times mistris Sanders, / A greater summe than that at a command, / Mary perhaps the world may now be chang'd'), Mistress Saunders is concerned about domestic hierarchy, rather than her subjection within the household. 'I am a woman,' she states, 'and in that respect, / I am well content my husband shal controle me.' The problem for her is this: 'But that my man [i.e. servant] should over-awe me too, / And in the sight of strangers, mistris Drurie, / I tell you, do's grieve me to the heart.'[49]

This early representation of Mistress Saunders as an ideal household mistress and mother undergoes a change as the play progresses. Having thus established Mistress Saunders' exemplary maternal role, careful domestic industry, and commitment to societal and cultural as well as political values in the form of household hierarchy,[50] the play proceeds to recount the degeneration of Mistress Saunders' exemplary qualities. Importantly, it does so through staging another scene that involves one of the Saunders children, who now appears on stage unsupervised. The play does not specify whether this child is the same one who appeared in scene II and asked for supper as well as some clothing items. Having the same actor play the same child in both scenes can be quite effective as it allows for an explicit contrast to be made between the same child first with his mother's supervision and then without.

The appearance of one of the Saunders children in scene XI visually stages the change in the nature of Mistress Saunders' housewifery and the decline in her watchfulness over the children. It tropes, by extension, her withdrawal of the care and moral education specified as the mother's responsibility in the conduct and devotional literature of the period. Scene XI follows on the heels of the murder of Master Saunders. It opens with a tableau of disorder: two children, one of them the 'yongest' of the Saunders children, are 'playing in the street' (clearly seen as an improper thing to do by Roger, Master Browne's companion, when they spy the child outside the Saunderses' house).[51] The child, moreover, is out in the street when "Tis dinner time' and he should be in the house enjoying a meal with the family.[52] The 'games' he is playing with his friend are described by Roger as 'unlawful', for they involve, as the two boys describe them in their opening dialogue, playing for money.[53] Roger, of course, the man who makes all of these disapproving remarks and negative assessments of the child's behaviour, is one of those involved in the murder of the child's father. Moreover, his remarks to the child are motivated by a startled Master Browne, who finds it difficult to handle seeing the boy whose father he has just murdered: Roger, failing to see the boy at first and wondering why Master Browne 'stop[s] on the sudden', describes the man's appearance as 'gastly'.[54] All of this makes Roger an unreliable and untrustworthy observer. His point of view would have hardly been expected to win the support of the original audience, who have just seen him offer his murderous help to Master Browne – as the latter concealed himself in preparation to kill Master Saunders – Roger eagerly inquiring, 'Shall ye not need my help sir?'[55]

There is, however, a sense that the child realises that he is engaging in a transgressive and unlawful act. Even before Roger and Master Browne appear on stage, the anonymous playwright is careful to make the child voice his awareness of this transgression. Choosing the place 'at our doore' for the game the two boys are playing, young Saunders answers a query from his friend who, too, is aware that Master Saunders will not be pleased to find them playing: 'What if your father find us?', a question which receives the ironic (because innocently unaware that the father has been murdered and will never come home) answer, 'No hees at Woolwich, and will not come home tonight.'[56] It is understandable then that the Saunders child immediately subscribes to Roger's notion of the impropriety of game, time and place and offers a bribe: 'Gaffer if you'le not tel my master of me, / Ile give you this new silke poynt.'[57] With no mother around to check his behaviour, the child leaves to play somewhere else and Master Browne and Roger proceed on their way to meet Mistress Saunders, now too distracted by the murder and too far removed from her initial role as careful mother to look after the child. Nothing could trope the degeneration in her housewifery and her maternal role more than this contrast the scene sets up between a child's transgressive behaviour checked and another that goes unseen and thus uncorrected.

Clearly drawing on the tradition of the genre of the mother's legacy, in its final movement the play seeks to restore order by restoring Mistress Saunders to her former household industry and role as an ideal Protestant mother. Having received her sentence to 'to be hang'd til you be dead', Mistress Saunders is asked to wait for her children, who come to see her and ask for her blessing: 'Your children hearing this day was the last / They should behold their mother on the earth / Are come to have your blessing ere you dye, / And take their sorrowful farewell of you'.[58] This anticipated entrance of the children, whose number is not specified anywhere in the text and whose genders are revealed in scene II as being, at least, one boy and one girl, transforms the scaffold that is about to send their mother to eternity into a traditional deathbed scene. Robson has explored a number of early modern treatises that seem to draw a parallel between the gibbet and the deathbed.[59] While Robson's ultimate aim is to show how the murder pamphlets she examines seem to suggest that 'it is possible to lead a "bad" life and make a "good" death', my purpose is to show how the play reinserts Mistress Saunders' dying moments not only within the tradition of the *ars moriendi* and the discourse of good death, but also within the genre of the mother's legacy, which, too, featured mothers dying a good death.[60]

At the point of the children's entrance on stage, calling out to the 'liminal woman':[61] 'oh mother, mother ... ere you die, / Give us your blessing', the gallows turn into a deathbed scene and the genre of the mother's legacy forcefully enters the text (in fact, the children's asking for the mother's blessing evokes the genre's two early examples, discussed above), marking the restoration of order through the transformation of Mistress Saunders back into the ideal mother.[62] All the elements of the genre discussed at the beginning of this essay are present: the maternal voice ('oh my deare children'); the moral instruction ('follow virtue, and beware of sin'); and the philosophy of *contemptus mundi*, the disdain of worldly things as inferior to heavenly rewards ('Behold (my children) I wil not bequeath, / Or gold or silver to you').[63] Instead she will bequeath them a devotional book, 'Therein you shall be richer than with gold, / Safer than in faire buildings: happier / Than al the pleasures of this world can make you'.[64] Clearly linking this scene on the scaffold with other mothers' legacies, the play stages a mother who is about to leave her legacy with her children literally as a dying woman. Dorothy Leigh, the author of the first female-authored mother's legacy, was ill and decrepit, she did not know exactly when she was going to die: likening herself to the 'labourous Bee', she says, 'She looketh out and seeth death, / Ready her to devour.'[65] Similarly, Elizabeth Grymeston describes herself as 'a dead woman among the living'.[66] Elizabeth Jocelin had a feeling that she was not going to survive the experience of childbirth, an understandable fear given the perils associated with giving birth in the early modern period: women at that time faced a 1 per cent risk of dying in each of an average of six to seven pregnancies.[67] Mistress Saunders, however, is the mother of the mother's legacy par excellence. She is *condemned* to die, and what separates her from death is this final interaction she has with her children: her children's plea for the mother's blessing, 'ere you die, / Give us your blessing', has a chillingly urgent feel to it.[68]

To complete the elements of the genre, the play has Mistress Saunders actually produce a book of meditations, a physical book, reminiscent of those documents – *The Mothers Blessing* and *The Mothers Legacie to her Unborn Child*, among others – that mothers passed on to their children on their deathbeds. In preparation to seeing her children for the last time, Mistress Saunders asks the Keeper to 'bring me / Those books that lie within my chamber window'.[69] While the play seeks to portray Mistress Saunders as one of those repentant condemned criminals who frequently turned up on scaffolds with Bibles, prayer books and books of meditation as visual markers of their repentance and reincorporation into the fold of the righteous, *A Warning for Fair Women* has another aim.[70] By depicting the mother passing on John Bradford's book to her children, 'here I give to each of you a booke / Of holy meditations, *Bradfords* works', and instructing them to 'sleepe not without them when you go to bed, / And rise a morning with them in your hands', the play visually and ideologically casts Mistress Saunders in the devotional role of the mother depicted in the mothers' legacies.[71] Moreover, this tableau of dutiful motherhood links back to Mistress Saunders' appearance in scene II, when she was one such mother concerned about her child's education and her household's orderliness. In the latter gifting scene, the play follows the representation of Anne Saunders in Arthur Golding's earlier pamphlet account of

1573, in which Anne bequeaths to each of her children 'a copie of M. Bradfordes meditations'.[72] In both the play and Golding's text, Bradford's book serves a totemic purpose, one of several 'tokens of unfayned repentance' expressed by Saunders.[73] Bradford's *Meditations*, thus, was more important for, and impactful because of, what it represented than what its pages actually said. Of course, by visually handing the *Meditations* over in this highly performative way, the play implies that Saunders had read it, or at least understood the spiritual counsel and succour its contents would provide her children. In this the play's most poignant of redemptive moments, the mothers in the audience are encouraged to do likewise.

Conclusion

The appearance of a religious book on stage is not, of course, unique to this play. The anonymous play *The Tragedy of Arden of Faversham* (1592), for instance, has its anti-heroine, Mistress Arden, appear on stage with a prayer book which she then proceeds to tear apart so she can replace the pages of the holy book with the pages of her devotion to her adulterous lover, Mosby: 'See Mosbie I will teare away the leaues. / And al the leaues, and in this golden couer, / Shall thy sweete phrases, and thy letters dwell, / And thereon will I chiefly meditate, / And hould no other sect, but such deuotion'.[74] 'A flagrant adulteress,' as Elizabeth Williamson writes, 'Alice Arden uses her prayer book to impress her lover with her lack of reverence for this emblem of domestic loyalty.'[75] Similarly, the later Caroline play *The Antipodes* (1640) by Richard Brome has an old woman who is depicted as persistent in her 'profane and diabolical courses', and cannot bear to see her maid with a devotional book, responding to the maid's invitation to read with her by 'strik[ing] down' the book and protesting: 'No, no, I cannot – read your meditations.'[76] In both of these instances, a prayer book and a book of meditation are used to trope the moral corruption of the women who assault them. *A Warning for Fair Women*, however, uses the devotional book in different ways. Not only does it employ the book to achieve the opposite effect to that aimed at in *Arden of Faversham* and *The Antipodes*, troping the repentance and conversion, rather than the corruption and prodigality, of Mistress Saunders. Nor does the play only, as Williamson writes, by placing the book specifically identified as 'Master Bradfordes book' in Mistress Saunders' hands, allow her to 'identif[y] herself with the writings of a Protestant martyr, [thus] reinscrib[ing] the values that were threatened by Anne's initial transgression, and in so doing foreground[ing] her role as a very contemporary reader'.[77] Instead, and far more importantly, it inserts the entire denouement of the play within the ranks of the mother's legacy as a genre, recuperating the devotional identity of this mother who has gone astray back into the fold of godly mothers dying exemplary deaths.

Notes

1 Henry Hitch Adams, *English Domestic or Homiletic Tragedy 1575–1642* (New York: Columbia University Press, 1943).
2 Frances E. Dolan, *Dangerous Familiars: Representations of Domestic Crime in England, 1550–1700* (Ithaca, NY: Cornell University Press, 1994); Viviana Comensoli, *'Household Business': Domestic Plays of Early Modern England* (Toronto: University of Toronto Press, 1996).
3 Mihoko Suzuki, 'Gender, Class, and the Social Order in Late Elizabethan England', *Theatre Journal* 44.1 (1992), 31–45; Peter Berek, '"Follow the Money": Sex, Murder, Print, and Domestic Tragedy', *Medieval and Renaissance Drama in England* 21 (2008), 170–88.
4 Frances E. Dolan, 'Moral Agency and Dramatic Form in *A Warning for Fair Women*', *Studies in English Literature, 1500–1900* 29.2 (1989), 201–18; Lena Cowen Orlin, *Private Matters and Public Culture in Post-Reformation England* (Ithaca, NY: Cornell University Press, 1994); Susan Dwyer Amussen and David E. Underdown, *Gender, Culture and Politics in England, 1560–1640: Turning the World Upside Down* (London: Bloomsbury, 2017).
5 Dolan, *Dangerous Familiars*, pp. 1–19.
6 Ann C. Christensen, *Separation Scenes: Domestic Drama in Early Modern England* (Lincoln: University of Nebraska Press, 2017).
7 Richard Helgerson, *Adulterous Alliances: Home, State, and History in Early Modern European Drama and Painting* (Chicago: University of Chicago Press, 2000).
8 Foucault writes that 'the public execution is to be understood, not only as a judicial, but also as a political ritual. It belongs, even in minor cases, to the ceremonies by which power is manifested.' Michel Foucault, *Discipline and Punish: The Birth of the Prison* (London, 1977), p. 47.
9 See J. A. Sharpe, '"Last Dying Speeches": Religion, Ideology and Public Execution in Seventeenth-Century England', *Past and Present* 107 (1985), 144–67; Susan Dwyer Amussen, 'Punishment, Discipline, and

Power: The Social Meanings of Violence in Early Modern England', *Journal of British Studies* 34.1 (1995), 1–34; Thomas W. Laqueur, 'Crowds, Carnival and the State in English Executions, 1604–1868', in A. L. Beier, David Cannadine and James M. Rosenheim (eds), *The First Modern Society* (Cambridge: Cambridge University Press, 1989), pp. 305–55.

10 James Alsop, 'Playing Dead: Living Death in Early Modern Drama' (unpublished PhD thesis, University of Exeter, 2014), p. 61. Quoting from James Shapiro, '"Tragedies naturally performed": Kyd's Representation of Violence', in David Scott Kastan and Peter Stallybrass (eds), *Staging the Renaissance: Reinterpretations of Elizabethan and Jacobean Drama* (New York: Routledge, 1991), pp. 99–113 (103–4).

11 Lynn Alison Robson, '"No Nine Days Wonder": Embedded Protestant Narratives in Early Modern Prose Murder Pamphlets, 1573–1700' (unpublished PhD thesis, University of Warwick, 2003), p. 234. I am grateful to Robert W. Daniel for bringing this thesis to my attention.

12 *Ibid.*, p. 287.

13 *Ibid.*, p. 285.

14 *Ibid.*, p. 250. For discourses surrounding the 'good' death, see Klaus P. Jankofsky, 'Public Executions in England in the Late Middle Ages: The Indignity and Dignity of Death', *Omega: Journal of Death and Dying* 10.1 (1979), 43–57; Linda McCray Beier, 'The Good Death in Seventeenth Century England', in Ralph Houlbrooke (ed.), *Death, Ritual and Bereavement* (London: Routledge, 1989), pp. 43–61.

15 Robson, '"No Nine Days Wonder"', p. 250.

16 The genre has received some welcome scholarly attention. For a study that positions this genre against the male-authored advice book see Christine W. Sizemore, 'Early Seventeenth Century Advice Books: The Female Viewpoint', *South Atlantic Bulletin* 41.1 (1976), 41–8. For the genre's engagement with contemporary political and religious debates see Catherine Gray, 'Feeding on the Seed of Woman: Dorothy Leigh and the Figure of Maternal Dissent', *English Literary History* 68.3 (2001), 563–92. For examinations of the significance of the last speeches of condemned female criminals from a feminist point of view see Frances E. Dolan, '"Gentlemen, I Have One Thing More to Say": Women on Scaffolds in England, 1563–1680', *Modern Philology* 92.2 (1994), 157–78.

17 For the titles that make up the genre and an excellent exploration of the various surviving mothers' legacies, see Jennifer Heller, *The Mother's Legacy in Early Modern England* (Farnham: Ashgate, 2011); Elizabeth Clarke, 'The Legacy of Mothers and Others: Women's Theological Writing 1640–1660', in Christopher Durston and Judith Maltby (eds), *Religion in Revolutionary England* (Manchester: Manchester University Press,

2006), pp. 69–90; Helen Ostovich and Elizabeth Sauer (eds), *Reading Early Modern Women: An Anthology of Texts in Manuscript and Print, 1550–1700* (London: Routledge, 2004), chapter 3.
18. Dorothy Leigh, *The Mothers Blessing* (London, 1616), sig. A8^r.
19. Heller, *Mother's Legacy*, p. 1.
20. Antonia Fraser, *The Weaker Vessel* (New York: Alfred A. Knopf, 1984), p. 69.
21. Heller does not find it 'implausible ... that Leigh's text had a strong impact on Jocelin's decision to write'. Heller, *Mother's Legacy*, p. 85.
22. Heller estimates that there were approximately twenty early modern advice texts that fall under the umbrella of the mother's legacy. *Ibid.*, p. 1.
23. *Ibid.*, p. 1.
24. *Ibid.*, p. 2.
25. Sylvia Brown, 'Introduction', in *Women's Writing in Stuart England: The Mother's Legacies of Elizabeth Joscelin, Elizabeth Richardson and Dorothy Leigh*, ed. Sylvia Brown (Stroud: Sutton, 2000), pp. v–x (v).
26. *Ibid.*, p. 2.
27. In fact, writers of mothers' legacies themselves encouraged others to write. Dorothy Leigh, for example, while aware that she is embarking on an 'unusuall custome of women [i.e. writing]', urges her children to do the same: 'I thought it fit to giue you good example, and by writing to intreate you, that when it shall please God to giue both virtue and grace with your learning, he hauing made you made you men, that you may write and speake the Word of God without offending any, that you would remember to write a booke vnto your children, of the right and true way to happinesse, which may remiane with them and theirs for euer.' Leigh, *Mothers Blessing*, sig. A3^v.
28. Heller describes the dying mother as a 'liminal woman'. Heller, *Mother's Legacy*, p. 5.
29. *Ibid.*, p. 181.
30. *Ibid.*, p. 182.
31. Leigh, *Mothers Blessing*, sig. B2^v.
32. *Ibid.*, sig. A6^v.
33. Elizabeth Jocelin, *The mothers legacie, to her vnborne childe* (London, 1624), sig. A1^v.
34. John Morgan, *Godly Learning: Puritan Attitudes towards Reason, Learning and Education, 1560–1640* (Cambridge: Cambridge University Press, 1986), p. 142. For a study that argues that the godly household predates puritanism, see Margo Todd, 'Humanists, Puritans and the Spiritualized Household', *Church History* 49.1 (1980), 18–34.
35. William Gouge, *Of Domesticall Duties* (London, 1622), sig. Mm4^v.
36. *Ibid.*, sig. Mm5^r.

37 Raising religious children was, of course, not easy. For the complexities surrounding godly parenting see chapter 9.
38 *A warning for faire women* (London, 1599), sig. B2^v. The original play has no act/scene divisions or pagination.
39 Ibid., sig. B2^v.
40 Ibid., sigs B3^v, C1^v.
41 Ibid., sig. C1^v.
42 Ibid., sig. C1^v.
43 Natasha Korda, *Shakespeare's Domestic Economies: Gender and Property in Early Modern England* (Philadelphia: University of Pennsylvania Press, 2011), p. 27.
44 Samuel Rowlands, *The Bride* (London, 1617), sig. D4^r.
45 Thomas Tusser, *Fiue hundreth points of good husbandry united to as many of good huswiferie* (London, 1573), sig. C5^r.
46 *A warning for faire women*, sig. C1^v.
47 Ibid., sig. C2^r.
48 Ibid., sigs C2^{r-v}.
49 Ibid., sig. C2^v.
50 It was a common notion in early modern England that the household was a micro-state and that order in the household ensured order in the state. See Susan Dwyer Amussen, *An Ordered Society: Gender and Class in Early Modern England* (New York: Basil Blackwell, 1988), esp. pp. 1–33.
51 *A warning for faire women*, sigs F4^{r-v}.
52 Ibid., sig. F4^v.
53 Ibid., sigs F4^{r-v}.
54 Ibid., sig. F4^v.
55 Ibid., sig. E4^v.
56 Ibid., sig. F4^r.
57 Ibid., sig. F4^v.
58 Ibid., sigs I2^v, K2^v.
59 See Robson, '"No Nine Days Wonder"', esp. pp. 234–93.
60 Ibid., p. 235. For the religious tradition of 'dying well' in England see chapters 13 and 14.
61 I borrow this phrase from Heller, *Mother's Legacy*, p. 5.
62 *A warning for faire women*, sig. K2^v.
63 Ibid., sigs K2^v, K3^r, K2^v. Saunders' words perhaps deliberately echo those of the Apostle Peter when healing a crippled man in Acts 3:6: 'Silver and gold have I none, but such as I have, that give I thee' (Geneva Bible).
64 Ibid., sig. K2^v.
65 Leigh, *Mothers Blessing*, sigs A8^{r-v}.
66 Elizabeth Grymeston, *Miscelanea* [sic]. *Meditations. Memoratives* (London, 1604), sig. A3^r.

67 Heller, *Mother's Legacy*, p. 55.
68 *A warning for faire women*, sig. K2^v.
69 *Ibid.*, sig. K2^v.
70 Examples are examined by Robson, '"No Nine Days Wonder"', pp. 234–93.
71 *A warning for faire women*, sig. K2^v.
72 Arthur Golding, *A briefe discourse of the late murther of master George Saunders* (London, 1573), sigs B1^{r-v}.
73 *Ibid.*, sig. A8^r.
74 *The lamentable and true tragedie of M. Arden of Feuersham in Kent* (London, 1592), sig. C5^r.
75 Elizabeth Williamson, 'The Uses and Abuses of Prayer Book Properties in *Hamlet*, *Richard III*, and *Arden of Faversham*', *English Literary Renaissance* 39.2 (2009), 371–95 (388).
76 Richard Brome, *The Antipodes* (London: Nick Hern, 2000), IV.i.15; IV.i.15; IV.i.20.
77 Williamson, 'Prayer Book Properties', p. 388.

6

Devotion, marriage and mirth in *The Puritan Widow* (1607)

Robert O. Yates

Thomas Middleton's *The Puritan Widow* (1607),[1] as scholars have noted, invites readings of its satirical elements as well as its confusing, even 'flawed', dramatic form.[2] The readings of satire illuminate the play's treatment of religious and political debates. Donna Hamilton, for instance, says the play's satire is 'unrelenting and comprehensive', before claiming that the 'main targets [of the satire] are Puritans and Catholics'.[3] *The Puritan Widow*, Hamilton notes, satirises both religious groups by associating Catholic beliefs and rituals, such as festive practices, icons and praying for the dead, with puritan ones, especially an individual's personal religious identity guided by the Word of God. Additionally, Jennifer Panek draws attention to the jest book *The Merrie Conceited Jests of George Peele* (1605) and how it structures the plot of the play, especially its fraught ending:

> While this unexpected denouement would constitute a failed comic ending in a play which offers the fantasy of a widow as a reward for a penniless but audacious young man, *The Puritan* [*Widow*] instead allows for an ending which undercuts the conventional fifth-act marriages of comedy by juxtaposing their closure with the movement toward open-ended freedom found in the play's jest-book source.[4]

Panek notes the importance of how the jest book influences the play's narrative – specifically how the fifth act conveys ambivalence around the remarrying widow. Panek carves out space to consider the relations between the logics of jesting, merriment and popular festivities and the representations of widowhood in *The Puritan*

Widow. Building on this work, I argue that by situating the play's titular widow, Lady Plus, within discourses of mirth and festive practices, her character's identity sustains conflicting roles of devoted wife, puritan and lusty widow. The hybridity of *The Puritan Widow*, which draws from conventions of city comedy and popular and religious discourses of marriage, as well as practices of popular festivities, creates the conditions through which Lady Plus paradoxically contains these seemingly contradictory titles. *The Puritan Widow* invites readers to consider how playing with genre might slip into theorisation of subjectivities and identities, which persistently defy clean categorical lines.

Lady Plus, in the home, garden and city

The Puritan Widow presents Lady Plus resisting various pressures to remarry at the beginning of the play by citing reasons of religious and marital devotion. Mourning her husband, she cries, 'O, I shall never forget him, never forget him. He / was a man so well given to a woman – O.'[5] Her brother-in-law, Sir Godfrey, reasons with her, saying, 'Methinks you are well read sister, and know that death / is as common as *Homo* a common name to all men.'[6] Unsurprisingly, Sir Godfrey's observation that death is a universal human experience fails to comfort his sister-in-law. But his primary consolation follows a few lines later: 'My brother has left you wealthy. You're rich ... I say you're rich. You are also fair.'[7] Sir Godfrey couples these observations with insistence that Lady Plus should remarry: 'For what / should we do with all our knights, I pray, but to / marry rich widows, wealthy citizens' widows, lusty fair- / browed ladies.'[8] Lady Plus rejects Sir Godfrey, insisting, 'Marry again? No, let me be buried quick then.'[9]

The primary problem of *The Puritan Widow* emerges in these first few lines: the widow must remarry. This is something the play then seeks to ardently resolve. Scenes later, Lady Plus meets the 'citizen scholar' George Pieboard, who seeks to hoodwink her into marriage in order to gain her wealth. While Pieboard's schemes fail on the one hand – she does not marry him – on the other hand, his machinations create the conditions through which Lady Plus and her daughters conclude the play on their way to three wedding ceremonies. The unnamed Nobleman, who disrupts and exposes Pieboard's plot just as Lady Plus and her family walk to the church, insists, 'And now, widow, being so near the church, 'twere great pity, nay, uncharity to send you home / again without a husband.'[10] The Nobleman replaces Pieboard and his fellow trickster with two suitors, who Jennifer Panek argues are 'as unsympathetic as they are dramatically insignificant'.[11] As Panek suggests, the play resolves in the dissonance of three unsatisfactory marital matches, but the ending also achieves closure in its promise of the marriage of two maids and a wealthy citizen's widow.

Tracing Lady Plus's relationship to remarriage (which exchanges one devotional role as chaste widow for another as obedient wife) sheds light on the ending's indeterminacy as well as its generative potential. Lady Plus's initial desire to remain a widow engenders popular early modern discourses that a widow should remain unmarried to demonstrate loyalty to her husband, to preserve her sexual purity, and thereby to secure her devotion to God. '[T]here are a few voices of dissent,' writes Panek, 'which describe a culture which tolerated and even encouraged remarriage for both sexes, but they are outnumbered by those who claim that widows were enjoined to celibacy and remarriage was condemned'.[12] In the first act, Lady Plus embodies such a position, effusively claiming that her late husband is 'unmatchable, unmatchable'.[13] In fact, the thought of remarriage prompts Lady Plus to pre-emptively curse herself, underscoring that the choice to remain a widow could say as much about the wife as the husband:

> O, may I be the by-word of the world,
> The common talk at table in the mouth
> Of every groom and waiter, if e'er more
> I entertain the carnal suit of a man.[14]

The prayerful 'O' and the sexual connotation of the word 'common' blur language of religious devotion with that of sex, highlighting the competing forces influencing Lady Plus's desires. The religious and sexual images climax in the reference to the 'talk at table in the mouth', as visions of Holy Communion mingle with the consumption of Lady Plus in the mouths of 'every groom and waiter'. It is here, at the festive table, that I draw our attention to *The Puritan Widow*'s hybridity. The play continues as we might expect a city comedy – Lady Plus and the two maids will marry – but the play remains focused on reforming Lady Plus's devotional desires through a series of mirthful encounters of jests and festivities.

While literary scholars have labelled the play as a 'scurrilous city comedy' and a satire, tracing references to jests and festivities might help us consider how *The Puritan Widow* deploys common tropes of the widow as an 'enabler rather than a preventer of remarriage' but then subverts these gestures through its ending.[15]

The vehicle of Lady Plus's movement from widow to remarried wife is the trickster George Pieboard, who exploits knowledge for personal gain. Pieboard, a 'scholar and a graduate', enters the stage in act 1, scene 2, and bemoans his life as an academic to his friend Peter Skirmish, explaining that learning grants taxonomy but lacks economy:

> I'll not be afraid
> to say, 'tis a great breeder but a barren nourisher, a
> great getter of children, which must either be thieves
> or rich men, knaves or beggars.[16]

His poverty established, Pieboard suggests that he and Skirmish should turn to more nefarious methods for making a living:

> For since the law lives
> by quarrels, the courtier by smooth Godmorrows, and
> every profession makes itself greater by imperfections,
> why not we then by shifts, wiles, and forgeries?
> ... And for our
> thriving means, thus, I myself will put on the deceit of
> a fortune-teller, a fortune-teller.[17]

Pieboard justifies deception through an imperfect analogy with the law, courtiers and 'every profession': they all benefit from 'imperfections'. Next, Pieboard makes 'imperfections' and 'shifts, wiles, and forgeries' synonymous, ignoring legal or religious arguments to the contrary. As the debt collector Puttock says later in the play, 'Troth, I have wondered how slaves could see into our breasts so much when our / doublets are buttoned with pewter.'[18] Pieboard's actions justify Puttock's suspicion, but Puttock's suspicion also reveals fear of his own exposure as a hypocrite. Puttock's friend Ravenshaw says, 'they will / publish our imperfections, knaveries, and conveyances / upon scaffolds and stages'.[19]

While *The Puritan Widow* comically critiques scholars, it also suggests Pieboard is a playful, rather than simply dangerous, presence within the play. Satire destabilises his identity as a criminal; like

Twelfth Night's Feste, Pieboard seeks to make a living through his available resources: wit and language. For instance, in the third act, cornered by debt collectors Ravenshaw and Puttock, he says, 'Extremity is touchstone unto wit, ay, ay,' as he barely escapes from them.[20] Pieboard lacks morality, but *The Puritan Widow*, as Donna Hamilton posits, is 'comprehensive' in the way it reveals the hypocrisy of all its characters. If we read Pieboard as a character who, like Feste, wields the power of jest but bears no claim to power otherwise, then a clearer link between Pieboard and the Nobleman emerges. Pieboard paves the way for the Nobleman, who saves Lady Plus (and in turn the city) through the redemptive marital union. To achieve this, he enacts a series of tricks that lead Lady Plus away from the solemnity of her home into the fecundity of her garden, where her sexual desires are reawakened.

Most notably, Pieboard's scheme to 'nim' Sir Godfrey's golden chain illustrates his employment of jesting and its effect of creating a community bent on reincorporating Lady Plus into the marriage state. As Pieboard and Skirmish decide to plot against Lady Plus, they discover that Skirmish's 'sworn brother, Captain Idle' is in prison for petty crime and cannot pay the fine to make bail.[21] Pieboard and Skirmish postpone their earlier plan and proceed to the prison to visit Idle, only to find that Idle's cousin and servant to Sir Godfrey Nicholas St Antlings is also at the prison. Idle does not welcome Nicholas, however, saying, 'This is double torture now. This fool by th' book / Does vex me more than my imprisonment.'[22] Nicholas, like his master, identifies as a puritan, and the scene proceeds with Pieboard persuading Nicholas to help steal Sir Godfrey's golden chain by replacing the word 'steal' with the synonym 'nim'. Nicholas refuses to steal the golden chain because 'That's the word the literal, thou / shalt not steal. And would you wish me to steal then?'[23] Pieboard reasons:

> PIEBOARD: No, faith, that were too much, to speak truth.
> Why, wilt thou nim it from him?
> NICHOLAS: That I will.[24]

In the same way that 'steal' slips into 'nim', puritanism slips into Catholicism in Pieboard's plot, as Hamilton has noted:

> Organizing these characters' overriding materialism around this nimming event, Middleton plays ironically on the equivocating style for which the Jesuit 'plotters' had become so well known.[25]

The Gunpowder Plot of 1605 prompted Parliament to pass four statutes, which included: 'An act to declare 5 November an annual day of thanksgiving, an act to punish those involved in the Plot, and two acts setting forth measures for "discovering and repressing" and "avoiding the dangers that may grow by popish recusants"'.[26] In these four statutes, a 'day of thanksgiving' for James I's life joins with acts of punishment and repression of subversive religious subjects (Catholics and those deemed extreme Protestants). *The Puritan Widow* expresses the potential of language to dissolve what at first seem to be two ends of a binary – Catholicism and puritanism – and unite them into one common object which contains some political and, in Pieboard's case, rhetorical end.

In addition to the verbal and theological slippage, the nimming event undercuts the notion that Pieboard commits an illegal act and instead suggests that he seeks in some way to entertain the participants. And yet, as Pieboard makes his plan more festive – he will not steal but rather hide Sir Godfrey's chain – he edges closer to achieving his overarching goal of courting Lady Plus. Pieboard says, 'Nay, I'll come nearer to you, / gentleman, because we'll have only but a help and a / mirth on't.'[27] Instead of keeping it 'outright', Pieboard's new plan requires that the chain go 'missing':

> When thou hast
> the chain, do but convey it out at backdoor into the
> garden, and there hang it close in the rosemary bank
> but for a small season. And by that harmless device, I
> know how to wind Captain Idle out of prison, the knight
> thy master shall get his pardon and release him, and
> he satisfy thy master with his own chain and wondrous
> thanks on both hands.[28]

The analogy between the exercise of political force of the four statutes and the coerciveness of Pieboard's plan to put 'mirth on't' appear starkly within this passage: both situations provide festive occasions – a celebration for the king and a celebration of a found necklace – which employ 'mirth' to mask the violence of either forcing or inducing the erasure of difference in religious (Catholic or puritan) as well as social (widow or wife) terms.

The nimming plot achieves its goal of awakening Lady Plus to erotic desire, as well as building upon popular traditions of mirth and festivity by shifting the action of the play into Lady Plus's garden. The image of the 'garden' recalls Northrop Frye's concept of the 'green world'. On Peele's, Greene's, Lyly's and Shakespeare's comic form, Frye writes:

> Thus the action of the comedy begins in a world represented as a normal world, moves into the green world, goes into a metamorphosis there in which the comic resolution is achieved, and returns to the normal world.[29]

The Puritan Widow, however, as a city comedy varies from Frye's structure in that although Lady Plus's devotional identity undergoes a 'metamorphosis' – evidenced by the first indication that she is sexually interested in a man as she imagines him within the quasi-green world of her garden – her awakened desire precipitates into the promise of marriage as she prepares to leave her house and enter the streets to reach the church.

The topsy-turvy nature of Lady Plus's desire maps on to domestic, garden and street spaces in *The Puritan Widow*. For instance, in act 4, scene 2, Lady Plus asks where she might find Sir Godfrey. Her servant Frailty says he is in the garden with a 'wondrous rare fellow, mistress, very strongly / made upward, for he goes in a buff jerkin'.[30] Captain Idle, the man Frailty describes to his mistress, has dressed as a conjurer and will 'fetch Sir Godfrey's chain again, if it hang between heaven and earth'.[31] Lady Plus, still in her home, ruminates on the image of the conjurer Idle. She first remarks, 'How happy were that woman to be / blessed with such a husband, a man o' cunning,' which is an affirmation of the supposed conjurer's intellect.[32] Lady Plus, however, interrupts herself by asking: 'How / does he look, Frailty? Very swartly, I warrant.'[33] Once she learns that the conjurer is 'fair', her daughter confirms: 'So fair and yet so cunning. That's to be wondered / at, Mother.'[34] Lady Plus identifies a male subject as desirable – first by noting his intellect and then through racialised language – within the green world of the garden. *The Puritan Widow* simultaneously induces Lady Plus into erotic desire through the jest of Captain Idle and Pieboard and then censures her for these feelings – the Nobleman chides, 'An impudent fellow best woos you, a flattering lip best wins you, or in a mirth, who talks roughliest is most sweetest.'[35] Finally, the logic of mirth in this play forces Lady Plus into remarriage while silencing her original expressed desires of remaining a devoted widow.

Lady Plus's gradual and then precipitous incorporation into the mirthful occasion also heralds her decline away from independence and an ability to speak her own desires. As noted above, Lady Plus begins the play stating that she will not desire a husband, much less remarry, but Pieboard's jests induce Lady Plus's expressions of bodily and intellectual desire for Captain Idle. Later in that scene, Pieboard, dressed as a fortune teller, explains that she must remarry, and she reasons, 'Well, seeing my fortune tells me I must marry, let / me marry a man of wit, a man of parts.'[36] Pieboard establishes festive events to induce erotic feelings, but in the final scene of the play, once Pieboard's scheme comes to light, Lady Plus says, 'Is't possible we should be blinded so and our / eyes open?'[37] Here, Lady Plus temporarily breaks from desire for Captain Idle and feelings of mirth more generally – she says her eyes are 'open' – but she does not restate her desires from the beginning of the play. Instead, the Nobleman rebukes Lady Plus: 'Widow, will you now believe that false which / too soon you believed true?'[38] A few lines later, the Nobleman compels Lady Plus and her daughter Frank to marry Muckhill and Tipstaff, characters defined by being 'of estimation both in court and city'.[39] As *The Puritan Widow*'s plot becomes more mirthful, Lady Plus is transformed from a subject expressing desires to a subject provided with desires. The Nobleman orders Lady Plus to 'bestow your eyes and your purest affections upon' Muckhill in the closing lines of the play, where Lady Plus and her daughters leave their arguably non-male-led home and enter the city streets in the direction of the church, a fully patriarchal space.[40]

Mirth, festival books and festive practices

I have argued that the 'flaws' in dramatic form of *The Puritan Widow*, particularly its ending, might be better understood as instances of Middleton playing with traditions of mirth and jest. Further, I aim to convey that through the hybridity of city comedy and references to textual and theatrical practices of festivity and mirth, *The Puritan Widow* surprises readers in its display, silencing and then preservation of Lady Plus's expressed competing desires through its enforcement of mirth. In this next section, I examine the festival book *A Relation of the Late Royall Entertainment ... at Cawsome House neere Redding: to our most Gracious Queene, Queene Anne* (1613) by Thomas Campion.[41] I argue mirth might compel, coerce or even physically force subjects to join within a community of merriment by (1) evoking erotic desire and (2) asserting the pre-eminence of social order. In this way, I suggest that devotion to mirth might serve the needs of various forms and figures of authority. Campion, according to David Lindley, 'attracted the praise of George Peele in his *Honour of the Garter* (1593)'.[42] Peele is the playwright later satirised in *The Merry Conceited Jests of George Peele* (1607), which Middleton drew upon to craft *The Puritan Widow*.[43] I make no claim to the relations of these texts other than that they share similar expressions of and policing of human subjects through mirth. I conclude this section by returning to Lady Plus to consider how we might read her expressions of erotic and religious desire in relation to her devotion to mirth.

A Relation of the Late Royall Entertainment begins with a description of Cawsome House, setting the scene for readers to imagine the moment Queen Anne approached the place where her daughter Elizabeth would be married in 1613. Campion writes:

> [A]t the further end whereof, upon the Queenes approach, a Cynick appeared out of a Bower, drest in a skin-coate, with Bases of greene Calico, set thicke with leaues and boughs: his nakednesse being also artificially shadowed with leaues; on his head he wore a false haire, blacke and disordered, stucke carelessely with flowers.[44]

What ensues is a dialogue between one Cynick and a Traueller, the latter of which works on behalf of the Queen and her train to allow them to continue toward the house. Cynick attempts to prevent them from moving forward by exclaiming:

> Here is no passage; see you not the earth furrowed? The region solitaire? ... here a kingdome I enjoy without people; my selfe commands, my selfe obeyes ... neither feare I, nor hope, nor ioy, nor grieue: if this be happinesse, I haue it; which you all depend on others seruice, or command, want: will you be happy? ... turne Pallaces to Hermitages, nosies to silence, outward felicitie, to inward content.[45]

Cynick, in addition to preventing the group proceeding, critiques society at large. He is content with himself in his bower, and even seems to suggest that the Traueller's 'outward' happiness does not reflect an inner contentment.

As a rebuke, the Traueller invites the Cynick into mirth by first referencing his body and then comparing his soul to an instrument out of tune, which implicitly suggests, compels even, Cynick into a community of souls where he might find harmony with himself through others. The Traueller exclaims, 'Thou art yet yong, and faire enough, wert thou not barbarous; thy soule poore wretch is farre out of tune, make it musicall, come, follow me, and learne to liue.'[46] While Cynick in the next line says, 'I am conquered by reason,' the first part of the Traueller's argument is that Cynick's body is young and fair enough. Enough for what? Sir Godfrey, we remember, uses similar appeals to Lady Plus, calling her 'rich', 'fair', and encouraging her that 'Nor are your years so far entered' to the extent that she 'will be sought after and may very well answer another husband'.[47] In other words, while the force of what I call devotion to mirth leads toward some form of social formation – marriage, in the case of Lady Plus, and the wedding train and society at large for Cynick – preceding it is an acknowledgement and sometimes embrace of physical beauty and erotic potential.

The logics of enforced mirth and their effects amplify when we attend, as many scholars have reminded us, to the performance practices that travelled from non-theatrical to theatrical spaces. Erika T. Lin, for instance, argues that generative cultural and literary readings become available when we reflect on these festive occasions incorporated within early modern drama, but such a reading requires and demonstrates 'the importance of moving beyond the representational narrative'.[48] Here I draw on Lin's article 'Popular Festivity and the Early Modern Stage', in which she argues for the festive qualities of *George a Greene* (1598) – another play which 'does not depict actual holiday observances taking place within the fictional narrative'.[49] Lin's analysis of three popular practices – communal feasting, festive combat and the wearing of livery – not only prove generative for her project of developing a 'theoretical framework for understanding how amateur performance traditions' circulated through London's commercial stage, but helps readers trace ways by which Pieboard induces Lady Plus into situations and affects of mirth.[50]

Communal feasting, festive combat and the wearing of livery linked common festivities in parishes with the early modern professional stage. Festivity, as practice, functioned in various spaces, whether religious, political or theatrical. For the purpose of this essay, I want to think about the ways in which references to feasting, combat and livery guide *The Puritan Widow* into discourses of devotion and sexuality, in turn shaping our understanding of Lady Plus's marriage. Like *George a Greene*, *The Puritan Widow* does not take place within a setting or time specifically marked by a holiday or religious festival, but the references to combat, feasting and livery would have been recognised as festive contexts by early modern audiences. Lin describes the first of these – combat – as an important aspect of early modern festivity:

> The leader of summer festivities was usually known as the 'Summer Lord' or 'Robin Hood' ... The Robin Hood of the summer games was not a subversive outlaw, but was chosen from the ranks of respectable parish leaders. He and his band of merry men solicited money for the community's needs through a variety of techniques, including what Johnston refers to as 'the combat game' – that is, 'a wrestling match or an archery contest or a fight with staves'.[51]

Within these amateur festive practices, a person of rank and honour – 'parish leaders' – dons the role of 'Robin Hood', gaining money for the community not through theft (as we might expect from the reference to Robin Hood), but through a series of mirthful games. *The Puritan Widow* experiments with this formulation by allowing Pieboard to think he is a subversive outlaw, only to deny him the pleasure of fulfilling that role.

Where Pieboard begins as a 'subversive outlaw', in the end he becomes an instrument that reinforces the 'needs' of the powerful members of 'the community'. He is a parish 'Robin Hood' serving the needs of the community to remarry Lady Plus and marry her two maiden daughters. As I have discussed, Pieboard seeks to secure Corporal Oath's, Peter Skirmish's and his own financial success. He pretends to be a fortune teller and tells Lady Plus that: 'For your part and your daughter, if there be not once this day some bloodshed before your door whereof the human creature dies, the elder two of you shall run mad.'[52] Pieboard's attempt at telling the future of a plot he has already planned aims at first to simply bolster Lady Plus's confidence in him as a fortune teller. He plans to use Oath and Skirmish's staged fight to gain Lady Plus's trust, but in a soliloquy at the end of the act, he confides to the audience that he has yet again changed the plan:

> And to confirm my former
> presage to the widow, I have advised old Peter Skirmish,
> the soldier, to hurt Corporal Oath upon the leg, and in

that hurry I'll rush amongst 'em, and instead of giving
the corporal some cordial to comfort him, I'll pour into
his mouth a potion of a sleepy nature to make him
seem as dead.[53]

Pieboard drugs Oath into a slumber so that later in the play he can 'resurrect' the corporal as a demonstration of his power and further secure Lady Plus's trust.

Pieboard's jest of a staged fight renders unintended consequences for the broader community. He first deceives Lady Plus and her family for the sake of his and his friend's plot, but then he betrays his friends in order to increase the effectiveness of the performance. 'These empty creatures, / Soldier and corporal, were but ordained / As instruments for me to work upon,' Pieboard says to himself after the staged fight.[54] Lin writes, 'The fight transforms these "strangers" into neighbors; combat is not disruptive, but instead promotes conviviality.'[55] Pieboard does indeed gain Lady Plus's trust and 'conviviality' as a result of the staged combat, but he also creates tension between himself and his original conspirators. After hearing Pieboard's premonition of violence and seeing the staged combat, Lady Plus invites him into her home, which establishes necessary conditions for the continuation of the induced marriage plot.

The play's second festive element – feasting – further incorporates Lady Plus into festive participation, which drives her from widowhood. When Pieboard first meets with Lady Plus, he tells her that 'I truly know by certain / spiritual intelligence that he [Lord Plus] is in purgatory.'[56] Although Lord Plus appeared moral, he in fact 'got his wealth with a hard gripe', or by exploiting the weak. Lady Plus counters Pieboard's accusation by referencing 'high days': 'Dine quickly upon high days, and when I had great guests, would e'en shame me and rise from the table to get a good seat at the afternoon sermon'.[57] Lady Plus argues for her husband's holiness: on holidays, he went to church as quickly as possible; therefore, he displays outward signs of true devotion to God. Pieboard responds with a common rejoinder which draws a distinction between the appearance of holiness and the practice of it: 'Church, ay, he seemed all church, / and his conscience was as hard as the pulpit.'[58] In other words, Lord Plus was outwardly 'holy' by foregoing festive occasions and attending church, but internally his 'conscience' was 'hard', or corrupt, because of his business dealings. Lady Plus's reference to feasting and festivity ironically incorporate her into Pieboard's scheme, as it exposes her husband's hypocrisy.

The 'nimming' and eventual recovery of Sir Godfrey's golden chain is a second occasion where references to festivity – in this case, feasting and livery – incorporate Lady Plus's family into Pieboard's plot. When Sir Godfrey discovers his golden chain is missing, he despairs, saying: "'Twas worth above three hundred crowns. / Besides, 'twas my father's, my / Father's father's, my grandfather's huge grandfather's.'[59] Although Lady Plus says that he can still 'read' – another satirical reference to how puritans privileged the written Word of God – Sir Godfrey dismisses her attempts to soothe him: '[W]ould you had me lost more? / My best gown, too, with the cloth of gold lace? / My holiday gaskins and my jerkin set with pearl? / No more?'[60] Sir Godfrey associates his golden chain, which Hamilton notes performs in some way as an image of the rosary, with other meaningful possessions: pieces of festive clothing.[61] Furthermore, the recovery of Sir Godfrey's chain parallels a moment of spiritual redemption: 'Sister, the rosemary bank. Come, come, / there's my chain, he says', which climaxes with a call for feasting.

> Ay, and a banquet ready by this time, Master
> Sheriff, to which I most cheerfully invite you and your
> late prisoner there. See you this goodly chain, sir?
> Mum, no more words. 'Twas lost and is found again
> ... Come, my inestimable bullies,
> we'll talk of your noble acts in sparkling charneco, and
> instead of a jester, we'll ha' the ghost i'th' white sheet
> sit at upper end o'th' table.[62]

The entire occasion of the golden chain parodies the Christian salvation narrative: humans lose that which connected them to the Father, only to find redemption on a 'tree'. Sir Godfrey also celebrates redemption through feasting, but instead of a 'jester', he calls a 'ghost'. The 'ghost i'th' white sheet' refers not to a literal ghost, of course, but to Corporal Oath, whom Pieboard drugs in order to stage a resurrection later in act 4. The scene, principally through Sir Godfrey, secures an allusion to the Holy Trinity only to undercut it through the audience's seemingly omnipotent knowledge that the ghost is in fact the jester.

In addition to feasts and combat, festive occasions also organised communities through clothing. The bestowing of livery – 'distinctive clothing marked out by color, cut, and insignia [which] identified persons as members of particular households' – could signify a 'stable social identity' in festive contexts.[63] Late medieval and early modern parishes, as Lin notes, sold livery such as badges – 'cognizances in their hats' – during festivals to raise money for the church and incorporate parish members into seasonal festivities. Lin writes: 'Parishes might sell anywhere from a few hundred to a few thousand badges bearing the insignia of Robin Hood or the May Lord.'[64] These festive buttons and other items of clothing mirrored formal livery which a lord might use to mark members of his household staff. Lin argues that the historical practice of livery took two forms in the theatre: the price of admission serves a similar function as a badge, and costumes signify membership of the actors. By associating audiences with the actors, livery 'appropriated the authority of festive traditions' in order to shape the community of the public theatre.[65] Livery could incorporate subjects to positively shape community, but livery could also shame and punish subjects who did not pay for the parish festivities. Lin cites Philip Stubbes, who recorded in his memoir that those who refused to purchase livery badges at parish events were 'mocked, & flouted at, not a little'.[66] The festive practice of livery, therefore, shaped community through exclusion and inclusion: it marked its members visually, and it marked outsiders through its absence. *The Puritan Widow* integrates the plasticity of livery to secure Lady Plus as a desirable object of the community.

While bestowing, buying and wearing livery established social connections – albeit coercively, in some cases – *The Puritan Widow* presents the removal of livery as a way to discipline community and indicate that which is valuable.[67] The play's deployment of its third and final festive element – livery – demonstrates that rank, gender and the capacity for childbearing are essential factors in a subject's value to the community. Nicholas, Sir Godfrey's servant, for instance, performs a function but lacks value (as compared with Sir Godfrey or Lady Plus) within the festive plot. We learn explicitly that Nicholas wears livery at the moment of his expulsion from the community. When Sir Godfrey discovers that Nicholas 'nimmed' his golden chain, he promptly removes his crest from Nicholas's back:

Deemed always holy, pure, religious,
A puritan a thief? When was't ever heard?
Sooner we'll kill a man than steal, thou know'st.

Out, slave, I'll rend my lion from thy back
With mine own hands.⁶⁸

Sir Godfrey's lines contain none of the playful ambiguity between 'nim' and 'steal' present in earlier acts. His removal of livery from his puritan servant emphasises that Nicholas is expendable. We might say that livery becomes what Ann Rosalind Jones and Peter Stallybrass call a 'material mnemonic' for some puritans' troubled relationship with festive practices, a term which extends Jones and Stallybrass's case that livery underscores servitude.⁶⁹ In *The Puritan Widow*, the moment of Nicholas's shame and servitude foils Lady Plus's reincorporation into society, perhaps distracting viewers from the way that the currents of festive power circulate and discipline various bodies depending on their subjectivity.

The final stage-picture of *The Puritan Widow* is that of a family surprised it has been drawn into a wild and coercive marriage plot but then also submissive to the Nobleman's sudden appearance and authority. The Nobleman concludes the play by referencing the divine, telling Lady Plus that her marriage will be 'a happy change which makes e'en heaven rejoice'.⁷⁰ And, yet, despite the Nobleman's admonition and Lady Plus's silence – or perhaps because of them – the ending feels flimsy. An alternative reading that I have argued in this essay takes its cue from the play's print history. First printed in quarto in 1607, *The Puritan Widow*'s title page reads:

THE
PVRITAINE
or
THE VVIDDOVV
of VVatlingstreete.
Acted by the Children of Paules.
VVritten by VV. S.
Imprinted at London by G.ELD.
1607.⁷¹

Between 1607 and 1734, the play was reprinted eight times as *The Puritan*, *The Puritan Widow*, and *The Puritan; Or, the Widow of Watling Street*. The erratic titles, similar to the variety of forces of mirth working to induce Lady Plus into remarrying, fail to agree on one subject. Instead, the play through its hybridity of city comedy, jest books and popular performance practices invites us to ask – who actually is Lady Plus?

Notes

1. Throughout this essay I quote Thomas Middleton, *The Puritan Widow*, ed. Donna B. Hamilton, in *Thomas Middleton, Volume 1: The Collected Works*, ed. Gary Taylor and John Lavagnino, 2 vols (Oxford: Oxford University Press, 2007), pp. 509–42, hereafter *Works*.
2. See Jennifer Panek, *Widows and Suitors in Early Modern English Comedy* (Cambridge: Cambridge University Press, 2004), pp. 141–2.
3. Donna B. Hamilton, 'Introduction', in Middleton, *Works*, pp. 509–11 (509).
4. Panek, *Widows and Suitors*, p. 150.
5. Middleton, *The Puritan Widow*, 1.1.9–10.
6. *Ibid.*, 1.1.13–14.
7. *Ibid.*, 1.1.59–61.
8. *Ibid.*, 1.1.66–7.
9. *Ibid.*, 1.1.80. For a statistical survey which examines why widows did and did not marry during this period see Barbara J. Todd, 'The Remarrying Widow: A Stereotype Reconsidered', in Mary Prior (ed.), *Women in English Society, 1500–1800* (London: Routledge, 1991), pp. 54–92. I am grateful to Robert W. Daniel for this reference.
10. Middleton, *The Puritan Widow*, 5.4.76–8.
11. Panek, *Widows and Suitors*, p. 142.
12. *Ibid.*, p. 6.
13. Middleton, *The Puritan Widow*, 1.1.86.
14. *Ibid.*, 1.1.98–101.
15. Jeffrey Knapp, *Shakespeare's Tribe: Church, Nation, and Theater in Renaissance England* (Chicago: University of Chicago Press, 2002), p. 145.
16. Middleton, *The Puritan Widow*, 1.2.64–6.
17. *Ibid.*, 1.2.76–8; 84–5.
18. *Ibid.*, 3.3.13–15.
19. *Ibid.*, 3.2.11–12.
20. *Ibid.*, 3.4.97.
21. *Ibid.*, 1.2.119–20.
22. *Ibid.*, 1.4.51–2.
23. *Ibid.*, 1.4.143–4.
24. *Ibid.*, 1.4.145–7.
25. Hamilton, 'Introduction', p. 511.
26. *Ibid.*, p. 509.
27. Middleton, *The Puritan Widow*, 1.4.160–1.
28. *Ibid.*, 1.4.168–75.
29. Northrop Frye, *The Anatomy of Criticism* (Princeton, NJ: Princeton University Press, 2000), p. 182.
30. Middleton, *The Puritan Widow*, 4.2.6–7.

31 *Ibid.*, 4.2.8–9.
32 *Ibid.*, 4.2.11–12.
33 *Ibid.*, 4.2.12–13.
34 *Ibid.*, 4.2.19–20.
35 *Ibid.*, 5.4.19–20.
36 *Ibid.*, 4.2.259–60.
37 *Ibid.*, 5.4.48–9.
38 *Ibid.*, 5.4.50–1.
39 *Ibid.*, 5.4.88–9.
40 *Ibid.*, 5.4.86.
41 Thomas Campion, *A Relation of the Late Royall Entertainment Given by the Right Honourable the Lord Knowles, at Cawsome House neere Redding: to our most Gracious Queene, Queene Anne, in her progresse toward the Bathe* (London, 1613).
42 David Lindley, 'Campion, Thomas (1567–1620)', ODNB. https://doi.org/10.1093/ref:odnb/4541. Accessed 12 March 2019.
43 Reid Barbour, 'Peele, George (*bap.* 1556, *d.*1596)', ODNB. https://doi.org/10.1093/ref:odnb/21768. Accessed 12 March 2019.
44 Campion, *A Relation*, p. 1.
45 *Ibid.*, p. 2.
46 *Ibid.*, p. 3.
47 Middleton, *The Puritan Widow*, 1.1.60–5.
48 Erika T. Lin, 'Popular Festivity and the Early Modern Stage: The Case of George a Greene', *Theatre Journal* 61.2 (2009), 271–97 (281). See also Erika T. Lin, 'Festivity', in Henry S. Turner (ed.), *Early Modern Theatricality* (Oxford: Oxford University Press, 2013), pp. 212–29.
49 Lin, 'Popular Festivity', p. 273.
50 *Ibid.*, p. 273.
51 *Ibid.*, p. 283.
52 Middleton, *The Puritan Widow*, 2.2.232–5.
53 *Ibid.*, 2.2.295–301.
54 *Ibid.*, 3.1.64–6.
55 Lin, 'Popular Festivity', p. 287.
56 Middleton, *The Puritan Widow*, 2.1.153–4.
57 *Ibid.*, 2.1.189, 207–9.
58 *Ibid.*, 2.1.216–17.
59 *Ibid.*, 3.2.27–30.
60 *Ibid.*, 3.2.35–8.
61 Middleton, *The Puritan Widow*, note 58, p. 527.
62 *Ibid.*, 4.2.180–1, 349–55.
63 Lin, 'Popular Festivity', pp. 291, 293.
64 *Ibid.*, p. 294.
65 *Ibid.*, p. 296.

66 *Ibid.*, p. 295.
67 Gowing explains: 'Clothed, early modern bodies were expected to be clearly marked by gender, rank and marital status, and until 1604, sumptuary laws attempted to regulate strict relations between rank and dress.' Laura Gowing, *Common Bodies: Women, Touch, and Power in Seventeenth-Century England* (New Haven, CT: Yale University Press, 2003), p. 32.
68 Middleton, *The Puritan Widow*, 5.4.70–4.
69 See Ann Rosalind Jones and Peter Stallybrass, *Renaissance Clothing and the Materials of Memory* (Cambridge: Cambridge University Press, 2000). They write that livery is 'a form of incorporation, a material mnemonic that inscribed obligation and indebtedness upon the body' (p. 20).
70 Middleton, *The Puritan Widow*, 5.4.105.
71 W[illiam] S[hakespeare], *The puritaine, or The vviddovv of VVatling-streete* (London, 1607), frontispiece. For the play's initial attribution to William Shakespeare see Donna Hamilton, 'The Puritan Widow', in *Thomas Middleton and Early Modern Textual Culture: A Companion to the Collected Works*, ed. Gary Taylor and John Lavagnino (Oxford: Oxford University Press, 2007), pp. 349–60.

Part IV: Devotional identities in the prison

7

'O this dark dungeon!': Murderers, martyrs and the 'sacred space' of the early modern prison

Lynn Robson

I want to begin with a glimpsed act of devotion. On the evening of 3 December 1517, just hours before Richard Hunne's corpse was found hanging in his cell in the Lollards' Tower of St Paul's Cathedral, he was seen 'telling his beads'.[1] Recounted in the inquest testimony of one of his jailers (which was then printed in *The enquirie* twenty years later) this captured image of Hunne seems an unequivocal act of orthodox devotion, which sanctifies the profane space of his prison cell. However, this representation is distanced from the reader: it is a memorial reconstruction of the last sighting of a man whose life, death and posthumous representation contain nothing but ambiguity and complication, in which he flickers in and out of focus. Was he Catholic or Lollard? Was he murder victim or suicide? Was he heretic or martyr? John Foxe's comment that Hunne was 'halfe a Papist; at least no full Protestant' not only expresses the contemporary conflict over the meaning of his life and death, and his ambivalent confessional identity, but also foreshadows the historical controversy that has followed him to the present day.[2]

Praying over his rosary, Hunne's devotions make him appear pious, but also exemplify his withdrawal into a secret sacred space, a place of unknowability. Readers (like the jailer) can only *infer* the meanings of Hunne's devotional acts; his spiritual condition and the meaning of his apparent piety are closed off. *The enquirie*, published when the lines between Catholic and Protestant were becoming more sharply drawn, and in the immediate aftermath of Tyndale's execution, frames Hunne's story as one of murder and martyrdom. The pamphlet's compiler uses the inquest's verdict that Hunne's hanging was faked post-mortem after he was tortured and throttled to prove that he was a murder victim. For Protestants, Hunne was a martyr, 'for to dye an heretique with the Papistes, what is it els (to say truth) but to dye with God a Martyr?'[3] A week after his death, Hunne's corpse was put on trial in the Lady Chapel of St Paul's and his copy of Wycliffe's Bible was the prize exhibit. Found guilty of heresy, Hunne's corpse was burned at Smithfield on 20 December.

Lines of demarcation converge in the different representations of Hunne's death: Lollard and Catholic, heretic and martyr, suicide and murder victim, making him a *liminal* figure. The cell he inhabited either is sanctified by his spiritual reformation, concealed his torture or was defiled by the violence he may have enacted on his own body. It is physical, spiritual, textual spaces, and the thresholds between them, their merging and separation, their shaping by urgent confessional allegiances and associated acts that formed the devotional identities of prisoners that this essay explores.[4] The readers' glimpse of Hunne's devotions, in what is probably the earliest example of the Protestant-influenced prose murder pamphlet, is richly suggestive. It foregrounds the physical environment of the prison cell and questions what effect the devotional actions of the criminal/sinner within it might have on the construction of profane and sacred spaces. The final sight of a living, pious Hunne, focused on his devotions and the health of his soul, is framed in a prison cell whose name confirms his confessional identity. The Lollards' Tower was the Bishop of London's prison, its likely inhabitants considered 'profane' by the pre-Reformation Tudor Church. It was part of St Paul's Cathedral: situated at the south-western corner of the great medieval church, it abutted the much smaller church of St Gregory's, which was itself 'really part of the cathedral'.[5] Here the Lollards' Tower assumes an ambiguous identity: it sits on architectural borders between the sacred and profane, but it also seems like a threshold to St Gregory's. Its name also represents the profound changes the Reformation made to ideas of sacred space. When Hunne was imprisoned, Lollards were on the margins of English religious life, criminalised by secular and ecclesiastical authorities. By the time his story was printed in 1537, monasteries and chantries were being demolished and St Paul's future was as a Protestant cathedral. Catholic priests and laity were dispossessed of their sacred spaces and they, like Protestants (albeit for different reasons), had to reimagine sacred space. Hunne's 'halfe a Papist', not quite Protestant, identity is indicative of early modern spiritual experiences; whilst Foxe's description suggests a state of flux, it also establishes divisions which demonstrate that the identities of heretic and martyr had changed places.

The theory and theology of prison space

For Reformed theologians, a true church was wherever God's Word was rightly preached, because 'not church buildings but we ourselves are temples of God,' and consequently 'we must guard against either taking them to be God's proper dwelling place, whence he may more nearly incline his ear to us ... or feigning for them some secret holiness or other, which would render prayer more sacred before God'.[6] As 'the sacred is ... experienced from *within* the profane', it is the *activities* of the inhabitants of the space that sanctify it.[7] Even in the 1620s and 1630s when the sacred exclusivity of churches was re-established by consecration, decoration and liturgical rituals,[8] Laudian preachers still acknowledged that God is everywhere: 'wee have here built a place, an house for the Lord. Now if we get not God into it what are we the neare for all the cost? Let our next care be to get God, and keepe God in it.'[9] If God must be 'got' into the church then it is not his natural dwelling. The actions that will 'get God in' and consecrate the space are reading 'the Word' and prayer. John Donne declared that 'holy persons and holy places ... must accompany one another'. Holiness is first conferred by 'the saints of God meet[ing] within the walls' and, 'as the Congregation sanctifies the place, the place may sanctifie the Congregation too'.[10] The *ritual* of consecration is confirmation of sanctity rather than its origination.

Early modern prison cells are transformed to sacred spaces by showing the sanctity of the individuals inhabiting them, which in turn is confirmed by their observed devotional acts. As Mircea Eliade argued, those actions make the boundary between profane and sacred permeable:

[The] threshold that separates [sacred and profane] spaces ... indicates the distance between the two modes of being, the profane and the religious. The threshold is the limit, the boundary, the frontier that distinguishes and opposes two worlds – and at the same time the paradoxical place where those worlds communicate, where passage from the profane to the sacred world becomes possible.[11]

Eliade imagined sacred and profane spaces as distinct but with the capacity to flow into one another in a moment of flux; a movement that is simultaneously temporal, physical and spiritual and marked by recognisable devotional actions. Prison cells were thresholds between life and death, whether the prisoner was a recusant, a murderous apprentice, a Jesuit priest or an adulterous wife; whether they were conceived as monastic cells or churches with tiny congregations. The flow of pious feeling across an internal, invisible threshold is manifested in the surrounding physical space. The connection between profane incarceration and the consecration of space achieved by an individual's pious actions is found in elite and popular texts. In 1541, Thomas Wyatt wrote to the Privy Council from the Tower, 'God knowethe, what restles tormente yt hath byne to me sens my hether commynge to examen my selfe, perusing all my dedes to my remembraunce.'[12] Wyatt's cell is a site of contemplation, of spiritual audit, born of the 'tormente' to his 'sens', and the result of his self-examination is the power to refute the 'eville interpretation' of his actions by 'a malicious enimye'.[13] It is the *sanctity* of Wyatt's hard-won spiritual self-knowledge that makes his 'declaration' persuasive. This letter from an elite writer crosses the threshold of his cell to reach an elite audience.[14] However, it is only cheaply printed pamphlets that have the capacity to reach a varied readership in a variety of spaces; to cross prison thresholds into domestic spaces where they might function themselves as devotional objects.

Profane spaces: early modern prisons

Although physically intimidating and solidly present in early modern London, prisons were not separated from the city's streets and several of them (Newgate, Ludgate and the Westminster gatehouse), originally situated within London's walls, marked the threshold of the city. As London life flowed in and out of them, so too did the accounts of prisoners' experiences. Prisons were profane spaces: dilapidated, dark, dirty, noisome; inhabited by the desperate, the debauched and the miserable. Such were the conditions that prisoners were more likely to die from jail fever than for any crime they might have committed. Used as holding pens for those awaiting trial, punishment or execution rather than places of sustained incarceration,[15] the difference between relative comfort and misery was dependent on rapacious jailers who themselves depended on the money they could extract from prisoners for 'garnishing', basic domestic comforts and food.[16]

In 1623, John Taylor listed eighteen prisons, ranging from the 'house of fame' that was the Tower to the 'theevish den' of Newgate, and the 'holes' of St Katherine's and East-Smithfield.[17] Those incarcerated in them, whether they were debtors, thieves, murderers, recusants, dissenters, prostitutes, counterfeiters or gamblers – the criminal, or the merely unfortunate – agreed about their miserable physical conditions. The 'hot gospeller' Edward Underhill, imprisoned during Queen Mary's reign, calls Newgate a 'lothsome jayle', full of 'evylle savers and great unquyettness off the logeynges'.[18] A petition from debtors in eight London prisons identifies their dwellings as 'local hells' full of 'stench, horror and darknesse'.[19] Geoffrey Mynshull describes with some passion how the King's Bench Prison 'stinckes worse than the Lord Mayors dogge house'.[20]

Mynshull's pamphlet vividly captures the transformative experience of imprisonment. He writes that 'the strangeness of the place' had so 'transported' him that he was unable to 'follow that study wherein I take delight'.[21] In a chaos of 'discontentments' and 'fantasies', his prison became an 'infernall island' where the 'inchauntments are so strong that it transformeth all that come thither'.[22] This imagery estranges the prison from city life, emphasising the distance between inside and outside. However, prison can also be a heightened and maddening version of London, a 'Microcosmos', 'a little commonwealth' where it is possible to 'learne more lawe' than one could at 'Westminster for a hundred pound', or more villainy than can be learned at 'twenty dycing howses, Bowling allyes, Brothelhouses or Ordinaryes'.[23] The permeability of prisons shows that cross-contamination is part of their profanity. In 1582, the Jesuit priest Robert Parsons complained about the overcrowded conditions in London's prisons – 'very full replenished and stuffed upp with Catholiques' – and particularly about 'oure Bridewell an infamous place of light housewyves & lewed folke', into which 'a gentle woman borne, confessing the Catholique faithe some what zealouslie, was thrust by the Superintendent of London'.[24] The 'gentle' Catholic woman is in danger of being transformed into a 'light housewife' by her surroundings through a combination of physical and spiritual contamination. The imagery of flux and contamination, of microcosm and macrocosm, that represents the distressing somatic and psychological experiences of the prison means it is understood as a diseased body, 'unwholesome, full-stuffed, humorous', with 'a Hole in the posteriors of it, whence it vents many stinking, noisome and unsavoury smells', which spread 'perpetual sickness and disease'.[25]

If the prison-body is imagined as leaky and noxious then the individual incarcerated within its contaminating embrace becomes the redeemable soul, and this metaphorical logic creates the prison cell as a potentially sacred space. The transformation from profane to sacred space is confirmed by the observed/imagined pious activities of the prisoners. The idea that the prison cell is a site of spiritual transformation is as pervasive as the difficulty of finding apt metaphors to convey its physical horrors. The playwright Thomas Dekker spent seven years in the King's Bench Prison for debt. In *Dekker his Dreame* (1620), he represents the sensory horrors of his imprisonment in familiar terms: his imprisonment is a 'sleepe', in a 'cave ... of dreadfull enchauntments', a 'deepe Lethe of forgetfulnesse [that] seized al my sences, drowning them in, and burying mee to the World, in the lowest grave of oblivion', in which he met 'nothing but frightful Apparitions'.[26] However, his suffering is counteracted by 'a Dreame, which presented to my waking Soule infinitie Pleasures', amongst which was a 'Poeticall Enthusiasme', which opened to him 'the great Volumes of Heaven and Hell' and 'in which he read many Wonderfull Things'.[27] It is not only an imaginative transformation, as actions of reading, writing and contemplation transform the physical space the prisoners inhabit. So, 'sequestration from the world' allows a prisoner to 'converse with God'.[28] The prison cell is legible and transformable, but only if the prisoner engages in internalised spiritual exercises. Seeing 'himselfe as in a glasse what his excesse hath brought him to' means that physical incarceration is understood as the threshold to spiritual liberty:

> It is not imprisonment that afflicts thee, but the evill which is in thy selfe ... comfort thy selfe that one day thou shalt be infranchised and goe to that place and mansion house which is prepared for thee, where all scores shall be payd, all cares banished, and all teares wiped away.[29]

All of these examples are drawn from pamphlet narratives written by those who were considered unlikely to die for their crimes. The imagery intensifies in the accounts of the transformative experiences of murderers and recusants, who face the prospect of execution. It is no surprise to find a contest for the representation of sacred space in religious polemic: the contest for appropriation of the prison cell as a sacred space mirrors the gains and losses of the English Reformation.

Sacred space: martyrs, murderers and prison cells

Jacques Brousse's account of the life of Father Benet of Canfield describes how Benet and a companion travelled to 'an old and infamous prison called Newgate', because it 'was filled with Priests'. In that profane space, Benet and his friend were 'put ... in the haven of our soules health' and 'reconcil[ed] to the holy Church'. Benet noted with satisfaction that the day of his confirmation as a Catholic was the 'saints day of St Peter *ad vincula*', one of the Bible's most famous prisoners.[30] Father Benet (William Fitch) came from a Protestant family in Canfield. His conversion took place in 1585–86, after which he emigrated to France and entered the Capuchin order in Paris.[31] In the aftermath of his involvement in a political scandal at the French court, he returned to England in 1599 and was swiftly arrested and imprisoned, first at Nonsuch Palace, then in the Tower and finally in Wisbech Castle.[32] In 1603, Benet was released at the specific request of King Henri IV, and returned to France.[33] It was a sign of his devotional identity – a breviary – that was instrumental in Benet's arrest and he would have expected to face the martyr/traitor's death allotted to Catholic priests discovered on English soil.[34]

The description of Father Benet's cell in Wisbech Castle is familiar: 'unwholsome and unco[m]fortable', it was far from 'all that might yielde assistance and comforte', and he shared it with other Catholic priests and laity.[35] Benet recreated his prison as a monastic space, a devotional act representing a double loss: the loss of the monasteries from England's sacred landscape and Benet's personal absence from his French monastery. He wore his Capuchin habit and 'practic[ed] all the austerities of his rule, as fastings, disciplines & other mortifications, whereby the Catholiques receaved very greate comforte and contentment'.[36] His prison became 'a Cloistre for the austeritie of his profession, and a pulpit ... drawing many soules out of the sinke of heresie'.[37] The physical sufferings caused by his devotions made even Protestant ministers (who flocked to 'converse' with him) remonstrate against his chosen privations. Benet's devotions prove a piety that derives from his ordination, but the physical sufferings which form part of his devotions intensify his sanctity. It is his sufferings in particular that 'get God' into Benet's cell. This is a common theme in accounts of the experiences of imprisoned Catholics. At their most extreme, the physical torments inflicted on recusants (priests and laity) are depicted meticulously in Verstegan's *Theatrum Crudelitatum* (1592), which concentrates on the tormented, defiled bodies and the bravery of these martyrs.[38] As Robert Southwell wrote in *An Epistle of Comfort* (1587), physical suffering is an act of devotion: not only is it an 'honour' to be imprisoned 'for the Catholicke fayth', but 'tormentes in a good cause are tolerable'.[39] Southwell represents prison cells as places of sanctuary 'away from the onions and garlicke, and flesh pottes', a 'retyringe place' where 'if your bodye be chastised, your soule is cherished, and the pyning of one is the pamperynge of the other'.[40]

Insistence on the transformational power of an individual's piety flows between Catholic accounts of imprisonment and martyrdom and the Protestant-inflected pamphlet narratives of penitent murderers. However, although imprisoned recusants bring piety into their cells with them, it is the *achievement* of penitence whilst incarcerated that transforms murderers' cells to sacred spaces. Murderers are deeply profane from the moment they commit their crime/sin, and the physical thresholds they cross as they move from murder room to prison and to court intensify that profanity. Once they reach the condemned cell, their 'dying room', the final threshold they cross is spiritual and invisible. Their entry into this secret sacred space is manifested through a transformation of the physical space they inhabit, and in the devotions they then perform.

These differing confessional narrative conventions are comparable to the different theological perspectives on the operation of grace. For Catholics, grace was something bestowed by God in response to pious actions, such as prayer, confession and even the endurance of torture. For Protestants, it was possible to perform such pious actions *only if* grace has been bestowed. In the imagery of the prison cell, the transformative power of piety radiates from the Catholic prisoner – 'if you be combred with darknesse, yourselves are lampes to light it' – and the 'presence of Gods prisoner in the most infamous dungeon, maketh it a courte and resorte of angels' where 'God himself delighteth to walk'.[41] The torture undergone by recusants focuses attention on their bodies, and that is matched by an imagined embodiment of God in their cells. In contrast, it is the *internal* change in the penitent Protestant murderers that transforms their understanding of their physical surroundings. God is never imagined walking around their prison cells; the moment the threshold between condemned sinner and redeemed sinner is crossed is hidden from the observers and from the reader.

The penitent murderer is created and recreated as a figure for pious contemplation, whose spiritual reformation transforms the physical realities of a cell, enabling its description as 'the best room that ever I came in'.[42] In 1537 Hunne's ambivalent devotional identity had limited his use as an example but, in 1573, Arthur Golding's representation of Anne Saunders, an adulterous, murderous wife, set the stereotype for subsequent generations of murder pamphlet writers.[43] Thirteen of *A briefe discourse*'s thirty-two octavo pages are devoted to a description of Anne's journey towards and performance of penitence, followed by seven pages of interpretation and exposition. Brought to an acknowledgement of her sinfulness through the operation of 'Gods good working', Anne is able to 'utte[r] such certayne tokens of unfayned repentance by all kinds of modestie and meeknesse'.[44] Her prison cell transforms to a church with a congregation as Anne brings together her children and her husband's family to beg their forgiveness. Anne's devotional act of 'kneeling mildely upon her knees, with an abundance of sorrowfull teares' elicits a response: her husband's family also kneel, 'praying to God with hir and for hir'. Prayer is matched with an interpretation of 'the Word' as Anne bequeaths to each of her children 'a copie of M. Bradfordes meditations'.[45]

Golding's commentary on Anne's penitential performance stresses God's transformative power, as he alone 'rayseth them by their overthrowe, amendeth them by their wickednesse, and revyveth them by their death'.[46] Such dramatic transformations, proceeding from God's grace alone, demonstrate 'the execution of his judgementes' and should 'by the terrour of the outward sight of the example, drive us to the inward consideration of our selves'.[47] Golding collapses the distance between murderer and reader, emphasising that outward devotional actions must be combined with inward contemplation. Arnold Cosbie, condemned for the murder of Lord Burgh in 1591, spent his time in prison 'meditating upon the New Testament ... he sometime red and sometime wrote such things as might best content his sinfull mind'.[48] Confessing his sins, begging for the forgiveness of his victim, praying and praising God, Cosbie went steadfastly to his death, passing from the sacred space he had created in his condemned cell to the gibbet, which became his deathbed. However, the narrative convention of devotional reading is dramatically breached in *A Pittilesse Mother*.[49] A Catholic 'gentlewoman', Elizabeth Vincent, murdered her two children on Ascension Day 1616. Awaiting her trial, she 'refused to looke upon any Protestant booke, as Bible, Meditation, Prayer booke, and such like'.[50] Immediately after her arrest, she was detained in a local inn (the Bell in Acton) where the Constable and other 'Good Christian' neighbours attempted to transform this profane space into a sacred one by seeking Elizabeth's conversion. Despite their 'good admonitions' and 'great pains', their efforts foundered on Elizabeth's 'erronious Opinions', which she 'stubbornely' maintained.[51] Elizabeth's adherence to her Catholic identity establishes a secret sacred space that is impervious to persuasion and her withdrawal into it is condemned by the pamphlet's Protestant polemic. In the depiction of Protestant murderers, this withdrawal across an internal threshold is indicative of deepening piety. As with the moment of penitential transformation, it is marked by devotional actions, but the full significance of these is withheld from the reader. The inference is that this is a space and time in which the penitent murderer communes directly and deeply with God. Elizabeth Caldwell, another would-be spouse murderer, is described 'continually meditating on the Bible', enhancing her piety by 'exclud[ing] herselfe from all companie'.[52] This withdrawal enables her representation as a preacher, transforming her reported gibbet speech from confession to sermon. In 1684, John Hutchins' 'frequent retiring to Places of as much secrecy as the Prison would allow' for private prayer and meditation was noted with approval.[53] Henry Jones left behind traces of his occupation of a secret sacred space. Although following the established pattern of reading and praying, much of his experience was hidden from his spiritual guides, but the prayers he had written were discovered in the prison after his execution and printed in *The Bloody Murtherer or Unnatural Son* (1672).[54]

Thomas Savage's story closes the circle of argument that opened with Richard Hunne and his rosary. Just as Hunne's devotional acts demonstrated his piety and sanctified his cell at a time when confessional identities were blurred, the same is true of Thomas Savage, a sixteen-year-old apprentice who murdered a maidservant in his master's house after she discovered him stealing some money.[55] In 1668, blurry confessional thresholds were not between Catholic and Protestant, but between Protestant and Protestant. After Savage's condemnation he was visited in prison by a succession of ministers, each of whom had been ejected from his parish on Black Bartholomew's Day in 1662 for refusal to abide by the Act of Uniformity and use the newly revised *Book of Common Prayer*. These criminalised dissenting ministers are the authors of *A Murderer Punished and Pardoned* (1668), and their narrative demonstrates that their 'dissenting' piety is more powerful than the 'Anglican' version that failed to keep Savage in church on Sundays. The representation of Savage's penitential journey once again shows a conflict over the appropriation of sacred space and the individual whose spiritual condition creates it. Early in the narrative, Savage is described entering at one door of a church only to leave immediately at another in order to avoid hearing the sermon. His headlong dash through the church not only works as a metaphor for Savage's spiritual ignorance but also suggests that this consecrated *Anglican* space made no impact on him whatsoever. His precipitate dash from the church leads him to the alehouse, which transforms to a 'baudy-house', and the profane taint of these spaces leads him to the 'murder room', the kitchen in his master's house where he kills his fellow servant. Savage's flight from the murder room leads to the prison, courtroom and condemned cell. His spiritual transformation turns his cell into a sacred space – in effect the church he fled from so precipitately at the beginning of his story – but now it is a dissenting one. As Thomas Savage says to his spiritual guides, 'I bless God that ever I came into a Prison.'[56]

An intensive programme of Bible reading and prayer transforms Savage from one who 'seemed but little sensible of what he had done' into a true penitent.[57] Savage's spiritual state sanctifies his surroundings and redefines his role within that space. Having first thought of Newgate as 'a hell upon earth' he sought 'heaven' with the other prisoners, but his reformed soul leads him to refuse their offer of a card game on 'the Lords day'. Reproving them, Savage declares that 'for my part I had profaned the Sabbath enough already'.[58] His devotional act is a rejection of profanity.

Everything in Savage's temporarily sanctified cell is rededicated. The coffin placed there with him, as a powerful memento mori, becomes 'the ship ... in which I must launch out into the Ocean of eternity'. It does not 'trouble and amaze him' but is 'a comfortable place' Savage desires to inhabit. Even his clothes are transformed, from 'dying cloaths' to 'my living cloaths ... out of which I shall go to eternal glory ... the best cloaths that ever I put on'.[59] Again, Savage's withdrawal into a secret sacred space is emphasised: on 'the last Lords day he lived ... he desired to be alone, and spent it wrestling with God by prayer, and in other duties in order to his preparation for his great chaunge by death'. Whatever happened during this time transformed those gathered to watch him die:

> All the company were exceedingly melted, and their hearts beyond ordinary measure warmed and raised, that the room did ring with sighs and groans, and there was such a mighty presence of the Spirit poured out upon him, and on those that joined with him, that we do not remember the time whenever we had experience of the like.[60]

The music of Savage's sacred condemned cell is 'sighs and groans' rather than harmonious choral singing. In each version of Savage's story, his cell is represented as a site of struggle, not just between God and the devil but also between competing ideals of Protestant piety and the devotions they inspire. *A Murderer Punished and Pardoned* also represents Savage occupying his condemned cell alone, although in reality it would have been crowded with those awaiting execution. This fictional convention of penitent murderer narratives returns us to the lonely final devotions of Richard Hunne but also to Father Benet's monastic cell. In the rhetoric of penitential devotions and sacred space, the usually sharp demarcations between religious confessions can to some extent be erased.

The representation of prisons as exceptional spaces – exceptionally dirty, noisy and smelly, but also spaces where exceptional things can happen – crosses early modern social, political, cultural and religious divisions. It is as prevalent in the heterogeneous, popular world of Protestant-inflected murder pamphlets as it is in the illicit world of smuggled stories of Catholic suffering and martyrdom. The writers insist on the transformation of profane into sacred space, in which rituals – reading, praying, writing – mark the movement across thresholds, including the movement from sacred to secret-sacred. The condemned cell is not permanently changed into a sacred space, it is one only temporarily: its sanctity is produced by the piety of its inhabitant and once he or she leaves then it flows back into profanity, but retains the potential to be transformed again.

Randolph Yearwood, the 'collector' of *The Penitent Murderer*, exhorts the reader not to treat it as 'a bare story or a piece of News, and so having read and seen it, there is an end: But read and consider, read and pray that this great and extraordinary passage of divine Providence may profit thy Soul'.[61] Yearwood claims that a pamphlet – that most profane of early modern printed texts – can act as a spiritual guide when other more conventional texts might struggle to gain a reader's attention. 'I grant you use prayer', Yearwood averred, 'and you read Sermon-notes sometimes, and the Scriptures themselves among your people at home; but how often? and how earnestly is that exercise?'[62] *The Penitent Murderer* finds space for itself where other more obviously godly works are excluded. Moreover, it and other pamphlets like it might be read more often or even *instead of* 'Scriptures' and 'sermon-notes'. It is transformed from a 'profane' to a 'sacred' text, carrying godliness across thresholds: from the prison into the booksellers and, finally, into the home.

Notes

1 *The enquirie into and verdite of the quest paneld of the death of Richard Hunne which was found in Lolars Tower* (Antwerp, 1537). The publication date is conjectured from the reference to William Tyndale's execution, 6 October 1536.
2 Quote: John Foxe, *Acts and Monuments of the English Martyrs* (1570), p. 977. *John Foxe's The Acts and Monuments Online*. www.dhi.ac.uk/foxe. Accessed 18 January 2018. For the varied interpretations of Hunne's identity see Richard Wunderli, 'Pre-Reformation London Summoners and the Murder of Richard Hunne', *Journal of Ecclesiastical History* 33 (1982), 209–24; John Fines, 'The Post-Mortem Condemnation for Heresy of Richard Hunne', *English Historical Review* 78 (1983), 528–31; S. J. Smart, 'John Foxe and "The story of Richard Hunne, martyr"', *Journal of Ecclesiastical History* 37 (1986), 1–14; Susan Brigden, *London and the Reformation* (Oxford: Clarendon, 1989), pp. 98–103; G. W. Bernard, *The Late Medieval Church: Vitality and Vulnerability before the Break with Rome* (New Haven, CT: Yale University Press, 2012), pp. 1–16; Richard Dale, 'The Death of an Alleged Heretic, Richard Hunne (*d*.1514), Explained', *Reformation and Renaissance Review* 15.2 (2013), 133–53.
3 Foxe, *Acts and Monuments*, p. 977.

4 'Sacred' and 'profane' derive from a preoccupation with space. *Sacer* describes objects and places; *profanus* refers to the area outside the *sacrum*, the sacred place. Mircea Eliade (ed.), *The Encyclopaedia of Religion*, 13 vols (New York: Macmillan, 1987), XII:526.
5 Findlay Muirhead (ed.), *London and its Environs* (London: Macmillan, 1927), p. 244. Built in 1010, St Gregory by St Paul's was destroyed with the rest of the cathedral in 1666.
6 John Calvin, *Institutes of the Christian Religion*, ed. J. T. McNeil, trans. F. L. Battles, Library of Christian Classics vol. 22 (Philadelphia: Westminster, 1960), book III, pp. 893–4.
7 R. W. Scribner, *Popular Culture and Popular Movements in Reformation Germany* (London: Hambledon, 1987), p. 2.
8 Andrew Spicer and Sarah Hamilton (eds), *Defining the Holy: Sacred Space in Medieval and Early Modern Europe* (Aldershot: Ashgate, 2005), p. 208.
9 Jeremiah Dyke, *A Sermon Dedicatory preached at the consecration of the Chapell of Epping in Essex* (London, 1623), p. 17.
10 John Donne, *Encaenia* (London, 1623), pp. 2–3.
11 Mircea Eliade, *The Sacred and the Profane: The Nature of Religion*, trans. Willard R. Trask (New York: Harper & Row, 1957), p. 25.
12 'A Declaration made by Sir Thomas Wiatt knight of his innocence being in the Tower upon false accusation ... made until the Councell the yeare of our Lorde 1541', in *The Complete Works of Sir Thomas Wyatt The Elder*, ed. Jason E. Powell, 2 vols (Oxford: Oxford University Press, 2018), I:294. Brigden describes Wyatt as 'a prisoner of memory, the memory that was the territory of guilt and self judgment'. Susan Brigden, *Thomas Wyatt: The Heart's Forest* (London: Faber & Faber, 2012), p. 1.
13 Wyatt, *Works*, I:294.
14 For more on elite writers and 'carceral imagination' see Molly Murray, 'Measured Sentences: Forming Literature in the Early Modern Prison', *Huntington Library Quarterly* 72.2 (2009), 147–67.
15 For changes in early modern attitudes to imprisonment see Thomas S. Freeman, 'The Rise of Prison Literature', *Huntington Library Quarterly* 72.2 (2009), 133–46.
16 Garnishing was the notorious practice of demanding payment for removing prisoners' chains on their arrival at the prison.
17 John Taylor, *The praise and vertue of a jayle* (London, 1623), sigs B3^v–B4^r.
18 'Autobiographical Anecdotes of Edward Underhill', in John Nichols Gough (ed.), *Narratives of the Days of the Reformation* (Westminster, 1859), pp. 132–76 (149).

19 *The Humble Remonstrance and Complaint of Many thousands of poore distressed Prisoners* (London, 1643), sigs A3^v–A4^r.
20 G. M., *Certaine characters of prisons and prisoners* (London, 1618), sig. B3^v.
21 Ibid., sig. A2^r.
22 Ibid., sig. B2^r.
23 Ibid., sig. B3^r.
24 Robert Parsons, *An epistle of the persecution of Catholickes in England* (Douai, France, 1582), p. 79.
25 William Fennor, *The comptors commonwealth; or, A voiage made to an infernall iland* (London, 1617), sigs C1^{r-v}.
26 Thomas Dekker, *Dekker his Dreame* (London, 1620), sigs A4^{r-v}.
27 Ibid.
28 John Lenthall, *The Representation of the Case of Sir John Lenthall* (London, 1654), sig. G2^r.
29 G. M., *Certaine characters,* sigs B3^r, B4^r–C1^v.
30 Jacques Brousse, *The life of the Reverend Fa. Angel of Joyeuse with the lives of Father Benet Englishman* (Douai, France, 1623), p. 48.
31 Stephen Innes, 'Fitch, William [Name in Religion Benet of Canfield], Capuchin Friar 1562–1610', *ODNB*. https://doi.org/10.1093/ref:odnb/4550. Accessed 2 November 2018. Also see Paul Strauss, *In Hope of Heaven: English Recusant Prison Writings of the Sixteenth Century* (New York: Peter Lang, 1995), p. 3.
32 Father Benet and Father John Chrysostom were arrested when they mistook a jail for an inn and stopped to ask for directions.
33 Brousse describes Benet meeting Lord Cobham and Sir Francis Walsingham during his imprisonment at Nonsuch. Even Queen Elizabeth was anxious to catch a glimpse of him as he left. Brousse, *The Life*, p. 107.
34 *Act against Jesuits and Seminarists* (London, 1585), 27 Eliz c2.
35 Brousse, *Life of the Reverend Fa. Angel of Joyeuse*, p. 108.
36 Ibid., p. 108.
37 Ibid., p. 110.
38 Richard Verstegan, *Theatrum Crudelitatum Haereticorum Nostri Temporis* (Antwerp, 1592).
39 Robert Southwell, *An Epistle of Comfort, to the Reverend Priests, & to the Honorable Worshipful, and other of the lay sort* (Paris, 1587?), sigs A3^{r-v}. This was possibly printed in London, maybe at Arundel House, in 1587.
40 Ibid., sig. N6^r.
41 Ibid., sigs N6^v, N8^r.
42 Randolph Yearwood, *The Penitent Murderer* (London, 1657). Yearwood was the Lord Mayor's chaplain.

43 Arthur Golding, *A briefe discourse of the late murther of master George Saunders* (London, 1573).
44 *Ibid.*, sig. A8^r.
45 *Ibid.*, sigs B1^{r-v}. Either John Bradford's *A frutefull treatise and ful heavenly consolation against the feare of death* (London, 1560, 1564), *Godlie meditations upon the Lords prayer* (London, 1562), or *Godly meditations uppon the ten commaundements* (London, 1567). Bradford (*c.*1510–55) was a Protestant minister. Imprisoned for preaching sedition in 1553, he was burned at Smithfield on 1 July 1555. See D. A. Penny, 'Bradford, John (*c.*1510–1555)', *ODNB.* https://doi.org/10.1093/ref:odnb/3175. Accessed 14 March 2018. For the dramatisation of Saunders' story on stage see chapter 5.
46 Golding, *A briefe discourse*, sig. B3^v.
47 *Ibid.*, sig. B4^r.
48 *The manner of the death and execution of Arnold Cosbie* (London, 1591), sig. A2^v.
49 *A Pittilesse Mother: That most unnaturally at one time, murthered two of her owne children at Acton within sixe miles from London upon Holy Thursday last 1616* (London, 1616).
50 *Ibid.*, sig. B1^v.
51 *Ibid.*, sig. B1^r.
52 Gilbert Dugdale, *The Practices of Elizabeth Caldwell* (London, 1604), sig. B2^r.
53 *A True Account of a Bloody and Barbarous Murder Committed on the Body of John Sparks Waterman by John Hutchins* (London, 1684), p. 3.
54 *The Bloody Murtherer; or, Unnatural Son* (London, 1672), p. 22.
55 R[ichard] A[lleine], *A Murderer Punished and Pardoned* (London, 1668). The story was reprinted in ever-expanding versions in 1669, 1671 and 1679; each publication date marks a sensitive moment in the dissenters' campaign to reverse the Clarendon Code. *The Murtherer Turned True Penitent* was printed in 1688, and a final version, *The Life and Death of Thomas Savage*, was printed in 1720.
56 *Ibid.*, sig. C4^r.
57 *Ibid.*, sig. A4^r.
58 *Ibid.*, p. 19.
59 *Ibid.*, pp. 32–3.
60 *Ibid.*, p. 28.
61 Yearwood, *Penitent Murderer*, sig. A5^v.
62 *Ibid.*, sig. E5^r.

8

Editing devotional identity: the compilation and reception of the prison prose of George Fox's *Journal* (1694)*

Catie Gill

George Fox's autobiographical writings make clear how entirely he committed his life to Quakerism. 'Great and deep sufferings' characterised Fox's religious travail, as William Penn noted, looking back over his friend's life.[1] An antagonistic figure, Fox, as his most recent biographer has shown, was 'temperamentally unable to admit failure', and yet the prison experience was apt to bring him to a point of reflection where he 'evaluated his earlier position'.[2] This essay explores the autobiographical writings of this most dogmatic of Quakers through his reflections on prison sentences that occurred during the Commonwealth period: Derby (forty-nine weeks), Carlisle (seven weeks) and Launceston (thirty-six weeks).[3]

The text thought to be Fox's first autobiographical account of his spiritual journey, called the *Short Journal* (*c*.1664), opens 'George Fox, So Called of the World but the world knows neither him nor his {new} name, Here are some of his sufferings y^t hee hath suffered by the world and their Professors, Priests & Teachers,' as though to foreground what awaits the reader is a story of surviving hostility.[4] Summarising where Fox sits in the tradition of spiritual autobiography, Kathleen Lynch astutely headlined the 'litany of beatings, stonings, jailings, and seemingly indefatigable journeys from place to place' that Fox endured as being the mainstay of the narrative, and its most striking content.[5] Finding meaning to 'suffering' in 'the world',

---

* This work was generously supported with a grant from the Hodgett Trust.

as Lynch and indeed Fox observe, means perceiving God's design in conjunction with finding a pattern to frequent incarceration.

One premonition encapsulates the carceral in Fox's autobiographical writings: he remembers, 'I then felt & saw I was a prisoner above 10 miles before I {came to Ives where we} was taken.'[6] This moment is significant because Fox's vision indeed predicts what is to come: a lengthy sentence in Launceston Castle Prison. It is also important for the other element that will be scrutinised in this essay: the matter of textual variation. While Fox's spiritual forewarning appears in the manuscript account, the final published text of 1694 omits this detail.[7] Fox's autobiography exists in three extant forms: first in the 1660s *Short Journal*, second in the 1670s version (which today is known as the Spence Manuscript, after its nineteenth-century owner), and third in the 1694 autobiography, known as the *Ellwood Journal* (hereafter *EJ*) because Thomas Ellwood made the text publication-ready.[8] The *Short Journal* (hereafter *SJ*) and the Spence Manuscript have for the purposes of this essay been accessed in modern editions, the latter of which takes the title of the *Cambridge Journal* (hereafter *CJ*). The interconnectedness between *SJ*, *CJ* and *EJ* is complex; working out what is common to all, or missing from one, is a critical enterprise. It is a worthwhile endeavour because when the same incident is put through a number of revisions, what emerges is a difference not only in phrasing, but often in emphasis.

What this essay proposes to do is first establish the principles which can be discerned in Thomas Ellwood's compilation of the parts of the *Journal*'s narrative devoted to the imprisonment in Derby, Carlisle and Launceston, especially the most significant discrepancies.[9] The impulse behind exploring textual revision is that it allows for an assessment of broader questions, such as whether Fox's life narrative was tampered with by Ellwood in order to sanitise his legacy. I will, however, demonstrate that there is clear evidence that Ellwood wished to preserve much of the distinctiveness of Fox's manuscript. Contemporaries, though, thought differently, and Friends had a reputation for meddling before publication. The Church of Ireland clergyman Charles Leslie, for instance, complained of the Quaker tendency to 'leave out these now unsavoury Passages' that did not fit the image that Friends wished to project.[10] While I will be defending Ellwood from some of the harsher judgements made of his editorship, he is not entirely exempt from a charge of altering 'unsavoury Passages'. What this study amounts to ultimately is a discussion of the degree to which the representation of Fox's imprisonment has been censored in the 1694 Ellwood edition, and the effects these changes had on the reception of the text.

'Nothing may be omitted fit to be inserted, nor anything inserted fit to be left out'[11]

The decisions that the compiler, Thomas Ellwood, made in relation to the *Journal* cannot fail to have significance, given the text he inherited: a roughly written manuscript, dictated by Fox but penned largely by Thomas Lower, which is a scrapbook of contemporary pamphlets and letters as well as an autobiography. There were 'many errors and mistakes in the printing and writing', Fox explained, clearly indicating that he did not envisage that the manuscript would be printed in the condition in which he left it.[12] Once Ellwood's work of compilation was complete, he passed on the text to the Second Day Morning Meeting, a censoring body that could change texts to make them publication-ready.[13] The records make clear that on one occasion a passage of the *Journal* was cut because of the likelihood that it would cause offence.[14] Because the minutes 'tell nothing of their detailed action', more about contemporary sensitivities to Fox's writings can be determined by looking at Ellwood's choices than by looking at the meeting's influence.[15]

While the detailed work of comparing *CJ* and *EJ* began in the nineteenth century, and was continued especially aptly by Henry Cadbury in the twentieth, it is only in recent years that a technique for reading textual variation emerged.[16] As Meg Twycross, Hilary Hinds and Alison Findlay aver, their online text of Fox's *Journal* does not seek to verify 'what really happened' when there are divergences, highlighting instead problems with 'the reliability of memory'.[17] They illustrate this method when assessing what occurred in the courtroom. Fox's response when being cross-questioned on a charge of blasphemy in Lancaster, 1652, for instance, leads Hinds to focus on the defendant's wordplay, how he 'reframed the matter', rather than trying to retrieve the truth of events from records not designed for veracity.[18] Rather than approaching this narrative as a digest of Fox's theological views, Hinds exposes how the attitudes being conveyed are textually mediated. Other work on sensitive trials conveyed in John Foxe's martyrology, *Acts and Monuments*, can similarly be read as 'steer[ing] readers to the truth by navigating them through the treacherous possibilities contained in the interrogation'.[19] Consequently, my account of Fox's imprisonments when dealing with variants does not seek to propose that one record is to be preferred over another.

The trials of Fox in the early years of the 1650s resulted in imprisonment on three occasions, so let us begin with a summary of events before moving on to a comparison of the textual variations. In Derby, Fox was first examined on a matter relating to his conduct, as he had interrupted a local minister, and was then tried on a charge of blasphemy (*SJ*, pp. 4–5; *CJ*, I:1–14; *EJ*, pp. 30–59). In Carlisle, where there was a similar pattern of a public disputation leading to an examination, Fox faced the death penalty as a blasphemer (*SJ*, pp. 32–3; *CJ*, I:115–27; *EJ*, pp. 108–18). 'They asked mee if I were the sonne of God, I said yes' (*SJ*, p. 32).

In Launceston, the charges initially arose as a result of Fox, William Salt and Edward Pyot distributing Quaker writings in Cornwall, but then escalated as Judge Sir John Glyn reacted to the Quakers' refusal to remove their hats (*SJ*, pp. 42–7; *CJ*, I:205–44; *EJ*, pp. 172–229).[20] A further dimension was added when Major Peter Ceely moved the court to consider his accusations. These involved charges that were plainly false: first, that Fox had boasted he could raise a large number of men to revolt against the government (the number being anywhere from four hundred to forty thousand, depending on the account), and second, that Fox had struck him.[21] Fox positioned himself, from the trial at Derby onwards, as responsible for 'ye defence of ye faith' (*SJ*, p. 4).

It is generally agreed that Ellwood 'took more liberty with his source than most modern editors would do', and that such interventions were in fact a feature of other life-writing.[22] Even though Ellwood is sympathetic to the historical record and the need to preserve Fox's visionary and stalwart character, his changes register on occasion priorities that seem designed to soften the image of the Quaker leader when he was responding to persecution. Cadbury's 'The *Editio Princeps* of Fox's Journal' tables six headings under which Ellwood's changes to Fox's manuscript can be arranged. They are: 'Ellwood's Editorial Style', 'Ellwood's Editorial Caution', 'Naming of Persons', 'Language', 'Other Sources' and 'Major Decisions', but this focus on style fragments events and obscures where major changes concentratedly occur. We could anticipate, given the sensitivity of texts dealing with arrests, trials and prison sentences, that Ellwood would intervene more here than in other parts of the *Journal*. Cadbury's digest confirms this expectation, but the textual variations between *CJ* and *EJ* are in fact sometimes attributable not to Ellwood's political or moral sensitivities about prison scenes, but to aesthetic concerns. Two aspects – how language dates a writer as much as his or her attitudes, and what Bruce Hindmarsh terms the 'adversarial' nature of religious identity – receive careful consideration by Ellwood.[23]

Three key passages in Fox's account of his forty-eight-week Derby sentence show the significance of either shortening or lengthening an account of an incident as it is transmitted from manuscript to printed text. While in Derby, Fox became sensitised to the treatment of criminals awaiting execution, and the first of the cuts that Ellwood makes to Fox's prose occurs in an emotive section. In the manuscript, the dead men's 'spiritts appeared to mee', but this ghostly encounter has been cut from *EJ* before publication (*CJ*, I:14). This incident is the one and only spectral occurrence in the prison scenes; as it is a unique, it is not easy to determine precisely why Fox's words seemed to Ellwood unprintable.[24]

In contrast to the previous example, Ellwood expands the account from the manuscript in three places, and each is interesting for what it shows about his practices. While Fox's *SJ* was wholly narrative reflection, by the time he was retelling his life story (about ten years later) for the Spence Manuscript he was drawing both on the *SJ* and on a variety of letters and Quaker published texts, which explains why in general the account that was written later was also longer. In the Derby narrative, several texts that relate to the trial and the sentence are interwoven into the account; interestingly, a similar method of authenticating suffering through corroborative documents is taken in *Acts and Monuments*. In the printed text compiled by Ellwood, some extra material not in the Spence Manuscript is provided.[25]

The first example of Ellwood going beyond the materials is when an illustration of a point in the main narrative comes from a text that is not in the Spence Manuscript. Fox explains, 'I saw ye Power of God went away from them as ye Waters ranne from ye Town {damn when ye floode gates were uppe},' which is a vision of God's judgement on Derby (*CJ*, I:9). There is more context in the printed text than the original manuscript, as Ellwood supplies a copy of Fox's warning to the town, beginning 'Ô Darby! As the Waters run away' (*EJ*, p. 52). In the second example of Ellwood enlarging the record, Fox is being tried. The *Ellwood Journal* has a couple of supplementary questions that were posed to Fox during his nine hours' examination, and his answers in the 1694 text thicken the detail of the record at this point (*CJ*, I:2; *EJ*, p. 31). The reader of the published text thus gets to witness more of Fox disputing with his interrogators, but also, given this was a blasphemy trial, more of the magistrates' perturbation. This seems an especially interesting amplification, therefore. In his 1696 text, the anti-Quaker Charles Leslie insists that Fox was guilty as charged because no innocent person would 'dodge, and shift' as much as he does when being tried for blasphemy.[26] If Ellwood thought that supplying more evidence of Fox at trial would better make the case for his innocence, then Leslie's response shows that sceptical readers conclude otherwise. The third example of Ellwood amplifying the original is when Fox explains that he will not serve as a soldier; as there is no clear equivalent in the manuscript, Cadbury insists that Ellwood was not using Spence but another source at this point.[27]

The three examples that have been extrapolated so far therefore point to only one instance of censorship, in Ellwood's treatment of the Derby imprisonment, but to far more instances of Ellwood combining sources to provide a fuller account for the reading public. Cadbury finds four more changes to phrasing, and two can be explained away as aiding the clarity of the piece.[28] The two other examples both work more judgementally, and so bear some brief discussion. In the first, Fox's words move a believer (once a soldier) to a new spiritual understanding. 'I spoake to him & opend his understanding' is the phrase used in the manuscript, while the printed text says 'his Understanding was opened' (*CJ*, I:12; *EJ*, p. 45). The effect of the passive 'was opened' is to assign more influence to God than to Fox, and so to establish divine power. It can be seen clearly that Ellwood's modification is more orthodox than Fox's sense of himself as ministering to the soul of this man, because he makes the same decision later. Conversing with the Welshman Rice Jones, Fox's version reads '{& soe I brought ye power of ye Lorde over his imaginations & whimsys}', while Ellwood wrote 'and so was the Power of the Lord brought over his *wicked Imaginations* and *Whimsies*' (*CJ*, I:11; *EJ*, p. 47).[29] As before, 'brought over' acts in the same way as 'was opened' in tempering the sense of Fox's activity.

It is the case that while these changes seem incriminatingly to point to Ellwood diverging from the text at sensitive points, this prison narrative is so rich a source in terms of unusual occurrences that the charge of editorial censorship must be somewhat reduced. Unquestionably, what Fox is recalling of the Derby event is what Quakers termed 'spiritual warfare'. Fox shows how clearly his purpose was made evident: 'the Lord had said to me before, That *I was not to be removed from that Place yet, being set there for a Service, which he had for me to do*' (*EJ*, p. 46).[30] This spiritual purpose is manifested by the narrative in accounts of an unbeliever (the keeper), or people lacking conviction (John Fretwell, Baptist conversants), helping Fox to realise the Lord's power was at work (*EJ*, pp. 37, 46–7). Still other incidents have a sense of menace or peril, such as the threatening behaviour by a 'Conjurer', and Fox's incarceration in a squalid part of the prison; but the narrative makes clear God has saved his prophet, and smitten his enemies (*EJ*, p. 48). While Ellwood does trim the original, he nevertheless respects Fox's insight into how providence ensures his survival. Some local colour is lost in transmission, but not this pious message.

The Carlisle events add only one subtle example of an Ellwood omission, but ample evidence of his additions.[31] It does need to be observed that the act of turning a manuscript into a printed document requires careful judgement. The Carlisle episode is a good example, as Ellwood has to slot the sentences running vertically into those running horizontally, so bringing order to a disorderly text (see figure 8.1).[32] In terms of Ellwood's omission, this occurs when Fox and other Friends are beaten by the jailer. While Ellwood's account conveys this factually – 'he would *beat Friends* with a great *Cudgel*' – the narrative has lost the colloquial colour of the manuscript's 'hee beate frends ... as if hee had beene beatinge a packe of wooll' (*EJ*, p. 112; *CJ*, I:126). In terms of additions, Ellwood has presented contemporary documents by Justices Pearson and Benson that were not in the original, so broadening the historical record of Friends' efforts to combat injustice. The Carlisle imprisonment also makes Fox recall how other Friends have suffered, and so a pattern of persecution begins to emerge.[33] Indeed, in Carlisle as in Derby, Fox was put into a '*Filthy, Nasty*' '*place so bad*' it was unfit for habitation, with the jailer finally being put into the prison over which he once presided (*EJ*, pp. 112, 117). Admonitory passages, a frequent motif of sufferings narrative, are recalled in part because they 'reassured Quakers of their own spiritual position and testimonies in the face of suffering and adversity', as Naomi Pullin has observed.[34]

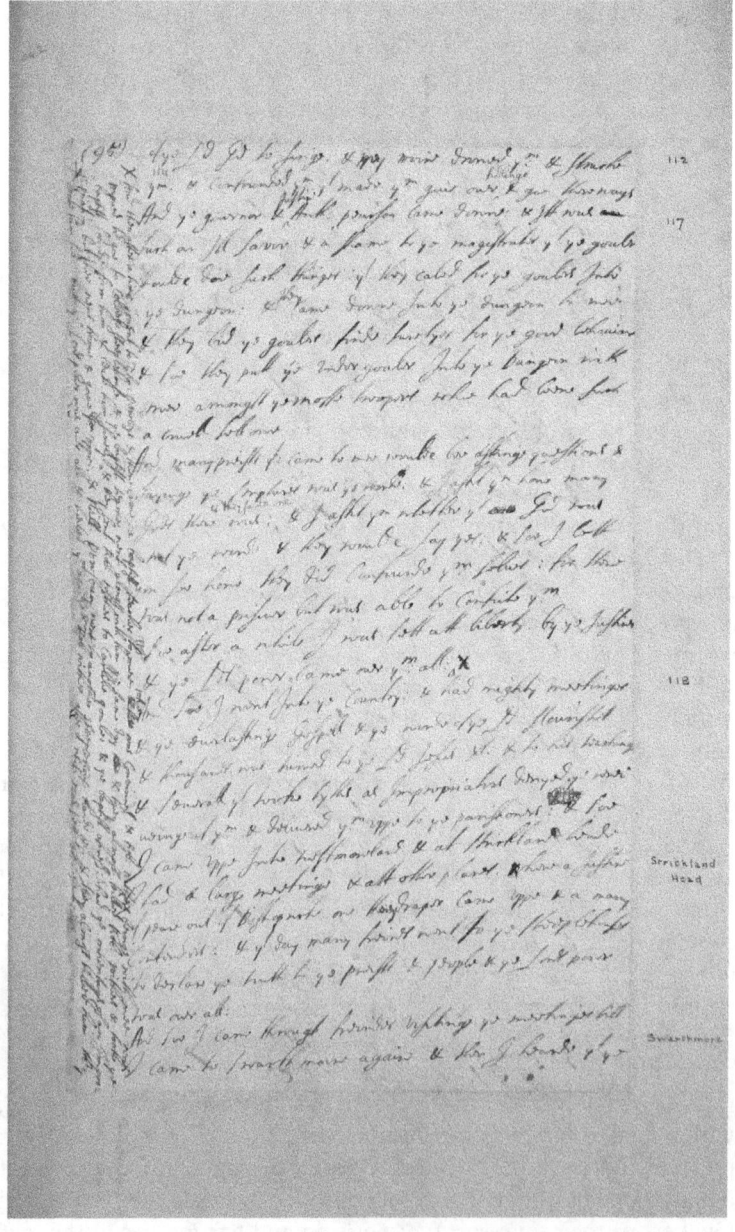

Figure 8.1 Page from the Spence Manuscript.

It is possible to establish how writing the autobiography helped Fox achieve perspective on events. One passage from 1659 summarises the era: 'this time they was Crucifeing ye seed'; only very rarely does Fox look with a wide lens out to the political context, and draw conclusions (*CJ*, I:343). The end of the decade seems indeed to be the time for it, as Fox also summarises Quaker hardship 'in the dayes of Oliver and his sonne Richard' in a brief paragraph from the *Short Journal* (*SJ*, p. 56). These 1659 phrases suggest that Fox wants to frame his experiences with respect to bigger historical forces, such as the change of government. My next example, from the Launceston episode, is important because it shows the effect of rewriting. Fox's first lengthy autobiographical text knows that the meaning of survival at Launceston has yet to be understood: 'So truth came over, and many Miracoulous deliverance I had wch would make a great volumn if they should be declared' (*SJ*, p. 47). But by the 1670s Fox reflected that 'I sawe y^t was ye Lord alone, y^t did preserve mee out of & over their bloody handes: for ye Devill had a great enmity to mee' (*CJ*, I:231). With no authorial equivalent, unless it is in a now lost source, Ellwood picks up on Fox's point about the Devil's enmity, and adds that he 'stirred up his *Instruments* to seek my *hurt*. But the *Lord* prevented them; and my Heart was filled with *Thanksgivings* and *Praises* unto him' (*EJ*, p. 189). In addition to extending the teleology, Ellwood's variant returns the praise to God, which is in turn characteristic of changes he made elsewhere. It seems that from Fox beginning to comprehend his purpose in the *SJ* to Ellwood compiling the *Journal* for publication there is greater clarity about teleology.[35]

It seems certain that because Ellwood was keenly scrutinising Fox's prose at points relating to an arrest, trial or imprisonment, owing to the inherent sensitivity of the material, these sections also enact numerous aesthetic or stylistic changes. Most of the changes Ellwood enacts are indeed of a rather technical nature, relating to matters such as subject–verb agreement or the use of the past or the pluperfect tense; he changes 'atop of' to 'over' and inverts some phrases.[36] These emendations are indicative of a desire on Ellwood's part to subtly modify Fox's prose, but if this design might seem to be about avoiding extensive archaism, there is one exception. Ellwood in fact often assigns a more dated word, 'hath', in place of 'has', which goes against the other evidence that his intention was to avoid formulations that by the 1690s were quaint.[37] The majority of the changes that Cadbury identifies are made in the interests of clarity. A couple are a little vindictive: while Fox names William Salt and Humphrey Norton in his manuscript, Ellwood removes these now ex-Quakers from the record; he also takes care to ensure that if Fox says someone is 'now living' this is verifiably accurate.[38]

A couple of the more heavy-handed changes to the Launceston section relate to matters of judgement, and engage with the Quakers' reputation.[39] In *EJ*, there are many instances where Ellwood's wording eliminates what is particular to Fox's voice. Yet overall, it can be said of Ellwood's efforts that he was both a sympathetic and talented compiler. Moreover, in the prison scenes from the years 1650–56, Fox emerges as a combative figure just as surely in *EJ* as in *SJ* and *CJ*, justifying the observation of his most recent biographer that Fox's relationship to the authorities fits the description of 'anarchism'.[40]

'That all may know the Dealings of the Lord with me'[41]

Near the end of Fox's life, before delivering a speech in London, he reflected:

> Since I came abroad to declare the everlasting truth, I have been a sufferer very much, by times, above these thirty years, in gaols, and prisons. And my body has been spoiled for the testimony of Jesus. So ... it was hard for me to come [to] this journey.[42]

The image of the pious sufferer that Fox movingly depicts here is easier to assimilate into 1690s culture than the image of the spiritual warrior he cultivates in his autobiographical writing. In the *Journal*, Fox determinedly seeks to overcome the enemies of truth. Anti-Quaker writing responds to this aspect of Fox's self-characterisation by focusing on the threat he posed to the establishment in the early stages of Quakerism, and even in their own times.

The final section of this essay notes a 'clash of ontologies, through contrary formulations of what is religiously true and real', by assessing how Fox's self-image was received after the *Journal*'s publication.[43] Even though Quakers were now apparently in a new age of compassion (the Toleration Act had been passed five years before the *Journal*'s publication), the forty-year-old association between Quakerism and lawbreaking still pertained. As is becoming clear in studies of the effects of the 1689 Toleration Acts, the pressures on dissenters did not wholly subside; their suffering, especially for the tithe, was not completely behind them.⁴⁴ The Anglican apologist Charles Leslie would therefore have been playing to contemporary fears when he wrote that as Quakers continued to see themselves as above the law, they were still dangerous: 'while they make themselves Gods, [Quakers] think their Governors to be Serpents'.⁴⁵

Finally, then, it is of interest that even though history is often written from the point of view of the powerful, not the oppressed, the opposite can be true of persecution. Whereas another critic, Francis Bugg, accuses Quakers of 'Contempt of Government' in much the same way as Leslie, who charges them with obstinacy and perversity – 'Very many of them [i.e. Quakers] did Provoke sufferings to themselves on Purpose' – it is the case that by exalting in the oppression of others he looks vengeful.⁴⁶ Quakers were a little more sensitive to changing mores than Leslie. This point can be demonstrated by tracing the alterations that Fox's *Journal* underwent between the period of its composition and publication with respect to persecutors. Ellwood indeed displays unease at some of the more vengeful of Fox's judgements. In the Launceston section, Ellwood shows how Fox was finally released from his long imprisonment as a result of the diligent efforts of Colonel John Desborough's deputy; Fox's manuscript, by contrast, identified God's judgement on the parliamentarian when noting that '[Desborough] ... left us in prison {but after when ye Kinge came in hee was cast Into prison himselfe}' (*EJ*, p. 217; *CJ*, I:241).⁴⁷ This gloating comment appears only in the manuscript, and was cut by Ellwood before publication. Ingle notes that Fox 'seemed to delight in cataloguing misfortunes befalling those who crossed him', but the actions of Ellwood and the Second Day Morning Meeting curbed this tendency a fraction.⁴⁸

The main strategy of Charles Leslie was to draw attention to the continuing threat to order that the Quakers posed. He regarded Quakers as enthusiasts and fanatics who were merely simulating respectability. Though he does not seem to have known that Ellwood was involved in preparing the *Journal* for print, he was aware that the Second Day Morning Meeting acted censoriously. Leslie instructed elders not to doctor the text currently in their care, perceiving their intention as being to 'take out its Sting'.⁴⁹ Leslie's view that Quakers massaged their public image is only partially proven by what Ellwood enacts as the compiler of the *Journal*. Certainly, some of the rough edges have been smoothed off, but it cannot be said that in amending Fox's language in the sections on Derby, Carlisle and Launceston imprisonment Ellwood had removed the text's 'Sting'.

Notes

1. William Penn, *The Rise and Progress*, in *The Peace of Europe, and Fruits of Solitude and Other Writings*, ed. E. B. Bronner (London: Everyman, 1993), p. 303. See Catie Gill, 'William Penn as Preface Writer, Historian, and Controversialist', in Andrew R. Murphy and John Smolenski (eds), *The Worlds of William Penn* (New Brunswick, NJ: Rutgers University Press, 2019), pp. 265–82.
2. Homer L. Ingle, *First among Friends: George Fox and the Creation of Quakerism* (Oxford: Oxford University Press, 1994), p. 188. Ingle is suggesting that the *Short Journal*, written after imprisonment in Lancaster, has occasional moments of wistfulness, even regret.
3. The term of the Derby sentence: 'I was sett freely at liberty; who had been kept a year w^{t}hin three weeks', in George Fox, *The Short Journal and Itinerary Journals of George Fox*, ed. Norman Penney (Cambridge: Cambridge University Press, 1925), p. 5, hereafter *SJ*. For the other sentences, I have taken Nickalls' estimate of the length of the prison sentence. See George Fox, *The Journal of George Fox*, ed. John L. Nickalls (Cambridge: Cambridge University Press, 1952), on Carlisle: note 1, p. 159; on Launceston: notes 1 and 2, p. 242.
4. *SJ*, p. 1. When Penney uses {brackets} it is to indicate that there is a correction at this point in the manuscript.
5. Kathleen Lynch, *Protestant Autobiography in the Seventeenth-Century Anglophone World* (Oxford: Oxford University Press, 2012), p. 172.
6. George Fox, *The Journal of George Fox*, ed. Norman Penney, 2 vols (Cambridge: Cambridge University Press, 1911), I:208, known as the *Cambridge Journal* and hereafter *CJ*.
7. See George Fox, *A Journal or Historical Account of the Life, Travels, Sufferings, Christian Experiences and Labour ... of ... George Fox* (London, 1694), hereafter *EJ*. The passage would be on p. 177 after the words 'rude and violent'.
8. The so-called *Great Journal* (now lost) would have provided one more version of Fox's life story. See Henry J. Cadbury, *Annual Catalogue of George Fox's Papers* (Philadelphia, PA: Friends Bookstore, 1939), p. viii. See also manuscripts by Fox on sufferings, in George Fox, *Narrative Papers of George Fox*, ed. Henry J. Cadbury (Richmond, IN: Friends United Press, 1972), pp. 203, 207.

9 I say 'compilation' because editing is too minor a word for the processes in which Ellwood was involved.
10 Charles Leslie, *The Snake in the Grass* (London, 1696), p. xcvii. Leslie is referring to how Quakers, after the Restoration, attempted to 'stifle and conceal' their prior flattery of Oliver Cromwell.
11 The words of Thomas Ellwood. Cited in Fox, *CJ*, p. xxxix.
12 Harvey says 'doubtless' Fox expected his literary executors to make changes. Thomas. E. Harvey, 'Introduction', in Fox, *CJ*, pp. xii, xxvii.
13 On Quaker censorship see Thomas O'Malley, '"Defying the Powers and Tempering the Spirit": A Review of Quaker Control over Their Publications 1672–1689', *Journal of Ecclesiastical History* 33.3 (1982), 72–82; and Norman Penney, 'Geo. Fox's Writings and the Morning Meeting', *Friends' Quarterly Examiner* 36.141 (1902), 67–9.
14 Second Day Morning Meeting Minutes, vol. II (1673–92), pp. 66, 68, 75. Library of the Society of Friends, London. MMM, V2, 1692–1700.
15 Henry J. Cadbury, 'The *Edito Princeps* of Fox's Journal', *Journal of the Friends' Historical Society* 53.3 (1974), 197–218 (198).
16 For older work, see Charles J. Spence, 'A Brief Account of the Manuscript Journal of George Fox', *Essayist and Friends Review* 1.1 (1893), 5–8; W. S. Hudson, 'A Suppressed Chapter in Quaker History', *Journal of Religion* 24.1 (1944), 108–18; Cadbury, 'The *Edito Princeps* of Fox's Journal', pp. 197–218; and the introduction to Fox, *CJ*, pp. ix–xxx, xxxi–xlii. Recent work on textual variation includes: N. S. Firmin, 'Perceptions of the Quaker Movement in the 1650s' (unpublished PhD dissertation, University of East Anglia, 1985); Claus Bernet, 'Mark Swanner (1639–1713): The Man Behind Fox and Penn', *Quaker History* 99 (2010), 20–36.
17 See Meg Twycross, Hilary Hinds and Alison Findlay, '"The Journeys of George Fox, 1652–1653": Interim Report on a Research Project and Website', *Quaker Studies* 14.2 (2010), 224–35 (226); and visit: www.lancaster.ac.uk/quakers/project/proj_index.html.
18 See the account of the 1652 Lancaster trial in Fox, *CJ*, I:60–85. Hilary Hinds, *George Fox and Early Quaker Culture* (Manchester: Manchester University Press, 2011), p. 49. The significance of blasphemy charges against Fox has been summarised in Richard G. Bailey, 'The Making and Unmaking of a God: New Light on George Fox and Early Quakerism', in Michael A. Mullett (ed.), *New Light on George Fox, 1626–1691* (York: Ebor, [1993]), pp. 110–28. My principle in choosing the three cases from 1650–56 (Derby, Carlisle and Launceston), and consequently omitting Lancaster 1652, needs to be justified. I do so on the grounds that the Lancaster examination did not result in imprisonment, and so is not a strict point of comparison. It is also brief (in the *SJ*, it receives only one paragraph, p. 27). I have omitted examples of Fox's imprisonment

from Richard Cromwell's rule (1658–60), and the Restoration period (1660 onwards) because engaging with a different political moment would stretch the current analysis too far.

19 Sarah Covington, 'Foxe's Villainous Tribunals: Reading the Judicial Examinations in the *Actes and Monuments*', in Thomas P. Anderson and Ryan Netzley (eds), *Acts of Reading: Interpretation, Reading Practices, and the Idea of the Book in John Foxe's Actes and Monuments* (Newark, NJ: University of Delaware Press, 2010), pp. 176–207 (186). *Acts and Monuments* is further relevant because it continued to be published into the 1690s, perhaps even achieving its 'greatest dissemination' in the period when Fox's *Journal* was being read. See Peter Nockles, 'The Changing Legacy and Reception of John Foxe's "Book of Martyrs" in "the long Eighteenth Century": Varieties of Anglicanism, Protestant, and Catholic Response, c. 1760–1850', in Robert D. Cornwall and William Gibson (eds), *Religion, Politics and Dissent 1660-1832: Essays in Honour of James E Bradley* (Farnham: Ashgate, 2010), pp. 219–48; Elizabeth Evenden and Thomas S. Freeman, *Religion and the Book in Early Modern England: Making Foxe's Book of Martyrs* (Cambridge: Cambridge University Press, 2011), pp. 320–47 (338); Robert W. Daniel, '"To make a second Book of Martyrs": Re-appropriating Foxe in Nonconformist Prison Writings in Seventeenth-Century Britain', *Bunyan Studies* 23 (2019), 45–61.

20 I deem the prison term to have started when Fox is first interrogated. I take a signal from Fox's reflection on when the sentence ended (usually, a phrase about achieving liberty). The relevant pages in the original manuscript, held in Friends House, London, are: Derby, pp. 5–7; Carlisle, pp. 51–3, Launceston, pp. 68–76.

21 *Extracts from State Papers Relating to Friends*, second series, 1659–66 (London: Friends' Historical Society, 1911), provides the best snapshot of the authorities' fears about Quaker insurgency.

22 Henry J. Cadbury, 'An Obscure Chapter of Quaker History', *Journal of Religion* 24.3 (1944), 201–13 (211). See also Peter Lake, 'Reading Clarke's Lives in Political and Polemical Context', in Kevin Sharpe and Steven N. Zwicker (eds), *Writing Lives: Biography and Textuality, Identity and Representation in Early Modern England* (Oxford: Oxford University Press, 2012), pp. 293–318. For the notion that 'editorial hands were heavy in each publication', see Lynch, *Protestant Autobiography*, p. 28.

23 D. B. Hindmarsh, *The Evangelical Conversion Narrative: Spiritual Autobiography in Early Modern England* (Oxford: Oxford University Press, 2005), p. 28.

24 Ghost stories, however, were a potent part of the Protestant imagination. See Peter Marshall, *Beliefs and the Dead in Reformation England* (Oxford: Oxford University Press, 2002), pp. 232–64.

25 Maybe the documents were once contained within the Spence Manuscript – having been lost between Ellwood's and Spence's day. Ellwood seeks to verify Fox's writing – for instance, checking personal details and qualifying large claims – seeming to indicate conscientiousness in relation to the facts. On the phrase 'to this day' see Cadbury, 'The *Edito Princeps* of Fox's Journal', p. 205.
26 Leslie, *The Snake in the Grass*, p. ccix. He refers to Lancaster, not the Derby trial, but as both were blasphemy trials, the point I am making is valid.
27 Cadbury, 'The *Edito Princeps* of Fox's Journal', p. 210. A fourth, less interesting, example is when Ellwood gives more detail than Fox about the visit of his relations. See Fox, *The Journal of George Fox*, ed. Nickalls, p. 61.
28 Cadbury, 'The *Edito Princeps* of Fox's Journal', pp. 203–4.
29 *Ibid.*, p. 204. The Launceston section contains another amendment where Ellwood emphasises divine agency. It involves Elizabeth Trelawney's response to Fox. See Fox, *EJ*, p. 174, *CJ*, I:204.
30 See 'ye Lord said to mee yt I was not to be remooved from y^t place yet, but was sett as a King for ye bodie^s sake & for ye true hope {y^t doth purify} & ye true ffaith {y^t gives ye vicoty} & ye true Beliefe {y^t overcomes ye worlde}'. Fox, *CJ*, I:3.
31 Harvey's (not Cadbury's) variant: Fox, *CJ*, p. xx.
32 For reproductions of pages from the Spence Manuscript, visit https://www.lancaster.ac.uk/quakers/spence/spence_index.html.
33 Fox describes James Parnell's fate; Ellwood characteristically adds detail by naming the pamphlet dealing with Parnell's death and a woman's punishment in a scold's bridle: *The Lambs Defence Against Lyes* (1655).
34 Naomi Pullin, 'Providence, Punishment, and Identity Formation in the Late-Stuart Quaker Community, c. 1650–1700', *Seventeenth Century* 31.4 (2016), 471–94 (477). A pointing finger, the word 'examples' or the phrase 'take note of' are deployed in the margin to emphasise providential intervention.
35 Fox describes 1650s millenarianism reflectively, too. See *EJ*, p. 211.
36 Cadbury, 'The *Edito Princeps* of Fox's Journal', p. 202.
37 *Ibid.*, p. 202. 'Hath' when used by Fox in the Derby, Carlisle and Launceston episodes occurs as part of a warning, admonition or prophecy to a non-Quaker (Fox, *CJ*, I:6, 7, 22, 206, 218, 221, 240), or is biblical: 'he hath taken away my sin' (*ibid.*, I:2). Ellwood, by extension, might therefore use 'hath' where Fox uses 'has' in order to create a stronger link between Fox's words and the Bible.
38 Cadbury, 'The *Edito Princeps* of Fox's Journal', pp. 206, 205.
39 See Fox on Desborough in the next section of this essay.

40 Ingle, *First among Friends*, p. 213. Madeline Ward, *The Christian Quaker: George Keith and the Keithian Controversy* (Leiden, Netherlands: Brill, 2019), may throw new light on Fox's reputation, but was published too late to be included in this essay.
41 The opening line of Fox's autobiography in *EJ*, p. 1.
42 Michael P. Graves, *Preaching the Inward Light: Early Quaker Rhetoric* (Waco, TX: Baylor University Press, 2009), p. 222.
43 J. M. Mueller, 'Pain, Persecution, and the Construction of Selfhood in Foxe's *Acts and Monuments*', in Claire McEachern and Debra Shuger (eds), *Religion and Culture in Renaissance England* (Cambridge: Cambridge University Press, 1997), pp. 161–87 (162).
44 Erin Bell, 'Quakers and the Law', in Richard C. Allen and Rosemary A. Moore (eds), *The Quakers, 1656–1723: The Evolution of an Alternative Community* (University Park: Penn State University Press, 2018), pp. 263–86.
45 Leslie, *The Snake in the Grass*, p. 170.
46 Francis Bugg, *The Picture of Quakerism* (London, 1697), p. 97; Charles Leslie, *Satan Disrob'd from his Disguise of Light* (London, 1697), p. 12.
47 The Second Day Morning Meeting amended a section of the *Journal* about persecutors' deaths. See Cadbury, 'The *Edito Princeps* of Fox's Journal', p. 215.
48 Ingle, *First among Friends*, p. 251. One incident in the Launceston section shows Fox's detractors robbed of the power of speech; this incident appears in all three texts. See Fox, *SJ*, p. 46; *CJ*, I:226; *EJ*, pp. 185–6. Another instance of a person rendered speechless occurs in Alexander Jaffray, *The Diary of Alexander Jaffray*, ed. John Barclay (London: Darton and Harvey, 2nd edn, 1834), p. 367. My thanks to Robert W. Daniel for this reference.
49 'I set it down this particularly … [to] those who will watch the New Edition of Fox's *Works*, and they shall neither Add nor Diminish, without being told of it … the Design is either wholly to suppress it, or to take out its Sting.' Leslie, *The Snake in the Grass*, pp. cclxxvi. See also pp. cclxxv–cclxxvi.

SECTION II
Types

Part V: Devotional identities in spiritual autobiographies

9

Fathers and sons, conscience, and duty in early modern England

Bernard Capp

> He that his Father honour doth,
> God will forgive his sin,
> ...
> The fathers Blessing stays the house,
> his curse doth make it fall.
> A wise Child makes the father glad,
> ...
> The Ravens shall pick out their Ey[es]
> that do their Parents curse.[1]

This bleak warning, in a Restoration ballad, reflects the power of biblical strictures in shaping early modern ideas on parental rights and children's duty. 'Children', wrote Saint Paul to the Ephesians (Ephesians 6:1), 'obey your Parents in the Lord: for this is right,'[2] a text William Gouge placed at the beginning of his section on the duties of children in his influential devotional treatise, *Of Domesticall Duties* (1622).[3] The message appears simple enough. But in the post-Reformation age of religious division and strife, contemporaries were well aware of problems the Apostle chose not to explore. There was a potential tension between the two parts of the command, for what if obedience to parents would mean disobeying God's commands? Did obedience to God come first? Yet disobeying parents inevitably meant breaking the Fifth Commandment God had conveyed to Moses. And in his epistle to the Colossians, Saint Paul had declared unequivocally, 'Children obey your parents *in all things*' (Colossians 3:20, emphasis added).[4] Many households in early modern England,

and throughout Europe, were strained by religious differences between husbands and wives, parents and children, employers and servants. And many of those affected faced a struggle of conscience to identify the morally and spiritually correct way forward, for on this issue there were two competing fathers. God the Father had bestowed divine authority on the biological father, so how was a tormented son or daughter to honour and obey both?

This essay focuses on fathers and sons in the mid-seventeenth century, when the division between Catholic and Protestant was further complicated by the emergence of new sects and denominations. Religious tensions and conflict between parents and adolescent or young adult children could become a significant element in family life, one that remains relatively neglected in modern scholarship.[5] In this essay I explore how such children attempted to reconcile duty to parents with the devotion they owed God, in struggles recorded in their diaries and autobiographies. Many painfully forged their own devotional identities, following their new faith while still acknowledging a divinely ordained duty to their parents. But that duty was now radically redefined and circumscribed. They must still honour parents, and obey them in worldly matters, but they believed they could no longer accept traditional devotional duties, such as kneeling to ask parental blessing or attending family prayers.

Radical sects and divided families

The issue of incompatible religious duties, even among Protestants, had already surfaced before the English Civil War, within the Established Church itself. The autobiography of Laurence Clarkson (or Claxton), published in 1660, offers one such example. Clarkson was to end his days as a Muggletonian, but his religious odyssey began around 1630, when he was fifteen and still living with his parents in Preston. He and his elder brothers disliked the town's minister, refused to kneel to receive the sacrament, and would walk miles to hear fiery puritan preachers in other parishes. The minister eventually warned their father that his children were 'going into Heresie', which would bring trouble both for him and them, and public disgrace. All this 'did much incense our father', Clarkson recalled, 'but all to no purpose, for I thought it conscience to obey God before man'. Possibly Clarkson found it easier than others to resolve the conflict between competing moral and religious obligations, but his decision to forge his own path was not without its attendant problems. He remembered how his father would 'cast a strict eye over me', and make him read aloud from the Prayer Book and Bishop Bayly's *Practice of Piety*, a popular book of devotion, until they all fell asleep. The 'next thing I scrupled', he added, 'was asking my parents blessing', an issue that was to trouble Quaker converts a generation later. He thought God would not listen to the prayers of a 'wicked man' (his father), and that it would offend God even to ask his father's blessing. He was reluctant, however, to trigger the angry confrontations Quaker converts were prepared to face. Instead, 'often times in the winter mornings, after I have been out of my bed, I have stood freezing above, and durst not come down till my father was gone abroad'. Sadly for us, Clarkson does not explain how this situation developed over the course of the next decade, before his move to London in the early 1640s.[6]

From the 1640s, issues of conscience and duty more often reflected a rather different set of circumstances: a son or daughter drawn away by a radical sectarian preacher, in defiance of parental wishes. After the Restoration, movement was sometimes in the opposite direction, with the offspring of puritan families choosing to conform to the Established Church, whether through conscience, peer pressure, material calculation or some combination of these.

Many father–son conflicts relate to the Quakers, who were, numerically, the most successful of the new movements, the most confrontational and the most visible, fired by their early dream of converting the entire nation, and indeed the whole world. Many of the early converts were young, which often led to conflict within their parents' or masters' homes. The best-documented story is perhaps that of Thomas Ellwood, the son of a Cromwellian gentleman and magistrate. Ellwood first encountered the Quakers in the winter of 1658–59, and was immediately attracted. His father detested the movement and forbade Thomas to attend Quaker meetings. Thomas's defiance brought him numerous beatings at the hands of his enraged father. The Quakers rejected conventional social gestures of respect and politeness, such as doffing one's hat, using the formal 'you' rather than familiar 'thou' and kneeling to ask one's parents' blessing. All this, of course, created repeated flashpoints for angry confrontation. Thomas was very conscious that in defying his father he was breaking God's Fifth Commandment. Could his new faith really be God's truth, he asked himself, if it led him to break God's own

Commandment? He pondered Saint Paul's guidance to the Ephesians, with its frustratingly ambiguous message. He eventually concluded that God required obedience only when parental commands were 'in the Lord', and that his father's commands were not. Ellwood went on to play a prominent role in the Quaker movement,[7] but he always remained sensitive to the charge of having failed in his duty to honour and obey his father. Twenty years after his conversion he was stung into publishing a pamphlet, *A Fair Examination of a Foul Paper* (1693), to vindicate his conduct, insisting that he had always honoured, obeyed and supported his father in everything compatible with his faith. He had always tried to minimise conflict between them, and was deeply pained that his duty to God had proved impossible to reconcile with his filial duty.[8]

A common pattern emerges in these accounts of divided families. Young converts faced a struggle of conscience over the duty they owed to their parents and to God, while parents experienced a struggle between warring emotions. For their part, fathers enraged by their children's disobedience and betrayal were often at the same time distressed by the dangers they now faced. Torn between anger and love, their behaviour could be wildly erratic. Walter Ellwood would furiously assault his son, but he was deeply distressed when Thomas slipped away and Walter feared he might never see him come home again. Walter later pulled strings to secure his son's release from prison, and then tried to keep him out of danger at home until his fit of madness (as Walter saw it) had passed. Even so, Thomas's conversion eventually resulted in a permanent rupture between father and son.[9]

The story of another early Quaker convert, Elias Osborn, has a different narrative arc but reveals similar emotions at play. Born in 1643 in rural Somerset, Osborn lost his mother at two and was raised by a caring father, who would take him to puritan lectures and repeat the preacher's message as they returned home. By the age of twelve, however, Osborn was starting to think for himself, and began to criticise the preachers as Pharisees and hypocrites. Alarmed by this development, his father would exclaim, 'Lord, what will come of this Boy?' In the event, it was several years before Osborn's critical spirit manifested itself more overtly. He became dissatisfied by the Prayer Book services reintroduced after the Restoration in 1660, and when he encountered the Quakers shortly afterwards he soon became a convert. His father and other close kin were appalled, he recalled, and 'their Lowly, humble, and in some respect, self-denying Zeal, turned to a harsh persecuting Temper'. He found moral support from a Quaker widow in the parish. Osborn soon fell in love with the widow's younger daughter and married her, despite his father's strong opposition. In this case, however, parental hostility proved less extreme, or at least less permanent. His father gradually came to terms with both his marriage and his faith, and became a loving parent once more. Like Walter Ellwood, he also worried about his son's safety during the periods of persecution. In his memoir, Osborn describes how his father came to regret his earlier hostility, and would say, 'He had been an unnatural Father to me, and I had been a dutiful son to him.' It is striking to find Osborn raising the issue of conscience and family duty, and applying it to his father as well as himself. He was evidently anxious for it to be known that his father had acknowledged his own failings, and that as a son he had been faithful in his filial duty as well as his duty to God. As with Ellwood, and many others alienated from their parents, the issue remained permanently sensitive.[10]

Many young converts, whatever their new faith, felt a deep sense of unease over the competing loyalties they now faced. But a few, especially among the early Quakers, brought a more confrontational spirit even to family relationships. One striking example is the story of John Horsey. Raised in Somerset, Horsey moved to London in the mid or late 1650s to become an apprentice, and joined the Quakers. In 1663 he returned to Somerset to visit friends and family, and found a cold welcome from his father. Thomas Horsey, the veteran minister of Somerton, 'turned him out of doors, with terrible threatening'. John ignored the threats and a few days later felt moved by the Spirit to enter the parish church where his father was conducting the Sunday service, 'to proclaim repentance to him and the people'. This was a direct confrontation and challenge, son against father, Quaker against Anglican priest. Horsey's father, outraged, had him arrested and packed off to Ilchester gaol, and at the next quarter-sessions urged magistrates to commit him to Bridewell. They apparently viewed the call as vindictive, and set the young man free. Horsey's story, alas, did not end happily. The following year, back in London, he was imprisoned in Newgate, and was one of the first Quakers to be sentenced to transportation. An epidemic broke out among the prisoners crammed together in the ship that was to carry them, and Horsey was among the many to perish even before the ship had passed Gravesend.[11]

Conscience and conformity: the troubles of Isaac Archer

The Restoration created a related and equally difficult issue in many puritan families: compliance, not conversion. Compliance had been a key issue in the Henrician and Elizabethan Reformations, and again in the 1640s and after the Restoration. Many hundreds of ministers had stepped down or been ousted during these upheavals, with many others remaining in their posts, often uneasy about what they should do and how far compliance should go. There were also, especially after the Restoration, many families where the issue of compliance divided father from son. The story of Isaac Archer and his father William saw the familiar problem of incompatible obligations to the human and divine fathers played out in this context. And in this case Isaac could never bring himself to give his complete allegiance to either God or his father.

Isaac Archer's diary records his concerns in detail over many years, and also reveals much about his father's attitudes and emotions.[12] The only son of a deeply committed Independent minister, Isaac agonised over whether to conform to the restored Church of England. Such a step would save his place at Trinity College Cambridge and his dream of a clerical career, but it would also require him to disobey his father, and flout his judgement. Isaac had deep respect for his father, and was certain he was among the elect. Far less sure about his own condition, he struggled for years to find a sense of grace, and repeatedly turned to his father for help and guidance. He also had his own serious misgivings about the Anglican Church and its rituals.[13] All this tipped the scales towards obeying his father, but other factors complicated the issue. Isaac was an undergraduate, living in college, and in 1660 he came under huge pressure to conform. Henry Dearsly, a protective college fellow, went out of his way to make conformity as easy as possible, and Isaac referred to him gratefully as 'my father'. And it was this college father, of course, that he was seeing almost every day. Early in 1661 he was allowed to proceed BA without having subscribed to the articles accepting the royal supremacy, the Thirty-Nine Articles and the Prayer Book.[14] Moreover, his real father, though a spiritual colossus, was authoritarian, parsimonious and short-tempered. If Isaac refused to conform he would have no career and become wholly dependent on his father's unpredictable goodwill.[15]

Isaac Archer's crisis of conscience lasted for over two years, and arguably for a lifetime. He was often melancholy and troubled, doubtful about his salvation, and torn between conflicting pressures at home and in college. He became very conscious of the looming dilemma several months before the king returned. By January 1660 many people at Cambridge were happy at the growing prospect of the return of both monarchy and the old Established Church of England, or at least willing to swim with the tide. At home, by contrast, Isaac's father and his friends viewed events with growing dismay. In the period immediately following the Restoration Isaac led a double life, troubled in conscience and anxious to 'keep my good name, as I called it'. At Cambridge he attended nonconformist gatherings in the town, while in college he posed as a conformist.[16] When he went back home in April 1661 he tried to equivocate. He told his father that he was not conforming, when in fact he had been attending Prayer Book services, simply making a token gesture by not wearing a surplice. A huge row erupted when William discovered this deceit. Isaac had disobeyed him, and by breaking the Fifth Commandment had sinned against God. He vowed never to see Isaac again 'till I had humbled my selfe for my disobedience to him, and sin against God'. In future, he raged, Isaac could find his own livelihood, or leave college and become an apprentice, a prospect which horrified Isaac. Back at Cambridge, however, friends assured him that fatherly authority did not extend to matters of religion, and he knew of others in college who had 'crossed their parents in such things'. He persuaded himself he had therefore not committed the sin of disobedience, and it followed that he had not sinned against God.[17]

Over the next few months, father and son exchanged a series of heated letters, with Isaac now 'sawcily' defending the Prayer Book, even though he did not wholly believe his own arguments. He admitted later that his combative nature had been guiding his pen. All this drove his father to still greater fury. He told Isaac 'he never thought that one sprung from his loynes would plead for Baal, and that if he thought I adored those abominable idols, and danced to that molten calfe etc, he would come and stampe it to powder, and make mee drinke it'. That astonishing outburst gives us a flavour of the passions unleashed by their quarrel. William added that he would rather see his son dead than wearing a surplice, and that he should study the Fifth Commandment, to learn the duty of obedience.[18]

William felt angry and betrayed but, as with Thomas Ellwood's father, rage was often tempered by the pull of parental affection. As Isaac recalled, his father 'for love's sake did intreat mee not to breake his heart, or goe against his mind. This did melt mee, and many struglings I had.' His conscience was deeply troubled, 'yet my desire of living in the colledge' and distrust of his father's vague and unreliable promise of maintenance weighed even more heavily.[19] In December 1661 his father warned that if he conformed he would have to shift for himself and discover 'how my idoll would maintain mee'. Isaac took this to mean he was being disowned and disinherited. He replied with a letter bidding his father adieu forever, which made his father still more angry and hurt. William later insisted he had been misunderstood and had never meant to disown his son, declaring (rather ambiguously) that 'he was more to mee then all the world'. In August 1662 he urged Isaac to leave Cambridge rather than subscribe to the new Act of Uniformity, promising an allowance if he did so. But he would still not commit to any specific sum, and Isaac refused. He pleaded conscience, though he later admitted that pride and resentment played a larger part. Isaac had argued that he and his father were both subjects of the King and duty-bound to obey his commands, whereupon William declared that his authority as a father outweighed the King's, 'for magistracy', he insisted, 'is founded upon family government'.[20] It was an extraordinary and indeed seditious claim.

It was, in any case, already too late to turn back, for Isaac had been conforming since Easter. The college authorities had displayed considerable skill in drawing him into the fold. They allowed him to return and promised to support him, since his father would not. Within a few months they had persuaded Bishop Wren to ordain him deacon and priest while still under the canonical age of twenty-one, and found him a small living in the college's gift.[21] Isaac went on to a long but deeply uneasy career in the Anglican Church. He continued to struggle with his conscience, and remorse prompted numerous lamentations in his diary. 'The Lord in mercy forgive my unnaturall carriage to a good father', he wrote on one occasion, 'who mourned over my sinful behaviour!' Moreover, he still felt uneasy about the restored Church. As a minister, he would rush through services, leaving out substantial parts of the liturgy to ease his conscience. Sometimes he omitted everything except the psalm and the lessons, and commented wryly that the congregation never complained. Whenever possible he hired a curate to read the service, and confined himself to preaching, behaving more as a parish lecturer than a vicar.[22]

William Archer gradually came to terms with the situation, up to a point. He sent his son advice on preaching and copies of his old sermons as models, and gave feedback on a few of Isaac's own sermons.[23] But the situation always remained difficult, in both spiritual and family terms. In 1664, when he could not find a reader, Isaac said he would now be willing to drop out of the Anglican Church if his father would promise to maintain him. But his father would still not guarantee any fixed level of support, so Isaac would always remain dependent on his goodwill.[24] William, a staunch parliamentarian, apparently saw arbitrary rule as the appropriate form of government within the household. Isaac did not agree.

There were new sources of tension in the years that followed. In 1664, for example, William blocked his son's marriage plans. Isaac had fallen in love with the daughter of a nonconformist minister, seemingly an ideal match, but his father regarded her portion as too small. Isaac then refused to marry the woman his father suggested.[25] Three years later he did marry, without William's approval, which provoked another bitter row. They eventually patched things up once again, and Isaac commented that his father's heart was softened 'so as to give mee an estate, and forgive mee the wrong I had done him; and, I know not how, my heart was inclined to love, and obey him'.[26] But there was to be no happy ending. When William died in 1670, he left behind a bombshell in the form of a vindictive will. He bequeathed the estate not to Isaac, now his only surviving child, but in trust to Isaac's children, to inherit at twenty-one. Isaac was to have no access to the estate or any income from it. It was a vengeful act, all the more perverse because Isaac had no living children, which threw everything into legal confusion. The restrictive provisions were eventually declared void, and Isaac was able to gain possession of the estate. He tried to convince himself that the episode had been a remarkable illustration of divine providence. God had punished his sin of disobedience, and then, in the light of his penitence, had forgiven him.[27]

After his father's death Isaac went over their letters again, mulling over their long and difficult relationship. He tried to acknowledge 'the good I have gotten by his savoury counsels'. He was mortified by a passage where his father had warned that disobedience to parents would prove a 'sting to the conscience all one's days'. Isaac commented ruefully, 'I find it a sting indeed, now he is dead.' He burned many of his father's letters and his own, unwilling for them ever to be read by others. For many years, well into the 1680s, he continued to brood over his former disobedience.[28]

Isaac Archer's lifelong anguish over the Fifth Commandment, spelled out in perhaps unparalleled detail, underlines the strength of its hold. Thomas Ellwood, Elias Osborn and many others felt similar anxiety and guilt. They, however, became certain they were following God's light in converting to their new faith. Isaac Archer, by contrast, always remained full of doubts. He admired his father as a devout, steadfast and scrupulous Christian, with an intellect and judgement far superior to his own. And he recognised that his own decisions had been influenced, to a troubling extent, by worldly concerns. Had his conscience guided him right? Or, as he feared, had self-interest silenced what his conscience and his father had been telling him?

Authority and love: the father's conflict

We hear William Archer's words only as they were mediated by his son within his diary. Seldom, if ever, do we hear from the parents themselves as children struggled with issues of conscience over family and religious obligations. What we do sometimes hear, however, are the worries of godly parents troubled by offspring who proved ungodly and reprobate. It was not unusual for children raised in deeply religious households to rebel in adolescence, presenting their parents with difficult decisions about how to respond. Ralph Josselin, a parish clergyman in Essex, and Henry Newcome, a prominent nonconformist minister in Manchester, provide two striking and well-documented examples of such a situation. Both had sons who rebelled against the values of the godly household in which they had been raised. Both fathers struggled for years with warring emotions of love, anger, hope and despair. And both worried endlessly about how best to help and reclaim their wayward offspring.

Josselin's second son John, born in 1651, appears to have been a troubled child from an early age. His family sent him to London in January 1667, aged fifteen, to be apprenticed, but he soon abandoned his place and returned home, to the family's dismay.[29] In October 1668 Josselin's diary records mournfully that John had gone back to London 'under a sentence of death, having no hopes in him as formerly, the lord trieth my faith, and the hopes for mercy from god for him'. This bleak assessment suggests that he already saw his son as spiritually lost. It was not long before John had dropped out of his apprenticeship and returned home again, hoping to earn a livelihood trading in the country. His swearing and debauchery reduced Josselin to despair. 'A sad weeke with John,' he sighed in February 1671, 'his cariage intolerable, uncertain what to resolve. Lord direct mee.'[30] Over the next few years Josselin recorded with dismay his son's lying, stealing, idleness, lewdness, disobedience and drunkenness. 'John is John,' he wrote despondently, 'but I will hope in god'.[31] There were flashes of hope, and once he was amazed to find his son writing out sermons, but such hopes were soon dashed. John 'sets himself on evill', he wrote on one occasion, and 'all our endeavours have the sentence of death on them'.[32] In October 1674 Josselin presented his son with an ultimatum, in the presence of his wife and four daughters. If John would mend his ways, Josselin would forgive all past offences and make him his heir; if he continued in his 'ill courses', however, he would be disinherited. John submitted, and a few weeks later he was brought to acknowledge his 'debauchery'. But there was no sign of the promised amendment, and in January 1675 'John [was] declared for his disobedience no son.' Yet even now Josselin was prepared to allow him £10 a year if he would enter service and behave responsibly, and 'if he so walkt as to become gods son, I should yett own him for mine'.[33] Love still battled with anger in Josselin's heart, along with despair; 'oh why is my son a shame of youth, my soules greife', he cried to God a few months later. On one occasion John was almost killed in a quarrel with one of his drinking companions, and in December 1675 the diary records: 'this weeke John wholly out in his filthy courses, I am resolved to leave him to thee oh god, only I will pray for him'.[34] John married in 1681, without telling his parents, but there is no indication that this led to any significant change. Even so, Josselin could never quite abandon his delinquent son. John was now his only surviving son and when Josselin died, in 1683, he left him the bulk of his estate, despite their stormy history.[35]

The troubled relationship between Henry Newcome and his second son Daniel, born in 1652, offers many parallels to this story. In September 1668 Newcome and his wife took Daniel to London to be bound apprentice. He had arranged a prospective master, a milliner, who appeared civil and good-natured but, as Newcome quickly realised, was not at all religious. Moreover he dealt only in wholesale trade and Newcome knew Daniel would never have the capital to set up in wholesale business himself. So he took Daniel away and placed him with a more religious master. Daniel did not settle, however, poured out his woes and refused to be formally bound. He eventually changed his mind, which allowed his parents to return home. But in December Newcome received a letter with 'the saddest news that ever I had in my life', reporting Daniel's gross misconduct. 'It is a great sorrow, bitter, reaches to the very heart,' Newcome lamented, 'and it is a sorrow I can see no end of'. Things deteriorated further, and after Daniel had run away, twice, Newcome and his wife travelled back to London in 1670 to decide what to do. 'The poor child was gotten linked with vile knaves that had made a prey of him,' he wrote, 'and he could not stir in any place for them'. Daniel had presumably run up heavy gaming or drinking debts, but Newcome's anger was still outweighed by pity and love. Daniel could not stay in London and did not want to return home, so it was eventually decided to send him to serve a planter in Jamaica. Newcome described seeing him off 'with a rueful heart, and the sad cries of his poor mother I shall not quickly forget'.[36] He wanted the best for their child, and was by no means certain this was the best solution. As time passed without news, he began to fear Daniel's ship might have been involved in a fight with Barbary corsairs, reported in the newspapers, and that he might have been killed or captured and enslaved. Letters from Daniel eventually arrived, confirming he was safe but voicing a fear that he had been tricked and would be sold into servitude in Jamaica. Newcome was dismayed. If Daniel's fears turned out to be true, his fate would be on his father's conscience. In the event they proved unfounded, and when his master died in 1672, Daniel returned home safely.[37]

This was far from the end of his parents' worries. In 1675 Daniel married secretly. Newcome had no objection to the marriage, except that the bride was underage, but was deeply hurt that he had not been consulted. The following year brought further troubles. Daniel had run up heavy debts, and to clear them Newcome was forced to sell land that had been intended for his son's inheritance. In 1678 Daniel's young wife bore a daughter, Jane, but died a few weeks later. In 1680 we find Newcome wailing, 'I had much grief and sorrow about Daniel, sometimes in trouble, sometimes in sin, sometimes wronged, sometimes forsaken by his friends, and sometimes at variance with us, and sometimes not well.' Like Josselin, Newcome was torn by conflicting emotions, unsure how best to handle a wayward son.[38] Daniel had remarried within a few months, but he and his new wife proved abysmal parents. Little Jane was so badly ill-used that it became a public scandal, and Newcome and his wife 'were clamoured upon that no course was taken about her'. Eventually, in 1683, a neighbour stepped in and took the child away. Newcome, though mortified, acknowledged that the intervention had been necessary. He complained that Daniel and his new wife continued to behave 'wretchedly and rudely, after their shameful abuse of the child. It is an affliction and shame to me'.[39] Early in 1684 Daniel fell ill, with a lingering sickness that was to prove fatal. Newcome's duty was now more straightforward: he must make his son ready to meet his Maker.[40] Daniel was eventually brought to acknowledge his sins and repudiate his former companions as 'wicked men, that derided religion, and made a mock of hell'. That gives us a glimpse of how completely he had rejected everything his father stood for. Newcome still hoped his son might recover, partly because of the guilt and shame he would face if he proved unable to prevent his son dying a notorious reprobate. Daniel's apparent belated penitence came as a huge relief, and when he died, on 8 February, Newcome could not help reflecting that by his death 'disgrace was prevented'.[41] Newcome's other son Henry had caused a different kind of heartache a few years earlier, by rejecting his father's nonconformist principles and becoming a minister in the Anglican Church. Newcome wrote sadly that 'his conformity is a kind of reflection upon me', but he proved far more forgiving than Archer's father.[42]

Fathers accepted their duty to protect, guide and support their children. Their duty was less clear, however, when they met with persistent defiance and delinquency. Newcome loved his son Daniel and longed to reclaim him, but he was also conscious that his wayward behaviour was bringing shame and scandal on the family and his ministry. Youthful converts struggled to reconcile duty to parents with their duty to God. Worried fathers faced a rather similar challenge: how to reconcile parental love with their duty to uphold God's commands. They might cling to the principle of hating the sin while loving the sinner, but for how long could that position be sustained? It exposed them to charges of connivance, double standards and hypocrisy. Josselin and Newcome found it painfully hard to answer such questions.

Fathers and sons, then, both faced problems in accommodating family ties and responsibilities to the duty they owed God. The dilemma was most acute for sons (and indeed daughters), faced with the blunt instruction of the Fifth Commandment.[43] But society insisted that fathers also had obligations, a point stressed by the domestic conduct books of the age and reflected in its cultural values. When George Chute disinherited his eldest son in 1616, a friend told him sternly that God 'exacteth as well a duety from the father to the children, as from the children to the father'. He urged Chute to re-examine his conscience.[44] Religion was not at issue in this instance. When religion did divide families, issues of conscience over incompatible obligations became deeply painful for parents and children alike. Diaries and autobiographies were the chosen vehicles through which adult children recorded their spiritual struggles and sought to justify the new devotional identities they had fashioned, to themselves, to God and to others. Intended in part for the edification of family members and co-religionists, such self-writings, especially autobiographies, were frequently bequeathed to kin, and were often read and treasured for generations.[45]

Notes

1 *An Hundred Godly Lessons* (London, 1674–79), ballad. I owe this reference to Robert W. Daniel.
2 Exact wording appears in both the Geneva and King James Bibles.
3 William Gouge, *Of Domesticall Duties* (London, 1622), p. 427.
4 Exact wording appears in both the Geneva and King James Bibles.
5 On this theme see Bernard Capp, *The Ties that Bind: Siblings, Family, and Society in Early Modern England* (Oxford: Oxford University Press, 2018), pp. 124–41.
6 Laurence Claxton, *The Lost Sheep Found* (London, 1660), pp. 4–5.
7 Ellwood would go on to edit the Quaker leader George Fox's *Journal*. See chapter 8.

8 Thomas Ellwood, *The History of the Life of Thomas Ellwood*, ed. C. G. Crump (London: Methuen, 1900), pp. 9–41; Thomas Ellwood, *A Fair Examination of a Foul Paper* (London, 1693), pp. 20–1.
9 Ellwood, *History*, pp. 35, 67.
10 Elias Osborn, *A Brief Narrative of the Life, Labours and Sufferings of Elias Osborn* (London, 1723), pp. 16–23, 28–9. Cf. E. Pearman, 'Typological Autobiography in Seventeenth-Century England', *Biography* 8.2 (1985), 95–118.
11 Joseph Besse, *The Sufferings of the Quakers*, 2 vols (London, 1753), II:592; George Whitehead *et al.*, *A Brief Account of some of the Late and Present Sufferings of the People called Quakers* (London, 1680), p. 107.
12 See Isaac Archer, 'The Diary of Isaac Archer 1641–1700', in Matthew Storey (ed.), *Two East Anglian Diaries, 1641–1729* (Woodbridge: Boydell, 1994), pp. 41–185. All quotes from Archer's diary are taken from this edition.
13 *Ibid.*, pp. 64–5.
14 *Ibid.*, p. 68.
15 *Ibid.*, pp. 56–7, 82.
16 *Ibid.*, pp. 66–8.
17 *Ibid.*, pp. 69, 72.
18 *Ibid.*, pp. 69, 72–4.
19 *Ibid.*, pp. 72–3.
20 *Ibid.*, pp. 80–2.
21 *Ibid.*, pp. 78, 80–5.
22 *Ibid.*, pp. 80, 97.
23 *Ibid.*, pp. 86–7, 92–5.
24 *Ibid.*, pp. 97, 99, 102, 104.
25 *Ibid.*, p. 99.
26 *Ibid.*, pp. 113–15, 117.
27 *Ibid.*, pp. 115, 123–4, 136.
28 *Ibid.*, pp. 126–33.
29 Ralph Josselin, *The Diary of Ralph Josselin 1616–1683*, ed. Alan Macfarlane (London: Oxford University Press for the British Academy, 1976), pp. 532, 534, 538. See also Alan Macfarlane, *The Family Life of Ralph Josselin* (Cambridge: Cambridge University Press, 1970), pp. 120–4. Macfarlane suggests that sibling rivalry may explain John's truculent behaviour, though the diary provides no evidence, and John eventually asked to be buried by his brother.
30 Josselin, *Diary*, pp. 544, 551, 555, 557–8.
31 *Ibid.*, pp. 559–61, 564, 579.
32 *Ibid.*, pp. 568, 573, 579, 581.
33 *Ibid.*, pp. 580–2.

34 *Ibid.*, pp. 585, 590, 594–5.
35 *Ibid.*, p. 634; Macfarlane, *Family Life*, pp. 211–13.
36 Henry Newcome, *The Autobiography of Henry Newcome*, ed. Richard Parkinson, Chetham Society, 26 (London, 1852), pp. 170–84.
37 *Ibid.*, pp. 186–7, 192–5, 200.
38 *Ibid.*, pp. 215–17, 225, 234.
39 *Ibid.*, pp. 228, 245, 248.
40 For the religious tradition of 'dying well' in England see chapters 13 and 14.
41 *Ibid.*, pp. 252–4.
42 *Ibid.*, pp. 208, 254.
43 For troubled daughters, such as Anne Upcott and Agnes Beaumont, see Capp, *Ties that Bind*, p. 128 and sources there cited.
44 John Holles, *Letters of John Holles 1587–1637*, ed. P. R. Seddon, Thoroton Society, 31, 35, 3 vols (Nottingham, 1975, 1983), I:111–12.
45 For religious life-writings as familial and social documents see Andrew Cambers, 'Reading, the Godly, and Self-Writing in England, circa 1580–1720', *Journal of British Studies* 46.4 (2007), 796–825; Robert W. Daniel, '"Have a little book in thy Conscience, and write therein": Writing the Puritan Conscience, 1600–1650', in Jonathan Willis (ed.), *Sin and Salvation in Reformation England* (London: Taylor and Francis, 2016), pp. 245–58.

10

Dissenting devotion and identity in *The Experience* of Mary Franklin (*d.* 1711)*

Vera J. Camden

The 24 August 1662 was referred to by the English dissenters as Black Bartholomew's Day, when nearly two thousand puritan ministers were 'ejected' from their pulpits and their livings.[1] From the standpoint of the history of the English dissenters, 'The Great Ejection' is part of the defeat suffered by the Republican cause following the Restoration of Charles II. Robert Franklin (1630–1703), a Cambridge-educated Presbyterian minister, was among the ejected ministers. He was first imprisoned in 1670 and several times thereafter in the tumultuous years that include the Exclusion Crisis and end with the Revolution of 1688. Mary Franklin (*d.* 1711), whom Robert married in 1669, writes about her experience of these years later in her life. She takes up a notebook that had contained her husband's sermon notes, turns it upside down, and writes on its blank pages the story of her experience of these troubled years. Mary Franklin's granddaughter, Hannah Burton (1723–86), some one hundred years after the composition of her grandmother's narrative, admiringly creates its title page within the manuscript notebook: 'The Experience of my dear grandmother, Mrs Mary Franklin' (see figure 10.1), while further adding to the notebook's remaining blank pages a diary of her own experience as an eighteenth-century dissenting widow. This essay will discuss how Mary Franklin's *Experience* chronicles what it was like to be a dissenting minister's wife in Restoration London

---

* I would like to thank Valentino L. Zullo for his editorial assistance with this essay.

Figure 10.1 This page encapsulates the enduring legacy of Mary Franklin's papers, showing the handwritten title Franklin's granddaughter gave to her writings as well as the stamp of the Congregational Library that later received it.

amidst 'the great persecution of 1660–1688'.[2] In doing so, it reveals how Franklin's devotion protected her against the tribulations of persecution and defined her identity as a dissenter.

That Mary Franklin writes about her experience late in her life, possibly after the death of her husband but certainly after the storm of persecution has past, reveals her determination to document these events for her family but also for future readers. That Mary Franklin's narrative circulated following her death is confirmed by the fact that the esteemed divine Benjamin Grosvenor (1676–1758) cites it at length in the funeral sermon he preached for her. That her narrative is carefully preserved by her children is manifested in the fact that her granddaughter, Hannah Burton, finds this notebook amongst her grandmother's 'private papers', names it, and reflects upon its record of devotion in the pages of her own diary. That Samuel Palmer (1741–1813) commemorates the life of Robert Franklin drawing from these same valuable papers entrusted to him by 'Mrs. Hannah Burton' for the purpose of his accounts of the lives of nonconformist ministers (including the memoir of Robert Franklin himself that is now lost),[3] indicates their historical value to dissenting history. That an eighteenth-century fair-copy version entitled 'The Experience of a Minister's Wife, Who Lived in the Last Century' is extant proves the continued interest and afterlife of Mary Franklin's narrative as it circulated in manuscript.[4] That Hannah Burton's son-in-law, William Bailey, husband of her daughter Rebekah, entrusts the family papers to nineteenth-century collector Joshua Wilson, patron of the Congregational Library, sustains their value to the archives of dissenters.[5] That the editors of the *Transactions of the Congregational Library* at the dawn of the twentieth century produced an early 'edition' entitled 'The Experiences of Mary Franklin',[6] indicates, once again, the enduring interest of this historical and spiritual witness (see figure 10.1). Now, in the twenty-first century, these manuscript writings have been transcribed into an edition for scholars and readers alike, providing a rare glimpse into the faith and the fortitude of an early modern family, whose devotion – and identity – is defined by dissent.[7]

Mary Franklin's *Experience* shows – in a spare but richly dramatised account – how early modern household devotion evolved as a protected, even holy, space because of the call to worship according to one's conscience and not to the conformity of the Established Church. As Erica Longfellow asserts, 'from the 1640s onward, the notion that the conscience rather than the state should govern religious decision-making introduced the idea that this area of individual life was to be rightly protected from the state. A private life that encompassed both interiority and freedom from the state was slowly brought to birth.'[8] This essay shows how an early modern woman used her private devotions to create an identity that could defy, and defend itself against, public persecution. Dissent cost Franklin dearly, as we shall see, within her heart and in her household. Her pious interiority takes on quite a literal, concrete definition when conceived in terms of her household, and the immortal souls that dwell within, who when faced with destruction are sustained by the promise of a 'building of God, an house not made with hands' (2 Corinthians 5:1).[9]

Mary Franklin and the cost of dissent

Under the strictures of the Clarendon Code, in 1670, Robert Franklin was imprisoned for illegally holding conventicles and was sent to Aylesbury jail, some thirty miles from his home in London. He was separated from his young, pregnant wife, whom he had married the previous year. Robert will be imprisoned several times over the next two decades, while English dissenting congregations suffer continual persecution during the last decades of the Stuart monarchy. We know about Mary Franklin's experience of these two decades because, much later in life, she repurposes one of her husband's unfinished sermon notebooks to tell the story of what these years of persecution were like for herself and her family. She reports living under constant surveillance, the invasion of her home and harassment by the authorities. The narrative of her *Experience* chronicles in rare, often raw detail what happened to her while her husband was in and out of prison and she was left to defend home and family during the political and religious turmoil of Restoration London.[10] She would bear ten children, only three of whom survived to adulthood. Early in her narrative Franklin describes how she delivered a stillborn child during her husband's first imprisonment, while she was a new wife. She writes, 'It pleased God I went out my full time, and after very sore and hard labor I was delivered of a large man-child, but it was still-born, which was judged by most, to be occasioned by my grief that I had upon me by reason of my husband's being so far from me in my condition.'[11]

For Mary Franklin, piety takes on an unflinching demeanour when it is assailed by political and religious persecution. Devotion provides her, precisely, with an impenetrable defence against the assaults she suffers from external foes and internal temptations to discouragement. She thus connects the persecution she is suffering to the call of conscience and to the price of her piety. Her account captures how she braces for the spiritual battles that unfold around her daily in her home and congregation. She assesses the trials of her faith and corresponding fortitude of her household and her church. 'The people of God' must expect trouble and must identify with Christ not only in suffering but in wielding the 'sword' of the Spirit against the devil and his instruments. As Franklin knew from experience, peace was only periodic, however longed for. She writes:

> And when this storm was over, we enjoyed peace again for a little season. It hath been the usual lot of the church and people of God to enjoy but short uninterrupted visits from God, either with respect to the inward presence of his spirit, or his outward presence of his ordinances. For while there is a devil and wicked men his instruments, there being such an enmity in their natures, one against an other, the people of God must expect trouble. Our blessed Lord, that was our example and pattern in suffering of affliction, he hath told us that in the world we must expect trouble (Matthew 5); *in the world ye shall have tribulation* (John 16:33). But for our comfort he hath likewise told us that in him we shall have peace. Our blessed Lord hath likewise told, *think not* (saith he) *that I am come to send peace on earth: I came not, not to send peace, but a sword ... a man's foes shall be they of his own household* (Matthew 10:34–6).[12]

For Mary Franklin, as for her husband, devotion is above all an active expression of faith: spiritual or contemplative practices in the inner person show themselves in outer manifestations. Her suffering and her sacrifice are recorded as signs of her salvation as well as service to Christ. Devotion is a living, active defence of the faith, that is made particularly tangible in the creation of her manuscript: its preservation and circulation through the centuries perpetuates that active intervention. The dissenting doctrines that propelled her husband's arrests and two-decades-long intermittent imprisonment will at the same time serve to sustain her spirit. Scripture supports these doctrines and provides an interpretation of the events that now beset her ('in the world ye have tribulation') but it also provides her comfort ('but be of good cheer, I have overcome the world')

(John 16:33). These doctrines inspire her further to document the meaning of persecution within her own personal history.

Mary Franklin's *Experience* therefore stands out as a theological, historical and personal witness to these turbulent times for English dissenters as it interweaves domestic detail into devotional witness to God's grace and providence. For example, in the same way that, as N. H. Keeble points out, John Bunyan's *Prison Meditations* reveal a deepening devotion fostered by his imprisonment,[13] so too Mary Franklin's record of her trials – amidst the pervasive atmosphere of harassment and surveillance – reveals a deepening dependence on faith and the conviction that her suffering was made meaningful by her obedience to a higher law than the government's. Her record of this experience and these times is recollected in the tranquillity of a new and more tolerant political order. But its memories are fresh and meant to provide an enduring witness for generations to come.

The shape of Mary Franklin's *Experience*

Mary Franklin's narrative does not follow the expected format of the conventional spiritual autobiography, in which the sinner describes the profligacy of his youth, his conviction of sin and failed attempts at reform, and his ultimate embrace of unmerited grace and dramatic conversion, however prolonged.[14] This is the form that proliferated in the seventeenth century amongst those whom William York Tindall called the 'unremembered class' of 'mechanick' preachers, yet finding its enduring expression in John Bunyan's *Grace Abounding to the Chief of Sinners* (1666).[15] Mary Franklin declares, by contrast, that she cannot specify the time of her conversion:

> As for the time of my conversion, I cannot give account, being from my childhood instructed by my parents in the concerns of my soul. They took great care of me and the rest of their children, teaching us catechisms and the Holy Scriptures; as the wise man's counsel is to *train up a child in the way he should go, and when he is old he will not depart from it* (Proverbs 22:6).[16]

She cautions, however, that she does not 'rest upon my education'.[17] Rather, she daily seeks the Lord's will. Her brief account of her early life includes the providence of surviving and witnessing the Great Fire of London, yet despite the impressive impact of this conflagration, the momentum of Mary Franklin's narrative inexorably leads to her meeting and marrying her husband, Robert Franklin, who at that time was preaching in Blue Anchor Alley.

Mary Franklin propels her narrative towards the identification with the cause of the dissenters, going so far as to establish a 'pedigree' of her own heritage as having grandparents who were martyred as Protestants in the previous century. She says that her father 'used often to tell me that I had a great privilege above many others, that I might plead God's covenant, he being the God of my father; and my father's, father's God, to several generations; and that he was informed that some of his ancestors were martyrs for Jesus Christ'.[18] Franklin wants her family members, religious community and future readers to understand that she was not a convert to the cause of puritanism, but was born into this faith. Since childhood she was accustomed to hearing and admiring the ministers who had been punished for preaching, 'and from my childhood I had a love to good people, but especially ministers; my father's and grandmother's houses being both much frequented by such good company; and when any troubles arose, and they were threatened imprisonment for preaching, I thought if I might suffer with them I did not so much care, so I might not be deprived of their company'.[19] By this Franklin narratively establishes the providence that led her to Blue Anchor Alley, to the ministry of her husband, and to the call to sacrifice and suffer for the dissenters' cause.

Her narrative is therefore driven by a desire to describe and document the cost of dissent. Her devotion is double-edged: it is the cause of her persecution in the sense that she must follow her conscience and the cause of religious freedom that subjects the dissenters to government crackdowns, in whatever century. But at the same time this devotion to the dissenters' doctrine and church discipline, the call to gather for worship according to their own belief as is enjoined by scripture ('not forsaking the assembling of ourselves together' (Hebrews 10:25)), is the defence that best shields her from defeat and discouragement. Her narrative also seeks to document this devotional call and its cost in terms of God's providence amidst political turmoil. Thus, the driving purpose of her narrative is to testify to the events of her and her family's *experience* of persecution that culminated in her husband's repeated imprisonments, particularly those around what she describes as occurring 'when the troubles were about the Duke of Monmouth'.[20]

Keeble has persuasively shown that nonconformist writing of the Restoration years contrasted utterly with the spirit of the Restoration court and the great literature of 'the Age of Dryden and Pope': his insistence that the literature of this period is also exemplified in the works of Milton and Bunyan carries with it the realisation that the culture of nonconformity which was so productive under the pressures of the Stuart state also inspired above all things a 'heart religion' and an introspective faith that was fuelled by political contexts but preferred personal pilgrimage. 'Nonconformist writing was ... private in an age which was going public ... public affairs are dealt with from the point of view of one who experiences (and usually endures) their consequences.'[21] This particular pattern fostered in Mary Franklin the impulse to provide a record of her persecutions that resounds with her personal experience, including not only the reflections of her faith but also the domestic details that point to the plain speech that Bunyan also prefers as an anchor to his congregational witness.[22]

Mary Franklin's chronicle offers the reader domestic detail alongside the record of political persecution. She presents the reader with a window into the privacy of her home and family life, the very privacy that, ironically, she suffered to protect from the prying and pernicious eyes of government informers. Marginalia which include pencilled brackets and 'X's (see figure 10.2) tend to occur in the manuscript when there is a description of some aspect of her persecution, such as the time an informer comes in through the window and she forces him out; or the time the officers of the law wait outside her house with their carts for the Sabbath to be over so they can load up her goods and take them from her; or, indeed the time in the night when her husband is arrested under the 'Corporation Oath' and carted off to prison. The reader who thus marks particularly all such events of invasion, harassment and enforcement is interested in making note of such a vivid and immediate historical account of the persecution of this family during the decades of the seventeenth century. It was observed by Samuel Palmer when editing the *Nonconformist's Memorial* that Robert Franklin was particularly targeted and 'perpetually harassed' by frequent trials and imprisonments.[23] Mary Franklin notes nearly every such incident. She decidedly does not, as we have noted above, abide by the generic, repetitive structure of spiritual autobiography, which subsumes autobiographical particulars to the prevailing narrative conventions of doctrinal and spiritual edification. This is not her style of devotion, nor is it her about 10 months after the death of my dear father, there arose new troubles, by reason of informers, that went about to inform against ministers for their preaching, and got warrants from Justices to seaze upon their persons and goods, and amongst the rest God was pleased to count us worthy to suffer for his sake, but we haveing some warning before did remove some of our goods out of the house, the manner of their comeing was thus, Nov. 1684 being about +a clock+ Satturday in the afternoone, the door being some way or other curiesly left open, they got into the meeting place, which joyned near to our house, and I being in kitchen, with only my 3 children, one of them ~~~~ knockt at the kitchen door gently and pretended to have brought me a letter, but I looking through a hole made for the purpose I did suspect him, and I went and look through a place which looks into the meeting place where I saw more of them, then I knew we were beset, I immediatly laid up the bars of the doors, and run up to my husband (who was in his study) and told him that they were come, the mean while they did knock and thunder at the door as if they would have broke it down but not getting entrance that way, they got in the window of the hinges, and quickly got in there being no body to resist them, only a poor sickly child in the cradle, the other two children being in a great fright followed me up stairs. and when they were got in, they quickly came up to us, the informer had his drawn sword in his hand, he set his foot against the calling to convert wayward souls, as one might suggest of the evangelist Bunyan.

Mary Franklin perhaps believes that the primary readers of her narrative, including her family, will be of God's people. She is documenting for a dissenting reader the sacrifices she and others made to bring about the religious freedom of her current moment, in the post-1688 world of the Glorious Revolution. Her narrative dwells on the impact of her husband's ministry at Blue Anchor Alley (the street where they lived and worshipped, having added a room for the gathering of his congregation),[24] highlighting the details of her individual life keeping home and hearth safe for her children.

Mary Franklin reports the details of her domesticity predominantly to capture a harassed and harried household, absent her husband. No sooner does one child recover from an illness – 'Our child Betty was taken ill of a sudden in the night, her teeth set in her head, which we were forced to open with a spoon to get some thing down. We feared she had been struck with death' – than another child, the eldest daughter, Mary, suffers a fatal accident:

> The maid having taken from the fire a skillet of milk with bread in it, run against the child, and spilt it upon her; and the bread stuck upon her face and breast. We immediately stripped off her clothes and sent for a surgeon our uncle Smith; who, when he saw it, despaired of a cure, because he perceived the flesh was mortified and scalded as deep as her windpipe; of which, after nine days' illness of a fever and convulsion fits, she died.[25]

Such consolation as Mary Franklin can provide for the reader, as for herself, rests upon the report of her little daughter's faith and the miracle of her guardian angel appearing to take her away. Franklin states, 'she seemed to be in an agony, striking with her hand and crying God, no no! When none of us spoke to her; and immediately after she lift up both of her arms as if she had behold an Angel come to receive her up, and so departed.'[26] Franklin's trials reaffirm her faith; they are not seen as judgements. Furthermore, the devotion of her daughter into her dying hour reaffirms God's love. As a mother, Franklin does not for a minute relent from her sorrow; neither does she relent from the conviction that many of the domestic upheavals that beset herself and her family are provoked by the realistic threat that at any time, day or night, her peace might be disturbed by household invasion.

Mary Franklin's narrative breathlessly telescopes the sensation of being trapped within one's own home. In one striking paragraph concerning the 'troubles about the Duke of Monmouth' she documents date, time, actions, occasion and impact. I cite this passage at length to capture the precision of her account.

> November 1684 being about 4 o'clock Saturday in the afternoon, the door being some way or other carelessly left open, they got into the meeting place, which joined near to our house, and I being in [the] kitchen, with only my three children, one of them knocked at the kitchen door gently and pretended to have brought me a letter. But I (looking through a hole made for the purpose), I did suspect him; and I went and look[ed] through a place which looks into the meeting place, where I saw more of them. Then I knew we were beset. I immediately laid up the bars of the doors and ran up to my husband (who was in his study), and told him that they were come. The mean while they did knock and thunder at the door, as if they would have break it down. But not getting entrance that way, they got the window off the hinges, and quickly got in there being nobody to resist them; only a poor sickly child in the cradle. The other two children, being in a great fright, followed me up stairs; and when they were got in they quickly came up to us. The informer had his drawn sword in his hand, he set his foot against the chamber door where we were, and broke out a board of the door, and thrust back the lock with his hand, and came in, in a great fury, and laid hold of my husband, and told him, he was the King's prisoner, and would not suffer him to stir from them.[27]

The impact of such invasions on body as well as mind and soul are rendered with familiar metaphors: physical, marital and maternal function together to access an intimate vocabulary which itself challenges the existing hierarchies of conformist religious practices dictated, for instance, by the *Book of Common Prayer*. In the same way that Victoria Burke insists that 'the image of the believer as the spouse of Christ ... posed a political problem: such an intimate relationship of Christ and the believer by-passed authority and all constraint', so too Mary Franklin unfolds the disruptions of her world.[28] Her repeated descriptions of the disruption of nursing and how it necessitates premature weaning of her infants, among many other dangers and disasters that befall her, highlight the impact of the constant threat – and reality – of being invaded by government informers. The following passage shows the intertwining of her bodily fears when confronted with round-the-clock military surveillance with her prevailing comfort in the presence of God and the assurance of scripture that she is protected in her pregnancy:

> And at the same time our house was guarded by soldiers for a considerable time; every Lord's day they came by seven o'clock in the morning, and continued 'til seven at night. And though it was all the time of my lying-in, yet the Lord was pleased to support me that I got no harm, [n]or frights. He made good his word, *as the day is, so shall thy strength be* (Deuteronomy 33:25).[29]

Her sad conclusion, later in the narrative, is that such harassment hurt her more in her youth than later when she became used to such disruptions, but she still feels it enough to capture it now in her reminiscences.

> Some little time after there came forth new warrants to seize our goods, and the informers with some of the officers endeavoured often to get into our house, which occasion[ed] much disturbance to us. And at this time, I was with having a young child hanging on my breast, and I was forced to wean the child; my milk being disturbed, it did both me, and the child hurt. This being new work to me, I having not been much used to this kind of work, I was not so well able to bear it as, I bless the Lord, I have been since.[30]

Once such narrative thread has been established, her metaphors of her relationship to God become not only an imaginative comfort from which to draw her narrative, but also a way to describe the impact of the political force that now invades her home. The house is a place that is like the body and should be protected as a temple, a tabernacle for God.[31] For example, Franklin refers to her body as being made ill by her continual harassment and persecution. In one instance she states, 'An other time when by reason of some trouble I met with, which did very much discompose my spirits and all so caused some illness upon my body'.[32] She viscerally captures the suffering of her daughter Mary, who is burnt with a skillet of milk amidst household turmoil, yet keeps quiet: 'while the wounds were dressing she never cried out, but squeezed her fingers and bit in her pain'.[33] Thus her description of any psychical pain or physical suffering (illness, sick children, miscarriage, melancholia) becomes almost causally and even reciprocally associated with her description of persecution (home invasions, imprisonment, surveillance and official threats). From a political as well as a psychological standpoint, religious discourse fortifies her resistance to harassment and strengthens her resolve.

Mary Franklin also couches her world in the language of scripture, often choosing language that connects to her domesticity and the ways that her childbearing, struggles with low spirits and physical illness are relieved by answered prayer and scriptural messages. Kate Narveson points out how impactful the copying of scripture text was for the woman 'lay-writer' during the seventeenth century as an educative and devotional language that encouraged female composition and imitation, ultimately leading to a strong identification with biblical characters and appropriation of complex imaginative language.[34] Franklin's *Experience* reveals a deep saturation in biblical texts. When, for instance, she describes suffering from a 'private' melancholia that used to trouble her post-pregnancy lyings-in, she finds consolation in scripture. When a human 'relation' disappoints her, the scripture reaches her soul.

> It was my tenth child: but in the time of my lying-in, by reason of some private trouble I had, and it meeting with a melancholy humour which I used to be troubled with in my lyings-in, my spirits were extremely burdened, which did very much disordered my body, and hindered my rest for several nights. I endeavoured to seek help by making my complaint to a relation, where I hoped to have had some relief; but all to no purpose, my trouble was rather aggravated. Then I resolved to go to the Lord, and cast my burden upon him who hath in his word given encouragement to his [people] so to do *cast thy burden upon the Lord, and he shall sustain thee: he shall never suffer the righteous to be moved* (Psalm 55:22). *Commit thy works unto the Lord and thy thoughts shall be established* (Proverbs 16:3). *And call upon me in the day of trouble, I will deliver thee and thou shall glorify me* (Psalm 50:15). When the Lord had enabled me thus to do, in one night's time all my troubles was scattered and gone, and I was greatly composed and quieted. The Lord grant I may never forget this time for it, for it was very remarkable.[35]

The scripture from Isaiah in the following passage speaks directly to the ways that God promises to 'husband' the believer: the language of conjugal comfort and forgiveness consoles her flagging spirit, tempted perhaps by doubt and even despair.

> This day, January 18, I met with some great trouble, which did very much discompose my spirit, and also caused great illness upon my body. I had no rest until I went and laid open my case before the

Lord; and then I found ease, from that comfortable word in Isaiah: *for thy maker is thine husband the Lord of hosts is his name, and thy redeemer the holy of Israel, the God of the whole earth shall he be called. For the Lord hath called thee as a woman forsaken and grieved in spirit, and a wife of youth, whom thou hast refused saith thy God. For a small moment, have I forsaken thee, but with great mercies will I gather thee* (Isaiah 54:5–8).[36]

Mary Franklin's description of the realities of pregnancy, lyings-in, nursing, weaning and caring for her children coincides overwhelmingly with the years of persecution. She wishes for more 'weanedness' from the world, and its affections, including her attachment to her own infants, yet remains attuned to the needs of these children and the suffering that they too experience because of disturbances. As she writes, 'at this time I gave suck to my fourth child, Joanna, but these frights did so disturb my milk that I was forced to wean her; and after she was weaned, I bless the Lord, she did thrive better than before, and was bigger and stronger than any of the rest'.[37] Devotion here is defined as maternal diligence: her children's survival, safety and souls direct her testimony as much as any doctrine.[38] Keeble emphasises that the nonconformists' doctrines of divine love find inevitable expression in human relations. 'To know God is to enjoy his "intimate acquaintance" as a "friend" ... of his own household.'[39] Love between God and his people and between members of a household creates a sacred place.

Conclusion

It is notable that in her last will and testament, written in 1709, two years before her death,[40] Mary Franklin requests that at her funeral sermon the following scripture verse would be preached: 'For we know that if our earthly house of this tabernacle were dissolved, we have a building of God, an house not made of hands, eternal in the heavens' (2 Corinthians 5:1).[41] Benjamin Grosvenor preached an eloquent celebration of her life, echoing her belief that the body is a tabernacle that harbours the Holy Spirit of God and that the sufferings in our earthly tabernacle and in our earthly homes do not compare to the glories of our heavenly mansions. Yet Grosvenor cites Mary Franklin's *Experience* at length, sharing her shock and dismay at the invasions of her home, the sufferings of her imprisoned husband, and sacrifices her entire family and congregation had made in service to the 'dissenting' cause, and their own consciences. He hesitates to mention the particulars of their persecutions because of the pain it might cause, 'And now the account enters upon such a scene of troubles, difficulty and trials, that I neither know how to mention, nor how to let alone,' and yet 'Nothing could remove the scandal of them ... To see a poor family not only frightened and alarmed, but the house plundered, the goods seized, the persons carried prisoners, because they did not say the same prayers, nor worship God just at the same place.'[42] The preacher cannot resist praising the 'passive obedience' whereby 'a man chooses to suffer himself, rather than be made an instrument in the execution of such unrighteous orders of any prince in the world'.[43] Preaching, as he is, some two decades after the Glorious Revolution, Grosvenor celebrates that Mary Franklin's devotion, her practice of piety, was demonstrated in her defence of her home, family and church against forces that are fresh in his memory, forces that sinned 'against God, and against the whole genius, frame, spirit, and design of Christianity, the end of all whose commandments is *love out of a pure heart and faith unfeigned*'.[44]

But insofar as Grosvenor quotes verbatim and at length from her *Experience* of these times now past, it becomes clear that Mary Franklin's final and lasting demonstration of devotion was in her defence of her faith – and this she accomplished in the writing of her *Experience*. For it is in this monument made not of hands, but of words, that her own voice can now be heard – signalled in the poignant scripturally derived proclamation appended to the end of the *Experience*, and in a different hand, which reads: 'She being dead yet speaketh'.[45]

Notes

1. N. H. Keeble, *The Literary Culture of Nonconformity in Later Seventeenth-Century England* (Leicester: Leicester University Press, 2nd edn, 1991), pp. 30–2.
2. See Gerald R. Cragg, *Puritanism in the Period of the Great Persecution, 1660–1688* (Cambridge: Cambridge University Press, 1957).
3. Palmer describes the collection of papers, including the writings of Robert Franklin, thus: 'Several original letters of his, written to his wife from prison, are in the possession of Mrs. Hannah Burton, of

London, a grand-daughter of his, who has the other MSS. above referred to; as also a short Catechism, and a letter to Charles II, soon after the Restoration, congratulating him on that event, and urging him to improve it by promoting a reformation of religion.' Edmund Calamy, *The Nonconformist's Memorial*, ed. Samuel Palmer, 3 vols (London, 1802–3), III:294.

4 The papers held in the Congregational Library include a fair copy of the *Experience*, entitled 'The Experience of a Ministers Wife, Who Lived in the Last Century', written in an eighteenth-century hand, copied between 1772 and 1774, along with various hymns, prayers and spiritual letters. DWL, II.e.46.

5 In 1817 William Bailey would 'turn over two boxes of books and property' that he had found in the effects of his departed wife, Rebekah, to Joshua Wilson. See Mary Franklin and Hannah Burton, *She Being Dead Yet Speaketh: The Franklin Family Papers*, ed. Vera J. Camden (Toronto: Iter and the Arizona Center for Medieval and Renaissance Studies, 2020), pp. 46–50, 303–4. Joshua Wilson (1795–1874) 'devoted much time to the investigation of early dissenting history. He also collected works of protestant theology and hagiography' and published histories of dissenters. Alexander Gordon, revised by Mark Clement, 'Wilson, Thomas (1764–1843)', *ODNB*. https://doi.org/10.1093/ref:odnb/29694. Accessed 12 March 2018.

6 Mary Franklin, 'The Experiences of Mary Franklin', in T. G. Crippen (ed.), *The Transactions of the Congregational Historical Society*, vol. II (London, 1906), pp. 387–401.

7 See note 5.

8 Erica Longfellow, 'Public, Private, and the Household in Early Seventeenth-Century England', *Journal of British Studies* 45.2 (2006), 313–34 (320).

9 Franklin and Burton, *She Being Dead Yet Speaketh*, pp. 166, 265–94. All of Mary Franklin's biblical quotations, together with those in this chapter, are taken from the King James Bible.

10 Melinda S. Zook argues that 'the actions of women who sheltered Dissenting preachers, held conventicles in their homes and on their estates, cared for their brethren in prison, hawked anti-Catholic broadsides, or shuttled outlaws and rebels from London to Amsterdam, cannot be simply bracketed off as "religious behavior"'; such actions were 'neither simply political nor simply religious but intrinsically both'. Melinda S. Zook, *Protestantism, Politics, and Women in Britain, 1660–1714* (Basingstoke: Palgrave Macmillan, 2013), pp. 8–9.

11 Franklin and Burton, *She Being Dead Yet Speaketh*, p. 137.

12 *Ibid.*, p. 138.

13 Keeble, *The Literary Culture of Nonconformity*, pp. 229–31.

14 For an account that similarly does not conform to the typical spiritual autobiography see Agnes Beaumont, *The Narrative of the Persecutions of Agnes Beaumont*, ed. Vera J. Camden (East Lansing, MI: Michigan State University Press, 2nd edn, 2002).
15 William York Tindall, *John Bunyan Mechanick Preacher* (New York: Columbia University Press, 1934), pp. vii–viii.
16 Franklin and Burton, *She Being Dead Yet Speaketh*, p. 132.
17 *Ibid.*
18 Three generations back would suggest the line of martyrs reaches to the persecution of the Protestants under 'Bloody Mary', Queen Mary I of England (1516–58). See John Foxe, *Acts and Monuments of the English Martyrs* (London, 1563), esp. pp. 1091–1825.
19 Franklin and Burton, *She Being Dead Yet Speaketh*, p. 136.
20 *Ibid.*, p. 149.
21 Keeble, *The Literary Culture of Nonconformity*, p. 211.
22 Bunyan proclaims that he will be 'plain and simple and lay down the thing as it was'. He turns to the local, humble habitations that are filled with the Spirit of God: 'Have you forgot the Close, the Milk-house, the Stable, the Barn and the like where God did visit your soul?' John Bunyan, 'Preface', in *Grace Abounding to the Chief of Sinners*, ed. Roger Sharrock (Oxford: Oxford University Press, 1962), pp. 3–4.
23 Palmer, in Calamy, *Nonconformist's Memorial*, III:294. Recent histories of dissent also remark upon the exceptional degree of harassment that the Franklins experienced. See Raymond Brown, *Spirituality in Adversity: English Nonconformity in a Period of Repression, 1660–1689* (Milton Keynes: Paternoster, 2012), pp. 37–8, 69.
24 Franklin and Burton, *She Being Dead Yet Speaketh*, pp. 20, 148–9.
25 *Ibid.*, p. 139.
26 *Ibid.*, p. 140. See also Vera J. Camden, 'Attending to Sara Wight: "Little Writer" of God's Wonders', *Bunyan Studies* 11 (2003–04), 94–131; Peter Marshall, 'Angels around the Deathbed: Variations on a Theme in the English Art of Dying', in Peter Marshall and Alexandra Walsham (eds), *Angels in the Early Modern World* (Cambridge: Cambridge University Press, 2006), pp. 83–103.
27 Franklin and Burton, *She Being Dead Yet Speaketh*, p. 144.
28 The defence of such language of religious intimacy is defended, as Burke and Clarke point out, by none other than Robert Ferguson, the Earl of Shaftsbury's chief pamphleteer during the Rye House plot and the author of the Duke of Monmouth's 'Declaration' upon landing in the West Country in 1685. Victoria E. Burke and Elizabeth Clarke, '"Julia Palmer's Centuries". The Politics of Editing and Anthologizing Early Modern Women's Manuscript Compilations', in W. Speed Hill (ed.), *New Ways of Looking at Old Texts III: Papers from the Renaissance*

English Text Society (Tempe, AZ, Renaissance English Text Society, 2005), pp. 47–64 (57).
29 Franklin and Burton, *She Being Dead Yet Speaketh*, p. 138.
30 *Ibid.*, p. 139.
31 Mary Franklin's funeral sermon, preached by Grosvenor, was on this biblical verse, '*For we know, that if our earthly house of this tabernacle be dissolved, we have a building of God, an house not made with hands, eternal in the heavens*' (2 Corinthians 5:1). For the funeral sermon see Franklin and Burton, *She Being Dead Yet Speaketh*, pp. 265–94.
32 Franklin and Burton, *She Being Dead Yet Speaketh*, p. 151.
33 *Ibid.*, p. 139.
34 See Kate Narveson, *Bible Readers and Lay Writers in Early Modern England: Gender and Self-Definition in an Emergent Writing Culture* (Farnham: Ashgate, 2012), pp. 101–30.
35 Franklin and Burton, *She Being Dead Yet Speaketh*, p. 150. See also Alice Thornton for her account of childbearing and domestic cares: *My First Booke of My Life*, ed. Raymond A. Anselment (Lincoln: University of Nebraska Press, 2014).
36 Franklin and Burton, *She Being Dead Yet Speaketh*, p. 150.
37 *Ibid.*, p. 141.
38 It is notable that Joanna does survive into adulthood, as revealed by her husband's and her mother's will mentioning her inheritance. See ibid., pp. 165–7, 305–6.
39 Keeble, *The Literary Culture of Nonconformity*, p. 238.
40 Franklin and Burton, *She Being Dead Yet Speaketh*, pp. 165–7.
41 *Ibid.*, p. 166.
42 *Ibid.*, p. 288.
43 *Ibid.*, p. 288.
44 *Ibid.*, p. 288.
45 Franklin and Burton, *She Being Dead Yet Speaketh*, p. 152. This phrase, reputed to have been written by Grosvenor, is based on Hebrews 11:4: 'By faith Abel offered unto God a more excellent sacrifice than Cain, by which he obtained witness that he was righteous, God testifying of his gifts: and by it he being dead yet speaketh'.

Part VI: Devotional identities in religious poetry

11

Loyalist and dissenting responses to George Herbert's *The Temple* (1633) in the devotional writing of the 1640s–50s

Jenna Townend

John Barbon, the vicar of Dallington, Northamptonshire, published *Leitourgia Thieotera Ergia; or, Liturgie a Most Divine Service* in 1662. He was responding to a pamphlet written by the Independent minister Vavasor Powell, entitled *Common-Prayer-Book No Divine Service* (1660).[1] Barbon concludes his staunchly loyalist text by quoting George Herbert's 'The British Church' as an addendum, clearly finding its religio-political outlook to be well aligned with his own, and speaking on behalf of loyalists wishing to reclaim the Church from '*malevolent* men and *Schismaticks*', like Powell, by returning it to the perceived glory of the period before the Civil War.[2] The dissenting minister Nathaniel Whiting, also from Northamptonshire, found a similar perspicuity in *The Temple*, believing that Herbert spoke directly to the challenges endured by the modern saints. In *The Saints Dangers, Deliverances, and Duties* (1659), Whiting quotes Herbert's injunction in 'The Invitation' to 'Come hither all,' to encourage readers to recognise the danger of 'thin Congregations and empty seats'.[3] Barbon and Whiting held different doctrinal perspectives on the role and governance of the Church, yet they were united in both their belief of the applicability of Herbert's poetry to their particular cause, and their conviction that his words could help them negotiate the complex task of writing and asserting their devotional identities during a period when little could be wholly agreed upon.

The interpretive generosity of *The Temple* and the capacity for its appeal to consistently cross denominational and political boundaries are the matters I wish to explore in this essay. In past assessments of Herbert's reception during the mid-seventeenth century, there has been a strong focus on how writers took inspiration from him as a way of responding to the English Civil War within their religious lyrics, as in the cases of Henry Vaughan and Christopher Harvey.[4] I want not only to bring to light new examples that can contribute to this conversation surrounding how Herbert's poems were transformed by loyalist and dissenting readers,[5] but also to show that we have neglected two other key areas where Herbert's poems were appropriated within this context: prose texts and poetic forms. By broadening our understanding of how the appeal of *The Temple* can be understood within other forms of writing by Herbert's admirers, and by examining their appropriative strategies, it is possible to elucidate new detail concerning the roles that Herbert played in the expression of devotional identities during the 1640s–50s.

As the brief examples from Barbon and Whiting have already demonstrated, writers present a closeness to and familiarity with Herbert in their borrowings, often revealing an admiration for his devotional and social principles as well as for the manner and style of the poetry that expresses them. This recognition that Herbert's affability influenced writers' decisions to borrow from his poems helps to shape our conceptualisation of the topic of textual borrowings from *The Temple* into definitions of several roles that Herbert was asked to play. Although critics like Robert H. Ray have noted numerous instances of writers appropriating Herbert's poems during the Civil Wars, the precise reasons why an admirer might turn to *The Temple* as a source of inspiration in shaping and articulating his or her devotional identity has not been considered with sufficient subtlety.[6] This essay proposes three ways in which it is possible to frame the roles that Herbert played, which correlate with an admirer's use of *The Temple* in prose works, poetic content and poetic form. Herbert's admirers turned to his poetry as a means of positioning a spokesman by quoting from him in prose works, claiming an ally through the appropriation of his imagery and vocabulary in verse, and finding an exemplar in his poetic forms that could provide consolation. Exploring these three ideas shows the importance of paying close attention to the various roles that Herbert was asked to play as both his loyalist and dissenting readers worked to respond to, and make sense of, unprecedented religious and political changes. However, as this essay will show, just because some readers supported the loyalist cause does not mean that they took inspiration from Herbert in ways that were diametrically opposed to their dissenting counterparts, nor does it mean that all loyalist readers drew upon Herbert in the same way or for the same reason.

A spokesman in prose

Lines, stanzas, phrases and entire poems from *The Temple* were quoted in hundreds of seventeenth-century prose texts, where Herbert is called upon to provide anything from support for a position, authority, illustration or justification to satire, to list just some examples. Herbert's admirers undoubtedly recognised poetry's capacity to be used as an argumentative and persuasive tool, and calling on the poems of *The Temple* allowed them to position Herbert as a spokesman for their cause, whether that was ceremonialist or puritan in origin. For Herbert's admirers who were writing during the flux of the mid-century, their quotations of, and borrowings from, Herbert's poems often struck an argumentative tone that was directed at issues of immediate national concern. The Church of England clergyman Thomas Fuller found precisely this argumentative potential in *The Temple* as he addressed both his own congregations and the readers of his printed sermons, seeking to console those whose lives were being torn apart by the Civil Wars. During the 1640s, Fuller delivered a number of sermons which advocated peace through reformation, and made clear his hatred of the wars and the 'spirituall hardnesse of hearts' they had created.[7] While his sermons published in the first half of the 1640s were primarily concerned with promoting reconciliatory action through reforms, his sermons published after 1645 reveal a greater concern with accentuating the possible consequences of the schisms that the wars had created within England's religious and political landscapes. Fuller had taken up residence in Exeter in 1644 before moving to London in April 1646 following Exeter's surrender to the parliamentarian army.[8] His sermon *Feare of Losing the Old Light* was published in June 1646 and, in light of Exeter's surrender only two months earlier, Fuller reflects on the long-term implications of 'this troublesome Age'.[9]

Fuller questions the extent to which true knowledge and practice of Christianity are leaving England for America as a consequence of the partisanship fostered by the Civil Wars, lamenting that 'God knows what good effects to them our sad war may produce.'[10] Despite religion's 'favourable inclination to verge more and more Westward', Fuller tempers any anticipation of the devotional value of America by encouraging his congregation to consider the price that may be paid by English religion. Expressing his concern that 'we should make so bad a bargain, as wholly to exchange our Gospel for their Gold, our Saviour for their Silver',[11] Fuller draws his imagery from these lines of 'The Church Militant':

> Then shall Religion to America flee:
> They have their times of Gospel, e'en as we.
> My God, thou dost prepare for them a way,
> By carrying first their gold from them away:
> For gold and grace did never yet agree:
> Religion always sides with poverty.
> We think we rob them, but we think amiss:
> We are more poor, and they more rich by this.[12]

Clearly believing Herbert to be a spokesman for English religion and the importance of its preservation, Fuller borrows from the prophetic content of 'The Church Militant' to bolster his argument that, while there is an assumption that America's new-found prosperity will leave England in a favourable economic position, England is at risk of being left spiritually 'poor'. Spiritual, rather than economic, wealth is the currency with which England should be concerned, Fuller says, and he hopes that his sermon may be 'read with as much favour, as it was once heard with attention'.[13] His borrowing from 'The Church Militant' therefore has a role in both oral and print culture, offering spiritual guidance to congregations whilst simultaneously creating a public, textual record of the current threat posed to English religion, and the urgent need for spiritual arousal in the Established Church.

The ability to exploit the political and persuasive potential of sermons was not limited to admirers of Herbert who supported the loyalist cause. As Fuller's sermon demonstrates, a printed sermon could address an issue that was of transcontinental concern, yet retain immediate relevance for those who had heard it in person. However, invocations of Herbert within politically charged texts were not always concerned with such large-scale matters, and borrowings from *The Temple* could also speak directly to more local matters.

Giles Firmin uses Herbert for precisely this purpose in his sermon *Stablishing Against Shaking* (1656). Firmin was a Presbyterian, and on 17 February 1655 delivered his sermon at Shalford in Essex 'upon occasion of the *Quakers* troubling those parts', and his quotation from Herbert is used as a line of attack against the movement.[14]

Feeling compelled to rebut the doctrinal arguments of the Quakers who, Firmin says, had begun to 'send diverse of their Books into our Town, [and] invited my people to come and heare', Firmin rebukes them as false teachers, citing the Pauline authority of 2 Corinthians 11:13 on 'false Apostles' and 'Deceitfull Workers'.[15] Firmin then addresses the apparent attractiveness of the Quakers' pious behaviour. Attacking both the sin and the sinner, he points out that 'Quakers must wear no lace, drink water, [and] fast,' going on to sarcastically ask, 'Who would suspect a Devil in these, to teach things thus crosse to the flesh[?]' Declaring that 'Yes even here he is ... if it be a thing to crosse God, to set up some way of our own, we can then crosse our selves,' Firmin calls Herbert as a witness to this assertion by injecting a poetic caveat:

> so true is that which blessed *Herbert* in another case hath said,
> Oh what were man, might he himself misplace!
> Sure to be crosse, he would shift feet and face.[16]

His quotation of two lines from 'The Church-porch', which refer to man's inherent vulnerability and desire to be contrary,[17] serves two purposes as a means of attack and defence. First, it is an unmistakable attack on the Quakers' contrary nature and '*shift*[ing] *feet and face*', which Firmin argues deceives both their existing and potential followers. Second, it admonishes Firmin's congregation to be wary of the apparently pious activities of their Quaker neighbours in the area surrounding Shalford. The sermon's publication in 1656 means that this quotation from Herbert appears at the zenith of the Quakers' prominence.[18] As such, for Firmin's congregation and the readers of the printed sermon, remembering Herbert's advice could form part of their armoury against the insidious actions of the Quakers. After all, as the Church of England clergyman Francis Higginson puts it, Quakers and their pamphlets flew '*as thick as Moths up and down the Country*' during this time.[19] Firmin's sermon and his quotation from Herbert speak to the local listeners who first heard the sermon, and the readers who could peruse it in print, helping to shape a national response to the perceived threats posed by Quakers during the mid-seventeenth century.

An ally in verse

When it came to interrogating the religious and political controversies of the Civil Wars, Herbert's voice was heard not only in his readers' prose works. I want to now examine how his lyrics were incorporated into poetry. While it is appropriate to discuss Herbert as being claimed as a spokesman within the prose texts of his admirers, describing the practice of how writers borrowed from his poems in verse requires a term that acknowledges this similarity in genre: ally. I suggest that poets who borrowed from Herbert's imagery and vocabulary turned to him as a writer who could help them craft poetic responses to a particular historical moment, and who could therefore be claimed as an ally for what they saw as the correct position. In the broad aims of their texts, both loyalist and dissenting writers are united by a commitment to poetic edification and the winning of a readership to their particular religious or political outlook through the harmonies of verse. However, these writers each simultaneously seek to claim Herbert as an ally for their cause, believing that he spoke directly to their particular concerns.

The Church of England clergyman Edward Sparke sought to claim Herbert as his ally when it came to the debate between the merits of public and private prayer in his collection of devotional verses, *Appendix Sacra*, which was bound with his 1652 work *Scintillula Altaris*. This debate, which had raged since the early seventeenth century, is one of Sparke's main focuses in his poem 'Prayer'.[20] Ramie Targoff offers a neat summary of the two opposing viewpoints. Puritans and later dissenters held firm that 'private practices alone [were] capable of edifying the worshipper's internal self', and regarded the Prayer Book services as 'a depersonalized and mechanical performance'. Conversely, loyalists, like Sparke, 'considered set forms of prayer to empower rather than efface the expression of individual voice'.[21] For Sparke, it is within the organised services and prayers of the Church, not in extemporary private devotion, that true spiritual benefit is found. Sparke turns to Herbert for inspiration to help him assert this position at a time in the early 1650s when, as he saw it, defences of the Established Church were urgently needed.

However, if Sparke was to align Herbert with his own poetic comments on prayer, the contents of Herbert's poems on the topic – 'Prayer (I)' and 'Prayer (II)' – offer little in terms of doctrinal argument. Consequently, Sparke draws arguments, imagery and phrasing from multiple Herbert poems within his meditation on the superiority of public prayer:

> Yet though such private Prayer have its high praise,
> The Publike Forme 'tis that designe doth raise
> Even up to Heaven, whither with stronger wings
> It flies, and thence a fuller blessing brings;
> Such private Suitors like less stars do shine,
> In Constellations while more lights combine;
> Those, but like Planets oft excentrick move,
> But These fix'd stars, Heavens Galaxia prove:
> ...
> Such Pray'r is revers'd Lightning, and Heavens wonder,
> While the joint Amen's like a Clap of Thunder.[22]

Sparke clearly agreed with Herbert's belief, expressed in 'The Church-porch', that 'Though private prayer be a brave designe, / Yet publick hath more promises, more love.'[23] However, Sparke's use of two other Herbert poems, 'Prayer (I)' and 'The H. Scriptures (II)', bears closer examination. At the end of this section, Sparke adapts Herbert's image of prayer as 'Reversed thunder' in 'Prayer (I)', referring to it as 'revers'd Lightning'.[24] Reorienting the auditory element of Herbert's stormy imagery, Sparke avers that the 'joint Amen' which concludes a public prayer constitutes an emphatic punctuation mark; it is 'a Clap of Thunder' which seals the prayer and sends it heavenwards (something which, he implies, could not be offered by the solitary 'Amen' of private prayer). Given that Sparke positions himself against the puritans who denied him the use of the Prayer Book, he turns to 'The H. Scriptures (II)' as a poem that could help him respond to the threat of anti-scriptural religion, singling out Herbert's opening image for appropriation:

> Oh that I knew how all thy lights combine,
> And the configurations of their glorie!
> Seeing not onely how each verse doth shine,
> But all the constellations of the storie.[25]

Eschewing any sense of light as a metaphor for sectarian inspiration, Sparke turns Herbert's celestial imagery relating to the power of scripture into an extended metaphor for the power of the Established Church. Sparke concedes a degree of power to the prayers of those who engage in private devotion, but their prayers exist only as 'less stars do shine / In Constellations'. Extending the metaphor, Sparke explains that these individuals 'like Planets oft excentrick move' in unpredictable paths, presumably because their prayers lack the structure provided by the Church. Conversely, those who engage in the Established Church's public prayers are 'These fix'd stars', moving in harmony and eventually becoming 'Heavens Galaxia'. By combining elements of three Herbert poems, Sparke uses *The Temple* like a phrase book to bolster his own poetic argument, as well as presenting Herbert as his ally. To Sparke, Herbert had expressed his exact sentiments some twenty years earlier, and all he has done is tweak an argument Herbert would have agreed with for the present moment. When it came to the composition of religious verse – for Sparke and those like him – it was clearly how Herbert said things, as much as what he said, that appealed to his readers.

Articulating the communicative power of prayer was also a keen interest of puritan and later dissenter poets, as demonstrated by the verse of the puritan minister Faithful Teate. Teate's poem 'Prayer' appears in his lengthy metaphysical verse text *Ter Tria*. First published in 1658, *Ter Tria* contains tripartite sequences of poems that expound the importance of the 'Father', 'Son' and 'Holy Spirit'; the values of 'Faith', 'Hope' and 'Love'; and the acts of 'Prayer', 'Hearing' and 'Meditation'.[26] Herbert's interest in expressing prayer's capacity to bridge the space between the divine and the temporal is taken up in Teate's own poetic meditations on the topic. In three couplets, Teate uses metaphors that are extremely similar to the lines of 'Prayer (I)', where prayer is described as the 'Christian plummet sounding heav'n and earth / Engine against th'Almighty, sinner's tow'r':[27]

> Pray'r is Faiths *Bucket* (Pray'r doth upward move,
> Drawing its *waters* from those *wells above*)
> Chain'd to that *Bucket* of the *Blessing*, so
> That that *comes down*, as this doth *upward go*.
> ...
> Pray'r lifting up its *holy hands* can dart.
> To Heav'n that hand-granado of the Heart.[28]

Teate follows Herbert's example of parading, and then dissolving, the boundary between the 'here' and 'there' of earth and heaven, as well as demonstrating that prayer possesses a power akin to weaponry. Taking inspiration from Herbert's imagery, Teate reveals a shared interest in prayer's reciprocal capacity to allow the Christian to communicate with God and to receive the spiritual comfort that he provides.[29]

If Teate's appropriations of Herbert are taken together with Sparke's borrowings, it becomes clear that it was how Herbert expressed an idea, as well as that idea itself, that extended an appeal to admirers with vastly different doctrinal perspectives. Writers align themselves with Herbert's argument for prayer's communicative power, whether those prayers were formalised or extemporary, public or private. Writing from his anti-enthusiast position, Sparke found comfort in Herbert's argument that, whilst private devotional practices have their merits, devotees should be wary of believing that these alone could edify the internal self. Conversely, puritan poets like Teate believed that it was the activity, rather than form, of prayer that mattered most, maintaining that 'Some read, some sing, and some their pray'rs can say, / He's an Elias that his pray'rs can pray.'[30] The lyrics of *The Temple* were sufficiently open to interpretation to accommodate and bolster various devotional identities.

An exemplar in poetic form

While the content of Herbert's lyrics was a source of inspiration for a number of his admirers during the mid-century, others showed greater interest in the creative, devotional and even political potential of his poetic forms. However, despite their convergence around this central point of interest, writers' interpretive reworkings of Herbert's forms are as dynamic as the devotional experiences and identities they describe. For Herbert's seventeenth-century admirers, the exemplars of his typographically striking forms provide opportunities for experimentation and exploration within the bounds of an already established form. However, in light of the emphasis that has previously been placed on writers, like Henry Vaughan, who borrowed from Herbert's lyrics within the content of their own verse, it is first worth posing the question of why admirers might turn to his poetic forms, rather than his vocabulary.[31] Molly Murray has theorised the consolation that individuals incarcerated in early modern prisons could locate within the metre and rhyme of poetic forms, arguing that they could derive consolation from 'the regularity and order of poetic language'.[32] When it comes to *The Temple*, the poetic forms of individual verses undoubtedly had a role to play in providing consolatory experiences for readers. For loyalists writing during the mid-seventeenth century, the composition of poetry according to metrical patterns and rhyme schemes provided structure and control at a time when many individuals were subjected to persecution or exile. Herbert's poetic forms provided formal templates into which admirers could effectively insert their own poems, finding order and consolation as they did so. The use of Herbert's 'Heaven' as the exemplar for an anonymous poem entitled 'The Eccho', transcribed in British Library Harley MS 6918, neatly illustrates this point.

As the examples of Thomas Fuller and Giles Firmin show, Herbert's admirers were reading and drawing upon his poems in the midst of political turmoil, including events such as the ascendancy of the parliamentarian government, Charles I's execution and the burgeoning of sectarian religions. For loyalist writers who were facing the political uncertainty of the monarchy's future, Herbert's poetic forms offered a framework through which to explore both the limits of what poetic form can express and the consolation it can provide. Although I have been unable to trace the poem's original source, beyond the fact that it appears in both Harley MS 6918 and Huntington Library MS EL8838, and was written sometime during the 1650s, it is clear that, when it came to seeking reassurance of the legitimacy of the loyalist cause, the compiler found consolatory potential in the echoing form of Herbert's 'Heaven'. After all, with the poem's opening imperative to 'Name Eccho who this new Religion grounded? ____ Roundhead', and its assertion that puritans 'to the King ... say they are most loyall ____ lye all', the compiler confirms his or her opposition to the parliamentarians and desire to accentuate the dangers of the puritans' growing influence in England's religious landscape.[33]

In Herbert's 'Heaven', what readers hear is a homonym – either a single word or short phrase – that invites them to actively participate in the advancement of their knowledge of God's comfort by interpreting the devotional meaning that is contained within their questions and supplied by the echoing responses. In this way, Herbert's poetic form illustrates the possibility of anticipating the consolation that lies within God's provision of heavenly delights: 'Light, joy, and leisure; but shall they persever? / Ever.'[34] However, for the anonymous author of 'The Eccho', the mid-century's political and religious pressures opened the possibility of an explicitly political application of Herbert's poetic form. As is implied by the poem's name, and as is the case in the exemplar of 'Heaven', the echoing respondent is not an external body but a prolongation of the speaker's own words. Given that the impetus of 'The Eccho' is to legitimise royalist suspicions around the 'new Religion', this feature of Herbert's form creates, quite literally, an echo chamber in which the speaker can mock and ridicule dissenting beliefs. In 'Heaven', the homonymic echoes of Herbert's form serve to advance the speaker's devotional knowledge. In 'The Eccho', however, the homonymic responses turn inwards rather than outwards. That is, the speaker seeks only to confirm both his or her anti-puritan suspicions and the superiority of the loyalist position by extracting the sinful characteristics and actions he or she believes lie at the heart of puritan religious practices, as in the query of: 'How doe they prove themselves the Godly ____ odly.'[35] As Leila Watkins puts it, although 'the echoes in this poem aurally or visually match the words with which they rhyme, they semantically contradict them'.[36] As the speaker seeks consolation concerning the superiority of loyalist principles over those of the puritans, the original devotional premise of Herbert's poetic form is made satirical as well as polemical.

For the speaker of 'The Eccho', the chief concern centres around the apparent secrecy of the ways in which puritans practise their faith. Indeed, the reader can sense the implied eye-roll that accompanies the rhetorical question, 'Ist not absurdity they them deliver ____ Ever.' The speaker takes the echoing satire further, though, as his or her attention turns to the puritans' places of worship:

> But now in Chambers they doe Conventicle ____ tickle
> the holy Churches they are sure belyed _____ bellyed
> the godly number then will soon descend _____ end
> Our Churches in zeale they doe embrace them ___ race them.[37]

Chiming with contemporary stereotypes of sexual promiscuity within sectarian religions, the speaker voices the suspicion that conventicles are actually a cover for sexual encounters.[38] Extending the metaphor of sexual impropriety, the speaker expresses the fear that, as a result, the 'holy Churches' have been besieged or impregnated by the puritan faction, causing them to be 'bellyed', or swollen, with their devotional principles. The consequence, the speaker warns, will be the downfall of the truly godly, and the only remedy to this is to 'race', or cut away, the Church's attachment to puritans and their principles.

The outlook presented by the speaker of 'The Eccho' is not a happy one for loyalists, and it offers little consolation for the future of the Church. However, while the poem is not characterised by optimism, it does offer consolation to readers in the form of the self-affirmation that arises from renewing their conviction in the superiority of the loyalist cause. Indeed, at the final moment, the poem is turned into a loyalist prayer that the status quo may yet be preserved: 'God keepe the Church and State from these same men ____ Amen.'[39] The author of 'The Eccho', and the interests of the compiler who transcribes it, ameliorate the catechistical premise of the Herbertian exemplar, and expand its application beyond the accumulation of devotional knowledge by applying it as a way of affirming one religious perspective while ridiculing another. Herbert's poetic form is used to imagine and parody the perspective of doctrinal adversaries in order to assert the superiority of a particular devotional identity. The consolation that arises may be polemical and self-congratulatory, rather than edifying, but it is present nonetheless.

A critic of Catholicism?

So far, this essay's analysis has shown how, although loyalist and dissenting writers converged around the roles that they asked Herbert to play within their texts as a spokesman, ally or exemplar, the individual contexts in which the borrowings appear reveal diverse religio-political concerns. Indeed, writers have sometimes represented opposing sides of the same controversial matter, as in the cases of Sparke's and Teate's poems on prayer. However, a striking rapprochement emerges among those admirers who borrowed from Herbert's 'The Church Militant' during the mid-seventeenth century to express concern over the threat posed by Catholicism to English religion during such a time of flux. It is therefore significant that Catholic writers are noticeably absent from the topography of Herbert's seventeenth-century admirers. While Herbert's position as a Church of England minister presents an obvious obstacle to the posthumous appeal he could exert for Catholic writers, what makes their absence especially intriguing is the fact that Herbert's admirers clearly had no problem selecting the elements of his verse that were most aligned with their particular devotional position, while ignoring those that were not. For example, Faithful Teate must have objected to a poem such as 'Whitsunday', with its conspicuous attachment to the calendar of the Established Church, yet he found Herbert's expositions on the value of prayer to be well suited to his own outlook. Given the absence of contemporary textual evidence or comment on Catholic writers' responses to Herbert, it is risky to argue stridently for a rationale behind their apparent lack of interest in *The Temple*. However, the less-than-favourable picture of Catholicism presented in 'The Church Militant' may well have deterred Catholic writers from believing that they would find anything palatable in Herbert's poems:

> When *Sein* shall swallow *Tiber*, and the *Thames*
> By letting in them both, pollutes her streams:
> When *Italie* of us shall have her will,
> And all her calendar of sinnes fulfill;
> Whereby one may foretell, what sinnes next yeare
> Shall both in *France* and *England* domineer.[40]

For Herbert's loyalist and dissenting admirers, however, this account provided a foundation for expressing their disdain of the Catholic faith and warning of the threat it posed to English religion.

From its publication, 'The Church Militant' was consistently quoted as prophetic by writers who either used it to express concern over the departure of religion from England and Europe, or celebrated it as justification for the settlement and devotional activities of colonies in America.[41] In his account of the poem in *Herbert's Remains; or, Sundry Pieces of that Sweet Singer of the Temple* (1652), the episcopalian clergyman Barnabus Oley struggled to reconcile the poem's optimistic and pessimistic tenors. Quoting lines which contain both the promising revelation that America will 'have their times of Gospel, even as we' and the foreboding threat of what may happen 'when *Italy* of us shall have her will', Oley prefaces his borrowing with the question, 'Shall I say, I hope, or Fear Mr. Herberts lines pag. 190. should be verified?'[42] Oley's quotation from Herbert allows him to express hope that the prediction of America's 'times of Gospel' may be realised, but to attach his own hopeful caveat that it would not occur at the expense of England's religious decline. Having addressed his work 'to the Clergy Reader' at a time when loyalist supporters of the Established Church were enduring ecclesiastical exile, Oley's hope is that Herbert may provide a call to action and 'prove a true prophet for *poor America*, not against *poor England*'.⁴³

Such anxious interpretations of Herbert's 'Church Militant' were not confined to loyalist fears of the influx of Roman Catholicism, however, and later dissenters were equally concerned with the consequence of such an invasion: the migration of religion to America. In a prefatory epistle that Richard Baxter wrote for John Tombes's *Romanism Discussed* (1660), he attacks Catholics as those who 'confine the Church to their deluded Faction' and behave as enemies to '*Civil Peace* and *Government*'.⁴⁴ He exhorts readers to 'suffer not the sins of men professing godliness, to drive away the Gospel, and send it to *America* (according to Mr. *Herbert's* sad conjecture in his *Church Militant*)'.⁴⁵ By paraphrasing Herbert's warning that 'Then shall religion to *America* flee / They have their times of Gospel, ev'n as we,' Baxter implies that what was once Herbert's mere 'conjecture' is in danger of being fully realised, expressing concern not only that the Church in England will be polluted by the Catholic faith, but that the gospel may depart altogether.⁴⁶ Baxter and Oley position themselves in a diachronic relationship with Herbert's original poem. For both writers, Herbert's prophecy concerning religion's departure from England as a consequence of Catholicism should not be dismissed as speculation, and all devotees, whether loyalist or dissenting, must exercise urgent vigilance against Herbert's 'sad conjecture'.

In previous studies of Herbert's reception, scholars have (rightly) discussed how frequently his poems were appropriated and reworked by his loyalist and dissenting readers during the mid-seventeenth century, but that does not mean that Herbert's influence is found only in poetic texts, or that his poetry was consistently asked to perform the same job. The absence of concrete, contextual specificity within the poems of *The Temple* imbues them with a transferable potential and pliability: Herbert's forms, vocabulary, imagery and arguments could be borrowed and transferred to new devotional contexts, including both loyalist and dissenting responses to the conflicts of the mid-century. I have suggested three terms that can frame the various ways in which Herbert is used within prose texts, poetry and poetic form: as spokesman, ally and exemplar. By using these terms as stepping stones to understanding why writers turned to *The Temple* during the 1640s–50s, it becomes possible to see the remarkable dynamism of the uses to which Herbert's poems were put as his loyalist and dissenting readers sought to make sense of the unprecedented changes around them and to articulate their devotional identities. Moreover, posing questions concerning the roles that Herbert was asked to play by his admirers demonstrates that they were keenly aware of the benefits to be obtained when they linked themselves with Herbert through a textual borrowing, showing a consistent fascination with how that borrowing could further their devotional and political arguments and, in turn, the ways in which they communicated with readers. While uses of Herbert by loyalist and dissenting writers may have been motivated by common external pressures of responding to fears over the future direction of England's religion, the threat of Catholicism and persecution – both rhetorical and real – the forms which those uses took are multifaceted. Preserving an appreciation of that complexity is essential to understanding the dynamic roles that the poems of *The Temple* performed for Herbert's readers in the expression of devotional identity during the mid-seventeenth century.

Notes

1 Vavasor Powell, *Common-Prayer-Book No Divine Service* (London, 1660).
2 John Barbon, *Leitourgia Theiotera Ergia; or, Liturgie a Most Divine Service* (Oxford, 1662), p. 193, sig. A3^r.
3 Nathaniel Whiting, *The Saints Dangers, Deliverances, and Duties* (London, 1659), sig. C3^r.
4 Robert Wilcher, 'The "true, practice piety" of "holy writing": Henry Vaughan, Richard Crashaw, Christopher Harvey, and *The Temple*', in Donald R. Dickson and Holly Faith Nelson (eds), *Of Paradise and Light: Essays on Henry Vaughan and John Milton* (Newark: University of Delaware Press, 2004), pp. 50–70.
5 This essay uses the term 'dissenting' to describe writers, mostly clergymen, who chose not to conform to the religious rites and rituals of the Established Church in England during the 1640s and 1650s. These same writers later went on to become 'dissenters'; that is, they refused to abide by the Act of Uniformity (1662) and were ejected from their church livings. Conversely, the term 'loyalist' describes those who adhered to the Church of England and, often, supported the monarchy during the internecine fighting and Interregnum. These terms are not mutually exclusive, though, and attached to my use of them is the caveat that there were also dissenting individuals who held loyalist beliefs, and loyalists who sympathised with the dissenting position. For nuanced discussions of the religio-political allegiances during the Civil Wars see Gerald E.

Aylmer, 'Collective Mentalities in Mid Seventeenth-Century England', *Transactions of the Royal Historical Society*, 5th series, 36 (1986), 1–25; Michael J. Braddick, *God's Fury, England's Fire* (Penguin: London, 2009), pp. 262–303; Andrew Hopper, *Turncoats and Renegadoes: Changing Sides during the English Civil Wars* (Oxford: Oxford University Press, 2012), pp. 19–120.
6 Robert H. Ray, 'The Herbert Allusion Book', *Studies in Philology* 83.4 (1986), 1–167.
7 Thomas Fuller, *Truth Maintained; or, Positions Delivered* (Oxford, 1643), sigs C1^v–C2^r.
8 W. B. Patterson, *Thomas Fuller: Discovering England's Religious Past* (Oxford: Oxford University Press, 2018), pp. 119, 126.
9 Thomas Fuller, *Feare of Losing the Old Light* (London, 1646), sig. A3^r.
10 *Ibid.*, p. 12.
11 *Ibid.*, pp. 12–13.
12 George Herbert, 'The Church Militant', in *The English Poems of George Herbert*, ed. Helen Wilcox (Cambridge: Cambridge University Press, 2007), pp. 667–73 (II:247–54). All subsequent references to *The Temple*, where they are not quoted as part of another text, refer to this edition.
13 Fuller, *Feare of Losing the Old Light*, sig. A3^v.
14 Giles Firmin, *Stablishing Against Shaking* (London, 1656), frontispiece.
15 *Ibid.*, sig. A4^r, p. 11. Exact wording appears in both the Geneva and King James Bibles.
16 *Ibid.*, pp. 14–15.
17 See George Herbert, 'The Church-porch', in *Poems*, pp. 50–62 (II:23–4).
18 Kate Peters, 'The Dissemination of Quaker Pamphlets in the 1650s', in Roeland Harms, Joad Raymond and Jeroen Salman (eds), *Not Dead Things: The Dissemination of Popular Print in England and Wales, Italy, and the Low Countries, 1500–1820* (Leiden, Netherlands: Brill, 2013), pp. 213–28 (215).
19 Francis Higginson, *A Brief Relation of the Irreligion of the Northern Quakers* (London, 1653), sig. A2^r.
20 Edward Sparke, *Scintillula Altaris* (London, 1652), sigs A2^r–A3^r.
21 Ramie Targoff, 'The Poetics of Common Prayer: George Herbert and the Seventeenth-Century Devotional Lyric', *English Literary Renaissance* 29.2 (1999), 468–90 (469).
22 Sparke, *Scintillula Altaris*, sigs A2^v–A3^r.
23 Herbert, 'The Church-porch', 397–8.
24 George Herbert, 'Prayer (I)', in *Poems*, p. 178 (I:6).
25 George Herbert, 'The H. Scriptures (II)', in *Poems*, p. 210 (II:1–4).
26 Faithful Teate, *Ter Tria* (London, 1658), *passim*.
27 Herbert, 'Prayer (I)', 4–5.
28 Teate, *Ter Tria*, pp. 174–5.

29 See also Jenna Townend, 'An Imitative Series in the Poetry of George Herbert, *Faithful Teate*, and Julia Palmer', *Notes & Queries* 65.2 (2018), 212–13.
30 Teate, *Ter Tria*, p. 175.
31 Sean H. McDowell, 'Herbert as *Bardd* in the Imagination of Henry Vaughan', *George Herbert Journal* 34.1–2 (2010–11), 102–18.
32 Molly Murray, 'Measured Sentences: Forming Literature in the Early Modern Prison', *Huntington Library Quarterly* 72.2 (2009), 147–67 (161).
33 BL, Harley MS 6918, fol. 27^v. The *Catalogue of English Literary Manuscripts* dates this manuscript to the 1650s.
34 George Herbert, 'Heaven', in *Poems*, p. 656 (II:19–20).
35 BL, Harley MS 6918, fol. 27^v.
36 Leila Watkins, 'Forms of Exclusion: Early Modern Lyric and Religious Difference', *Modern Philology* 115.3 (2018), 348–70 (369).
37 BL, Harley MS 6918, fol. 27^v.
38 Joad Raymond, *Pamphlets and Pamphleteering in Early Modern Britain* (Cambridge: Cambridge University Press, 2003), p. 241.
39 BL, Harley MS 6918, fol. 27^v.
40 Herbert, 'The Church Militant', 241–6.
41 Helen Wilcox, '"Religion stands on Tip-toe": George Herbert, the New England Poets, and the Transfer of Devotional Modes', in Allan I. MacInnes and Arthur H. Williamson (eds), *Shaping the Stuart World, 1603–1714: The Atlantic Connection* (Leiden, Netherlands: Brill, 2006), pp. 147–73.
42 Barnabus Oley, *Herbert's Remains; or, Sundry Pieces of that Sweet Singer of the Temple* (London, 1652), sigs B3^v–B4^r; Herbert, 'The Church Militant', 235–58.
43 Oley, *Herbert's Remains*, sigs A1^r, B4^r.
44 Richard Baxter, in John Tombes, *Romanism Discussed; or, An Answer to the Nine First Articles* (London, 1660), sigs C1^r, B4^r.
45 *Ibid.*, sig. C1^r.
46 Herbert, 'The Church Militant', 247–8.

12

'Whom I never knew to Poetrize but now': grief and passion in the devotional poetry of Richard Baxter

Sylvia Brown

Richard Baxter remains best known as a voluminous writer of polemic and devotional prose. Yet he was also a poet, with two volumes of poetry printed during his lifetime as well as an articulated poetics which characterised the verses he wrote as 'Heart-Imployment', directed inwards as well as towards God.[1] That characterisation might suggest that Baxter understood his verse writing as a private devotional act. Even so, the publication of his *Poetical Fragments* (1681) and *Additions to the Poetical Fragments* (1683) represented a creative supplement to as well as an elaboration of the methods of his prose works of practical divinity.[2] Baxter's assessment of his own poetry was that it was 'fit for women and vulgar wits, which are the far greater number'; also for those 'afflicted, sick, [and] dying'.[3] As in his pastorate at Kidderminster and throughout his printed output of practical divinity, Baxter presented his printed poetry as a ministry to the troubled. Unlike his massively popular prose works, however, Baxter's poetry enjoyed a restricted afterlife, mainly in hymns, and his nineteenth-century editor William Orme, while declaring his prose writings 'full of poetry', also seemed to agree with Baxter himself that he was 'not skilled in versification'.[4] In his own preface to *Poetical Fragments*, Baxter unpromisingly declared, 'I have long thought, that a Painter, a Musician and a Poet, are contemptible, if they be not Excellent: And that I am not Excellent, I am satisfied.'[5] Yet devotional exercises, even poorly fashioned through verse, were not redundant. Baxter was prepared to be contemptible if he could be useful, stating, 'Common

Painters serve for poor men's work: And a Fidler may serve at a Country-Wedding.'[6]

Published in the year of his wife Margaret's death, *Poetical Fragments* was linked by Baxter himself to 'sorrows and sufferings': his own as a bereaved husband, but also those of his wife stretching back to when she was a member of his flock in need of spiritual consolation, and finally those of the 'near Friends in Sickness, and other deep Affliction' of the title page. In the preface, Baxter made a special plea for 'passions' as a key part of devotional identity: they were both the motive for spiritual song and an essential for spiritual life, without which 'it will be hard to have any pleasant thoughts of Heaven'.[7] Both *Poetical Fragments* and *Additions* versify Baxter's practical application of doctrine to daily devotional life and to the 'heart' through a vigorous miscellany of poetic spiritual autobiography, godly ballad and interior dialogues. Baxter wrote of a kinsman who had composed a poem for Margaret during a dangerous illness: 'I never knew [him] to Poetrize but now that tender love and passion taught him.'[8] This essay explores why these words might equally apply to the evolving devotional identity of Baxter himself. Baxter used the occasion of devastating personal loss to present to his readers a new kind of practical divinity: consolation – of self as much as others – through a poetics of the passions.

Baxter's poetry: fragments from a 'Broken-healed Heart'

Baxter composed poetry throughout his writing life: not in quantity, but with a catholicity of range, from his well-known verse epitaph for himself, 'Farewell vain world!' (which appeared in numerous Baxter publications and which he also translated into Latin),[9] to the psalms or hymns of praise 'for the use of ignorant Families that need them' appended to his immensely popular *Poor Man's Family Book* (1674).[10] Almost the last thing that Baxter wrote was poetry, his 'Paraphrastical Translation of the Psalms', which he had completed 'and written with his own hand fairly and accurately for the Press' just before his death.[11] The pieces collected in *Poetical Fragments* had been written over a number of years. Many are dated and linked to specific occasions, such as the previously printed 'Upon the sight of Mr. VINES His Posthumous TREATISE OF THE SACRAMENT, October 18. 1656. Who Dyed a little before'.[12] In the posthumously printed *Reliquiae* (1696), we learn from Baxter that he did not originally intend for that poem to be published, but 'having received the Printed Book from the Stationer as Gift, it renewed my Sorrow for the Author's Death; which provoked me to write that Poem the same Night, in the Exercise of my Sorrow, and gave it the Donor for his Book; and he printed it without my knowledge'.[13]

It was Margaret Baxter's death in 1681 (a difficult year for Baxter personally and nonconformists generally[14]) that prompted him to gather these fragments. His poetry collection was in fact one of a triad of publications in the year connected with his bereavement: *Poetical Fragments* 'Written partly for himself' and 'Published for the use of the Afflicted' appeared at the same time as *A Breviate of the Life of Margaret, the Daughter of Francis Charlton ... and Wife of Richard Baxter* 'for the use of all but especially their Kindred', as well as *The Last Work of a Believer*, the funeral sermon of Margaret Baxter's mother, reprinted 'at the desire of her Daughter, before her death'.[15] Baxter was explicit about his wife's death and his own passionate grief as justification for his venture into publication as a poet (as opposed to occasional strewer of verses amongst his greater prose works). Margaret Baxter died on 14 June 1681. The preface to *A Breviate*, dated 23 July, shows that he was already thinking about a volume of poems and even had the title in his mind:

> And if before I get over this (owned) Passion, I publish also a few *Poetical Fragments* partly suited to the condition of some sick, or sad afflicted Friends, and partly to my own; if thou accept them not, forgive them only and neglect them.[16]

In the preface to *Poetical Fragments* itself, he declared of the poems now published that:

> as they were mostly written in various Passions, so Passion hath now thrust them out into the World. God having taken away the Dear Companion of the last Nineteen Years of my Life, as her sorrows and sufferings long ago gave Being to some of these Poems ... so my grief for her Removal, and the Revived Sense of former things, have prevailed with me to be passionate in the open sight of all.[17]

Given this statement, and the title-page assertion that the book represents 'The Concordant Discord of a Broken-Healed Heart', it is striking that the contents include no poems explicitly expressing grief for a beloved wife; although the sequence 'The Complaint', 'The Answer' and 'The Submission' – all referencing unspecified physical and spiritual affliction – could certainly have been applied to Baxter's immediate case or any other reader's.[18] Baxter seems to have put together what poetry he had to hand, both unpublished and previously printed. 'Love Breathing Thanks and Praise' is a long, unfinished verse spiritual autobiography in which Baxter had 'purposed to have recited the most notable mercies of my Life'.[19] It ends abruptly with the Civil Wars, long before he met Margaret Charlton.[20] A number of the pieces recollect Baxter's love for Herbert's poetry: not only 'Divine Love's Rest', described explicitly as 'Written on Herbet's [sic] Poems', but also dialogic poems structured as conversations with both God and the self, such as 'The Resolution ... Written when I was Silenced'.[21] The latter poem is dated 3 December 1663; according to the *Reliquiae*, Baxter had in fact preached his last sermon in public on 25 May 1662.[22] Other dated poems in the collection can be connected to the death of Margaret Baxter's mother in January 1661.[23] Finally, while there is no elegy for Margaret, Baxter included a versified 'Covenant and Confidence of Faith' with the note that his 'Dear Wife' had subscribed it 'with a cheerful will' when she was suffering that same dangerous sickness that had prompted her kinsman to write her a poem, around 1659; and the entire collection ends, significantly, with the verses that were 'written on a fair Marble over the Grave where my Wife and her Mother are buried'.[24]

It is as if his publicly '(owned) passion' over his wife's death had given Baxter permission to collect, consolidate, print and share other passions that he had worked through in the past through verse. Arguably, the selection and publication (or republication) of certain pieces in 1681 carried a political charge: as in the recollection of a time when Baxter (long ejected) and his late friend Richard Vines were active preaching ministers, of 'One Church: for we agreed, / Both in one Method, and one Creed'.[25] A printed miscellany held together by the 'Revived Sense of former things' and compiled by a famously embattled nonconformist cannot escape being resistant, if not political. Baxter's poetry may be seen as part of the larger project undertaken by ejected ministers, to continue their pastoral work through available means and especially print, despite persecution.[26]

Reception and circulation

It is not surprising to read in Baxter's typically self-reflexive preface that he pretested the reception of *Poetical Fragments* in his circle of friends – and then ignored their discouraging feedback. The work was below him, said some, and those who spoke 'wiselier' (according to Baxter) thought that he was below the work.[27] Yet he was announcing forthcoming publication in the month after Margaret Baxter's death.

By November, the printed poems were in circulation, falling into the hands of one of the first Tory news sheets, *Heraclitus Ridens*. The issue of Tuesday 15 November 1681 introduced a satiric 'query': 'Whether Mr. *Baxter* were by Nature made more for Poetry or Divinity; and whether, though he took to the later so soon, and set up for the former so late, he be not yet at this day as good a Poet as Divine?' The implication was that Baxter was equally pernicious as a 'Divine' as in his somewhat surprising new role as a 'Poet'. Lest the reader miss the point, the following 'query' dredged up the old joke about the royalist Sir John Denham, who pleaded for a pardon for George Wither so that he would not be left as the worst poet alive: might he not 'if occasion were, sue for a pardon for Mr. *Baxter* upon the same reason?'[28] Three weeks later, *Heraclitus Ridens* still had not finished with Baxter's devotional poetry. Encountering recycled rhymes in 'a necessary House', one speaker in a satirical dialogue refers to the *Poetical Fragments*: 'Alas, thought I, Mr. Baxter's Rhapsodies have had a quick circulation, to come to their Journeys end already'.[29] The use of the word 'rhapsodies' is telling. Associated with enthusiastic and fanatic religion and used to denigrate the devotional identity of nonconformists,[30] it also had a whiff of passion beyond licit bounds, as in the criticism of the carnal poetry of the age – 'amorous lays of Wit, wanton Rhapsodies, and prophane Ballads' – by Baxter's contemporary, the Independent and fellow poet John Reeve.[31]

Undaunted by friends or enemies, however, Baxter went on to publish *Additions to the Poetical Fragments* two years later. This work has no preface, but pre-emptive words on the title page – 'Written for himself, and Communicated to such as are more for serious Verse than smooth' – suggest a consciousness of criticism. Yet, *Additions* differs in that it published new rather than collected poems. Dates printed at the close of poems about the action of 'Grace', the fleshly corruption of 'Man', and the imminence of death (which enjoyed a long afterlife in hymnals as 'The Exit' and 'The Valediction') indicate Baxter was writing them during the months of December and January 1682–83, yet another time of trial.[32] All his possessions had been distrained the previous October, forcing him to cast away 'multitudes of manuscripts' including 'Letters practical, and Cases of Conscience'.[33] Out of that suffering – and also 'waking torments Nephritick, and Colick, after other long pains and langour' – came *Richard Baxter's Dying Thoughts* and these further poems, both printed in 1683.[34] Between 1681 and 1683, it seems that Baxter started to think of himself as a devotional poet; or at least that publishing poetry could supplement his pastoral prose, despite the declaration that made the debut volume of his poetry seem like a valediction: 'my painful and spiritless Age is now unfit for Poetry'.[35] Two further editions of *Poetical Fragments* appeared in the seventeenth century: a second in 1689 and a third in 1699, both incorporating the *Additions*.[36]

The republication of Baxter's works in the eighteenth century did not, however, include his poetry, which would have to wait until 1821 for another edition.[37] Select verse quotations and even whole poems were reprinted for new purposes, notably as hymns in the growing canon of dissenting hymnody,[38] but Baxter was rarely considered *as a poet* during this century, with a few exceptions. An assessment from America in 1735 enthused over 'Baxter's 'Farewell vain World!' as 'the best Lines that were ever written';[39] but more characteristic is the faint praise of 'the plain, but weighty lines which he composed in view of his own sufferings and death'.[40] These are represented by a selection of stanzas from 'The Resolution' reprinted at the end of the first volume of *Biographical Collections*:

> Must I feel sickness and smart,
> And spend my days and nights in pain?
> Yet if thy love refresh my heart,
> I need not overmuch complain.[41]

In the nineteenth century, William Orme thought Baxter's poetry worth an extended 'critical examination' but not a reprint.[42] The hymn writer and poet James Montgomery reprinted a few selections from *Poetical Fragments* in his *Christian Poet*, but perhaps more importantly gave one of the first sympathetic critical assessments of Baxter as a poet: 'he speaks the language of a minute self-observer, and tells the experience of his own heart in strains, which never lack fervency, nor indeed eloquence, however unapt in the art of turning tuneful periods in rhyme'.[43]

Montgomery's assessment and Baxter's own classification of *Poetical Fragments* as practical divinity suggest an alternative framework for assessing his poetry: as not merely unskilful verse but rather an evolution of the complex devotional identity he presented to his readers in print. Baxter's *Compassionate Counsel to all Young Men*, published around the same time as *Poetical Fragments*, included the first version of Baxter's 'annotated' bibliography of his own works.[44] In this catalogue, *Poetical Fragments*, as well as the *Breviate* of Margaret Baxter's life and the funeral sermon on her mother, are classed as 'Practicals for the Faithful';[45] in other words, works of practical or 'case divinity'.[46] As exemplified by Baxter's popular *Christian Directory*, 'case divinity' applied articles of faith and doctrine to everyday life, encouraging self-examination: 'heart work' to activate the passions as well as the understanding and the will. If we follow Baxter's lead, we may consider (and judge) his poetry not so much a literary enterprise as a devotionally 'practical' one.

Baxter's poetics of passion

As Elizabeth Clarke argues of John Bunyan's poetry (which has also suffered from a tradition of unfriendly critical assessment), it is necessary to identify the alternative 'poetic values' of dissenting poets like Bunyan or Baxter if one is to understand 'what he thought he was doing when he was writing in verse'.[47] Bunyan and Baxter allied themselves with utility over rhetorical ornament, but usefulness included appealing to readers' affections and passion, which was the province of poetry. For both minister-poets, passion was the spark through which poetry could function alongside other awakening genres like sermons or the bracing tracts which Baxter classified in his catalogue as 'Practicals for the Unconverted'.[48]

Poetical Fragments' preface serves as an 'Apology for Poetry' and includes Baxter's own personal canon of excellent poets. There he declared 'various Passions' to be both the origin and publication prompt for his poems, and undertook a surprisingly eloquent defence of passion itself, despite the fact that it could hinder judgement so that one 'should be very suspicious of himself till it be laid'.[49] Baxter's weightiest work of practical divinity, *A Christian Directory*

(1673), contains an entire chapter of 'Directions for the Government of the Passions' (chapter VII), which begins from the premise that the passions are not sinful in themselves but become sinful or holy, as they are used.[50] They are classed in the realm of *adiaphora*, things indifferent that can be used well or badly.[51] Introducing his poetry, however, Baxter presents passion rightly used as almost a *necessity*. While passion can hinder reason, reason is also 'a sleepy half-useless thing' until some passion excites it: 'I confess, when God awakeneth in me those Passions which I account rational and holy, I am so far from condemning them, that I think I was half a Fool before.'[52] What had changed from the time Baxter wrote most of *A Christian Directory*, in 1664 and 1665,[53] and first published it in 1673, was the death of Margaret Baxter in 1681. In that year, as he wrote in the *Breviate*, he was writing 'under the power of melting Grief ... For passionate Weakness poureth out all'.[54] Perhaps his intense grief at the death of his wife had altered his devotional outlook and sense of self, showing him that passion was not always a governable adiaphoron, but could instead be more like a weeping wound.

Here Baxter differs from Bunyan in how passion authorises poetry. Where Clarke sees Bunyan using the affective mode of verse to 'entice' his readers, to make them 'fall in love' with salvation,[55] the passion that underpins Baxter's poetry incorporates the etymological sense of *suffering*. Suffering passion, moreover, not only caused Baxter to write poems. Suffering also justified their circulation to other afflicted readers: 'being suited to afflicted, sick, dying, troubled, sad and doubting persons, the number of such is so great in these calamitous times, as may render them useful to more than I desire'.[56] Baxter, in other words, expected his poems to be devotionally practical and popular.

In this, Baxter's poetry and poetics were distinguished from those of other Protestant poets (including Bunyan), who took the more Horatian line that the virtue of Christian poetry was to add delight to teaching.[57] In Baxter's canon, George Sandys is this kind of poet.[58] Yet while Baxter acknowledged the excellence of a range of poets from Abraham Cowley to Katherine Philips, it was George Herbert who was exemplary for him – 'none so savoury to me'.[59] Helen Wilcox and others have demonstrated that Herbert was the poet most admiringly invoked by later generations of dissenters, who responded to the simplicity and sincerity of the poems in *The*

Temple as well as their thoroughly scriptural language.[60] For Baxter, Herbert was the poet who:

> speaks to God like one that really believeth a God, and whose business in the world is most with God. Heart-work and Heaven-work make up his Books.[61]

The language is mirrored in the full title of *Poetical Fragments*: 'Heart-Imployment with God and It Self. The Concordant Discord of a Broken-healed Heart. Sorrowing-rejoycing, fearing-hoping, dying-living'. For Baxter, moreover, Herbert not only exemplified heart-sincerity but also the necessity of passion and sorrow for sincere belief. As early as the first edition of *The Saints Everlasting Rest* (1650), written 'in the time of his languishing', Baxter invoked the language of 'the Divine Poet' Herbert, quoting from 'Affliction' ('Sorrow was all my soul; I scarce beleeved, till Grief did tell me roundly, that I lived') and closing the volume with the full text of 'Home', in which the speaker longs for dissolution.[62] Herbert is exemplary – even though to Baxter there were others more excellent in wit and more accurate in verse composition[63] – because he is a 'Divine' through being a 'Poet', his poetry extending his pastoral vocation of turning the unpromising materials of the passions into belief. This is how Baxter's own poetry touches his practical divinity.

The words of the title page of *Poetical Fragments* nonetheless invoke passions scarcely held in check by oxymorons: the grief is still placed front and centre in the 'concordant discord' of 'sorrowing-rejoycing, fearing-hoping, dying-living'. An anonymous posthumous life of Baxter noted that although his wife's death 'occasion'd much Grief', he mourned 'not like an Infidel; hoping again to see her, and go to her, but not her to come to him'.[64] This litotic assurance suggests the real possibility that Baxter's passionate grief was excessive – something he himself 'confessed' in the prefatory statements to both the *Breviate* and *Poetical Fragments*. Why do you mourn if you have faith? This is the standard line, repeated in countless funeral sermons. Keith Condie discusses the importance of Baxter's emphasis on the catalysing effect of rationally managed passions in his ministry: 'the effective preacher (and writer) will be attuned to the normal operations of the soul's faculties and will use emotion to move truth into practice'.[65] Condie emphasises the ideal balance between reason and the passions throughout Baxter's writings, but acknowledges the possibility of instability in the 'inherently turbulent' nature of the emotional state.⁶⁶ Condie's analysis is based on the prose writings, but it is the *Poetical Fragments* where the balance is most precarious. Baxter's own directions for governing the passions characterised them as sinful when they are 'immoderate or excessive in degree' but holy when 'devoted to God'.⁶⁷ His passion-derived volume of poetry ran the risk of unbalancing the adiaphoron.

Margaret Baxter and the poetry of practical divinity

Margaret Baxter is at once strangely absent from the volume catalysed by her sorrows, sufferings and eventual death, and everywhere present in its paratextual elements. She is the presiding spirit of *Poetical Fragments*, both ghost and inspiration. This paradox may have had much to do with the difficulty of balancing the disturbing power of passion with its awakening potential.

As the *Breviate* presents her, Margaret Baxter was a complex figure. Richard Baxter had married late, after publicly declaring that a minister was better off without a wife, and this made their relationship 'the matter of much publick talk and wonder'.⁶⁸ Margaret Charlton's relationship with the already famous author of *The Saints Everlasting Rest* evolved from the pastoral support of a young convert to the intimacy of marriage, activating all the contemporary prejudices about godly ministers and their female followers.⁶⁹ Richard Baxter's correspondent Katherine Gell reported that some of her relatives were shocked at her meetings with a minister, believing 'that privat conferrence with a min[iste]r was much worse t[ha]n gaming or mixed daumcing or bare breasts or spo[t]ting painting'.⁷⁰ As *Poetical Fragments* was associated with passion, so too was Margaret Baxter, its genius. This association was problematic – Baxter believed women generally to be temperamentally more passionate and more given to religious melancholy, and Margaret to be a particularly acute case⁷¹ – but also productive in a 'practical' sense. When Margaret Charlton sought out Richard Baxter for spiritual help, this generated material that Baxter could use for others and indeed found its way into his printed output, not least the *Breviate*.⁷² It was the 'case' of her crisis of faith that caused the 'sorrows and sufferings' to which Baxter attributes the genesis of his own printed poetry collection. She was, moreover, a practitioner of case divinity herself. In the *Breviate*, Richard Baxter declared that she was 'better at resolving a case of conscience than most Divines that ever I knew in all my life', and that in the latter part of their marriage he took to consulting her on 'all, save secret cases'.[73]

Margaret Baxter was also bound up in Richard Baxter's positive representations of poetry in his *Poetical Fragments*, particularly as it overlapped with psalm-singing:

> It was not the least comfort that I had in the converse of my late Dear Wife, that our first in the morning, and last in Bed at night was a Psalm of Praise (till the hearing of others interrupted it).[74]

For Baxter, the singing of psalms was the least problematic way to 'poetrize', connected as it was with the authorising template of the scriptural psalms.[75] The intimacy of this image, however, while of a piece with what made Baxter distinctive and even popular,[76] touches on the problematic inter-involvement of Baxter's poetics of passion with the passion evoked by the figure of Margaret Baxter.

A passage from *The Christian Directory* is thought-provoking in this respect:

> Get but the Love of God well kindled in your Heart, and it will find employment, even the most high and sweet employment, for your Thoughts ... See but how a lustful lover is carried after a beloved silly piece of flesh? Their thoughts will so easily and so constantly run after it, that they need no spur! Mark ... how it feedeth and quickneth their invention, and elevateth an ordinary fancy into *a Poetical and passionate strain*! What abundance of matter can a Lover find, in the narrow compass of a dirty Corpse for his thoughts to work on night and day?[77]

This passage starkly lays out both the connection between passion and poetry and the enduring and problematic connection of the former with a corrupting and sexualised body. There is no question of Baxter's esteem for his own wife. *The Christian Directory* also advises that a man can have no better best friend than his own wife, while the *Breviate* persistently defends the person, memory and writing of Margaret Baxter against (acknowledged) public opinion that her marriage might have compromised his ministry. Yet, as far as they are authorised by 'passion' – with all that Baxter associates with that potentially unstable catalyst of human affections, actions and belief – there remains something finally unbalanced and unharmonised about Baxter's poems, a 'discord' not resolved in the devoted and devotional soul they seek to depict. The very last poem printed in *Poetical Fragments* remediates the verses inscribed on the marble monument erected by Margaret Baxter over the grave of her mother. As Baxter recounts in the *Breviate*: 'in the doleful-flames of London, 1666. the fall of the Church broke this great Marble all to pieces, and it proved no lasting Monument'. Baxter hoped that his 'Paper-Monument', 'erected ... in some passion indeed of love, and grief, but in sincerity of truth, will be more publickly useful and durable'.[78] In the end, it was the public usefulness as well as endurance of 'practical' print that Baxter invoked against the corruptions of the body and the world, the changeable sphere to which 'passion' belonged.

Poetical Fragments (1681) and the *Additions* (1683) can be understood as an experiment in giving more precedence to the passions – and poetry – than Baxter did elsewhere, occasioned by an unusual crisis of love and grief. However, remediating his own passionate suffering into print was the basis for Baxter's pastoral and authorial success from the publication of *The Saints Everlasting Rest* (1650) onwards. On this view, Baxter breaking into print as a poet mid-career was not a change of direction but rather an extension of his work in practical divinity. Baxter's poems of passion, which stem from a devoted husband in grief, are not 'private' but are justified by entering into circulation, where they must risk the mockery or neglect they seem to have suffered, and which Baxter predicted and even invited. 'And if my present grief may but excuse the Publication, he that needeth them not may let them alone.'[79]

Notes

1 The phrase 'Heart-Imployment' is taken from Richard Baxter, *Poetical Fragments* (London, 1681), frontispiece.
2 In addition to Baxter's *Poetical Fragments* and *Additions*, his posthumous *Paraphrase on the Psalms* (1692) constitutes a third volume.
3 Baxter, *Poetical Fragments*, sig. B1^v.
4 William Orme, *The Life and Times of Richard Baxter* (London, 1830), pp. 754–5.
5 Baxter, *Poetical Fragments*, sig. A5^r.
6 *Ibid.*, sig. A5^r.
7 *Ibid.*, sig. A4^r.
8 Richard Baxter, *A Breviate of the life of Margaret ... wife of Richard Baxter* (London, 1681), p. 31.
9 See Richard Baxter, *Reasons of the Christian Religion* (London, 1667), frontispiece; Baxter, *Poetical Fragments*, p. 134. For another Latin poem

along the same lines, see 'Munde dolose vale' in Baxter's *Methodus Theologiæ Christianæ* (London, 1681), p. 439.
10 See Richard Baxter, *Poor Man's Family Book* (London, 1674), sigs A7^v–A8^r.
11 Richard Baxter, *Paraphrase on the Psalms* (London, 1692), sig. A3^r.
12 Baxter, *Poetical Fragments*, pp. 120–6.
13 Richard Baxter, *Reliquiae Baxterianae,* ed. Matthew Sylvester (London, 1696), p. 122. 'Upon the sight' appears in Richard Vines, *A Treatise of the ... Sacrament* (London, 1656), sigs A2^r–A4^v. Also previously printed was 'Self-Denial. A Dialogue between the Flesh & the Spirit', ending with Baxter's covenant 'Renouncing Flesh', dated 29 October 1659. Baxter, *Poetical Fragments*, pp. 65–74. This dialogue first appeared appended to Baxter's *Treatise of Self-Denyall* (London, 1659), sigs Yy1^r–Yy4^v.
14 See Baxter, *Breviate*, sig. A1^v. On other deaths in Baxter's 'ancient family' in that year see N. H. Keeble, 'Baxter, Richard (1615–1691)', *ODNB*. https://doi.org/10.1093/ref:odnb/1734. Accessed 12 December 2018. For the renewed campaign to repress dissent in the aftermath of the Exclusion crisis see Richard Greaves, *Glimpses of Glory: John Bunyan and English Dissent* (Stanford, CA: Stanford University Press, 2002), pp. 401–6.
15 All three titles were entered in the Term Catalogue for Michaelmas (18 Sept.) 1681. Edward Arber, *The Term Catalogues, 1668–1709,* 3 vols (privately printed, 1903–06), I:457.
16 Baxter, *Breviate*, sig. A5^v, emphasis added. Baxter's use of the word passion here mixes the senses of 'suffering or affliction', 'overpowering emotion' and 'love'. See *Oxford English Dictionary Online* (hereafter OED), 'passion, *n.*', senses 3, 6 and 8, respectively. On the importance of 'passions' to Baxter, the man and the preacher, see Frederick J. Powicke, 'A Puritan Idyll', *Bulletin of the John Rylands Library* 4.3–4 (1918), 434–64 (435–6).
17 Baxter, *Poetical Fragments*, sig. A3^v.
18 *Ibid.,* pp. 89–96.
19 *Ibid.,* pp. 1–50 (50).
20 For 'Love Breathing Thanks and Praise' as a 'rambling, meditative poem' that occasionally threatens to break into the epic mode, see Sharon Achinstein, *Literature and Dissent in Milton's England* (Cambridge: Cambridge University Press, 2003), pp. 97–101.
21 Baxter, *Poetical Fragments*, pp. 51, 61. Compare with Herbert's speakers as entering into 'poetic conversations with God' in Helen Wilcox, 'Introduction', in *The English Poems of George Herbert*, ed. Helen Wilcox (Cambridge: Cambridge University Press, 2007), pp. xxi–xxxvi (xxi).
22 Baxter, *Poetical Fragments*, p. 61; Baxter, *Reliquiae*, II:384.

23 See 'The Lamentation [Jan. 18. 1660/1] For Sin afflicting the Sinner; especially by the grievous sufferings of Friends' and 'The Relief [26 January 1660/1]', in Baxter, *Poetical Fragments*, pp. 102–5, 105–19. See also Keeble, 'Baxter, Richard'.
24 Baxter, *Poetical Fragments*, pp. 81–3, 135. Also see Powicke, 'A Puritan Idyll', p. 440.
25 Baxter, *Poetical Fragments*, p. 125.
26 See Andrew Marvell's unsympathetic attack on print doing 'more harm than an hundred Systematical Divines', quoted in George Southcombe, 'Introduction', in *English Nonconformist Poetry, 1660–1700*, ed. George Southcombe, 3 vols (London: Pickering & Chatto, 2012), I:xi–xxxvii (xiii). For the printing of ejected ministers' 'Farewell Sermons' as politicized mourning see Achinstein, *Literature and Dissent*, pp. 38–42.
27 Baxter, *Poetical Fragments*, sigs A4^v–A5^r.
28 *Heraclitus Ridens: AT A Discourse Between Jest and Earnest*, concerning the Times, no. 42, 15 November (London, 1681), pp. 1–2 (2).
29 *Heraclitus Ridens*, no. 45, 6 December (London, 1681), pp. 1–2 (2). The recycled rhymes are in fact by another despised nonconformist poet, 'Democritus Flens', *ibid*.
30 See OED, 'rhapsody, *n.*', senses 2.a and 4, but also the complaint of 'Oliver Foulis' [David Lloyd] in *Cabala; or, The Mystery of Conventicles* (1664) that 'infinite more phanatick Rhapsodies [are] printed every day', p. 61.
31 [John Reeve], *Hymns and Spiritual Songs* (London, 1682), sig. A3^r. See Elizabeth Clarke, '"Truth in Meeter": Bunyan's Poetry and Dissenting Poetics', in Michael Davies and W. R. Owens (eds), *The Oxford Handbook of John Bunyan* (Oxford: Oxford University Press, 2018), pp. 325–42 (327–8).
32 Richard Baxter, *Additions to the Poetical Fragments* (London, 1683), pp. 18, 61, 69, 76.
33 Keeble, 'Baxter, Richard'; Richard Baxter, *Dying Thoughts* (London, 1683), sig. A3^v.
34 Baxter, *Additions*, sig. A4^v.
35 Baxter, *Poetical Fragments*, p. 50.
36 The third edition has a separate title page dated 1700 for the *Additions*.
37 See Richard Baxter, *The Poetical Fragments of Richard Baxter* (London: Pickering, 4th edn, 1821).
38 Clarke notes that 'Ye Holy Angels Bright', first printed in 1674 in *The Poor Man's Family Book*, 'became one of the best-loved dissenting hymns'. Elizabeth Clarke, 'Hymns, Psalms, and Controversy in the Seventeenth Century', in Isabel Rivers and David L. Wykes (eds), *Dissenting Praise: Religious Dissent and the Hymn in England and Wales* (Oxford: Oxford University Press, 2011), pp. 13–31 (27).

39 John Adams and Benjamin Colman, *Reliquiae Turellae, et Lachrymae Paternae* (Boston, 1735), p. 44.
40 Richard Baxter, *Biographical Collections*, 2 vols (London, 1766), I:169.
41 Ibid., I:169–70.
42 The 'critical examination' was published in the second volume of *Life and Times*, together with the twenty-three volumes of his *Practical Works of The Rev. Richard Baxter*, in 1830.
43 James Montgomery (ed.), *Christian Poet; or, Selections in Verse, on Sacred Subjects* (Glasgow, 3rd edn, 1828), p. 320.
44 See N. H. Keeble, 'A Baxter Bibliography', in N. H. Keeble, *Richard Baxter: Puritan Man of Letters* (Oxford: Clarendon, 1982), p. 157. *Compassionate Counsel* also appeared in the Michaelmas 1681 Term Catalogue, see Arber, *The Term Catalogues, 1668–1709*, vol. I.
45 Richard Baxter, *Compassionate Counsel to all Young Men* (London, 1681), sig. [*2]^r.
46 See the statement, 'There be not (I believe) more able men for case divinity and all practicalls in the World, then in this Nation.' R. H., 'To the Reader', in *The Good Old Way* (London, 1652), sig. A8^r. For an excellent discussion of Baxter's contribution to the print history of 'practicals' in this sense, see Isabel Rivers, *Books and Their Readers in Eighteenth Century England* (Leicester: Leicester University Press, 1982), pp. 131–2, 140–2.
47 Clarke, 'Truth in Meeter', pp. 326, 328. For a recent collection of a range of nonconformist poets see Southcombe, *English Nonconformist Poetry*, passim.
48 On the imperative of the minister to be engaging and thus truly 'popular' see Rivers, *Books and Their Readers*, p. 129. Also see this work for a discussion of Baxter's *Call to the Unconverted* as undoubtedly his most popular 'practical [manual] for the unconverted', pp. 139–40.
49 Baxter, *Poetical Fragments*, sig. A3^v.
50 See Richard Baxter, *A Christian Directory* (London, 1673), pp. 327–60.
51 Reason can also be used well or badly, as Baxter explores in the poem 'Wisdom', in *Additions*, p. 24.
52 Baxter, *Poetical Fragments*, sig. A4^r.
53 See Baxter, 'Advertisements', in *Christian Directory*, sig. A2^r.
54 Baxter, *Breviate*, sig. A1^v.
55 Clarke, 'Truth in Meeter', quoting Bunyan's 'Ebal and Gerizzim', p. 328.
56 Baxter, *Poetical Fragments*, sig. A8^v.
57 In understanding poetic passion actually to affect the soul, Helen Wilcox sees Baxter departing from the persistent puritan suspicion of poetry – even among those who, like Bunyan, acknowledged the usefulness of its affective power. Helen Wilcox, 'Voices and Echoes: Poetical

Precedents from Herbert to Bunyan', *Bunyan Studies* 22 (2018), 14–38 (16).
58 Baxter, *Poetical Fragments*, sig. A7^v.
59 *Ibid.*, sigs A6^r–A7^r.
60 See Wilcox, 'Voices and Echoes', p. 20; Achinstein, *Literature and Dissent*, pp. 205–6; also, most recently, Jenna Townend, '[S]weet Singer of our Israel': Psalms, Hymns, and Dissenting Appropriations of George Herbert's Poetry', *Bunyan Studies* 22 (2018), 39–62. For a discussion of Herbert's various admirers and imitators during the 1640s–50s see chapter 11.
61 Baxter, *Poetical Fragments*, sig. A8^v.
62 See Richard Baxter, *The Saints Everlasting Rest* (London, 1650), pp. 127, 853–6.
63 See Baxter, *Poetical Fragments*, sig. A7^r.
64 *Life and Death of … Richard Baxter* (London, 1692), p. 18.
65 Keith Condie, 'Affection and Intellect in the Thought of Richard Baxter', in Alec Ryrie and Tom Schwanda (eds), *Puritanism and Emotion in the Early Modern World* (Basingstoke: Palgrave Macmillan, 2016), pp. 13–46 (43).
66 *Ibid.*, p. 46.
67 Baxter, *Christian Directory*, p. 274.
68 Baxter, *Breviate*, p. 46.
69 *Ibid.*, pp. 33–4. See also Powicke, 'A Puritan Idyll', pp. 443–4.
70 Quoted in Alison Searle, '"My Souls Anatomiste": Richard Baxter, Katherine Gell and Letters of the Heart', *Early Modern Literary Studies* 12.2 (2006), 1–26 (19). For a discussion on Katherine Gell's sermon notes see chapter 3.
71 *Ibid.*
72 Baxter, *Breviate*, pp. 34, 46.
73 *Ibid.*, pp. 67, 68.
74 Baxter, *Poetical Fragments*, sigs A5^v–A6^r.
75 See prefatory remarks in Baxter's *Paraphrase on the Psalms*, sigs A5^r–B4^v.
76 For Baxter's 'readiness to take his readers into his confidence and address them in disarmingly direct and frank ways' see N. H. Keeble, '"Loving & Free Converse": Richard Baxter in His Letters' (Friends of Dr Williams's Library, 45th Lecture, 1991), pp. 1–24 (9–10).
77 Baxter, *Christian Directory*, p. 299, emphasis added.
78 Baxter, *Breviate*, pp. 94–5.
79 Baxter, *Poetical Fragments*, sig. A8^v.

Part VII: Devotional identities in the *ars moriendi*

13

'My sick-bed covenants': scriptural patterns and model piety in the early modern sickchamber

Robert W. Daniel

In 1698 the Church of England clergyman Thomas Gipps heaped scorn on *Reliquiae Baxterianae* (1696) – the autobiography of the eminent dissenter Richard Baxter – for its insistence 'on the most trifling and dirty parts of his [Baxter's] Actions, even how well his Physick wrought' during his various illnesses.[1] Such criticisms were not targeted at the sickbed writing of dissenters alone. Years earlier, the Cheshire Presbyterian and ejected minister Henry Newcome admonished other writers whose:

> whole discourse is, how they are held and handled [by physicians], where their pain is, and how it works them. And a story they can make of all passages [of sickness], as if nothing else was minded by them. And they spend their time in groaning and complaining, and in using means to get up again.[2]

These views were so widely shared that in 1713 Jonathan Swift – the dean of St Patrick's Cathedral, Dublin – condemned diarists of the previous century, and his own, who 'without any Ceremony, will run over the History of their Lives: will relate the Annals of their Diseases, with the several Symptoms and Circumstances of them'.[3] Despite their different religious positions, Gipps, Newcome and Swift all agreed that there was more medicine than religion in the prosopography of the sick. It is true that such 'patient narratives' have proved invaluable sources to scholars of early modern medicine.[4] There was also, however, a great deal of devotion, and devotional writing, in the sickbed accounts of early modern England. Despite a reinvigorated interest in the religious rituals of the sickchamber, there is still much to be learned about the devotional identities of those who practised them.[5]

In this essay I explore how the acts and attitudes during infirmity, in manuscript and printed accounts by both men and women, can be seen as often theologically cohesive. Patients demonstrated a precise and widely shared biblicism – that is to say, they used the same scriptures – in their sickbed writings.[6] This created a common devotional identity that ran across denominational, social and political lines, and at times crossed the confessional divide. By identifying and examining these shared scriptural patterns, I show how the ill incorporated broad and attested doctrinal behaviours during their illnesses. This is not to suggest that all sickbed practices were homogeneous, but rather that some were more significant and more frequently performed than others. This essay also demonstrates how popular sickbed piety was as likely to reject as to reflect the devotional models espoused in printed 'how-to' manuals.

Central to the composition of sickness accounts was the influence and inclusion of scripture. This is unsurprising. The puritan luminary Edmund Calamy, minister of St Mary Aldermanbury in London, was typical of the period in teaching that: 'The Word of God is the *sick Saints salve,* the *dying Saints cordial;* a most precious medicine to keep Gods people from perishing in time of affliction.'[7] What is striking, however, is the way specific scriptures were repeatedly used to enact specific activities in the sickchamber: from demonstrations of patience to covenanting, will-making, restorative prayers and thanksgiving praises after recovery. This essay, thus, demonstrates the ways in which similar devotional identities were distilled as much as disseminated in accounts of illness.

Patience during illness: Psalm 116

From the outset, accounts of illness were always careful to emphasise the sufferers' patient posture in their faith in, and submission to, the divine will of God. Here patients were not meant to rail against their ailments and the pain these were causing them. Instead, they were expected to display the key scriptural attribute of 'patience',[8] taken from Psalm 116:13:

> I will take the cup of salvation, and call upon the name of the Lord.[9]

Printed devotional texts aligned this scripture with the quality of enacting 'patience' during infirmity. William Perkins in *A Salve for a Sicke Man* (1595) stated that instead of demonstrating 'impatience and griefe' sufferers should consider Psalm 116:13, which taught 'patience' in that 'all things in sicknes ... come to passe unto us by the prouidence of god'.[10] In his *A Manual of Directions for the Sick* (1648), the late bishop of Winchester Lancelot Andrewes quoted Psalm 116:13 in a section entitled 'Concerning the Patience and Thankfulness required in the sick'.[11] This emphasis on suffering 'patiently', however, was not an innovation brought about by the Reformation. It was a recycled remnant from the medieval *ars moriendi*, which had labelled 'impatience' as one of the five grievous temptations of the deathbed.[12]

Due to its ubiquitous usage in printed manuals, expressions of 'patience' became synonymous with (and shorthand for) adherence to Psalm 116:13. When the Essex minister Ralph Josselin lost his eight-year-old daughter Mary in the summer of 1650, he stated in his diary that she 'was patient in the sicknesse, thankefull to admiracon'.[13] Lucy Hutchinson, a gentlewoman and religious Independent, wrote of her husband the regicide Colonel John Hutchinson that 'he was very patient under sickness or pain, or any common accidents'.[14] In 1671 the Particular Baptist Hanserd Knollys described how his son Isaac 'exercised very great patience under his very great pain, soreness, and burning Feaver'.[15] In 1680 Mary Penington stated in a manuscript account of her life that 'I had nothing to do in sickness, but to suffer patiently.'[16] The Kentish gentleman and lawyer-poet Thomas St Nicholas cited Psalm 116:13 directly in his manuscript hymn composed after his recovery from a 'burning feaver' in 1667.[17] He prayed for the same endurance to be continued in any future afflictions:

> Help me to take salvation's cup,
> And make it my endeavour
> When I lie down, when I rise up,
> To praise thy name for ever.[18]

There were notable exceptions, however, to this performance of stoic *apatheia*. Elizabeth Wallington, mother of the woodturner and diarist Nehemiah Wallington, was remembered as screaming on her sickbed, 'No more, Lord, no more; no more, Lord, no more!' She openly questioned the cause of her suffering: 'Lord, what have I done, what is my sin ... that thou dealest thus with me?'[19] Nehemiah took such disturbing cries of impatience as a warning. The accounts of Josselin, Hutchinson, Knollys, Penington and St Nicholas, whose religious beliefs were otherwise divergent, suggest that Elizabeth's outbursts were neither common nor acceptable amongst the godly sick.

This did not mean that patients were prohibited from expressing their suffering – through groans, cries and screams of anguish.[20] What the pious objected to was a rebellious attitude towards suffering – where the sick felt angry with God for causing their pains, or felt they did not deserve it. Expressions of 'patience' were important, not just because they manifested a scriptural principle, but because they demonstrated that the sick had total trust in God. They also reveal how biblical notions were embedded within accounts of 'lived religion' in ways that are not always clearly signposted to modern readers.

Will-writing during illness: Isaiah 38

Another way the sick pointed to God's Word was demonstrating how illness (fatal or temporary) was a sign from Jehovah to make a last will and testament. They did this by citing Isaiah 38:1:

> In those days was [King] Hezekiah sick unto death. And Isaiah the prophet the son of Amoz came unto him, and said unto him, Thus saith the Lord, Set thine house in order: for thou shalt die, and not live.

Once a set of earlier prayers of 'satisfaction' for the dead in the Catholic *Dirige*, Isaiah 38 was transformed under reformed theology.[21] Several writers now cited it as a timely reminder of the need to make a suitable will during illness.

The Presbyterian minister Philip Henry made his will on 17 February 1665 after a restless night of pain in his limbs. As he explained in his diary: 'I made my will, not knowing but it [his pain] may bee a Summons to Death, however tis not amiss to have my house alwayes in order.'[22] Similarly, the Independent Welsh clergyman Vavasor Powell exclaimed in 1658 that, afflicted by a strange sickness, and reading Isaiah 38 in his bedchamber, 'I was much troubled about my Will, and was afraid the Lord would have taken me away before I had finished it.'[23] This sickbed piety was performed as much by parishioners as by preachers. In his recovery hymn, St Nicholas used Isaiah 38 to note how the Almighty had nudged him not to die intestate during his illness:

> sent'st a summons, seemed to say,
> 'Now set thine house and heart
> In order ...'[24]

Not only the ill, but those attending them, could be reminded of this duty in the same way. Lady Mary Rich, countess of Warwick, after 'readeing of Hesekias message' felt stirred to consider 'how I should be prepared for it [will-writing during sickness]' during one of her nightly Bible readings whilst caring for her crippled husband.[25] This practice was even carried across the Atlantic by the English émigré Richard Mather. He used Isaiah 38 in the preamble to his will to justify why he had written it during his declining health.[26] In such ways, a number of early modern men and women made will-making during illness a devotional activity as well as a worldly duty.

Prescriptive literature, however, appeared at odds with this practice of last-minute will-making. One reason was that patients might be too ill to start, let alone finish, a will, and even if one was completed, the mental state of the testator during its writing was frequently questioned.[27] Another reason was a wish to challenge the folkloric belief that writing a will would hasten its author's death. A further reason was to prevent a will's financial concerns superseding spiritual ones during illness.[28] The Bishop of Bangor Lewis Bayly admonished readers, in his bestseller devotional guide *The Practise of Pietie* (1613), to 'make thy Will in thy health time', and confuted the popular superstition by insisting that 'it will neither put thee further from thy goods, nor hasten thee sooner to thy death'. He posited that making a will in full health would 'bee a great ease to thy minde in freeing thee from a great trouble [during illness], when thou shalt haue most need of quiet: for when thy house is set in order, thou shalt be better enabled to set thy soule in order, and to dispose of thy journey towards GOD'.[29] Those like the Elizabethan devotional writer William Perneby, by contrast, was ready to acknowledge in *A Direction to Death* (1599) that making a will during illness would still bring financial, spiritual and relational peace within the household. 'Now by making of a will in sickenes (if then it be made)', Perneby argued, 'a man may so dispose of his goods, as thereby he may greatly glorifie the name of God, which gaue them; throughly breake off strife and dissension betweene them, which shall haue them, and singularly quiet himselfe that is to depart from them.'[30]

Several established and ejected clergymen conceded how culturally engrained this practice of scripturally attested last-minute will-making had become. Oliver Heywood in *Meetness for Heaven* (1679) agreed that 'When King *Hezekiah* was sick unto death God sends him this Message; *Set thine house in order, for thou shalt dye and not live, Isa.* 38.1. (*i. e.* Make thy Will, and dispose of thy domestical concerns).'[31] These instructions were reiterated in the 1559 and 1662 versions of the Prayer Book. Ministers were advised, when visiting their sick parishioners, to '*let him then be admonished to make his will ... to take order for the settling of their temporal estates*'.[32] Whatever their religious position, all could agree that it was better to make a will during illness than not at all. After quoting 'Isa. 38.1' in the margins of *A Salve for a Sicke Man*, Perkins wrote that 'if the Will be unmade, it is with godly advise and counsell to be made in the time of sicknesse'.[33] These accounts by Independent, Presbyterian and Church of England authors aptly show how such scriptures were not *adiaphora*, but central to people's conceptualisation of what constituted integral sickbed devotion.

Sickbed covenants: Psalm 39

Patients were very good at hedging their bets. An additional way the sick could point to scripture was by not only making a will in the event they should die, but making a sickbed covenant should they live. During the Reformation the tradition of covenant-making was rejected by Protestants on the grounds that sin was unavoidable. It was believed that such promises displayed an unwarranted faith in one's own willpower.[34] By the late sixteenth century, however, the practice was creeping back, and, as Alec Ryrie demonstrates, by the 1630s it was 'almost within the pale of Protestant acceptability'.[35]

The biblical precedent for sickbed covenanting was Psalm 39:1–13, where a sickly King David pledged:

> I said, I will take heed to my ways, that I sin not with my tongue: I will keep my mouth with a bridle ... O spare me, that I may recover strength, before I go hence, and be no more.

David's prayer served as both a request for, and attestation of, deliverance from illness (as the following Psalm 40 testifies).[36]

Sick patients used it to bargain with the Almighty for their health by way of making similar reformatory vows.[37] In the 1620s the Northamptonshire gentlewoman Elizabeth Isham fell ill with 'one [of the] greatest colds since I can remember', which she feared was actually a sign of having contracted the 'pestilence' that was ravaging a nearby town.[38] In her manuscript autobiography, 'A Booke of Rememberance', Isham records calling out to God, 'if it be thy will spare me, that I may recover my strength: psal [3]9.1[3] before I go hence and be no more seene'.[39] Similarly, in his recovery hymn St Nicholas invoked this biblical passage paraphrastically:

>   spare a little, and give space,
> Like a most tender father,
> That, in thy strength and by thy grace,
> I might some new strength gather
> Ere I go hence, and shall no more
> Upon this earth appear.[40]

adding that:

> My sick-bed covenants might not break,
> Nor give my tongue the lie![41]

On his sickbed in 1682, Andrew Rivet, a French physician, asked his family to make a covenant on his behalf using Psalm 39:13, during a potentially fatal illness, likely typhoid. He implored his niece to cry out on his behalf, 'O Return! Return! Confirm me wit[h] thy strength, before I go hence, and be seen no more.'[42] Even the 1662 version of the Prayer Book seemed to endorse the legitimacy and effectiveness of such scriptural covenants. In its rubric for the 'Visitation of the Sick', the minister was to call out to God on behalf of the ill: 'O Lord ... strengthen *him*, wee beseech thee ... before *he* go hence, and be no more seen.'[43]

Yet again, such devotions jarred with the guidance found in printed conduct literature. Several ministers were suspicious of sickbed vows, viewing them as easy to make and much harder to keep. The Essex divine John Beadle wrote in his *Diary of a thankful Christian* (1656), that 'How many are there that on their sick dayes make new promises, but being recovered, forget God[?]'[44] The Northamptonshire preacher and poet Nathaniel Whiting stated in his *The Art of Divine Improvement* (1662): 'Make good your sick-bed thoughts, and purposes ... what you then purposed, now practise: [for] sick people usually have the best minds, but the worst memories'.[45] Baxter simply warned that 'Sick bed Promises are usually soon forgotten.'[46] Bayly pointed out that such resolutions were detrimental and demoralising, so much so that people had 'vow[ed] that they will vow no more' – and this included during illness.[47]

Regardless of these warnings, scriptural covenanting remained a substantive part of the sickbed devotion practised by lawyers (St Nicholas), physicians (Rivet) and gentlewomen (Isham). This was because, as the Scottish Presbyterian minister Zacharie Boyd had argued in *The Balme of Gilead Prepared for the Sicke* (1629), 'it is [biblically] lawfull for a man, beeing in danger of death to begge his lyfe from his GOD'.[48] Psalm 39 had sufficiently demonstrated this. Crucially, like other personal vows, these covenants were to be written down and kept with other devotional writings.[49] They were thus mnemonic aids, seriously made, not to be easily forgotten.

Curative prayers: various scriptures

Patients also used prayers to aid their recovery. One popular prayer was inspired by the episode of Christ's healing of the Roman centurion's servant struck with 'palsy' (Matthew 8:5–13, Luke 7:1–10). The dramatic pathos of this scene evidently struck a chord with carers of the chronically sick. It was frequently invoked as a curative prayer for a series of ailments. The puritan lawyer Robert Woodford wrote in his diary on 18 March 1638, 'O Lord heale my poore Child [John] that is sick if it be thy will, I humbly sue unto thee as the Centurion & health & sicknes are thy servants say but to this goe & it goeth to that Come & it cometh, say but the word & my child shall be healed.'[50] After convalescence, Woodford's son was restored. This prayer was said not only by fathers over their sick sons. The roles were also transferred and spoken by husbands over their wives. The Sussex clergyman William Turner tells the story of one Mrs Savage, the wife of a London schoolmaster and minister, who had suffered 'Lameness in her Hand since Childhood'. Turner records that one day 'Her Husband proceeded Reading [the Bible] till he came to the Faith of the Centurion about his Servant, when on a sudden she felt a Pain in her Knuckles and Fingers, and pulling off her Glove, her Hand instantly stretched out straight, and became like the other; and she was immediately cured.'[51] The restorative properties of this prayer were also used by clergymen for their spouses. When Isaac Archer's wife, Anne Peachy, fell ill with a 'tertian ague' at the start of January 1667, the uxorious Archer was confident of the remedy. In his diary he recalls, 'I begged of Christ, who had diseases under his command, as the centurion, Matt 8.9, to rebuke the distemper, and so he did.'[52]

Other scriptural prayers were used with more precision. Patients reminded God that he had intervened in specific situations before and implored him to do so again. One example is where Christ cured a Canaanite woman's daughter of possession, prompted by the sincere faith of her mother (Mark 15:21–8). When one of her young daughters fell ill in the 1650s Elizabeth Egerton, Countess of Bridgewater, thought this passage highly apposite. Egerton wrote in her manuscript book of devotions, 'A Prayer in the Sicknesses of my girl Frances … O Almighty and eternall God … heal her from her great paine & sicknesse … say unto me, as thou didst to the woman at Canaan, o woman great is thy faith, and be it unto thee even as thou wilt, & immediately the child was made whole from that hour.'[53] Sadly, the infant later died. Alice Thornton recalls when Christ 'Cureth the Bloody Issue' (Matthew 9:18, Mark 5:25) when she herself was recovering from a miscarriage.[54] Isaac Archer quotes the healing of Peter's wife's mother from fever (Luke 4:38) when he prayed in 1678 for his daughter's release from the same affliction.[55] Though not all scriptural prayers were equally popular, the frequent usage of some may have stemmed from those found in the Elizabethan Prayer Book.[56] The prayers of Woodford, Archer, the Savages, Thornton and Egerton serve as a reminder of how the incantatory use of scripture to cure various afflictions was not only sanctioned during the Reformation, but still being practised well into the late seventeenth century by both religious conformists and dissenters alike.

Recovery praise: Psalm 116

It might be tempting to assume that few recovered from their illnesses during this period, given the perceived backwardness of medicine and the high mortality and morbidity rates, but the truth is that many sick patients were restored to health. Until recently, scholars have tended to overlook the behaviours and pious postures of these survivors.[57] If the sick recovered from their illnesses, they used the Bible once more to celebrate and commemorate those recoveries. These often took the form of psalm-singing and reading. Psalm 116 appears to have been a favourite and was employed in various ways. We saw earlier how this scripture was used to instil patience during suffering. It seems fitting that it would also be used to signify a resolution to that suffering. This was a psalm whose speaker travelled from sickness to convalescence – from 'the pains of hell' to praises in 'the courts of the Lord's house' (Psalm 116:3, 19).

When Isaac Archer overcame a 'violent feaver' in April 1667 he immediately 'thought upon Psalm 116:8' ('For thou hast delivered my soul from death, mine eyes from tears, and my feet from falling'). This scripture so impacted Archer – he states it 'affected mee much' (an often repeated phrase when the sick read the Bible) – that he rendered up a thanksgiving to 'solemnly blesse God for my recovery from that dangerous feaver; and desire to walke more closely with him'.[58] When the Leeds antiquarian Ralph Thoresby fell ill in 1698, Oliver Heywood wrote in a letter of encouragement that he would 'pray for a perfect recovery', adding that once healed Thoresby should 'say and act as David, Psalm cxvi. 16' ('O Lord, truly I am thy servant ... thou hast loosed my bonds').[59]

As Heywood's letter indicates, sickness was a communal affair in early modern England. This meant that family, neighbours and friends were partakers in not just each other's illnesses but their recoveries too. Psalm 116 was used by Lady Anne Clifford to share in the joy of her grandchild John Tufton's restoration to health. Clifford records in one of her manuscript 'summaries' that when Tufton had 'escaped death very Narrowly, by a dangerous sickness he had in France' in 1662, the news 'caused me to have in a thankfull remembrance Gods great Mercies to me & Mine ... Psalm 116.v.12' ('What shall I render unto the Lord for all his benefits toward me?').[60] In using Psalm 116, these individual citations (from Archer, Heywood and Clifford) share a unified purpose – as articles of praise said for potential or actual recoveries from illness. Their thanksgivings were fit vehicles of devotion as they were both authored and authorised by God. These examples suggest the multifarious ways the Bible was used to express both general and personal devotional meanings, not just during sickness but after it had passed.

The Bible beyond words

What of those who were unable to quote scripture because they had suffered a stroke, had damaged vocal cords or were catatonic?

Communicating scriptural principles was crucial, so vocally challenged patients tried to respond in physical rather than verbal gestures. This applied to both High and Low Church adherents alike. When suffering from 'palsy', the Canterbury widow Hope Winter in 1625 'made little or noe answer by word' when the scriptures were being read to her. Instead 'by her jesture [of] her *hand* or her *countenance* she manifested her devotion and good understanding of what was then read'.[61] As the Cornish Quaker Richard Samble said of his fellow believer Christopher Bacon, as he lay on his sickbed in 1678, 'he could not speak many Words more' but 'lifting up his Hands, whereby Friends understood that his Life was fresh and green in the everlasting Love of God'.[62] The same gesture was performed by Lady Alice Wandesford when she fell ill in 1659. Surrounded by her household, Wandesford's maid Dafeny plangently prayed that her mistress 'would give them some sign that she found comfort of God's spirit in her soul with a taste of the joys of heaven', which Wandesford 'immediately did' and 'lift[ed] up both hands unto heaven three times'.[63] Again, this kind of sickbed piety was replicated in New England. The Massachusetts minister Richard Mather did not 'speak much in his last Sickness either to Friends or to his Children' in 1669. Instead, Richard attempted to express meaning whereby he 'lifted up his hands' as an affirmative to catechistical questions put to him.[64] Though the raising of hands in an act of prayer or praise during infirmity was also employed by those who could speak, it took on a new significance for those who could not.[65]

Such gesticulations were in keeping with printed advice manuals. The importance placed on such physical signs during sickness was explained by the Middlesex devotional writer John Norden in *A Pathway to Patience* (1626). In a section entitled 'Comfort for the Sick', Norden reminded his readers that 'for the satisfaction of such as visite a sicke person, if he [the sufferer] can but showe it [their piety] by the tongue in speaking, though weakely', that was to be welcomed. If the sick person was unable to perform this, Norden recommended the 'lifting up [of] his hands, or eyes' because this would 'argue the inward heart wel prepared' for heaven.[66] These sickbed gestures were further affirmed and inculcated in woodcut illustrations in works of popular piety (see figures 13.1 and 13.2). Whether by sign or word, such actions were intended to be a clear affirmation of the sick person's faith and his or her posture towards suffering, which served as a model for others to follow.

ARS MORIENDI

Figure 13.1 Woodcut scene of a man in his sickbed from the ballad *An hundred godly lessons* (1684–95?).

Figure 13.2 Woodcut scene of a woman in her sickbed from an earlier edition of *An hundred godly lessons* (1674–79). In both this woodcut and the one in figure 13.1, the sick patients are raising their hands, presumably in prayer.

Conclusion

This piety had a price. Accounts emphasised the obligation of, but also the possible health risk in, speaking and gesturing during sickness. Not knowing if their sickbeds would become their deathbeds, patients made sure others were left in no doubt of their devotion. This meant, however, that spiritual advice often clashed with the medical advice of physicians. During an extreme attack of gout, Powell's doctor insisted that he should be 'kept from speaking much'. Yet so zealously was he affected for the glory of God 'that neither his pains, bodily weakness … could possibly restrain him' as he broke forth into 'high and heavenly praises, sometimes by prayer, [and] sometimes by singing'.[67] When the ejected clergyman Thomas Tregross lay sick in 1671, 'his physician desired him to desist, lest he should spend his spirits too much'; whereupon he replied, 'Give me leave to speak … suffer me to speak as much as I can.'[68] One can only speculate how much these pious exertions increased patients' suffering, hampered their recovery and hastened them to death. Such acts, however, may have also calmed their spirits and allowed them vital fellowship with those around them.

Whatever the risks and benefits, a biblical paradigm of sickbed piety – and writing about it – had gradually become commonplace from the Reformation onwards. This ensured that a systemic devotional identity during illness was widely circulated, printed and read. The reason, as Matthew Henry explained, was because people were to be 'more desirous to be told how we may carry our selves well in our sickness, and get good to our souls by it, than whether we shall recover by it'.[69] It was the manuscript and printed accounts of the period's 'divers sickly and ill' lay men and women that had achieved this.[70] It was these model patients, perhaps more than the clergy, who had made piety within the sickchamber so recognisable and thus repeatable.

Notes

1 Thomas Gipps, *Remarks on remarks; or, The Rector of Bury's sermon vindicated* (London, 1698), p. 61.
2 Quoted in David Harley, 'The Theology of Affliction and the Experience of Sickness in the Godly Family', in Ole Peter Grell and Andrew Cunningham (eds), *Religio Medici: Medicine and Religion in Seventeenth-Century England* (Aldershot: Scolar, 1996), pp. 273–92 (279).

3 Quoted in Michael Rosenblum, 'Swift's "Holyhead Journal" and Circumstantial Talk in Early Modern England', *Eighteenth-Century Studies* 30.2 (1996), 159–72 (164).
4 See Grell and Cunningham, *Religio Medici, passim*; Ian Mortimer, *The Dying and the Doctors: The Medical Revolution in Seventeenth-Century England* (Woodbridge: Royal Historical Society and Boydell, 2009).
5 For recent studies see Andrew Cambers, *Godly Reading: Print, Manuscript and Puritanism in England, 1580–1720* (Cambridge: Cambridge University Press, 2011), pp. 63–71; Hannah Newton, *The Sick Child in Early Modern England, 1580–1720* (Oxford: Oxford University Press, 2012); Olivia Weisser, *Ill Composed: Sickness, Gender, and Belief in Early Modern England* (New Haven, CT: Yale University Press, 2016), pp. 46–80; Hannah Newton, *Misery to Mirth: Recovery from Illness in Early Modern England* (Oxford: Oxford University Press, 2018).
6 I, like Hannah Newton, use the term 'patient' to denote not only those who resorted to physicians during their illnesses, but also those who saw themselves as 'patients' under the care of a providential God. See Newton, *Misery to Mirth*, pp. 1–30.
7 Edmund Calamy, *The Godly Mans Ark* (London, 1657), p. 94.
8 Godly sufferers were 'patient' in both senses of the word. They were to demonstrate the quality of 'enduring pain ... without discontent or complaint (OED, 'patient, *adj.*' sense 1.a); and be a 'patient' 'undergoing the action of another' (OED, 'patient, *n.*', sense 2†.a) – that is, as a passive recipient of God's correction for sin through sickness.
9 All biblical quotations in this essay are taken from the King James Bible.
10 William Perkins, *A Salve for a Sicke Man* (London, 5th edn, 1611), p. 116. Also see William Cowper, *Three Heauenly Treatises* (London, 1609), p. 324.
11 Lancelot Andrewes, *A manual of directions for the sick* (London, 1648), p. 24. Such calls were reinforced in the 1559 and 1662 versions of the Prayer Book's 'Order for the Visitation of the Sick'. The rubric encouraged sick parishioners to suffer 'patiently' no less than five times, ending with a reading from Psalm 71, whose 14th verse rang: 'As for me, I will *patiently* abide, always[s].' Church of England, *The Book of Common Prayer: The Texts of 1549, 1559, and 1662*, ed. Brian Cummings (Oxford: Oxford University Press, 2009), pp. 164–8, 442–6, hereafter *BCP*.
12 Ralph Houlbrooke, 'The Puritan Death-bed, *c.* 1560–1660', in Christopher Durston and Jacqueline Eales (eds), *The Culture of English Puritanism, 1560–1700* (Basingstoke: Macmillan, 1996), pp. 122–44 (130–1). For

'patience' in the Catholic sickchamber see William Palmes, *The life of Mrs Dorothy Lawson, of St Antony's, near Newcastle-on-Tyne*, ed. G. B. Richardson (London, 1855), pp. 46–7.

13 Ralph Josselin, *The Diary of Ralph Josselin, 1616–1683*, ed. Alan Macfarlane (London: Oxford University Press for the British Academy, 1976), p. 74.

14 Lucy Hutchinson, *Memoirs of the Life of Colonel Hutchinson*, ed. N. H. Keeble (London: Phoenix, 2000), p. 20. Lucy adds that he was frequently 'rheumatic' and 'troubled with weakness and toothaches'. *Ibid.*

15 Hanserd Knollys, *The life and death of ... Hanserd Knollys*, ed. William Kiffin (London, 1692), p. 39.

16 Mary Penington, *Some Account of Circumstances in the Life of Mary Penington from her Manuscript, left for her Family* (London, 1821), p. 56.

17 Birmingham University Library, MS 5/iv/23, p. 207.

18 *Ibid.*, p. 208.

19 Quoted in Paul S. Seaver, *Wallington's World* (London: Methuen, 1985), p. 27.

20 As Jeremy Taylor argued, in his section on 'Impatience', the sick man 'cries so loud to God, that it pierces the clouds; and so hath every sorrow, and every sicknesse: and when a man cries out, and complains but according to the sorrowes of his pain, it cannot be any part of a culpable impatience, but an argument for pity'. Jeremy Taylor, *Holy Dying* (London, 1651), p. 83. In this way, sounds of groaning and crying were believed to be a divinely ordained form of communication, which generated pity in onlookers. For examples see Newton, *Misery to Mirth*, p. 116.

21 For the use of Isaiah 38 in the prayers of Catholics and early Protestants see Micheline White, 'Dismantling Catholic Primers and Reforming Private Prayer: Anne Lock, Hezekiah's Song and Psalm 50/51', in Jessica Martin and Alec Ryrie (eds), *Private and Domestic Devotion in Early Modern Britain* (Abingdon: Routledge, 2012), pp. 93–113.

22 Philip Henry, *Diaries and Letters of Philip Henry, M.A. of Broad Oak, Flintshire, A.D. 1631–1696*, ed. Matthew Henry Lee (London, 1882), p. 168.

23 Edward Bagshaw, *The life and death of Mr Vavasor Powell* (London, 1671), p. 93.

24 Birmingham University Library, MS 5/iv/23, p. 207. Like so many others, however, St Nicholas died without writing a will.

25 BL, Additional MSS 27351–5, fol. 145ʳ.

26 Mather wrote, '*the will of God* [is] *that a man should set his House in order before he depart this life*, [Thus] *Do* [I] *make this my last Will*

    and Testament'. Increase Mather, *The life and death of that Reverend Man of God, Mr. Richard Mather* (Cambridge, MA, 1670), p. 34.
27 See Peter Carlson, 'The Art and Craft of Dying', in Andrew Hiscock and Helen Wilcox (eds), *The Oxford Handbook of Early Modern English Literature and Religion* (Oxford: Oxford University Press, 2017), pp. 634–49 (641–4).
28 For the multifarious motivations behind will-making, see Christopher Marsh, 'Attitudes to Will Making in Early Modern England', in Tom Arkell, Nesta Evans and Nigel Goose (eds), *When Death Do Us Part: Understanding and Interpreting the Probate Records of Early Modern England* (Oxford: Oxford University Press, 2000), pp. 158–75.
29 Lewis Bayly, *The practise of pietie* (London, 3rd edn, 1613), p. 811.
30 William Perneby, *A direction to death* (London, 1599), p. 236.
31 Oliver Heywood, *Meetness for heaven* (London, 1679), p. 64.
32 *BCP*, pp. 166, 445.
33 Perkins, *A Salve for a Sicke Man*, pp. 145–6.
34 Alec Ryrie, *Being Protestant in Reformation Britain* (Oxford: Oxford University Press, 2013), pp. 132–3.
35 *Ibid.*, p. 139.
36 For similar sickbed prayers see Isaiah 38:1–4 and Job 10:20–1.
37 For a broader discussion of sickbed vows see Newton, *Misery to Mirth*, pp. 138–45.
38 Elizabeth Isham, 'Booke of Rememberance', in *Constructing Elizabeth Isham Project*, ed. Alice Eardley (University of Warwick, 2009), fol. 7^v. http://web.warwick.ac.uk/english/perdita/Isham. Accessed 13 March 2018.
39 *Ibid.*, fol. 8^r.
40 Birmingham University Library, MS 5/iv/23, p. 207. For a Scottish sickbed covenant see Alexander Brodie, *The Diary of Alexander Brodie*, ed. David Laing (La Crosse, WI: Brookhaven, 1982), p. 481.
41 Birmingham University Library, MS 5/iv/23, p. 207.
42 Nehemiah Coxe, *A believers triumph over death* (London, 1682), p. 72. Sickbed covenants were also made by parents on behalf of their sick children or, occasionally, by servants on behalf of their sick masters. See BL, MS. Add. 88897/1, p. 73; Lady Anne Harcourt, 'The Diary of Lady Anne Harcourt', in *The Harcourt Papers*, ed. Edward H. Harcourt, 14 vols (London, 1880–1905), I:169–96 (172).
43 *BCP*, p. 448. The text further reinforced the effectiveness of this prayer by stating, 'O Lord, that there is no word impossible with thee … thou canst even yet raise *him* up, and grant *him* a longer continuance amongst us.' *Ibid.*
44 John Beadle, *The journal or diary of a thankful Christian* (London, 1656), p. 2. The same minatory messages were expressed by clergymen

who preached before Parliament during the 1640s. Their admonitions resonated with their listeners as often these preachers had been present at the sickbeds of Members of Parliament. See Jeremiah Burroughs, *Sions joy* (London, 1641), p. 63; Cornelius Burges, *Two sermons preached* (London, 1642), pp. 40–1.

45 Nathaniel Whiting, *The art of divine improvement* (London, 1662), p. 82. Whiting added that 'all the sick-bed resolutions vanish into air'. *Ibid.*
46 Richard Baxter, *Reliquiae Baxterianae*, ed. Matthew Sylvester (London, 1696), p. 90.
47 Bayly, *Practise of pietie*, p. 900.
48 Zacharie Boyd, *The balme of Gilead prepared for the sicke* (Edinburgh, 1629), p. 97.
49 For the imperative to write out and keep personal covenants see Richard Alleine, *Vindiciae pietatis* (London, 1665), p. 209.
50 Robert Woodford, *Robert Woodford's Diary, 1637–1641*, ed. John Fielding (Cambridge: Cambridge University Press, 2012), p. 190.
51 William Turner, *A compleat history of the most remarkable providences* (London, 1697), p. 112.
52 Isaac Archer, 'The Diary of Isaac Archer, 1641–1700', in *Two East Anglian Diaries 1641–1729*, ed. Matthew Storey (Woodbridge: Boydell, 1994), pp. 41–200 (153).
53 BL, MS Egerton 607, fol. 21^v.
54 BL, Additional MS 88897/2, fol. 59^r. I am grateful to Hannah Newton for this reference.
55 Archer, 'Diary', p. 156.
56 In the rubric for the 'visitation of the sick', the minister was to pray over the ailing parishioner: 'Mericifull God, and saviour. Extend thy accustomed goodnes to this thy servant whiche is greved with syckenesse, visit him O Lorde, as thou diddest visit Peters wifes mother [Luke 4:38], and the capiteines servant [Matthew 8:5–13, Luke 7:1–10].' *BCP*, p. 165. This passage was removed in the 1662 Prayer Book.
57 See Newton, *Misery to Mirth*, pp. 7–9, *passim*.
58 Archer, 'Diary', p. 154.
59 Joseph Hunter (ed.), *Letters of eminent men, addressed to Ralph Thoresby*, 2 vols (1832), I:336.
60 BL, MS Harl 6177, p. 164.
61 Quoted in Elizabeth A. Hallam, 'Turning the Hourglass: Gender Relations at the Deathbed in Early Modern Canterbury', *Mortality* 1.1 (1996), 61–82 (75), emphasis added.
62 Richard Samble, *Richard Samble's testimony concerning Christopher Bacon* (London, 1678), p. 4.

63 Alice Thornton, 'A Book of Remembrances', in Elspeth Graham *et al.* (eds), *Her Own Life: Autobiographical Writings by Seventeenth-Century Englishwomen* (London: Routledge, 1989), pp. 145–62 (153).
64 Mather, *Mr. Richard Mather*, pp. 27–8. The raising of hands in prayer was also the appropriate expression of piety and sought-after redemption at the scaffold. See *The cruel mother … with the manner of her execution and demeanour there* (London, 1670), p. 8.
65 A five-year-old Richard Evelyn is recorded as having requested, due to the 'agony' of his ague, 'whether he might pray to God with his hands unjoined'. Richard was permitted to 'keep his hands in [the] bed' because he still had the ability to speak. John Evelyn, *The Diary of John Evelyn*, ed. Austin Dobson, 3 vols (Cambridge: Cambridge University Press, 2015), II:129.
66 John Norden, *A Pathway to Patience in … Sicknesse* (London, 1626), pp. 86–7. The lifting of hands or eyes, however, was a problematic gesture. It was explicitly proscribed as potentially idolatrous in popular devotional works such as William Perkins, *The whole treatises of the cases of conscience* (Cambridge, 1608), p. 150; and Henry Ainsworth, *Annotations upon the second book of Moses* (Amsterdam, 1617), sig. O3^v. This was, in part, due to the fact that Catholics in their sickbeds also lifted their eyes to heaven and raised their hands to pray, make the sign of the cross or to kiss their crucifixes. See Palmes, *Mrs Dorothy Lawson*, pp. 50–1; and chapter 14.
67 Bagshaw, *Mr Vavasor Powell*, p. 190.
68 Edmund Calamy, *The Nonconformist's Memorial*, ed. Samuel Palmer, 3 vols (London, 1802–3), I:366. This is not to suggest that physicians were attempting to silence, or did not take part in, sickbed devotions. On the contrary, some physicians read scriptures for and prayed with the sick at their bedside. See Sophie Mann, 'Physic and Divinity: The Case of Dr John Downes M. D. (1627–1694)', *Seventeenth Century* 31.4 (2016), 451–70 (458).
69 Matthew Henry, *Commentary on the Whole Bible: Vol II–III*, ed. Anthony Uyl (Ontario: Devoted, 2017), p. 123.
70 Phrase occurs in Josselin, *Diary*, p. 159.

14

'Now the Lord hath made me a spectacle': deathbed narratives and devotional identities in the early seventeenth century

Charles Green

In act 3 of *The Second Part of King Henry VI*, the murdered Duke of Gloucester, 'laid fair', 'dead in his bed', is made a disturbing spectacle for the King and his allies. The original 1594 quarto text of the play, titled *The First Part of the Contention betwixt the Two Famous Houses of York and Lancaster, with the Death of Good Duke Humphrey,* makes it clear that this elaborate prop would have functioned something like a stage within a stage when the play was first performed, enclosed by curtains used to maximise viewers' intrigue and horror. Coming, finally, 'to survey his dead and earthy image', the lugubrious Henry ponders its relevance to his own state, in the many senses of that word:

> That is to see how deep my grave is made,
> For with his soul fled all my worldly solace;
> For, seeing him, I see my life in death.

These lines are steeped in those of 'The Order for the Burial of the Dead' from the *Book of Common Prayer*: 'As is the earthy, suche are they that are earthy'; 'In the mideste of lyfe we bee in death' – language that gestures outwards from the play's fraught historical setting and into the post-Reformation world of its first audiences.[1] While within the wider play, as Andrew Gordon and Thomas Rist have argued, the political consequences of Gloucester's death ('the event that split apart a troubled commonweal') are manifest in 'divergent practices of remembrance' on both sides, Henry's distorted liturgy transposes this epicentre of division into the recognisable terms of Shakespeare's England, in which a diverse range of cultural scripts for dying and remembering competed for precedence.[2]

Over the 1590s and into the seventeenth century, a vast devotional and didactic literature on dying well – or *ars moriendi* – was written, printed and sold on London's bookstalls, building on late-medieval and Calvinist precedents such as Thomas Becon's bestselling *Sicke Manns Salve* (1595), as well as Catholic devotional texts like Robert Parsons's *Booke of Christian Exercise Appertaining to Resolution* (1582), appropriated in a 'perused' form two years later by the Calvinist Edmund Bunny.[3] Generically and confessionally diverse, the *ars moriendi* reminded readers that 'the life of a Christian should be continually exercised in the meditation of Death'; last-minute repentance was unwise, particularly for those whose vocations made sudden death an everyday risk, and despite the fact that Christ himself had saved a repentant criminal on the cross.[4] Robert Southwell's *Epistle of a Religious Priest vnto his father* (1597), a private exhortation to convert to the Roman faith (and another 'visibly Catholic' publication printed two years after Southwell was martyred at Tyburn), contains an extraordinary evocation of its addressee's future deathbed, universalised in printed form:[5]

> If you were layed on your departing bed, burdened with the heavy load of your former traspasses, and goared with the sting and pricke of a festered conscience: If you felt the crampe of death wresting your hart stringes & ready to make the rufull divorce between body and soule: If you lay panting for breath, and swimming in a colde and fatall sweat, weried with struggling against your deadly panges: O how much wold you give for an hower of repentance at what rate woulde you valew a days contrition.[6]

The nature and availability of the 'good death' was thus a matter of serious concern to contemporary readers of English *ars moriendi* texts.[7] But this literature also points to the contested social, confessional and political dimensions of that concern. Those at the deathbed would watch its protagonist closely, aware that in speech and comportment he or she showed outward signs of an inner faith whose strength would be tested, and on which salvation might depend. Even theologians espousing a strictly predestinarian soteriology, which held one's status of election or reprobation to be immutably (and, ultimately, inscrutably) writ in 'the book of life', contributed towards this focus: William Perkins's 'Survey, or Table Declaring the Order of the Causes of Salvation and Damnation', and Arthur Dent's *Plaine Mans Path-way to Heaven* (1601), promised readers that they '*may clearely see, whether* [they] *shall be saved or damned*' through certain 'signs'.[8] Moreover, adapting Paul's famous analogy from 1 Corinthians 9:24, Perkins shows how the deathbed in particular remained a uniquely indicative microcosm of an auspicious lifelong faith: 'as men that are appointed to runne a race, exercise themselves before in running, that they may get the victory: so should we beginne to die now while we are living, that we may die well in the end'.[9] Interpreting such arguments on the spiritual battlefield of the deathbed could require highly trained forms of what Erin Sullivan calls 'emotive improvisation', to 'read' verbal and bodily 'signs' in theologically applicable ways.[10]

Such scrutiny could also expose individuals, and the spiritual health of their associates, to unwelcome conjectures, including accusations of last-minute conversion or apostasy. Responding – sometimes pre-emptively – to such polemics, Christian communities in late sixteenth and early seventeenth-century England began ever more to narrativise deathbeds in printed form, packaging them within and alongside funeral sermons, early biographies and didactic texts more recognisably belonging to the *ars moriendi* tradition. While plays, scaffold speeches, martyrologies and ballads scripted the deaths of historical characters, convicted felons, heretics and saints, deathbed narratives made available to a growing reading public the final moments of a diverse range of ordinary Christian subjects.[11] This essay surveys a cross-section of deathbed narratives printed in English between 1592 and 1646, about individuals from a spectrum of social classes and confessional identities. It has two chief objectives, out of which come two main arguments. The first is to read behind some of these works and into the discursive and polemical contexts that, I argue, first catalysed their publication. The second is to offer a fresh account of the deathbed narrative as an emergent devotional subgenre that combined many shared features across the confessional divide that gave rise to it (whilst remaining highly expressive of devotional identity): a didactic purpose informed by *ars moriendi* precedents, a specific narrative arc, inventive and extensive uses of print, and a flexible prose style shaped by a number of biblical, dramatic and literary analogues. Away from the open theatricality of the playhouse and the scaffold, deathbed narratives stage exemplary domestic piety both to edify wider communities and to construct enduring histories about private sites of public intrigue and scandal.

The late-Elizabethan deathbed: print and the polemics of dying

Up to the final years of Queen Elizabeth's reign, as Patrick Collinson and Jessica Martin have shown, it was extremely uncommon for funeral sermons on ordinary Christian folk to be printed. Over the first few decades of the new century, however, such texts – particularly about women – grew rapidly in popularity, reaching something of an 'apotheosis' in 1640 with the publication of *The House of Movrning*: a folio anthology of forty-seven funeral sermons on unremarkable individuals, whose subtitle purposes it distinctively as an *ars moriendi* text.[12] Throughout this period, the question of how far a funeral sermon should praise a deceased person or discuss his or her conduct was also a live one, given especially what Martin describes as a 'new Protestant culture' of suspicion for 'all works commemorating the lives of the dead'.[13] For preachers who did so, justification could be found in the example of the church fathers, who had written encomia in the classical tradition of the funeral oration, which praised virtue in order to encourage its imitation in others.[14] Over time, it became conventional to divide funeral sermons into the sermon proper and a short biographical section, or eulogy; though the proportion made up by each remained a point of some contention.[15] According to Collinson, the publication that first 'pointed to a new literary fashion' of commemorating and biographising the common sort, 'and perhaps even initiated it', was *Deaths Advantage Little Regarded*, an edition of two funeral sermons on the Lancastrian puritan Katherine Brettergh, printed in 1602.[16] Not only were these sermons about a relatively obscure layperson; both contain substantial eulogies, and they were appended by a thirty-eight-page account of her 'Christian Life and death', during which she is said to have overcome 'a bitter conflict' with Satan, 'to the great glorie of God, and comfort of all beholders'.[17] By the 1680s, Ralph Houlbrooke notes, 'there was a growing scepticism about the value and meaning of deathbed testimonies, a greater reluctance to publish them, and a growing readiness to discount or pass over the last scene when assessing the whole of an individual's life performance'.[18]

One notable precedent here is *A Christall Glasse for Christian Women* (1592), published ten years earlier by the puritan pamphleteer Philip Stubbes. A much shorter black-letter tract, it describes the death of Stubbes's wife Katherine, which also featured 'a most wonderfull combat betwixt sathan and her soule', here 'set downe word for word as she spake it, as neere as could be gathered'.[19] Beyond their broadly thematic and didactic titles, a number of similarities between these two texts are readily apparent, and would continue to characterise such publications into the seventeenth century. Both insist upon the open publicity of the deathbed chamber: Stubbes alludes to 'them that were present (as there were many both worshipful & others)' almost incidentally, and the names of 'divers other well affected' visitors of Brettergh are at one point listed in a margin note.[20] Such publicity reflects broader customs about the government of the bedchamber at birth and death: whereas gossips and midwives took great care to ensure the confidentiality and homosociality of the birthing chamber (even to the extent of blocking keyholes), at the deathbed that dynamic would be reversed, the community invited into the same domestic space.[21] A second similarity is closely related to this one: deathbeds, as public contexts, are described in somewhat liturgical terms, their protagonists performing central roles in community worship. Both Stubbes and Brettergh are said to have sung psalms once their spiritual travails had subsided, with Brettergh afterwards leading her deathbed assembly in communal prayer.[22] Indeed, comparisons between deathbeds and pulpits were becoming relatively common in the period. Addressing his St Paul's congregation in 1627, John Donne, who favoured this analogy, asks that 'When you come to hear us here, who are come from God, heare us with such an affection, as if we were going to God, as if you heard us upon our death-bed, for we are bound to the same truth, and sincerity here, as if we were upon our death-bed.'[23] What is perhaps most striking about this aspect of deathbed narratives and printed funeral sermons is that they bulked large in female subjects, offering to those women, and the reading public, unique kinds of homiletic ministry and posthumous authorship.[24]

The key difference between the texts, in addition to length, is their approach to the authenticity they assert. The larger part of

Stubbes's narrative is divided into direct transcriptions of his wife's extemporised confession and, later, her rebuttal of Satan:

> And wheras before shee looked with a sweete, louely and amiable countenaunce, red as the Rose, and most beautifull to beholde, nowe vpon the sudden, she bent the browes, shee frowned, and looking (as it were) with an angry, sterne, and fierce countenaunce, as though shee sawe some filthy, vgglesome and displeasant thing: shee burst foorth into these speeches following, pronouncing her wordes (as it were) scornefully, and disdainfully, in contempt of him to whom shee spake.[25]

But in *Deaths Advantage Little Regarded* a more discerning and collaborative approach is evident. Harrison admits that he 'cannot rehearse the least part of those heauenly speeches' Brettergh 'vttered'; yet, he confronts his auditory, *'if you yet doubt of this point, I could shew the testimony of the best learned to approve it'*.[26] The preface to the 'Christian Life and death' corroborates this:

> And this I assure the Reader, that howsoeuer I may sometimes misse the forme of words which possibly the Gentlewoman vsed in her speech; yet haue I faithfully set downe the substance of the matter, and for the most part also faithfully related the words themselues, ... testified by persons of good and honest report, as they are named in the margent: out of whose fresh memories the substance of that which I publish was presentlie set downe.[27]

The three large texts and numerous commendatory verses that make up *Deaths Advantage Little Regarded* are in constant dialogue, establishing and substantiating particularities about Brettergh's life and death, such as her habit of reading eight Bible chapters a day.[28] While fragments of voice are still conveyed ('once when she should have said, *Leade us not into temptation*, she made a stop, saying *I may not pray; I may not pray (being interrupted, as she said, by Satan)*'), her spiritual turmoil is filtered predominantly through an intricate weave of third-person narratives. Harrison's preface reveals that this strategy, and the printing of the work in the first instance, were undertaken 'to cleere her from the slanderous reports of her popish neighbors, who will not suffer her to rest in her graue, but seeke to disgrace her after her death'.[29] This objective is also reflected in his decision to preach on Isaiah 57:1 ('mercifull men are taken away, and no man understandeth that the righteous is taken away from the evil to come'), a text often used in polemical commemorations of the time, and whose themes are further explored by Leygh.[30] Claiming, in an unprecedented way, the cultural capital of the printed funeral sermon, and buttressing it with 'The Christian Life and death of Mistris Katherine Brettergh', this innovative and popular publication represents a forceful response to a 'shrewd polemical sally' against her deathbed conduct.[31]

About the 'popish neighbours' responsible some information survives. As Steve Hindle points out, Brettergh's local community contained an influential Catholic recusant faction led by the seminary priest Thurston Hunt and Edward Norris, a local landowner.[32] Hunt was a close associate of another Catholic priest, Robert Middleton, alongside whom he was tried and executed in Lancaster some two months before Brettergh's death.[33] The strong feelings aroused by this process are suggested in a contemporary commemorative song:

> Huntes hawtie courage staut, with godlie zeale soe true;
> Myld Middleton, O what tonge can halfe they virtue shew;
> At Lancaster lovingly, these marters tooke their end
> In glorious victorie, true faith for to defende.[34]

Brettergh's death thus stood in direct contrast with the extraordinary spectacle of Catholic martyrdom, stoically endured on the Lancaster scaffold. Leaving this aside, and the possibility that she indeed did suffer diabolical assaults on her deathbed, there are clear circumstantial reasons for her becoming personally embroiled in a local religious propaganda war. Her husband, William Brettergh, who was high constable of West Derby, had only the previous year provoked riots through an aggressive policy of apprehending Catholic recusants in two parishes under his jurisdiction.[35] Her brother was the famous puritan iconoclast John Bruen, whose household was many times involved in stirring up religious unrest in the region, such as the smashing of stained-glass windows at St Andrew's Church in Tarvin. Like his sister, Bruen was later also commemorated in an innovative hagiographical biography.[36]

While no evidence can confirm what specific aspersions were cast on Katherine by local Catholics (or how), this context points to the conditions under which deathbed publications were assembled, spurred by the snowballing nature of third-party intrigue and readers' appetites for such materials. A wide range of contemporary analogues reinforces this point. The public executions in England of men like Hunt and Middleton were themselves scrupulously narrativised in

English martyrologies from continental presses, by writers such as Thomas Worthington and John Wilson.[37] Likewise, English Protestants – particularly those of noble birth – could easily become the subjects of polemical conversion narratives while abroad in Catholic Europe. When in late 1605 the Jacobean grand tour of Pickering Wotton (Henry Wotton's nephew) was suddenly halted by fatal illness, handwritten accounts of his deathbed conversion began circulating widely, to the extent that the subject was 'argued over for years afterwards'. One such text, purporting to contain the actual words Wotton spoke, would even be subjected to a close reading exercise by William Bedell when in 1607 he took up Henry Wotton's chaplaincy in Venice.[38] Perhaps the best-known English target to be thus accused over the following years is John King, Bishop of London, whose 'Supposed Apostasie', promulgated in Richard Broughton's *The English Protestant's Plea* (1621), among various other texts, led John's son Henry to preach a riposte at King James's insistence. Henry was also compelled to make this his first printed sermon, appending it with 'The Examination of Thomas Preston', which tersely and categorically refutes the claims made against his father.[39] The sermon went into three editions within weeks of its launch.[40]

Scripting deaths and devotional identities: Lady Magdalen Montague and Mr Thomas Peacock

If polemical piety catalysed the development of deathbed narratives in these years, it also provided publication strategies and behavioural models that became broadly influential to English devotional practice. Richard Smith's *The life of the most honourable and vertuous lady, the Lady Magdalen Viscountesse Montague* portrays the death of a prodigious Catholic noblewoman and patron who died in Battle, East Sussex. Originally published 'soone after her death' in Latin in 1609, in a biographised adaptation of a funeral sermon, it was later translated into English by Cuthbert Fursden and sold as a stand-alone biography in 1627. In the same way, William Harrison had reprinted 'The Christian Life and death of Mistris Katherine Brettergh' as a single publication of comparable length, retitled *The Life and Death, of Mistris K. Brettergh*, in 1612. The publication strategy of Montague's *Life* is otherwise highly similar to the above examples – a fact in keeping with Montague's longstanding support for English recusant printing, which she had even previously undertaken to house within her London lodgings.⁴¹ Fursden's dedication to Montague's *Life* offers an apology for the 'rudenes of the stile' which he justifies by insisting on its fidelity; likewise, Smith's dedicatory epistle claims 'the truth' as the work's 'principall ayme': 'I write nothing, but what my selfe haue seene, or haue receyued from the mouth of this Lady her selfe, or of other witnesses worthy of credit.' He also vindicates the work with immediate reference to patristic funeral orations about 'such pious women of their tymes'.⁴²

Roughly four pages of Smith's text are concerned explicitly with Montagu's deathbed; but the fact of her death overshadows the earlier chapters through digressive reflections on her loss that build anticipation towards that climactic scene: 'O what iewell of chastity did the earth loose! how much did heauen gaine by her death!'⁴³ A similar technique is used in Izaak Walton's 'Life and Death of Dʳ Donne, Late Deane of St Pauls London', the latter third of which holds the image of its dying protagonist in view as a centre-point for general reflections on his life.⁴⁴ Smith's deathbed narrative itself follows the same general structure as those depicted by Stubbes, Harrison and Leygh, in that it stages a trial of faith and fellowship ultimately overcome in a peaceful and well-documented passing. But the chief point of disputation between deathbed protagonist and bedside congregation is here of a different kind: 'for her merit, and our edification', God 'did prolong her infirmity for eleuen whole weekes'; during which, Smith recalls, 'oftentimes euen in her extremest torments', 'she beseeched, praying God to increase both her paine and patience'.⁴⁵ Her emphasis on the divine authorship of this suffering creates a framework within which she models Christianised versions of stoic *apatheia* and the devotional tradition of *contemptus mundi*:

> from the beginning of her sicknes, to vs who much desired her life, she seemed too much to desire her death; & therfore when we did propose vnto her the examples of *S. Paul, S. Martin*, and others, who for the consolation of their friends were content to liue, she would humbly answere: *The will of God be done*.⁴⁶

Even at the height of her suffering, Montague continues to use her position to pursue Catholic ministry: 'Sometimes she enquired the estate of other sick persons; & as occasion was presented, she did exhort Catholikes to constancy in their fayth, and sometimes also she spake to Heretikes of imbracing the Catholike fayth'.⁴⁷ A codicil to her will notes also that she 'did in her last sickness give and bequeathe by worde to divers p[ar]ticuler p[er]sons sithens the makinge of hir last will and Testament'.[48] Foreseeing death, even in contradiction to the reassurances of her physicians, Montague asks five priests to say mass for the Blessed Virgin in a constant relay, following which 'the very pangs of death did assault her, neyther did they euer leaue her, till they bereaued her of this motall life'.[49] As with Brettergh's deathbed, the author is careful to (twice) note the precise time at which Montague dies, holding a crucifix and 'a hallowed light, which she held so fast euen after her death, that without force it could not be wrested frō her'. Her bowels were buried in situ at Battle, where she died, but her body was taken to Midhurst, and 'there layd in the Sepulcher of her husband'.[50]

Disputation and dialogue are common features in these works, the primary means through which theological and experiential perspectives, physical decline, and spiritual insight are modelled and reproduced in omniscient narrative or scripted text. This reflects the range of *ars moriendi*, biblical and literary precedents from which deathbed narratives draw. The final example I will discuss is the most allusive and stylistically eclectic and dramatic. It was printed, like the English *Life* of Magdalen Montague, long after the death of its protagonist, and fifteen years after the death of its author, Robert Bolton. This is *The Last Conflicts and Death of Mr Thomas Peacock, Batchelour of Divinity, and fellow of Brasen-nose Colledge in Oxford* (1646). Intriguingly, a 'Post-script to the Reader' states that this book was originally censored by the licenser, refused 'as too precise for those times', and printed only when such licensing gave way to looser regulation after the outbreak of the English Civil War.[51] Bolton's own life is well documented thanks to his printer, biographer and executor, Edward Bagshaw, who noted his youthful affinity for Roman Catholicism, 'stage plays, cards and dice'. Bagshaw is, however, careful also to recount Bolton's later conversion to hard-line Calvinism – a conversion sparked by his friendship with one Thomas Peacock.[52]

Accordingly, Bolton's deathbed narrative on Peacock is modelled on the most important *ars moriendi* text in the Calvinist tradition, Thomas Becon's *Sicke Manns Salve*. Becon's 'quasi-dramatic' style derives particularly from the Book of Job, in which the faith of the ruined eponymous character is repeatedly questioned and tested in 'cycles' by four well-meaning interlocutors (counting Elihu). Becon's text seems to provide something of a rationale for a long-unquestioned tendency in Reformation history to describe deathbeds in the terminology of theatre.[53] While, as Beaty notes, the sprawling length, 'extreme scripturalism' and doctrinaire polemics of the *Sicke Manns Salve* attenuate its devotional qualities, Bolton's *Last Conflicts and Death* might be read as an abbreviated, accessible and personalised adaptation of its drama.[54] The deathbed congregation is again in evidence, including the godly divine John Dod (who delivers an initial homiletic address to Peacock), 'a worthy Governour of a Colledge' and 'some of his best friends', who are the first to question Peacock in a passage of pure dialogue that follows an initial address to the reader.[55] When Dod later returns, he engages Peacock, who refuses to believe himself among '*those that are elected*', in an intense theological debate that follows the same prose–dialogue format:

> Would you believe your self, or the Physician touching the estate of your body? *The Physician.* Believe not your self then, now you are sick, yet shall be restored? *It is impossible.* Why so? If you had sinned so much as you could, you could not have sinned to much as *Adam*, yet he is in Heaven. *It repented him.* Doth not it you? *No.* Doth your sicknes or sinne more trouble you, or had you rather have grace, or health? *Grace.* Well then. *But it cannot be.* God will wash you. *I have no water.*[56]

Drama, in Alison Shell's words, 'subjects personality to exegesis' – an insight borne out by the near-equivalence of doctrine and dialogue fashioned within this text.[57] Dod teases out, exhaustively, the tenets of a version of Protestant orthodoxy from a voice characterised by something like the 'spiritual schizophrenia' of Becon's protagonist, Epaphroditus.[58] Bolton's rapid-fire dialogue creates a vividly dramatised form of 'emotive improvisation' within scriptural exegesis, creating an experiential, vicarious *ars moriendi* text populated by recognisable figures from seventeenth-century England. Reaching the end of the debate, Peacock reflects: '*I thank God* (saith he) *he hath begun to ease me ... Now the Lord hath made me a spectacle.*'[59] Sure enough, Peacock's deathbed soon becomes a platform for his own ministry and testimony, delivered to 'many young Gentlemen, to whom he said, Live in Gods fear, that you may die in his favour: Otherwise the Oxe and the Asse will condemn you; I spent my time foolishly and prodigally'.[60]

Admonishing the reader of *The Last Conflicts and Death* to 'take heed of small sinnes' in his preface, Bolton cites the cautionary story of Francis Spira, an Italian lawyer said to have abjured a lifelong conviction of election on his deathbed, which went on to become the subject of international speculations, retellings and dramatisations.[61] Spira appears as Philologus in Nathaniel Woodes's 1581 play *The Conflict of Conscience*, printed with alternative 'elect' and 'reprobate' endings – an interactive textual experience in which players and readers could act out the knotty emotional and spiritual scenarios of the deathbed.[62] While, as this essay has shown, controversy and conflict scripted Christian deaths into literary forms, those forms would map passageways to reconciliation – with God, the wider community and the readers of the 'lives' they would become.

Notes

1 These allusions are noted by Roland Knowles in *King Henry VI, Part 2*, in *The Arden Shakespeare*, ed. Ronald Knowles (London: Bloomsbury, 3rd edn, 2013), pp. 264–5.
2 Andrew Gordon and Thomas Rist, 'Introduction', in Andrew Gordon and Thomas Rist (eds), *The Arts of Remembrance in Early Modern England: Memorial Cultures of the Post Reformation* (Farnham: Ashgate, 2013), pp. 1–19 (9).
3 Becon's work was first printed in 1561, though its composition date is uncertain. See Ian Green, *Print and Protestantism in Early Modern England* (Oxford: Oxford University Press, 2000), p. 361. Nancy Lee Beaty collates and compares the works of Parson and Bunny in *The Craft of Dying: The Literary Tradition of the Ars Moriendi in England* (New Haven, CT: Yale University Press, 1970), pp. 157–96.
4 John More, 'The Printer to the Christian Reader', in *A lively Anatomie of Death: Wherein you may see from whence it came, what it is by nature and what by Christ* (London, 1596), sig. A1^r. On Christ's pardon see Thomas Tuke, *A Discourse of Death, Bodily, Ghostly, and Eternal* (London, 1613), p. 18. Tuke's subtitle specifies the tract's suitability for '*Souldiers Warring, Seamen sayling, Strangers trauelling, Women bearing, nor any other liuing that thinkes of Dying*'.
5 See Arthur F. Marotti, 'Southwell's Remains: Catholicism and Anti-Catholicism in Early Modern England', in Cedric C. Brown and Arthur F. Marotti (eds), *Texts and Cultural Change in Early Modern England* (London: Macmillan, 1997), pp. 37–65 (54).
6 Robert Southwell, *An Epistle of a Religious Priest vnto his father: exhorting him to the perfect forsaking of the world* (London, 1597), pp. 23–4.

7 For a recent overview see Peter Carlson, 'The Art and Craft of Dying', in Andrew Hiscock and Helen Wilcox (eds), *The Oxford Handbook of Early Modern English Literature and Religion* (Oxford: Oxford University Press, 2017), pp. 634–49.
8 The 'Survey' was first printed with Perkins's *Works* (Cambridge, 1612) as a foldout page between pp. 10–11; Arthur Dent, *The Plaine Mans Path-way to Heaven. Wherein every man may clearely see, whether he shall be saved or damned* (London, 1601), e.g. pp. 32–3. As Carlson notes, John Calvin himself said that 'we have been inscribed in the book of life if we are in communion with Christ', opening up the interpretive space such intricate theological texts sought to map. Carlson, 'Craft of Dying', p. 638.
9 William Perkins, *A Salve for a Sicke-Man; or, A treatise containing the nature, differences, and kindes of death; as also the right manner of dying well* (Cambridge, 1595), p. 46. 1 Corinthians 9:24: 'Know ye not that they which run in a race run all, but one receiveth the prize? So run, that ye may obtain' (King James Bible).
10 Erin Sullivan, *Beyond Melancholy: Sadness and Selfhood in Renaissance England* (Oxford: Oxford University Press, 2016), p. 9.
11 On ballads and other cheap print focusing on individual deaths, see Tessa Watt, *Cheap Print and Popular Piety 1550–1640* (Cambridge: Cambridge University Press, 1991), pp. 106–14.
12 The subtitle reads: '*Furnished with Directions for, Preparations to, Meditations of, Consolations at the Houre of Death*'. See Patrick Collinson, *Godly People: Essays on English Protestantism and Puritanism* (London: Hambledon, 1983), pp. 521–3; Jessica Martin, *Walton's Lives: Conformist Commemorations and the Rise of Biography* (Oxford: Oxford University Press, 2001), p. 24.
13 Martin, *Walton's Lives*, pp. 18–19.
14 See, for example, William Walker, *A Sermon Preached at the Funeralls of the Right Honourable William Lord Russell, Baron of Thornhaugh ... the 16 of September, 1613* (London, 1614), sig. B2^r. This justifies Walker's emulation of 'Funerall Orations' with reference to examples by Nazianzen, Ambrose and Bernard. This example and subject are discussed in Barbara K. Lewalski, *Donne's Anniversaries and the Poetry of Praise* (Princeton, NJ: Princeton University Press, 1973), pp. 175–9.
15 Ralph Houlbrooke notes that biographical material, known as the 'lean to', could take up as much as a quarter of a funeral sermon. Ralph Houlbrooke, *Death, Religion, and the Family in England 1480–1750* (Oxford: Clarendon, 1998), p. 311.
16 Collinson, *Godly People*, p. 521. The full title of the book, by William Harrison, is *Deaths Advantage Little Regarded, and the soules solace*

against sorrow. Preached in two funeral Sermons at Childwal in Lancashire at the burial of Mistris Katherin Brettergh (London, 1602).

17 See title page to 'A Brief Discovrse of the Christian Life and death, of Mistris Katherin Brettergh', in Harrison, *Deaths Advantage Little Regarded*, sig. M4ʳ. It is not entirely clear who wrote this biographical sketch of Brettergh.

18 The exception, as Houlbrooke notes, was amongst dissenting communities. Houlbrooke, *Death, Religion, and the Family*, pp. 213, 323.

19 Philip Stubbes, *A Christall Glasse for Christian Women. Containing, A most excellent Discourse, of the godlie life and Christian death of Mistresse Katherine Stubbes* (London, 1592).

20 *Ibid.*, sig. B1ᵛ; 'The Christian Life and death, of Mistris Katherine Brettergh', p. 36. The bedside visitors include William Harrison himself.

21 See Andrea Brady, *English Funerary Elegy in the Seventeenth Century: Laws in Mourning* (Basingstoke: Palgrave Macmillan, 2006), p. 188. Of course, this dynamic could be complicated by instances of sudden death and – especially – death in childbirth. For examples see Andrea Brady, '"A Share of Sorrows": Death in the Early Modern Household', in Susan Broomhall (ed.), *Emotions in the Household, 1200–1900* (Basingstoke: Palgrave Macmillan, 2008), pp. 185–202 (194). I am grateful to Robert W. Daniel for this reference.

22 'The Christian Life and death, of Mistris Katherine Brettergh', pp. 36–7.

23 John Donne, *LXXX Sermons Preached by that Learned and Reverend Divine, Iohn Donne, Dr in Divinity, late Deane of the Cathedrall Church of S. Pauls* (London, 1640), p. 475.

24 For recent work on this more generally, see Lucinda M. Becker, *Death and the Early Modern Englishwoman* (London: Routledge, 2017).

25 Stubbes, *A Christall Glasse*, sig. C2ᵛ.

26 Harrison, *Deaths Advantage Little Regarded*, p. 82.

27 *Ibid.*, sigs M8ʳ⁻ᵛ.

28 *Ibid.*, p. 79; William Leygh, 'The Soules Solace Against Sorrow', in *Deaths Advantage Little Regarded*, p. 70; 'The Christian Life and death, of Mistris Katherine Brettergh', p. 8.

29 Harrison, *Deaths Advantage Little Regarded*, sig. A4ᵛ.

30 Brady offers several examples in *English Funerary Elegy*, p. 13. Harrison's sermon text (Isaiah 57:1) is taken from the Geneva Bible.

31 Peter Marshall describes accusations of 'bad deaths' and last-minute conversions thus in *Beliefs and the Dead in Reformation England* (Oxford: Oxford University Press, 2002), p. 267. *Deaths Advantage Little Regarded* would go into a fifth edition by 1617; see Collinson, *Godly People*, p. 521.

32 Steve Hindle, 'Brettergh, Katherine (1579–1601)', *ODNB*. https://doi.org/10.1093/ref:odnb/3351. Accessed 25 November 2018.

33 Privy Council records note that they were sent back to the county due to their 'lewde and outragious' behaviour under questioning in London. The National Archives, PC 2/26, pp. 107–8.
34 BL, Add. MS 15, 225, fol. 31. Quoted in Dominic Round, 'Venerable Robert Middleton, Martyr', *The Venerabile* 22.2 (1963), 94–102 (102).
35 William Brettergh is the author of the dedicatory epistle included before William Leygh's sermon. See Harrison, *Deaths Advantage Little Regarded*, sigs G4^{r-v}.
36 Hindle, 'Brettergh, Katherine'; and Steve Hindle, 'Bruen, John (1560–1625)', *ODNB*. https://doi.org/10.1093/ref:odnb/3767. Accessed 5 February 2019. Also William Hinde, *A faithful remonstrance of the holy life and happy death of John Bruen of Bruen Stapleford* (London, 1641). For more on Brettergh and Bruen see Robert N. Watson, *The Rest is Silence: Death as Annihilation in the English Renaissance* (Berkeley: University of California Press, 1994), pp. 305–15.
37 For example, Thomas Worthington, *A Relation of Sixteene Martyrs Glorified in England in Twelve Monethes* (Douay, France, 1601); John Wilson, *The English Martyrologe, Conteyning a Summary of the Lives of the Saints of England, Scotland and Ireland* (St Omer, France, 1608). See also Martin, *Walton's Lives*, p. 130.
38 Bedell's analysis is cited and discussed in Edward Chaney and Timothy Wilkes, *The Jacobean Grand Tour: Early Stuart Travellers in Europe* (London: I. B. Tauris, 2014), pp. 50–3.
39 Henry King, *A Sermon Preached at Pavls Crosse, the 25. of November. 1621. Upon Occasion of that False and Scandalous Report (lately Printed) Touching the Supposed Apostasie of the Right Reuerend Father in God, Iohn King, late Lord Bishop of London* (London, 1621), sigs M1^r–M3^r.
40 See Mary Hobbs, 'Introduction', in Henry King, *The Sermons of Henry King (1592–1669), Bishop of Chichester*, ed. Mary Hobbs (Rutherford: Scolar, 1992), pp. 15–58 (16–17).
41 Elizabeth Patton, 'Women, Books, and the Lay Apostolate: A Catholic Literary Network in Late-Sixteenth-Century England', in Leah Knight, Micheline White and Elizabeth Sauer (eds), *Women's Bookscapes in Early Modern Britain: Reading, Ownership, Circulation* (Ann Arbor: University of Michigan Press, 2018), pp. 117–34 (132–4).
42 Richard Smith, *The life of the most honourable and vertuous lady, the Lady Magdalen Viscountesse Montague*, trans. Cuthbert Fursden (alias John Fursdon) (London, 1627), sigs A2^v–B3^v.
43 Smith, *Lady Magdalen*, p. 22.
44 Walton's 'Life' was first printed in Donne, *LXXX Sermons*, sigs A4^v–C1^v.
45 Smith, *Lady Magdalen*, p. 40.
46 Ibid., p. 41.
47 Ibid., p. 40.

48 The National Archives, PROB 11/111, fol. 232.
49 Smith, *Lady Magdalen*, p. 42.
50 *Ibid.*, pp. 42–3.
51 See Collinson, *Godly People*, p. 521; Nigel Smith, *Literature and Revolution in England, 1640–1660* (London: Yale University Press, 1994), p. 24.
52 Quoted in Stephen Wright, 'Bolton, Robert (1572–1631)', *ODNB*. https://doi.org/10.1093/ref:odnb/2806. Accessed 5 February 2019.
53 For example, David Cressy refers its 'social drama' in *Birth, Marriage and Death: Ritual, Religion, and the Life-Cycle in Tudor and Stuart England* (Oxford: Oxford University Press, 1997), p. 2; Ralph Houlbrooke describes the 'final drama of the death-bed', intensified as a result of 'diminished ritual support' left by the Protestant Reformation in 'The Puritan Death-bed, *c.* 1560–1660', in Christopher Durston and Jacqueline Eales (eds), *The Culture of English Puritanism, 1560–1700* (Basingstoke: MacMillan, 1996), pp. 122–44 (123–4). In the *Craft of Dying*, Beaty describes the character of Moriens in the earliest *ars moriendi* text, the *Tractatus (or Speculum) artis bene moriendi*, as the 'chief actor in the drama of death', p. 6.
54 See Beaty, *Craft of Dying*, pp. 112–35. Other analogues she proposes for Becon's work are the Book of Jeremiah, Plato's *Phaedo*, and 'genuine drama', p. 114.
55 Robert Bolton, *Last Conflicts* (London, 1646), pp. 6–7 (Dod's initial address), pp. 7–29 (dialogue with friends).
56 *Ibid.*, pp. 32–3. This disputation runs pp. 30–47.
57 Alison Shell, *Catholicism, Controversy and the English Literary Imagination, 1558–1660* (Cambridge: Cambridge University Press, 1999), p. 28.
58 Beaty, *Craft of Dying*, p. 143.
59 Bolton, *Last Conflicts*, p. 46.
60 *Ibid.*, pp. 60–1.
61 *Ibid.*, sigs A3^{r-v}.
62 See Sullivan, *Beyond Melancholy*, pp. 171–90.

Afterword

N. H. Keeble

I cannot praise a fugitive and cloister'd vertue, unexercis'd &
unbreath'd, that never sallies out and sees her adversary, but slinks
out of the race, where that immortall garland is to be run for, not
without dust and heat.[1]

Milton's famous repudiation of the monastic life as cowardly and
self-interested represents the spiritual demands of Christianity as a
strenuous competition with evil – an *agon* – to be contested in the
arena of the everyday world: 'our faith and knowledge thrives by
exercise, as well as our limbs and complexion'.[2] In his early 'Nativity
Ode' (1629) he presents a Herculean Christ-child, a 'dreaded infant'
able 'in his swaddling bands' to see off the 'damned crew' of pagan
deities,[3] and thereafter, from the Lady in *Comus* (1637), through
Satan, Adam and Eve in *Paradise Lost* (1667) and the Son in *Paradise
Regained* (1671) to the imprisoned Samson, every one of his dramatic
and epic designs centres upon the psychology of temptation represented in a contest with an adversary, upon trial, testing. And no
wonder: 'that which purifies us is triall'.[4]

That sense of striving, of tenacious spiritual effort, may be
Miltonic, but it is not peculiarly Miltonic. It recurs throughout the
period's sermons and guides to godliness, which, like Milton, draw
on the Pauline image of the Olympic race for the prize or crown of
salvation,[5] on images of journeying from Exodus and the prophets,
of pilgrimage from Hebrews 11:13–14,[6] and of combat and battle,
again drawing on Paul, this time on the image of the armour of

faith and of righteousness.⁷ The conspicuous example is, of course, the seventeenth century's most enduringly influential prose work (other than the King James Bible), *The Pilgrim's Progress* (1678). Its climactic moments and exemplary figures are martial: Christian confronting Apollyon, 'harnessed ... from head to foot, with what was proof' from the armoury of the Palace Beautiful; Valiant-for-Truth fighting so vigorously with his '*right* Jerusalem *blade*' that his sword cleaves to his hand with blood; Great-heart the giant slayer, the exemplar of a Christian minister.⁸ This is a Christianity engaged (in the words of another Bunyan title) in *The Holy War* (1682): bracing, active, dynamic, tenacious, assertive, if not revolutionary, rather than retired, meditative, contemplative, reflective. 'The Soul of Religion', says Christian in discrediting Talkative, 'is the practick part'.⁹ The true pilgrim, alert and engaged at all times, keeps on going: the 'Plain, called *Ease*' is 'but *narrow*' and to rest on the '*inchanted ground*' would be disastrous.¹⁰ '*Departing from iniquity*', wrote Bunyan elsewhere, 'is not a work of an hour, or a day, or a week, or a month, or a year: *But it's a work will last thee thy life time.*'¹¹ With this emphasis, the century's many works of evangelistic, practical and pastoral theology are exercises in what we would now call psychological analysis and counselling, remarkable for their clear-sighted address to fallible human nature and to the emotional and spiritual trials of everyday experience. 'It was never the will of God that bare *speculation* should be the end of his *Revelation* or of *our belief*. Divinity is an *Affective practical* Science,' asserted the puritan divine Richard Baxter.¹²

Wayfaring and warfaring are outdoor activities. Apart from the episodes of ministerial and congregational instruction in the Interpreter's House and Palace Beautiful, and his confinement in the prisons of Doubting Castle and Vanity Fair (reflections of nonconformist experience), Christian is never indoors. In the less heroic and more domestic part II of *The Pilgrim's Progress*, Christiana is still admonished, '*The bitter is before the sweet:* Thou must through Troubles ... enter this Celestial City.'¹³ In all this, there seem to be few opportunities to withdraw, to retire, to be alone, to reflect and meditate, even to pray.

In the many and varied contexts and occasions discussed in the essays in this collection, however, we are in a very different physical space – enclosed, private, engaged on a range of essentially sedentary, often silent, occupations: reviewing sermon notes, casting up 'spiritual accounts', reflecting on personal experience, writing conversion narratives, keeping diaries, reading, discussing, praying and meditating. The typographical features of a printed text might enact this interiority and its relationship to the outer world, as Michael Durrant demonstrates in an acute bibliographical analysis of (in a striking phrase) the 'looping teleology' of Katherine Sutton's *A Christian Woman's Experiences* (1663).[14] We are, however, admitted to these interiors, physical and experiential, largely because, while the printed homiletic and didactic literature of instruction is not neglected, these essays also draw on unprinted family records, private papers, letters, diaries, notebooks and the many other forms of introspective and meditative writing that sustained personal faith, created devotional identities and enabled spiritual growth. By turning to these archives, these essays contribute to our growing realisation that the motor of individuals' intellectual and religious development in early modern England was as much manuscript exchange and epistolary networks as it was printed books.[15]

This scribal devotional world is characteristically familial. Families recur throughout these essays as creators, audiences, distributors and preservers of devotional exercises and papers. The astonishing sixty volumes of sermon notes in the Gell archive from the period 1644 to 1707 were a focus of the devotional life not only of the individual who first took the notes but also of the family members who reviewed them through several generations – and not only them: these notes (we may reasonably suppose) provided matter for meditation, reflection and discussion also for the family's religious friends.[16] Other forms of writing might serve similar purposes. When, in 1782, Hannah Burton began to keep her diary, it was in the same notebook as, a century earlier, her admired grandmother the nonconformist Mary Franklin had written her own spiritual autobiography and narrative of witness under persecution, to which Burton gave the title 'The Experience of my dear grandmother, Mrs Mary Franklin'. A personal and (one may suppose) reassuring and sustaining devotional relationship is established across the generations by thus creating a book of family testimony, strengthened yet further by the fact that this same notebook was originally used for the sermon notes of Mary Franklin's husband, the Presbyterian minister Robert Franklin. It was not only the family that read, and preserved, Franklin's narrative. That its text was included in an eighteenth-century commonplace book along with hymns and prayers is clear evidence of its being copied and circulated for devotional and edificatory ends.[17]

The spiritual significance of the home was underscored by such printed texts as Baxter's *Poor Man's Family Book* (1673) and *The Catechizing of Families* (1684). Indeed, the familial and personal recur throughout Baxter's oeuvre. It was the death of his wife that prompted him to publish his poems; their context is the marital home and their business spiritual instruction and encouragement arising from his experiences as a husband as well as a Christian pastor.[18] He published a *Breviate of the Life of Margaret ... Baxter* (1681), and had intended also to publish lives of other members of his household – his stepmother, mother-in-law and housekeeper – until dissuaded by friends.[19] The printing house that put devotional works into the public sphere was itself a domestic as well as a professional space that might incorporate the author into its 'wider family'.[20] And when the very different world of the theatre takes up cases of conscience and religious commitment it is again in family contexts, in such domestic tragedies and comedies as *A Warning for Fair Women* (1599) and *The Puritan Widow* (1607), discussed in this collection.[21]

The period's religious groups and congregations have a similar character. Meeting *house* came to be the accepted designation for a building used for worship by nonconformists, the term connoting the nature of its members' relationship one to another. Gathered churches assiduously preserved records of their decisions and doings; the particular church was defined by a shared religious experience demonstrable by reference to a written record.[22] Attentiveness to inner spiritual experience and the quality of devotional commitment was fostered by the common practice in gathered churches of requiring from prospective members personal professions of faith and, often, narrative accounts of their conversion experiences,[23] a practice that played a very significant role in the development of what in the next century became the secular genre of autobiography.[24] Although quite different in its preconceptions and practices, Nicholas Ferrar's community at Little Gidding was just as surely a devotionally defined association or voluntary society, or (indeed) extended family, as any gathered church or Quaker meeting of those tellingly styled 'Friends', and just as surely dependent upon written texts, individual commitment and shared devotional practice.[25] It was as an orderly household that, in a poem entitled 'The Familie', Ferrar's friend, the parish priest George Herbert, represented the harmonious ideal of a church meeting in a truly Christian spirit.[26]

Such covenanted worshipping communities may have been religiously and devotionally demarcated, but they were not isolated from the public sphere. The life of Nicholas Ferrar, no less than the lives of Mary Franklin and Oliver Heywood, was shaped by the religious politics of the period. The complexities of the period's ecclesiological and theological disputes, and the heatedness – indeed cruelty and violence – of their political rivalries made it very difficult for individuals to identify reliable sources of advice and guidance, or to determine what was appropriate devotional behaviour. Devotional practices were hence inextricably bound up with cases of conscience, particularly in family contexts. The apparently straightforward injunctions to obedience delivered in the Fifth Commandment in Exodus 20:12, and by Paul in Ephesians 6:1 and Colossians 3:20, were in seventeenth-century practice far from straightforward to follow.[27] Conscience could bring obedience to God into conflict with obedience to parents, just as it could with obedience to rulers, Matthew 22:21 and Romans 13:1–3 notwithstanding.[28] 'A familie', said William Gouge in his *Of Domesticall Duties* (1622), 'is a little Church, and a little commonwealth,'[29] but in neither capacity could it function when relationships between parents (or, more strictly, fathers) and children were strained by differences over ecclesiastical allegiances, and so over religious practices and observances.[30] The Quakers disrupted not only church and state but many a family, as, after 1662, did questions of conformity and nonconformity: should one accept the state's, and a father's, right to insist on compliance with the established national church? And how far might a head of a household allow family devotions to assume the character of an illegal conventicle by admitting neighbours, and perhaps a nonconformist minister?[31] At the end of the century, the nonconformist minister Oliver Heywood published his own book of domestic instruction, *A Family Altar* (1693), to reinvigorate family worship in the changed circumstances following the 1689 Toleration Act that allowed (within strictly defined limits) public worship by nonconformists. No longer essential to the survival of nonconformity as an alternative to public congregational worship, nor as a refuge against persecution, the role of family worship stood in need of redefinition for nonconformists: in providing that, Heywood's book looks ahead to the more settled (although not uncontested) national religious life of the eighteenth century.[32]

When religious commitment fell foul of the authorities of the day, then prison became the dark mirror image of the home, its confinement a noisome and grotesque parody of domestic space, as its 'care' of prisoners was a parody of familial relations. Prisons, however, could serve quite as well as homes as places of devotion, of introspective reflection, of regeneration and redemption, perhaps, indeed, more effectively than homes precisely because those incarcerated there for the sake of conscience had need of assurance that their suffering was not in vain. *The Pilgrim's Progress*, after all, is narrated by a prisoner: it is a story of spiritual liberation. 'For though men keep my outward man / Within their Locks and Bars / Yet by the Faith of Christ I can / Mount higher than the Stars,' wrote Bunyan in his *Prison-Meditations* of 1665.[33] That is the great theme of the *Journal* of George Fox, its narrative taken up very largely with accounts of, and reflections on, his imprisonments and suffering, tending all to the demonstration that 'the power of the Lord is over all', the phrase that Geoffrey Nuttall took to encapsulate Fox's visionary spirituality.[34] These spaces, no less than the home, could become, in the words of the title to chapter 7 in this collection, 'sacred spaces', 'threshold[s] to spiritual liberty' as, in fulfilment of Matthew 18:20, they, no less than a domestic space or a meeting house, assumed the role of a church consecrated by the faith of those present.[35]

Sickness and death waited on seventeenth-century prisons (it is one of the wonders of the age how George Fox survived his repeated incarcerations over more than thirty years), but not, of course, only prisons. The sickbed and the deathbed are ever-present in the period's devotional literature. John Donne in his shroud, as engraved by Martin Droeshout and sculpted for his monument in St Paul's Cathedral, stands at the head of the century, enacting its belief in the edificatory, homiletic and devotional power of life's end if rightly anticipated, undergone, witnessed and recorded.[36] The most accomplished seventeenth-century contribution to the *ars moriendi* tradition, Jeremy Taylor's *Holy Dying* (1651),[37] begins with an extended meditation on the shortness and vanity of life, reinforced by subsequent reflections on the miseries, sufferings and sicknesses of human life: 'As our life is very short so it is very miserable, and therefore it is well it is short: God in pity to mankinde, lest his burden should be insupportable and his nature an intolerable load, hath reduced our state of misery to an abbreviation.'[38] This is a construction of human life intended to induce in the reader fervent devotional exercises and prayers, self-examination, patience, other-worldliness and heavenly-mindedness in the face of decay, mutability and mortality. Such spiritual exercises give us (again in a family context) the mother's legacy genre,[39] as well as the meditations on death in funeral sermons and the exemplary force of their short biographies of the deceased.

A striking feature of those funeral sermon biographies and of the vignettes and narratives of the pious and patient bearing of the invalid and dying, is that they are so often of ordinary people, or, at least, ordinary laypeople of the mercantile and professional classes.[40] Commonly, of course, members of the peerage and clerics are the subject, but by no means always: mayors, aldermen and other holders of civic office, physicians, merchants, and, often, women are commemorated.[41] The practices and literature of devotion have an insistently democratising effect. Bunyan may have been among the first early moderns to fictionalise ordinary lives, but he was certainly neither alone nor the first to record them. Indeed, there is the mighty precedent of John Foxe's 'Book of Martyrs', which, through its records of ordinary, suffering lives, did so much to create English Protestant identity.[42]

If we can detect in these devotional practices and writings a new valuation of non-elite people, we can detect also a new evaluation of the individual and of individual experience, and a new authenticity and circumstantial realism in the depiction of ordinary lives. Exemplary these characterisations may be, but far from the stereotypes of hagiography. One thing, though, they do all share. The much-promoted practice of introspective 'spiritual audit' had one of its roots in Calvinist theology and the desire to determine one's sincerity and ultimate destiny by assessing the nature and fervour of one's faith against marks of election, a desire that could all too easily generate debilitating anxiety and depression.[43] It had, though, another root in the experiential reality of the divine that defines the family of the faithful: 'The Spirit itself beareth witness with our spirit, that we are the children of God' (Romans 8:16).[44] This conviction may have been most obviously evident among the Quakers, but that experience, or the aspiration to that experience, is not confessionally or dogmatically bound.[45]

Of this there can be no better evidence than the fact that the poetry of George Herbert was a devotional touchstone for people of all religious persuasions.[46] What spoke across confessional boundaries was (and is) the fact that, in the words of Richard Baxter, '*Herbert* speaks *to God* like one that *really believeth a God*, and whose business in the world is most *with God*. *Heart-work* and *Heaven-work* make up his Books.'[47] That is as good a definition of the literature of religious devotion as can be had.

Notes

1. John Milton, *The Complete Prose Works of John Milton*, ed. Don M. Wolfe, 8 vols (London: Yale University Press, 1953–82), II:515.
2. Milton, *Complete Prose*, II:543.
3. John Milton, *Complete Shorter Poems*, ed. John Carey (London: Longman, 2nd edn, 1997), p. 115, lines 222, 228.
4. Milton, *Complete Prose*, II:515.
5. E.g. 1 Corinthians 9:24; Galatians 5:7; Philippians 2:16; Hebrews 12:1.
6. See further N. H. Keeble, '"To be a pilgrim": Constructing the Protestant Life in Early Modern England', in Colin Morris and Peter Roberts (eds), *Pilgrimage: The English Experience from Beckett to Bunyan* (Cambridge: Cambridge University Press, 2002), pp. 238–56, which lists representative titles employing this imagery on p. 242.
7. E.g. Romans 13:12; 2 Corinthians 6:7; Ephesians 6:11–13.
8. John Bunyan, *The Pilgrim's Progress*, ed. Roger Sharrock (Oxford: Clarendon, 1960), pp. 55–60, 290–1, 295.
9. Bunyan, *Pilgrim's Progress*, p. 79.
10. *Ibid.*, pp. 106, 136.
11. John Bunyan, *The Miscellaneous Works of John Bunyan*, ed. Roger Sharrock, 13 vols (Oxford: Clarendon, 1976–94), IX:276.
12. Richard Baxter, *Directions for Weak Distempered Christians* (London, 1669), pt. I, pp. 97–8.
13. Bunyan, *Pilgrim's Progress*, p. 180.
14. See chapter 2 (quotation from p. 52).
15. On networks, epistolarity, note-taking and family records, and their significance to religious life, see Anne Dunan-Page and Clotilde Prunier (eds), *Debating the Faith: Religion and Letter-Writing in Great Britain, 1550–1800*, International Archives of the History of Ideas 209 (Dordrecht: Springer, 2013); Meredith Marie Neuman, *Jeremiah's Scribes: Creating Sermon Literature in Puritan New England* (Philadelphia: University of Pennsylvania Press, 2013); James Daybell and Andrew Gordon (eds), *Cultures of Correspondence in Early Modern Britain* (Philadelphia:

University of Pennsylvania Press, 2016); Johanna Harris, *Godly Letters: Epistolary Style and Early Modern Puritanism* (London: Palgrave Macmillan, forthcoming); Alexandra Walsham, *Archives of Dissent: Family Memory and the English Nonconformist Tradition* (London: Dr Williams's Trust, forthcoming).

16 See chapter 3, esp. pp. 63–5, 69–71.
17 See chapter 10, esp. pp. 185–8.
18 See chapter 12, esp. pp. 223–5, 231–3.
19 Richard Baxter, *A Breviate of the Life of Margaret ... wife of Richard Baxter* (London, 1681), sigs A1^v–A2^r.
20 As demonstrated by Michael Durant on p. 56.
21 In chapters 5 and 6.
22 See Mark Burden, Michael Davies, Anne Dunan-Page and Joel Halcomb, *An Inventory of Puritan and Dissenting Records, 1640–1714* (2016). Available on Queen Mary University of London's website: www.qmulreligionandliterature.co.uk/online-publications/dissenting-records. Accessed 11 December 2019.
23 On this practice see Geoffrey F. Nuttall, *Visible Saints: The Congregational Way 1640–1660* (1957; repr. Oswestry: Quinta, 2001), esp. pp. 109–16.
24 See further: Patricia Caldwell, *The Puritan Conversion Narrative: The Beginnings of American Expression* (Cambridge: Cambridge University Press, 1983); Kathleen Lynch, *Protestant Autobiography in the Seventeenth-Century Anglophone World* (Oxford: Oxford University Press, 2012); D. Bruce Hindmarsh, *Spiritual Autobiography in Early Modern England* (Oxford: Oxford University Press, 2005); Owen C. Watkins, *The Puritan Experience* (London: Routledge & Kegan Paul, 1972).
25 See chapter 1, esp. pp. 27–8, 30–7.
26 George Herbert, *The English Poems of George Herbert*, ed. Helen Wilcox (Cambridge: Cambridge University Press, 2007), pp. 476–9.
27 Exodus 20:12: 'Honour thy father and thy mother'; Ephesians 6:1: 'Children, obey your parents in the Lord: for this is right'; Colossians 3:20: 'Children, obey your parents in all things: for this is well pleasing unto the Lord' (King James Bible).
28 Matthew 22:21: 'Render therefore unto Caesar the things which are Caesar's; and unto God the things that are God's'; Romans 13:1–3: 'Let every soul be subject unto the higher powers. For there is no power but of God ... For rulers are not a terror to good works, but to the evil' (King James Bible).
29 William Gouge, *Of Domesticall Duties* (London, 1622), p. 18.
30 Chapter 9 adduces many examples of divided households and competing loyalties from all religious persuasions.

31 The Conventicle Acts of 1664 and 1670 prohibited any gathering of more than five persons, not counting family members, for religious worship other than according to the *Book of Common Prayer*.
32 Heywood's devotional text is discussed in chapter 4.
33 Bunyan, *Miscellaneous Works*, VI:43.
34 In his introduction to George Fox, *The Journal of George Fox*, ed. John L. Nickalls (1952; repr. London: Religious Society of Friends, 1975), p. xix. This emerges forcefully despite, and sometimes because of, the significant redaction and revision of Fox's accounts by his 1694 editor Thomas Ellwood, for which see chapter 8.
35 These remarks are taken from chapter 7, pp. 137, 140–1. Mathew 18:20: 'For where two or three are gathered together in my name, there am I in the midst of them' (King James Bible).
36 The engraving appeared as the frontispiece to Donne's last sermon, *Deaths Duell* (1632). For it, and for the monument and its significance, see R. C. Bald, *John Donne: A Life* (Oxford: Clarendon, 1970), pp. 529, 533–6. Donne's *Devotions upon Emergent Occasions* (1624) seeks to wring from his own near-fatal illness just such spiritual benefit.
37 Pre-eminent it may have been, but Taylor's claim that his book was 'the first intire body of directions for sick and dying people that I remember to have been published in the Church of England' was, as his modern editor remarks, 'disingenuous', or, at least, rested heavily on the force of 'intire' and on a specific sense of 'Church of England'. Jeremy Taylor, *Holy Dying*, ed. P. G. Stanwood (Oxford: Clarendon, 1989), pp. 13, xiv.
38 Taylor, *Holy Dying*, p. 41. For remarks on the *ars moriendi* tradition in different contexts see chapter 5, pp. 98–9, and chapter 14, pp. 259–62.
39 On this genre see chapter 5, pp. 99–101.
40 Charles Green dates this development from the early seventeenth century. See chapter 14, p. 262.
41 For examples, see chapters 13 and 14.
42 David Manning comments on this precedent and legacy on p. 35, and Catie Gill on its continuing relevance on p. 155.
43 An example is the case of Katherine Gell, discussed by Ann Hughes on pp. 66–9. For a trenchant presentation of this as an inevitable consequence of theologies derived from Calvin, see John Stachniewski, *The Persecutory Imagination: English Puritanism and the Literature of Despair* (Oxford: Clarendon, 1991).
44 King James Bible.
45 This point is made, and discussed in relation to the Little Gidding community, by David Manning on pp. 28–30.
46 See chapter 11.
47 Richard Baxter, *Poetical Fragments* (London, 1681), preface, sig. A7^v, quoted by Sylvia Brown on p. 230.

Select bibliography

Achinstein, Sharon, *Literature and Dissent in Milton's England* (Cambridge: Cambridge University Press, 2003).
Adcock, Rachel, *Baptist Women's Writings in Revolutionary Culture, 1640–1680* (London: Routledge, 2015).
Adcock, Rachel, Sara Read and Anna Ziomek (eds), *Flesh and Spirit: An Anthology of Seventeenth-Century Women's Writing* (Manchester: Manchester University Press, 2014).
Aston, Margaret, *Broken Idols of the English Reformation* (Cambridge: Cambridge University Press, 2016).
Cambers, Andrew, *Godly Reading: Print, Manuscript and Puritanism in England, 1580–1720* (Cambridge: Cambridge University Press, 2011).
Cambers, Andrew, 'Reading, the Godly, and Self-Writing in England, circa 1580–1720', *Journal of British Studies* 46.4 (2007), 796–825.
Capp, Bernard, *The Ties that Bind: Siblings, Family, and Society in Early Modern England* (Oxford: Oxford University Press, 2018).
Chapman, Alister, John Coffey and Brad Gregory (eds), *Seeing Things Their Way: Intellectual History and the Return of Religion* (Notre Dame, IN: University of Notre Dame Press, 2009).
Clarke, Elizabeth, 'Elizabeth Jekyll's Spiritual Journal: Private Diary or Political Document?', *English Manuscript Studies* 9 (2000), 218–37.
Clarke, Elizabeth, *Politics, Religion and the Song of Songs in the Seventeenth Century* (Basingstoke: Palgrave Macmillan, 2011).
Clarke, Elizabeth, '"Truth in Meeter": Bunyan's Poetry and Dissenting Poetics', in Michael Davies and W. R. Owens (eds), *The Oxford Handbook of John Bunyan* (Oxford: Oxford University Press, 2018), pp. 325–42.
Coffey, John, *Persecution and Toleration in Protestant England, 1558–1689* (London: Longman, 2000).

Coffey, John (ed.), *Heart Religion: Evangelical Piety in England and Ireland, 1690–1850* (Oxford: Oxford University Press, 2016).

Coffey, John (ed.), *The Oxford History of Protestant Dissenting Traditions, Volume I: The Post-Reformation Era, c.1559–c.1689* (Oxford: Oxford University Press, 2020).

Coles, Kimberly Anne, *Religion, Reform, and Women's Writing in Early Modern England* (Cambridge: Cambridge University Press, 2008).

Corrigan, John (ed.), *The Oxford Handbook of Religion and Emotion* (Oxford: Oxford University Press, 2008).

Coster, Will, and Andrew Spicer (eds), *Sacred Space in Early Modern Europe* (Cambridge: Cambridge University Press, 2005).

Cressy, David, *Birth, Marriage and Death: Ritual, Religion, and the Life-Cycle in Tudor and Stuart England* (Oxford: Oxford University Press, 1997).

Davies, Michael, Anne Dunan-Page, and Joel Halcomb (eds), *Church Life: Pastors, Congregations, and the Experience of Dissent in Seventeenth-Century England* (Oxford: Oxford University Press, 2019).

Doran, John, Charlotte Methuen and Alexandra Walsham (eds), *Religion and the Household* (Woodbridge: Boydell (for the Ecclesiastical History Society), 2014).

Dunan-Page, Anne, and Clotilde Prunier (eds), *Debating the Faith: Religion and Letter Writing in Great Britain, 1550–1800*, International Archives of the History of Ideas 209 (Dordrecht: Springer, 2013).

Durston, Christopher, and Jacqueline Eales (eds), *The Culture of English Puritanism, 1560–1700* (Basingstoke: Macmillan, 1996).

Ezell, Margaret J. M., *The Oxford English Literary History, Volume V: 1645–1714, The Later Seventeenth Century* (Oxford: Oxford University Press, 2017).

Felch, Susan M., 'English Women's Devotional Writing: Surveying the Scene', *ANQ: A Quarterly Journal of Short Articles, Notes, and Reviews* 24.1–2 (2011), 118–30.

Gaudio, Michael, *The Bible and the Printed Image in Early Modern England: Little Gidding and the Pursuit of Scriptural Harmony* (Abingdon: Routledge, 2017).

Greaves, Richard, *Glimpses of Glory: John Bunyan and English Dissent* (Stanford, CA: Stanford University Press, 2002).

Green, Ian, *Print and Protestantism in Early Modern England* (Oxford: Oxford University Press, 2000).

Grell, Ole Peter, and Andrew Cunningham (eds), *Religio Medici: Medicine and Religion in Seventeenth-Century England* (Aldershot: Scolar, 1996).

Hall, David D. (ed.), *Lived Religion: Towards a History of Practice* (Princeton, NJ: Princeton University Press, 2007).

Hamlin, Hannibal, *Psalm Culture and Early Modern English Literature* (Cambridge: Cambridge University Press, 2004).

Hindmarsh, D. Bruce, *Spiritual Autobiography in Early Modern England* (Oxford: Oxford University Press, 2005).
Hiscock, Andrew, and Helen Wilcox (eds), *The Oxford Handbook of Early Modern English Literature and Religion* (Oxford: Oxford University Press, 2017).
Hunt, Arnold, *The Art of Hearing: English Preachers and their Audiences, 1590–1640* (Cambridge: Cambridge University Press, 2010).
Keeble, N. H., *The Literary Culture of Nonconformity in Later Seventeenth-Century England* (Leicester: Leicester University Press, 2nd edn, 1991).
Killeen, Kevin, Helen Smith, and Rachel Willie (eds), *The Oxford Handbook of the Bible in Early Modern England, c.1530–1700* (Oxford: Oxford University Press, 2015).
Knight, Mark (ed.), *The Routledge Companion to Religion and Literature* (Abingdon: Routledge, 2016).
Lake, Peter, and Michael Questier, *The Antichrist's Lewd Hat: Protestants, Papists and Players in Post-Reformation England* (London: Yale University Press, 2002).
Lewycky, Nadine, and Adam Morton (eds), *Getting Along? Religious Identities and Confessional Relations in Early Modern England* (Farnham: Ashgate, 2012).
Longfellow, Erica, *Women and Religious Writing in Early Modern England* (Cambridge: Cambridge University Press, 2004).
Lupton, Julia Reinhard, 'Religion and the Religious Turn', in John Lee (ed.), *A Handbook of English Renaissance Literary Studies* (Oxford: Wiley-Blackwell, 2017), pp. 70–85.
Lynch, Kathleen, *Protestant Autobiography in the Seventeenth-Century Anglophone World* (Oxford: Oxford University Press, 2012).
Marshall, Peter, *Beliefs and the Dead in Reformation England* (Oxford: Oxford University Press, 2002).
Martin, Jessica, and Alec Ryrie (eds), *Private and Domestic Devotion in Early Modern Britain* (Abingdon: Routledge, 2012).
McCullough, Peter, Hugh Adlington, and Emma Rhatigan (eds), *Oxford Handbook of the Early Modern Sermon* (Oxford: Oxford University Press, 2011).
Molekamp, Femke, *Women and the Bible in Early Modern England: Religious Reading and Writing* (Oxford: Oxford University Press, 2013).
Narveson, Kate, *Bible Readers and Lay Writers in Early Modern England: Gender and Self-Definition in an Emergent Writing Culture* (Farnham: Ashgate, 2012).
Rivers, Isabel, *Vanity Fair and the Celestial City: Dissenting, Methodist, and Evangelical Literary Culture in England 1720–1800* (Oxford: Oxford University Press, 2018).

Rivers, Isabel, and David L. Wykes (eds), *Dissenting Praise: Religious Dissent and the Hymn in England and Wales* (Oxford: Oxford University Press, 2011).

Ross, Sarah C. E., *Women, Poetry, and Politics in Seventeenth-Century Britain* (Oxford: Oxford University Press, 2015).

Ryrie, Alec, *Being Protestant in Reformation Britain* (Oxford: Oxford University Press, 2013).

Shagan, Ethan H., *The Rule of Moderation: Violence, Religion and the Politics of Restraint in Early Modern England* (Cambridge: Cambridge University Press, 2011).

Smith, Nigel, *Literature and Revolution in England, 1640–1660* (London: Yale University Press, 1994).

Walsham, Alexandra, *The Reformation of the Landscape: Religion, Identity, and Memory in Early Modern Britain and Ireland* (Oxford: Oxford University Press, 2nd edn, 2012).

Webster, Tom, 'Writing to Redundancy: Approaches to Spiritual Journals and Early Modern Spirituality', *Historical Journal* 39.1 (1996), 33–56.

White, Micheline (ed.), *English Women, Religion, and Textual Production, 1500–1625* (Burlington, VT: Ashgate, 2011).

Willis, Jonathan, *Church Music and Protestantism in Early Modern England: Discourses, Sites and Identities* (Farnham: Ashgate, 2010).

Willis, Jonathan (ed.), *Sin and Salvation in Reformation England* (London: Taylor and Francis, 2016).

Zook, Melinda, *Protestantism, Politics and Women in Britain, 1660–1714* (Basingstoke: Palgrave Macmillan, 2013).

Index

Abergavenny, Frances 99
Act of Toleration (1689) 79–80, 82, 86, 88–91
Act of Uniformity (1662) 72, 145, 176, 219 n5
Acts and Monuments see Foxe
Alleine, Richard 257 n49
Alsop, Eleanor 64, 69, 71, 75
Andrews, Lancelot 243
Angier, John 87
Anglicanism xviii, 26, 86, 145, 174, 176–7, 181
Anne of Denmark 122
Archer, Isaac 6, 40, 174–8, 248–50
Archer, William 174–8
articles of religion
   the Thirty-Nine Articles 174
Augustine of Hippo 26, 36, 48

Baptism/s 81, 89
Baptists 43–60, 157, 243
Bible, books of
   Colossians 169, 279
   Corinthians 40 n16, 40 n21, 188, 198, 202 n31, 209, 261, 271 n9, 282 n7
   Deuteronomy 196
   Ecclesiastes 34
   Ephesians 169, 172, 279, 282 n7
   Exodus 3–4, 275, 279
   Hebrews 191, 202 n45, 275, 282 n5
   Isaiah 197–8, 244–6, 255 n21, 264
   John 40 n16, 45–6, 70, 189–90
   Luke 41 n35, 45, 73, 248, 249, 257 n56
   Matthew 39 n9, 189, 248, 249, 257 n56, 279, 280
   Peter 39, 64
   Proverbs 42 n49, 190, 197
   Psalms 35, 47, 50, 52, 64, 69, 75 n5, 197, 242–4, 246–50, 254 n11
      see also singing
   Romans 279, 281, 282 n7
Bible, figures of
   Christ 45–6, 49, 195
   Elizabeth 73
   Jethro 3
   Mary Magdalene 45–6, 49
   Moses 3
   Zechariah 73
Bible, kings of
   David 35, 47, 50, 246, 250
   Hezekiah 244–6
   Solomon 37
Bible, readings of 144–5, 189–204, 241–58, 264

Bacon, Christopher 251
Bagshaw, William 73
Bagshaw, Edward 268
Barbon, John 205–6
Barton, William 3–4
Baxter, Margaret 13, 223–6, 228–9, 231–3, 278
Baxter, Richard 13, 17 n24, 63–8, 83, 218, 222–37, 241, 247–8, 276, 278, 282
Bayly, Lewis 171, 245, 248
Beadle, John 247
Becon, Thomas 260, 268–9
Bedell, William 266
Behn, Aphra xvi
Bentley, Thomas 30, 99
blasphemy 153–4, 156
Bolton, Robert 268–9
Book of Common Prayer *see* Prayer Book/s
'Book of Martyrs' *see* Foxe
Boyd, Zacharie 248
Bradford, John 10, 97, 107–8, 143
Breton, Nicholas 99
Brettergh, Katherine 262–5, 266
Brettergh, William 265
Brome, Richard 108
Broughton, Richard 266
Brousse, Jacques 141
Bruen, John 265
Bugg, Francis 161
Bunny, Edmund 260
Bunyan, John xvi, 190, 192, 194, 228–9, 276, 280–1
Burton, Hannah 185, 187, 277

Calamy, Edmund I 242
Calamy, Edmund III 65
Caldwell, Elizabeth 144
Calvin, John *including* Calvinism 9, 26–7, 31, 33, 38, 67, 87, 89, 260, 268, 271 n8, 281, 284 n43
Camden, William 36
Campion, Thomas 121–2
catechisms/catechizing 72, 86, 190, 199–200 n3, 216, 251, 278

Catholicism/Catholics 2, 4, 10, 26, 36, 90, 114, 118–19, 135–7, 139–44, 146, 216–18, 244, 260, 265–8
Charles I of England 214
Charles II of England 3, 199–200 n3
Charles V Holy Roman Emperor 36–7
Church of England 3, 72, 170–1, 174–5, 179, 187–8, 208, 210, 212, 217
  calendar 217
  clergy 1, 4, 27, 207, 209–10, 241
Chute, George 182
Civil War xvi, 3, 13, 170, 205–21, 225, 268
Clarkson, Laurence 170–1
Clifford, Anne 250
Collett, Anna 27, 34
Collett, John 27
Collett, Mary 27, 34
Collett, Susanna 27
confession/s *see* repentance
Communion *see* Lord's Supper
Cosbie, Arnold 143–4
Cosin, John 30
covenant/s 13, 33, 191, 225, 234 n13, 246–8
Cranshaw, William 10
Cromwell, Oliver 4, 159

de Valdés, Juan 31
Dearsly, Henry 174
Dekker, Thomas 140
Denham, John 226
Dent, Arthur 261
Devil *see* Satan
dissent/dissenters xvi, 3–4, 10, 13, 44, 54–5, 71–4, 79–92, 139, 145, 161, 175, 178, 181, 185–99, 205–19, 224–9, 241, 249, 276–80
Dod, John 269
Donne, John xvi, 137, 263, 267, 280
Dürer, Albrect 46

INDEX

Dutch Republic 43–4, 54
Dyke, Daniel 1
Dyke, Jeremiah 1, 14

Egerton, Elizabeth 249
election *see* salvation
Eliot, T.S. 25–6, 38
Elizabeth I of England 149 n33, 262
Ellwood, Thomas 11, 152–62, 171–2, 176, 178
Ellwood, Walter 172–3
Everard, Edmund 55

Farnworth, Ellis 77 n37
fast/s 64–5, 69, 72, 81–2, 86
Ferrar, John 27
Ferrar, Mary 34–5
Ferrar, Nicholas 25, 27–9, 31, 34, 36, 278–9
Firmin, Giles 209, 214
Fitch, William 141
Foucault, Michel 98
Fox, George 7, 11–12, 151–66, 280
Foxe, John 20 n51, 35, 135, 137, 153, 201 n18, 281
Frankland, Richard 94 n39
Franklin, Mary 6, 12, 185–202, 277, 279
Franklin, Robert 185, 187–8, 191–2, 277
Fuller, Thomas 207–8, 214
Fursden, Cuthbert 266–7

Gell, Elizabeth 70–1, 74
Gell, John 69, 71–4
Gell, Katherine 6, 10, 63–9, 71–4, 231
Gell, Temperance 65, 70–1
Gipps, Thomas 241
Goddæus, Henry 45–56
Golding, Arthur 107–8, 143
Goodwin, John 3–4
Gouge, William 101, 169, 279
grace 28–9, 33–4, 37, 45, 52, 66–7, 85, 88, 142–3, 174, 190, 226, 269
Grosvenor, Benjamin 187, 198–9

Grymeston, Elizabeth 107
Gurnall, William 67

Hampson, Robert 55
Harcourt, Anne 256 n42
Harrison, William 264, 266–7
Hartopp, John 71
Harvey, Christopher 206
Henri IV of France 141
Henry, Matthew 4, 253
Henry, Philip 4–5, 67, 244
Herbert, George xvi, 7, 13, 25–7, 31, 205–21, 225, 229–30, 279, 282
heretic/s 135–7, 261, 267
Heywood, Oliver 7, 10, 79–94, 246, 250, 279–80
Higginson, Francis 209
Hill, Thomas 65
Hollis, Elinor 65
Holy Spirit 13, 28, 198, 212
Holy Trinity 26, 126
Hooker, Richard 30
Hopton Hall 64, 70, 73–4
Horne, Robert 13
Horsey, John 173–4
Horsey, Thomas 173
Howe, John 83
Hunne, Richard 135–7, 143–4, 146
Hunt, Thurston 265
Hutchin, John 144
Hutchinson, John 243–4
Hutchinson, Lucy 17 n24, 243–4
hymn/s xvi, 3–4, 51, 200 n4, 222–3, 226–7, 235 n38, 243–5, 247, 277–8
see also singing

idolatry 175–6, 258 n66
Independents 4, 69, 89, 174, 205, 226, 243, 244, 246
Isham, Elizabeth xxi n9, 247–8

James I of England 266
Jocelin, Elizabeth 100–1, 107
Jones, Henry 144
Jones, Rice 156

291

Josselin, John 179
Josselin, Ralph 178–80, 182, 243–4

King, Henry 266
King, John 266
Knollys, Hanserd 43–4, 243

Laud, William *including* Laudianism 27, 30, 43, 137
Leigh, Dorothy 99, 101, 107
Leslie, Charles 152, 156, 161
letters 30, 55, 64–5, 67, 69, 100, 108, 153, 155, 175, 178, 180, 199–200 n3, 227, 277
Leygh, William 265, 267
life–writing *see* puritanism
Little Gidding 9, 25–42, 278
 see also Ferrar
London 4, 6, 43, 55, 71, 83, 98–9, 123, 136, 138–9, 160, 171, 173, 179–80, 185, 188, 190, 200 n10, 207, 242, 248, 260, 266–7, 273 n33
 Great Fire of 148 n5, 190–1, 233
Lord's Prayer 84
Lord's Supper 30, 86, 116
Lower, Thomas 153

Marshall, Stephen 70
Mary I of England 201 n18
Mather, Richard 245, 251
Middleton, Robert 265
Middleton, Thomas 10–11, 114–31
millenarianism 165 n35
Milton, John xvi, 2, 192, 275
Montague, Magdalen 266–8
Moore, Joseph 64, 72–4
murder 98–9, 104–6, 135–47
Mynshull, Geoffrey 139

Newcome, Daniel 180–1
Newcome, Henry 178, 180–2
New England 251
nonconformity *see* dissent/dissenters
Norden, John 251
Norris, Edward 265

Norton, Humphrey 160
Nye, Philip 69–70

Oley, Barnabus 217–18
Osborn, Elias 172–3, 178
Otefield, John 68, 70
Owen, John 71

Parsons, Robert 139, 260
Paul's Cross 10
 see also St Paul's Cathedral
Peachy, Anne 248–9
Peacock, Thomas 268–9
Peele, George 120, 122
Penington, Mary 243–4
penitence *see* repentance
persecution 3, 11–12, 55, 64, 71, 74, 79, 84, 90, 135–7, 151–62, 173–4, 187–99, 277
Pepys, Samuel xvi
Perkins, William 243, 246, 261
Perneby, William 245–6
Porter, Robert 63–5, 67–8, 70, 72–4
Powell, Vavasor 205, 244, 253
prayer/s 29–30, 65–6, 80, 84–92, 99, 116, 137, 143–4, 147, 210–17, 244, 246–9, 263, 277
Prayer Book/s 4–5, 28, 48, 72, 107–8, 144, 145, 171–2, 174, 175, 195, 210–11, 246–7, 249, 254, 257, 259, 284
preaching *see* sermons
predestination 28, 31, 44, 260–1
Presbyterians 4–5, 63–78, 79–94, 185–202, 209, 241, 244, 246, 248, 277
Privy Council 138, 273 n33
prophecy xvi, 165 n37, 218
Protestantism xvii, 4–5, 7, 26, 30, 36, 49
providence 33, 37, 85, 147, 157, 177, 190–1
purgatory 125
puritanism/puritans xvii, 26, 37–8, 66, 72–3, 79–94, 118–19,

292

INDEX

126–8, 169–84, 185–202, 210–16
Pyot, Edward 154

Quakers 87, 151–66, 171–3, 209–10, 279, 281

Reeve, John 226
repentance 35, 49–50, 52, 98, 107–8, 142–7, 173, 260, 264, 269
Rich, Mary 245
Rivet, Andrew 247–8
Rowe, Thomas 99
Rowlands, Samuel 103

the Sabbath 29, 145, 173, 192
Salt, William 154, 160
salvation 65, 68, 74, 99, 126, 175, 189, 229, 242–3, 260–1, 270, 275, 281
Samble, Richard 251
Satan 146, 159, 189, 209, 262, 264, 275
Savage, Sarah 67
Savage, Thomas 144–6
sermons 10, 63–78, 80–2, 88–9, 91, 100, 125, 144–7, 177, 179, 185, 187–8, 198, 207–9, 224–5, 228, 230, 261–6, 275–7, 281
Shakespeare, William 120, 131 n71, 259–60
sin 35, 68, 144, 181, 218
singing xvi, 7, 43, 51, 146, 232, 249, 253
Smith, Richard 266–7
Southwell, Robert 142, 260
Sparke, Edward 210–13, 216
Spira, Francis 270
St Paul's Cathedral 135–6, 280
St Nicholas, Thomas 3–4, 6, 243–4, 247–8
Stubbes, Katherine 263–4
Stubbes, Philip 127, 263–4
Sutton, Katherine 6, 9, 43–60, 277
Swift, Jonathan 241

Tallents, Francis 73
Taylor, Jeremy 255 n20, 280–1
Taylor, John 139
Teate, Faithful 212–13, 216–17
Ten Commandments
  the Fifth Commandment 169, 171–2, 175–6, 178, 182, 279
Teresa of Avila xviii
thanksgiving/s 29–30, 64–5, 72–3, 81–2, 89, 91, 119, 250
Thoresby, Ralph 250
Thornton, Alice 202 n35, 249
Tombes, John 218
Tregross, Thomas 253
Trelawney, Elizabeth 165 n29
Trinity College, Cambridge 174
Tufton, John 250
Turner, William 248
Tyndale, William 135

Underhill, Edward 139

Vaughan, Henry 206, 213
Vincent, Elizabeth 144
Vennar, Richard 30
Verstegan, Richard 142

Wallington, Elizabeth 243–4
Wallington, Nehemiah 71, 243–4
Walton, Izaak 267
Wandesford, Alice 251
Whiting, Nathaniel 205–6, 247
Whitley, Roger 17 n24
Wilson, John 266
Wingfield, Mary 55–6
Winter, Hope 251
Wither, George 3–4, 226
Woodes, Nathaniel 270
Woodford, Robert 248–9
Word of God *see* Bible; sermons
Worthington, Thomas 266
Wotton, Henry 266
Wotton, Pickering 266
Wyatt, Thomas 138

Yearwood, Randolph 147

EU authorised representative for GPSR:
Easy Access System Europe, Mustamäe tee 50,
10621 Tallinn, Estonia
gpsr.requests@easproject.com